A
FRAMEWORK
FOR SURVIVAL

Health, Human Rights, and
Humanitarian Assistance in
Conflicts and Disasters

E D I T E D   B Y

KEVIN M. CAHILL, M.D.

A Joint Publication of BasicBooks and the
Council on Foreign Relations

Library of Congress Cataloging-in-Publication Data
A framework for survival: health, human rights, and humanitarian assistance in conflicts
and disasters / edited by Kevin M. Cahill.
p.   cm.
Includes bibliography references and index.
ISBN 0–465–02513–7 (pbk.)
1. Disaster medicine—Congresses.   2. Medical assistance—Congresses.   3. Human
rights—Congresses.   I. Cahill, Kevin M.
RA645.5.F73 1993   92–55005
363.3'48—dc20   CIP

Designed by Ellen Levine

93 94 95 96 CC/HC 9 8 7 6 5 4 3 2 1

For Joan Durcan

*and all those who devote their
lives to the service of others*

CONTENTS

ACKNOWLEDGMENTS

This book was made possible by the generous contributions of many individuals and organizations.

Each of the participants accepted my invitation on short notice and came, often from long distances, and for no honorarium, because they shared my belief that the topics deserved attention and the timing was critical. I know my colleagues realize the depth of my respect and gratitude for their efforts, and I hope that my editing of their manuscripts into a cohesive book fulfills part of my debt to them.

The Board and staff of both the Center for International Health and Cooperation and the Council on Foreign Relations graciously supported the entire effort, willingly offering their resources and skills to assure success. I particularly thank Peter Tarnoff, president of the Council for his always gracious and gentle counsel. Enid C. B. Schoettle, director of the Project on International Organizations and Law at the Council on Foreign Relations, helped organize the symposium that led to this book. Ambassador A. A. Farah, Consultant Director for the Center for International Health and Cooperation, provided invaluable advice and practical support throughout the entire planning period for the symposium. Dr. Schoettle and Ambassador Farah were ably supported by Lawrence Hamlet and Renee Cahill. These friends made a complex and difficult task a pleasure.

Michael J. O'Neill, the former editor-in-chief of the *Daily News* and president of the Association of Newspaper Editors, graciously attended the entire symposium as official rapporteur; he then, typically and selflessly, reviewed all of the manuscripts and offered his sage and warm counsel in the midst of his own busy writing schedule.

The rapid editing was made pleasant and possible by David Haproff of the Council, and Jo Ann Miller and Michael Mueller of Basic Books. I would also like to thank George Craig and Stan Colbert of Harper-Collins for their interest and assistance throughout this project.

Essential funding for the symposium was provided by a major grant from the Ford Foundation to the Council on Foreign Relations, and from the Tropical Disease Center of Lenox Hill Hospital to the Center for Intenational Health and Cooperation. The Weisner Foundation and the Albert Kundstadter Family Foundation also made specific grants for the project.

FOREWORD

I t is really only in the last year or so that I have come to understand the importance of health issues in world affairs. Like so many others of my generation, I became involved in American foreign policy when security concerns and the East-West struggle were paramount. During my service in the U.S. government, we thought of little else than how to maintain the network of alliances—political, economic, and security—which West Europeans, Japanese, Canadians, and Americans built immediately after the conclusion of World War II.

Then, at the time of the Carter administration, human rights became part of America's international agenda and, increasingly, humanitarian assistance was recognized as an obligation of the developed countries in helping the many less favored nations of the world. Now that the Cold War has ended, the international community has begun to appreciate how linked the issue of world health is to questions of economic development and even democratic practices and institutions.

My pleasure at being asked to open this conference was enhanced by its sponsors, the Center for International Health and Cooperation—an important new organization—and the Council on Foreign

Relations, with which I have long been associated. However, neither this fine publication nor the work that preceded it would have happened without the vision, dedication, and drive of my friend, Dr. Kevin M. Cahill. He brought the topics and authors collected in this volume together in order to inform us about ways that government, private groups, and international organizations can begin to care better for the health and well-being of all.

Cyrus Vance

INTRODUCTION

In a world where chaos and conflict are endemic, at a time when violence and votes are sweeping away the political contours we once thought permanent, in countries battered by economic collapse, internecine wars, and revolutions, when great nations are disintegrating into unworkable ethnic enclaves, and survival seems secure only in clan structures, when hatred and massacres, hunger and epidemics run rampant, there is, nonetheless, a glimmer of hope in the growing recognition that, for better or worse, we are all neighbors on a finite globe, and that the oppression and starvation and illnesses of others are ultimately our own.

By building on common objectives and universally accepted values, by defining the core needs of all human beings and proposing ways to satisfy those needs, we may be able to create a better framework for survival in a new century. Focusing on health, human rights, and humanitarian assistance offers an innovative approach to foreign policy that may be more effective in many cases than the conventional military, economic, and geopolitical "solutions" that have so often been so flawed. Time is not on the side of those who believe we can maintain the status quo, that we can continue to confront reality with old rhetoric and allow the past to happen over and over again.

With today's instant communication, it is impossible to hide from distant catastrophes. Bloated bellies and destroyed societies are no longer only sad stories to be debated by statesmen far removed in time and space from the carnage. Now the images are on our television screens; they are a major force in our own and our children's continuous education. Unless we intend to give up being human, we can no longer feel warm and secure in our homes while disasters swirl through the cold world outside.

The fact that we know, instantly and vividly, that terrible wrongs are occurring creates a moral and legal burden that did not weigh on previous generations. No amount of sophistry can ever again dehumanize the horrors of war or the waste of innocent lives into dull statistics that soften the harsh fact that it is real people who suffer and die. We cannot simply talk about problems, deceiving ourselves that words—even heartfelt concerns—can substitute for corrective actions and compassionate deeds.

I have had the good fortune to work as a physician for more than three decades in troubled areas of Africa, Latin America, and Asia. I have shared in the human catastrophes that are an inevitable part of conflicts, and in the tragedies that follow earthquakes and famines, droughts and floods. For part of twenty-two consecutive years I directed medical teams in Somalia, helping to establish a national health service, while observing a political process that evolved from clans to nationhood and then reverted to the horrors that now shock the world. I learned the humbling lessons of Third World medicine, that politics and prejudice, racism and religion, weather and witchcraft, corruption and incompetence, were as much a part of most nations' health problems as the easily definable diseases we were taught in medical school. I also saw firsthand that economic embargoes are not abstractions, the antiseptic instruments of power politics. They are anesthesia supplies that do not come, respirators that cannot be repaired, and people that needlessly die. Yet during these long periods overseas, I also became aware of the unique role a physician may have, especially in societies where there are multiple reasons for suspicion or cynicism or even hatred.[1]

These experiences convinced me that those health care workers who have intimate contact with the human suffering of the masses as well as unusual access to foreign leaders could contribute to the solution of crises and conflicts in ways impossible for politicians, soldiers, and even diplomats. Humanitarian actions can open doors to negotiated settlements; even in the midst of violence, they can create corridors of human understanding that eventually become permanent bridges to peace.[2]

It was in this spirit of possibility—of seeking alternatives to the traditional tools of diplomacy—that we convened a symposium on health and human rights in conflicts and disasters which was held at the Council on Foreign Relations in New York City on September 14 and 15, 1992. The conference brought specialists in foreign affairs together with leaders in the fields of international law, medicine, and disaster aid. The premise was that both groups had a great deal to contribute to each other in the common cause of providing better assistance to the victims of wars and natural calamities and, more hopefully, in developing policy initiatives that can lead to the peaceful resolution of conflicts and the prevention of mass suffering.

The symposium was held against a background of a world in tumultuous and violent transition, emerging from the Cold War, groping for new relationships, new regional and international arrangements, and a new postindustrial global order. For forty-five years all foreign policy was shaped by a corrosive East-West competition for ideological, political, and military supremacy. This was the core assumption on which all national policies and international alliances were based. With the collapse of communism, this defining principle has now been swept away. Suddenly, the superpower struggle and the nuclear threat that bound nations together through military pacts or nonaligned groupings have been dissipated. An interdependent global economy of free markets, surging new technologies, and mass communications is now driving the international system.

The current crises in former Yugoslavia, Somalia, and many other areas are not isolated events, therefore, but part of a vast panorama of change signaling the turbulent passage of history from one age to another. Most of the old premises of the international system are under siege. Fundamental principles such as national sovereignty, ideas that have stood for hundreds of years, are being challenged by a wide range of developments from the communications revolution to popular mass movements. Countries like Germany and Japan, no longer requiring an American protector, are exploring new approaches in policymaking. It is not surprising, therefore, that there is considerable disarray in devising a common approach to problem areas such as Bosnia and the Balkans. Former clients of the Soviet Union, such as Cuba and North Korea, suddenly find themselves twisting in the wind without a military sponsor; their ideologies and policies are in ruins. Public opinion in many areas is demanding that the vital interests of individuals—their health, their living conditions, their social and political rights—have a higher priority than the arbitrary political and ethnic borders of nation states.

The United Nations, never really able to free itself from the Cold War restraints imposed by the Soviet Union and the United States, is now moving assertively into new areas. This has raised hopes in the North that it might, after all, be able to act more resolutely against threats to peace, human rights violations, and humanitarian emergencies. But all through the developing world there are smoldering concerns—in many cases deep resentments and fears—that the rich nations are merely using the UN to advance their own political and economic agendas at the expense of the world's poor countries.

Two levels of discourse are evident in the papers presented at the conference. At one level, the authors address the many technical and practical problems as well as policy differences involved in providing humanitarian assistance in major disasters and conflicts. At a deeper level, however, there is a palpable tension between the Western aid experts and the Asian and African delegates. Two different cultures are speaking, North and South, rich and poor, donors and recipients, so that identical issues are viewed through very different lenses and argued from very different reference points of history and philosophy. Even apparently altruistic efforts of assisting the poor are not accepted in all guises.

One of the principle areas of contention is the rapidly evolving concept that the ancient precepts of sovereignty must yield to human imperatives in cases of major disasters and violations of individual rights—that international agencies, foreign governments, or even nongovernmental organizations have a right to intervene without permission of the government involved. As Professor Richard Falk of Princeton University observes, humanitarian crises have now been internationalized "with the media dramatizing the commission of atrocities, generating public pressures to act, especially in settings where the citizenry of powerful countries in the West identify ethnically or religiously with the victims."

Former U.S. secretary of state Cyrus Vance opened the conference by arguing that health, human rights, and a safe environment do not stand on the outer banks of international relations but are pivotal concerns at the center. The work of building a new world order, he says, "cannot be confined to questions of military security." The grim health statistics in the developing world "divide the world of the North from South as effectively as the East/West separation of the Cold War years." He notes that diseases like AIDS cross continents and that medical care costs, environmental concerns, and rights violations are problems for both advanced and developing nations.

Secretary Vance also takes sharp issue with the view that a country's internal affairs and actions, such as human rights violations, should be exempt from international concern or even intervention: "Although our options may at times be limited, we should never stop trying to apply diplomatic, economic, and political pressures that will help the human family continue its passage toward a more open, more democratic and freer life." Several other speakers, particularly those representing the nongovernmental organization (NGO) community, make similar points, insisting that sovereign privilege must ultimately yield to humanitarian necessities. "Widespread violations of human rights and the deliberate endangerment of vast numbers of people," asserts the head of one NGO, "can no longer be tolerated."

These views may reflect popular Western opinion but they are vehemently opposed by representatives of developing nations who absolutely reject any suggestions that humanitarian law should prevail over a nation's sovereign rights. Their arguments reveal a strong undertow of resentment against Western assumptions of superiority and a profound suspicion of Western motives and methods. Abdulrahim Abby Farah of Somalia, former longtime UN under-secretary-general for African Affairs, admits that there have been situations when the principles of sovereignty and noninterference should not have been allowed "to paralyze humanitarian intervention." He notes, however, that the overwhelming view of the developing nations, as voiced during the General Assembly debate concerning humanitarian assistance in 1991, is that sovereign rights should not be violated "even in the name of the noblest gestures."

One reason these countries feel so strongly about sovereignty, of course, is that they have only recently won their independence from colonial masters. Understandably, they militantly guard their new freedoms and resist any outside intervention, however well intended, that appears to infringe upon those freedoms. A related reason, evident in these papers, is that the developing countries resent the continuing political and economic dominance of the West and profoundly suspect Western motives and methods. They feel that the political interests of the great powers continue to override humanitarian goals despite the end of the Cold War. Supposedly noble motives become clouded, and double standards are applied in the mobilization of emergency assistance.

Some Western speakers conceded the point. As Falk writes, geopolitics still "rules the roost," so that "the flow of force" is overwhelmingly from North to South and strong states are still "definitely off limits." Can anyone imagine, he asks, that the UN would ever intervene to protect native Americans in the United States or Canada? The distorting presence of geopolitical motives can be seen in the way the United States has mixed humanitarian responses with political agendas. One author claims, for example, that the United States was "indifferent or worse" to the breakup of Yugoslavia out of deference to Germany's regional ambitions, Croatian separatist sympathies, and an almost pathologic dislike of Serbia's Slobodan Milosevic. American foreign policy agendas were also cited as an important factor in the series of events that led ultimately to the plight of the Kurds and Shi'ites in Iraq. In the eyes of many observers, America's championship of humanitarian causes has merged with its political role as the world's only remaining superpower.

This development has contributed to strong misgivings in the developing world—and indeed among many humanitarian leaders in the West—about the increasing activism of the United States and other Western powers in the expanding humanitarian and peacekeeping initiatives of the UN. The trend is defended on the grounds that disasters in places like Somalia and the Sudan are so vast that only large nations and international organizations can provide the necessary logistical support. This rationale does not dispel two kinds of fear on the part of developing countries. One fear is that these operations increasingly blur the border between politics and disaster relief efforts, and this, in turn, tends to undermine the very perceptions of independence, impartiality, and selflessness that are vital to the NGOs and other humanitarian groups.

A major theme throughout this book is that health workers and humanitarian groups can indeed build bridges to peace in conflicts, but only if they are completely independent. The parties to a dispute must know that the aid agencies have no hidden political agendas. Because governments often provide massive logistical and even financial support in major disasters, NGOs and government agencies from the same country are often thrown together in the same operation. As foreign military cargo planes land supplies and foreign relief workers deliver them, two different functions are fused into one image. This can irrevocably alter the character of a relief effort, and, as one speaker

warns, NGOs run the risk of becoming "the tools or simply the contractors of donor governments."

A second, corollary fear voiced during the conference is that the
UN's independence is being seriously undermined by its increasing
reliance on a small number of major Western nations for large-scale
logistical and military support. Some claim the UN Security Council
is becoming a mere captive of the United States. And Farah reports
that the Group of 77 (G-77), the official organization of developing
nations, feels strongly that the "UN ought not to be commandeered
into an assistance brigade that delivers its gifts by coercion."

Ambassador Kofi N. Awoonor, Ghana's UN representative, goes
even further, charging that the "Security Council is being slowly
turned into a war cabinet which will mandate the use of military force
to police the world in the name of preventive diplomacy, peacekeeping, and peacemaking." Behind his statement are widely felt concerns
that the escalating use of armed forces in disaster assistance and peacekeeping efforts will tend to unbalance the UN, subverting its founding
mission and distorting its financial priorities. I suggest that unilaterally
expanding the military role of the UN to the inevitable detriment of its
humanitarian services will ultimately erode support for the very social
and economic development programs that offer the most promising
path to lasting peace.

A major complaint of many of our authors is that the whole thrust
of international policy seems to be on immediate emergency actions
when it should be on long-term foreign assistance, conflict resolution
and development programs that could prevent many disasters from
happening in the first place. Ambassador Awoonor argues that "development is the only instrument that will remove the stigma of charity
that accompanies all humanitarian relief efforts." He tells of a flood in
Bangladesh that claimed 200,000 lives; disaster workers arrived in their
"expensive tropical clothes" and then left when the emergency was
over. Only silence greeted Third World proposals for long-term solutions to the deadly floods that were sure to occur again and again. As
Awoonor contends, it is as if the "merchants of charity" need a continuing supply of disasters to perpetuate their "humanitarian industry."
Recurrent rescue operations—dramatic and often emotionally satisfying to distant donors—will remain our only option if we passively await
the inevitable consequences of neglect.

One can acknowledge the transcendental importance of long-term
solutions, but this does not diminish the terrible dimensions of
the immediate crisis of millions of people being killed or dying in

epidemics of violence and disaster. An urgent challenge confronting the international community is how such epidemics can be brought under control or prevented and how humanitarian efforts, when they are needed, can be marshaled, managed, and coordinated more effectively. In the final chapter, UN under-secretary-general Jan Eliasson emphasizes the need for cooperative action now: "We must clearly and compellingly demonstrate that the international community's conscience will respond with dispatch and generosity to the suffering and affliction of fellow men and women."

The papers presented here address a wide range of difficult issues that include: the different roles to be played by the UN, national governments, and NGOs; the relationship between humanitarian efforts and conflict resolution or other political agendas; the extent to which outside agencies should involve local governments and local professionals in relief work; and the problem of competition and conflicts among the different groups that frustrate effective relief efforts in emergencies. These and many other problems must be resolved before a consensus on a common humanitarian agenda for the world can be reached. But it is abundantly clear from these papers that even the profound differences that do exist are less significant than the mutual interests and common bonds that were discovered amidst the tension of debate at the symposium. A new path in foreign affairs has been probed, and a new foundation for future diplomacy might well have been found in the human tragedies and political failures of the past.

A Somali Postscript

Three months after editing this book I was working in a Somali refugee camp when American military forces landed on the strobe-lit, camera-crowded beaches of Mogadishu. That there are radically different approaches to resolving conflicts could not have been more apparent. I thought back to the conference room in New York where we had so recently struggled to blend legal, moral, political, and logistical concerns on health, human rights, and humanitarian assistance into a new and creative force in foreign affairs.

Those earlier deliberations seemed especially relevant and timely, reflecting a physician's profound mistrust of "quick fix" therapy, of the dangers in deceiving ourselves that dramatic displays can ever substitute for the tedious tasks required to truly rehabilitate a gravely wounded nation. Changing a humanitarian effort into a security action may offer a temporary respite from the pain of frustration, but it reflects an approach that, while gratifying the short-term needs of the healer, fails to resolve the problems of the patient. In fact, the vast scope of military action adversely alters the critical relationship between donor and recipient, drains the finite resources available, and imposes a transient mirage of well-being that simply cannot be sustained.

C. P. Snow once wrote that, in the relationship between science and government, "no one that I have read has found the right answers. Very few have even asked the right questions. The best I can do is tell a story." The Somali story is a sordid one, a shameful tale of selfish global politics gone awry, of superpowers using and then abandoning a client state, of a world silently watching as a corrupt regime annihilated its own population, and a once proud nation slipped into anarchy, with vast death and destruction in its wake. Somalia offers an almost perfect parable for this book; if there are no easy answers in Somalia at this time there surely are many legitimate questions—hard, demanding ones that are posed in every chapter of *A Framework for Survival*. How these questions are resolved in Somalia may well define future international law, the role of the United Nations, and the relationships of rich and poor nations.

Television and newspaper coverage of the military exercises created an impression of great victories over petty warlords and teenage thugs. No one seemed to ask why the situation had become so desperate before we finally responded, or what was to determine the end point of our visit. No one seemed to question the wisdom of a massive military response, or balance the costs of such an operation with the stated goals. Were 35,000 troops really necessary, and for how long would they remain? Would they merely secure the ports and food convoys, or did they intend to disarm a nomad population and impose a new government? It is conservatively estimated that the military expenses for the first two months will be many times greater than the entire international budget of the last three years for all humanitarian efforts combined.

As I write this, European nations—with minimal risks and maximum media rewards—are competing to have their own troops participate, and enormous financial donations are being sought to underwrite the military costs. But relatively little of this money will go to reconstruct Somalia. Who will bear the costs of restoring the country's civil infrastructure, of reestablishing a functioning society that needs everything from education to police, from housing to a court system, not to mention such essentials as food, crops, tools, and animals? Can we afford merely to indulge in self-gratifying relief operations without realizing that, if there is to be an end to dependence, we must provide opportunities for the Somalis to help themselves? Why not, for instance, create a Somali police force, and allow them to govern and decide who should be disarmed and how?

The relationship between the United States and the United Nations in the Somali military exercise contains the seeds of future disaster. Has the Security Council become a rubber stamp in an era when only one world power remains? Is it in the best, long-term interest of the UN, an organization founded on the premise that mankind could finally beat its swords into ploughshares, to so unbalance its activities in favor of military exercises? Can the UN intervene wherever there are violations of human rights or serious health hazards? What are the norms that the world will use in deciding where, when, and how to intervene? The current level of hunger and oppression in the southern Sudan, for example, may well be more extensive than the Somali disaster, but the television images of starving infants in Baidoa have made one a genuine humanitarian crisis, while ignorance and inattention leave an impression that the other does not exist.

As C. P. Snow advised, we must learn to ask the right questions if we are ever to find adequate answers. Somalia's tragedy may be a seminal one, and demand responses that are more complex and more difficult than an inappropriately vast and costly spectacle of American military might. The world clearly needs a better approach. This book poses many of the right questions for those who must try, each in his or her own way, to devise a blueprint for the future, one that will be built on the terrible realities of a Somali refugee camp as well as the valid concerns of diplomats in a conference hall.

Kevin M. Cahill

Meeting the Challenges of the Year 2000: Health Care and a New World Order

CYRUS VANCE

The period from late 1989 through 1992, scarcely more than a thousand days, will unquestionably be remembered as a time when unprecedented and unexpected events took place at every turn. And in the wake of those events, it will be remembered that literally scores of people began offering definitions of what has been called a "new world order." A number of them seem to have in mind only enhanced collective military security.

For my part, I am convinced that a "new world order" cannot be confined to questions of military security, nor can it be based on notions of the United States as world arbiter.

In that spirit, and recognizing that the world situation impels us to look for solutions that might have been previously impossible, let me offer a few suggestions.

I propose them as challenges for us to rise to as we move through space and time to keep our date with the millennial year 2000. A new world order for the twenty-first century, I believe, should be structured along the general lines of the 1991 Stockholm Initiative to meet the following six imperatives:

- International peace and security
- Sustainable economic development
- Curbing uncontrolled population growth and environmental degradation
- Providing adequate global health care
- Fostering democracy and human rights
- Strengthening key international institutions

International Peace and Security

The first and primary imperative of a new world order must be the maintenance of peace and security on both a global and a regional scale.

Although the Cold War may be over, we need to look no further than the nightly television news to recognize that national, ethnic, religious, and other conflicts—both across and inside national borders—continue to pose grave threats to peace and security.

The disintegration of Yugoslavia into bitter civil war tragically demonstrates how real and destructive these conflicts can be. The dissolution of the former Soviet Union, while thus far largely peaceful, contains serious flash points—some of which have already led to conflict. Other potential flash points also exist in Eastern and Central Europe. Nor is ethnic and religious conflict limited to Europe. We must never forget, nor can the world ignore, similar violence in Somalia, other parts of Africa, Central Asia, and the Indian subcontinent. In short, the end of the Cold War has by no means brought an end to violence and conflict on our planet.

Beyond maintaining appropriate military capabilities, we should begin our search for peace and greater security by strengthening the mandate and the capabilities of the institution that has the widest and potentially most effective reach—the United Nations.

The UN's collective security potential was demonstrated during the Gulf crisis. After Iraq's invasion of Kuwait, nations working within the UN framework impressively and effectively applied an unprecedented policy of embargo, containment, and enforcement. And when the war ended, there was no choice but to turn increasingly to the United Nations to provide long-term stability and humanitarian aid.

Yet, with new thinking in mind, imagine for a moment what might have been possible had the UN at the time of the Gulf War possessed the capability to head off Iraq's aggression.

In this connection, Prime Minister Ingvar Carlsson's Stockholm Initiative recommends the establishment of a global emergency system within the United Nations. This proposal has been reinforced by UN Secretary-General Boutros Boutros-Ghali in his August 1992 report, "An Agenda for Peace."

Under this proposal, which I support, UN political offices would be established inter alia in key locations, such as Iraq/Kuwait and South Korea/North Korea, to provide early warning of potential aggression and thus, it is hoped, deter potential conflict. But that alone would be inadequate. The UN also needs its own collective security forces—by which I mean earmarked forces that would be available on the call of the Security Council—to intervene when the Security Council so determines.

To make the global emergency system effective, the secretary-general should be granted greater leeway to deploy the organization's diplomatic, monitoring, and dispute-resolution capabilities whenever requested by a member state.

A UN with such capacity and authority could have posted buffer forces on the Iraq-Kuwait border, could have facilitated early peaceful discussion of the two countries' border disputes, and could have signaled clearly that Iraqi aggression would almost certainly trigger a collective response by the world community.

But the United Nations cannot be everywhere. To keep the peace, we also need to modernize regional security arrangements, particularly in volatile areas like the Middle East, the Horn of Africa, and South Asia, where no effective regional institutions now exist.

The Conference on Security and Cooperation in Europe—known as CSCE—has facilitated to a degree the post–Cold War thaw that is taking place in Central and parts of Eastern Europe. The North Atlantic Treaty Organization, of course, was the Western shield that kept a fragile situation stable until a thaw could take place. But it was CSCE, through treaties and confidence-building measures, that helped the former Soviet Union and Central and Eastern European countries to begin to work their way to democracy and free-market economies. But much more remains to be done.

As the Middle East peace process moves painstakingly forward, the CSCE model should be considered. Obviously, on one level, the meetings now under way are discussing Arab-Israeli relations and the issue of a Palestinian homeland. On another level, affected nations both inside and outside the region are beginning to tackle a broader range of issues, including regional security arrangements, human rights, environmental degradation, refugees, economic cooperation, and restraints on the development and transfer of all kinds of weapons.

As to the last of these, there is a crying need to rid the Middle East of all weapons of mass destruction and methods of their delivery as soon as possible. The radical limitation of conventional arms exports to the Middle East must also be addressed as a matter of top priority.

In the United States we regard it as quite normal that we should be beginning a major military build-down. With the fading Soviet threat, we are beginning to reduce strategic weapons and other military expenditures, and to reallocate the resources to domestic priorities. Yet in the Middle East and much of the rest of the world, arms sales continue minimally abated. Unfortunately, the United States and other arms-exporting nations persist in viewing such transfers as commercial opportunities rather than potential threats to regional and, as we have seen, our own security. We urgently need a convention limiting the sale of conventional arms, especially in the Middle East.

Sustainable Economic Development

Correspondingly, peace and development will be served if a prospective new world order includes a recommitment to international economic cooperation and increased development assistance.

Both the United States and other countries have had bouts of protectionist flu as economic pressures and changing world trading patterns have endangered the previous worldwide consensus on access to goods and money.

President Kennedy, when he signed the historic Trade Expansion Act of 1962, remarked that "a rising tide lifts all boats." The premise remains true, but sadly, its support is less widespread than one would hope.

The General Agreement on Tariffs and Trade (GATT) needs to be reinforced, not weakened, as seems to be the drift today. When the International Monetary Fund (IMF) and World Bank were created at Bretton Woods, the GATT was seen as the global trade organization that could accommodate the interests of both developed and developing countries, while holding back the protectionist and mercantilist forces that were so destructive in the past. But protectionist forces now seem, unfortunately, to be gaining strength, rather than waning.

The GATT, World Bank, IMF, and UNCTAD—the UN Conference on Trade and Development—all are important global institutions. They are complemented by regional trade and financial entities such as the European Community; the Asian, African, and Latin American development banks; and the European Bank for Reconstruction and Development.

Over the past several years fresh regional groups have taken on new life. That is good. But it would be tragic for all of us if this were to end up dividing the world into European, Asian, and North American economic blocs pitted against each other, while leaving the world's poor nations on the outside looking in.

Have-not nations cannot prosper absent a free and open international economic and financial environment. But such an environment alone will not ensure sustained growth. No viable new world order can be based on a trickle-down theory.

We must not forget, however, that the history of the past forty years has shown us a number of surprising economic success stories. The development process, once begun, takes on a dynamic momentum that carries it forward at a self-sustaining rate. Certain interrelated factors can be identified as reasons for success:

- Investments in human capital through better education, health care, population planning, and training
- Investments in infrastructure and industry that have the long-term prospect of bringing success in international markets
- Development of domestic agricultural production, distribution, and processing

By the same token, we have learned that grandiose projects such as dams, superhighways, steel mills, and modern airport complexes often do not make sense *unless* they are part of sound, overall plans for sustainable economic development.

We must face the dual realities that slow growth in both developed and developing nations illustrates a downside of interdependence, namely, that slow growth in each diminishes demands for products of the other. Similarly, we must also recognize that debt service continues to consume a major share of developing country resources. Even resource-rich but heavily indebted potential powerhouses such as Brazil will do well in the next decade not to lose ground. And it is evident that these issues are severely aggravated by problems of populations, environment, and refugees.

The common thread that links these complex intersecting factors is evident: no nation can resolve all its own problems without the help of other nations. *Common action and common security are essential.*

We have learned from hard experiences that multilateral global action is the only way we can achieve widespread sustainable economic growth and expanding investment.

The United Nations estimates that one billion people—one-fifth of the world population—now live in extreme poverty. Yet the World Bank estimates that with sufficient investment, this number could be reduced by almost half by the end of the decade.

Such an effort would require that all nations commit themselves to simple and discrete targets.

The worldwide cost of meeting key social development targets is estimated at $20 billion annually—the cost of sustaining the Persian Gulf War for a fortnight.

It is all a question of priorities: Do we care enough to make a similar investment in the future of humanity?

The long-cited target for development assistance is that each industrialized country provide seven-tenths of 1 percent of its GNP to international development. With slow world growth, this will be hard to achieve. As we know, a heavily indebted developing world will be hard-pressed to borrow enough money or generate enough wealth internally *unless* direct assistance is forthcoming and spent wisely. This is a reality we cannot avoid.

Confronting Critical Global Issues

There are three commanding, sensitive, and closely interrelated issues that both rich and poor must confront if a successful new world order is to emerge. I am talking, of course, about population, environment, and health care. A fourth critical issue, the adequacy of global and local food supply, is largely dependent upon the interactions of these three variables and the constructive interdependence of nations outlined above.

POPULATION

As to population, as nations develop, birthrates invariably recede— another reason why promoting economic development is in our long-term interest. Nonetheless, long-standing religious and social pressures will continue to make it difficult to curb population growth to the extent necessary to relieve pressures on both human health and the global environment.

It is sobering to realize that if current projections hold, the 1990s will produce the largest generation yet born—with some 1.5 billion children entering an already crowded world.

Population growth, by definition, tends to reduce standards of living except in nations that enjoy remarkable economic growth. Population growth also adds to environmental pressure—most directly, in areas where new deserts are created as forests are destroyed to provide land for cultivation. Such growth encourages exploitation of children, migrants, and others in the workplace. It pits neighboring countries against each other as they feel each other's population pressures.

It will take political courage, but leaders of both developed and developing nations must commit themselves to population planning programs as an integral part of their plans for economic development. A good place to start would be for the United States to renew its funding of the UN Fund for Population Activities.

ENVIRONMENT

In contrast to population, the related issue of the environment is on everyone's mind. But the question remains: Are we willing to invest the political and financial capital required to both restore and protect the health of the planet?

In the rush to development, humanity has already done irreversible damage to the planet. And both developed and developing countries are to blame.

More than half of Africa's arable land is at risk of becoming desert. One-third of Asia's and one-fifth of Latin America's land is in the same state. We learn daily of the environmental catastrophe that exists in the former Soviet Union and in much of Eastern and Central Europe.

We are aware, however, that further damage can be checked and some of the prior damage reversed, if we muster the political will to act.

Various ideas for future progress are already in place. Debt-for-environment swaps permit host countries to receive debt relief in return for protecting vital environmental resources. The Global Environmental Facility created by the UN and the World Bank has helped to raise public consciousness and to offer practical alternatives. There is an emerging international consensus that environmental impact assessments should be built in to economic development plans at both national and international levels.

Issues of global warming and ozone depletion, already high on the international agenda, must not be shunned or postponed simply because they are politically difficult. To come to grips with these challenges, the nations of the Northern Hemisphere alone will need to reduce emissions of carbon dioxide from the combustion of oil, coal, and other fossil fuels by perhaps 50 percent in the next twenty-five years or so. And we must eliminate the use of chlorofluorocarbons—or CFCs—and halons on a far more rapid and comprehensive scale than we have so far committed ourselves to.

The scope of the problem is illustrated by the stark fact that if just four industrializing countries—India, Brazil, China, and Indochina— were to increase their use of CFCs and halons up to the limit now *permitted* under the 1987 Montreal Protocol, the annual release of CFCs would *increase* by 40 percent rather than diminish.

Unfortunately, the 1992 UN Conference on Environment and Development was a more rhetorical than substantive success, in no small part hampered by the reactionary position of the United States. Yet the conference did provide an important beginning for change, much as the Helsinki Conference on Human Rights did some years ago. The industrialized countries must take the hard choices of environmental protection if they are to have any hope of persuading the poorer nations to join in.

PROVIDING ADEQUATE GLOBAL HEALTH CARE

Any new world order must also include provision for adequate global health care.

Dazzling accounts of organ transplantation and manipulation of the human genome fill our newspapers and periodicals. Yet, despite giant strides in medical research and development, the global delivery of adequate health care is lagging woefully behind ever-increasing demand. Complaints of failing health care systems are voiced daily around the world. In many countries we hear predictions that health care is rapidly becoming the number-one problem and that many of us, lay persons and doctors alike, are failing to meet our human responsibilities and the challenges at hand.

The facts are clear. In the United States we continue to face such long-standing problems as heart disease and cancer. In addition, new scourges, such as AIDS and widespread international drug abuse, beset us. And new challenges, such as providing maximum functioning and independence to rapidly expanding *elderly* populations, test our skills and political will. On the other side of the coin, difficulties in delivering adequate medical care to expanding *infant* populations, especially those in our own inner cities, continue to hobble us. We have yet to demonstrate maintenance of effort in the long haul.

However, it is in the developing nations of the world where health statistics document the growing disparity between the haves and have-nots, a gulf that divides the world of North from South as effectively as the East-West separation of the Cold War years. Throughout the tropics schistosomiasis, river blindness, pneumonia, and dysentery continue to cripple and kill. We have shown that great strides forward are possible: childhood immunizations, oral rehydration therapy for diarrhea, the conquest of smallpox—but unfortunately, we can balance tales of success with numerous failures.

Infant mortality and life expectancy rates in the developing world must by analyzed not merely as cold numbers in columns; they represent the tragic wastage of human lives, dreams, and potential in countries that can ill afford such a constant loss. AIDS is decimating whole areas of central Africa, disproportionately destroying the young, educated urban hope of that continent. In some areas over 30 percent of the entire population is infected with the fatal human immunodeficiency virus. There has been a resurgence of ancient scourges, with drug-resistant tuberculosis and malaria, as well as cholera, once again reaching epidemic proportions in Africa, Asia, and Latin America. Eradication and control schemes are paralyzed by lack of funds and an adequate cadre of skilled health workers.

And let no one think that these problems will be long confined to the developing nations of the world; infectious diseases simply do not recognize political borders, and the speed and frequency of air travel have broken the old quarantine barriers against contagious transmission.

We also confront the vexing issue of skyrocketing medical costs and the fact that those who suffer most are located not only in the developing countries but also among the poor, including the working poor, in the United States.

There can be no doubt that providing decent and humane medical assistance, particularly to the less-fortunate, will be a most pressing issue in any new world order.

For all these reasons, we must take the necessary actions to close the existing gap. But what should we do?

Recognizing the importance and complexity of these issues, let me, as a layperson, offer a few suggestions.

First, we must put increased emphasis on exploring the linkages among health care, population, and environment.

On population, I make three suggestions:

- Strengthen biomedical research on human reproduction.
- Strengthen psychosocial research on human reproduction.
- Foster incorporation of family planning into health services, especially in the field of primary care.

One vehicle for the achievement of all these objectives would be to broaden and invigorate the Human Reproduction Programme of the World Health Organization.

Second, as to environment, absent careful control of the way in which growth takes place, there are often negative environmental repercussions that adversely affect human health. Examples include lead poisoning; asbestosis; inadequate sanitation; and the direct and indirect threats to health posed by poorly planned, overcrowded urban environments. There are also potential dangers to health from larger environmental problems, such as damage to the ozone layer, toxic wastes, and the incalculable long-term consequences of damage to the ecosystems of the world's great oceans.

Unfortunately, at the UN Conference on Environment and Development, there was not a clear and strong call for significantly increased health-related research backed by concrete proposals for international collaboration. It goes without saying that assuring adequate funding is also essential.

Third, as to health care systems, I believe the international community must increasingly share experience and information on the comparative advantages and disadvantages of various systems, with a view to containing health care costs without compromising access to, and the quality of, medical care. Health care is a fundamental human need, and access to it is a fundamental human right. It must not be a privilege of the elite. Therefore, ways of providing access without generating unacceptable costs must be reexamined intensively and put into place.

In our own country excellent health is often available—to those who can pay for it. However, more than thirty million Americans have no medical insurance coverage whatsoever. This means that they do not receive care, they take their chances with charity care, or they exhaust their very meager savings.

Further, for many years health care costs in the United States have risen at a rate more than twice that of general inflation, and neither the private nor the public sector can allow this to continue. Retired people are losing their benefits, working people are making do with reduced benefits, and many small-business employers offer no health insurance coverage. The American public policy community presently is trying to find answers; but all the alternatives are crushingly expensive, and both the White House and Congress are deadlocked on what to do.

Most Western nations seem dissatisfied with their own systems, and many poor nations have no effective system at all. Each nation seems to stumble, by trial and error, through a succession of failures and shortfalls until it adopts a system that in the end is still not satisfactory. This will not do. The world community can and must demonstrate the political will necessary to develop effective systems, at acceptable costs, and with accessible services distributed equitably within societies.

Finally, further to the point that adequate health care is both a fundamental need and a human right, I suggest that doctors could be more active in addressing issues of health promotion and disease prevention as they relate to the wider national and world communities. If we are to contribute effectively to the urgent health needs of poor nations, we cannot merely transfer our elaborate, curative medical technology. It is an inappropriate system in many other lands and distracts from the basic public health needs of most developing countries. We must learn to put greater emphasis on sanitation and nutrition, safe water supplies, and basic education and vaccination programs, projects that may not be as dramatic as disaster relief efforts but hold the only hope for long-term improvement.

Governor Dean of Vermont, himself a physician, has emphasized that doctors' analytical skills and knowledge are badly needed in public life. He is not talking about the understandable need for doctors to organize to protect themselves against matters such as possible malpractice actions. Rather, he is talking about the need for doctors to take a more active role in the public processes concerned with satisfying the basic right of each individual to receive adequate health care. As we all know, good health not only affects the well-being of those who are fortunate enough to enjoy it; it also generates expanded productivity and enhanced economic growth and stability.

Finally, it should be noted that health and humanitarian assistance can be an effective tool in preventive diplomacy, not only providing immediate lifesaving help, but offering a common ground that can sometimes open the difficult doors to political negotiation. There is much sustained work to be done by both medical personnel and laypersons in addressing a wide range of serious health-related problems.

To do so will require a level of cooperation among different sectors of society rarely achieved.

Fostering Democracy and Human Rights

There is yet another issue that all too often is ignored. It is the erroneous belief that the internal affairs of other nations are not a proper subject for state-to-state discourse, and that internal events in other countries, such as human rights violations, are not our concern. I strongly disagree. Although our options may at times be limited in dealing with such questions, we should never stop trying to apply diplomatic, economic, and political pressures that will help the human family continue its passage toward a more open, more democratic, and freer life.

Those countries that have attempted to create economic development in a totalitarian framework have found it does not work. The human spirit, liberated, is capable of productivity and achievement undreamed of under the deadening hand of conformist control. Just as we have seen that economic and social policy steps are necessary for development, we have also seen that political steps contribute to development—the establishment of constitutional government, the rule of law, accountability of government officials, openness, and respect for human rights.

Moreover, I believe that, just as the United Nations should establish early-warning mechanisms to foresee and, if possible, forestall military conflict between nations, the UN must continue to expand and strengthen its machinery for monitoring and bringing pressure to bear on violations of political and human rights. As I mentioned above, the tragic ethnic conflicts that are devastating Yugoslavia, parts of the former Soviet Union, and, among other countries, Somalia are, at core, egregious violations of human rights.

The period beginning in late 1989 has been tumultuous. But it has demonstrated that the tide of history is not running in the wrong direction. Although some events are currently beyond our control, the tide still flows toward openness and freedom of the individual—concepts that lie at the heart of many religious and ethical traditions around the world.

Strengthening Key International Institutions

In the 1940s the international community held historic summits in San Francisco and Bretton Woods that helped establish a basis for a more enlightened world order. The Stockholm Initiative, to which I referred earlier, proposes that a comparable world summit on global governance be called to address the unprecedented challenges and opportunities that confront us today. The fiftieth anniversary of the UN in 1995 would be an excellent target date.

Such a global summit, which would have to be very carefully prepared through a process of consultation and negotiation among the participants, would, I suspect, lead not only the United States but most nations to the realization that it is incumbent on us to modernize institutions of cooperation—and to create new or modified instructions where needed. I refer particularly to the United Nations, which must be modernized, streamlined, and strengthened to meet the tasks that face it. This will require a number of changes, including broadening the UN's mandate at the Security Council level, strengthening the authority of the secretary-general, and overhauling the UN financial system.

I have suggested several structural changes that could be steps on the road to greater international peace and security . . . to shared and sustainable economic development . . . to curbing uncontrolled population growth and environmental degradation . . . to providing adequate global health care . . . to fostering democracy and human rights . . . and to creating a world order in which both law and justice become the norm, rather than the exception.

As we rush toward our date with the millennium, now less than three thousand days ahead, we have, I believe, an unparalleled chance to define that future. Let us seize the moment.

I

LEGAL AND ECONOMIC ISSUES

The history of civilization can be traced in evolving rules of law that document how various societies in different eras have tried to codify the obligations and rights of their citizens. Domestic ordinances and legislative statutes defining acceptable standards of conduct and behavior have been extended by intergovernmental agreements to protect those traveling in or trading with neighboring states, and to regulate relations among the states. Respect for such agreements enhanced peace and prosperity; their violation created tensions which at times erupted into local conflicts and war.

In our nuclear age, with its rapid travel and almost instant communications, local conflicts can imperil regional and even world peace; large-scale oppression, the violation of basic human rights, and the chronic suffering of the economically deprived are now universal concerns that can no longer be hidden by national frontiers.

In this section two world-renowned jurists reflect on the reality, as well as the limitations and potential, of international law. The former foreign minister of a major power and an African ambassador offer different perspectives on the emerging relationship of developed and developing nations. A distinguished professor then presents economic and philosophic arguments supporting the wisdom of investments in human resources.

1

Human Rights, Humanitarian Assistance, and the Sovereignty of States

RICHARD FALK

During the Cold War, the conduct of international relations was focused on the challenge of the "strong state," that is, the state with the capacity and ambition to project its influence beyond its sovereign territory by military means. In such a setting, peace and security concerns dominated the political imagination, and such ideas as "containment" and "deterrence" were at the core of policy. In the post-Cold War world,[1] the challenge of the "weak state" is moving to the center of concern. A weak state is a state that is in the grips of a war of internal fragmentation or that is in any sense ungovernable, either as a consequence of civil strife or overwhelming humanitarian crisis. Fashioning appropriate responses to the challenges posed by weak states remains controversial and reflects the transitional nature of the post-Cold War world. Unlike the simplicities of the Cold War, the distinctive nature of each weak state challenge makes issues of interpretation of crucial importance. This chapter discusses international humanitarian diplomacy as a central aspect of this developing world situation.

A Conceptual Orientation

World order thinking has been beset by core confusions arising from the failure to distinguish among five intersecting dimensions of concern:

1. *The Geopolitical:* The shaping of international diplomacy through the agency of initiatives, ambitions, and worldview of a leading state or states.
2. *The Statist:* The formal and functional ideas about territorial supremacy and the equality of states that are embodied in the doctrines and practice of state sovereignty, providing the cardinal principle of international relations since the Peace of Westphalia (1648), and continuing to be unconditionally acknowledged in the UN Charter and contemporary international law.
3. *The Normative:* The moral and, increasingly, the legal mandate given to the organized international community, and more controversially, to other actors, to protect civilian victims of official abuse, natural disaster, political chaos and strife, and circumstances of belligerency without the consent of the government that represents territorial sovereignty, thereby to engage in interventionary diplomacy that may include the use of force.
4. *The Logistical:* The combination of technical and military capabilities, at acceptable financial cost, to complete successfully the humanitarian mission within a finite time period and without a high risk of being drawn into a large-scale guerrilla war.
5. *The Psychopolitical:* The psychological underpinnings of political behavior, although frequently overlooked and notoriously difficult to assess, are of critical relevance. Although many elements could be discussed, matters of *perception, memory,* and *identity* will be mentioned here. Perception is the way in which issues of cause and responsibility are perceived by key leaders, by public opinion, and by the media. Memory refers to past occurrences that shape interpretations and policy debates. Identity is the relative degree of identification between the wider world community contemplating a response and the victim community.

Recalling the importance of "the lessons of Munich" during the Cold War, it is evident that for the British foreign secretary, the experience of the United Kingdom in Northern Ireland over the past twenty years or, for President Bush, the abortive effort by the United States to ensure stability in Lebanon after the 1982 war, have caused these leaders to feel reluctant about intervening to stop bloodshed in Bosnia. In the United States, the frequent references to "quagmire" in discussions of Yugoslavia are thinly disguised invocations of the long ordeal of the Vietnam War. Whether a particular historical memory serves to discourage the repetition of mistakes or as an unwarranted pretext for irresponsible behavior is a matter of severe controversy. What is evident and beyond question is the relevance of memory, and its interpretation, to the current debates about what to do in the face of humanitarian crises.

Matters of identity and identification are also important, since the North-South settings of many of today's humanitarian crises also raise issues of race, religion, and culture. The stronger the bonds of identification, the greater the pressure to act compassionately and effectively. As a corollary, the weaker these bonds, the greater the temptation to remain disengaged. Such a pattern fosters an impression of racism in relation to humanitarian diplomacy, especially as the most difficult challenges at present are arising in black Africa. Concerns about identity are further complicated by the fears—genuine or feigned—of weak states that their humanitarian crises are being exploited by geopolitical forces of regional or global scope, and by their insistence that international responses must under all circumstances respect their sovereign rights.

The inability to disengage the normative and psychopolitical from the geopolitical and the logistical generates much of the controversy about where to draw the line between sovereign rights and human rights. The controversy is partly conceptual and theoretical, attracting academic analysis and prescription, but it is partly political, pitting opposed world order tendencies against one another and placing geopolitical considerations into contention with statist considerations. It is necessary to comprehend all five dimensions in their contextual specificity if we are to develop a convincing world order approach to the array of agonizing humanitarian challenges being posed in this early post-Cold War period of world history.

Broad discussion of these underlying issues is also complicated by the urgency of ongoing crises of human rights abuse and humanitarian emergency in Yugoslavia, Somalia, Sudan, Iraq, and elsewhere in the world. These crises have been internationalized, with the media dramatizing the commission of atrocities, generating public pressures to act, especially in settings where the citizenry of powerful countries in the West identify ethnically or religiously with the victims. Responses engaging the geopolitical, the statist, the normative, the logistical, and the psychopolitical are being organized with a variety of consequences. The human suffering is so acute and the difficulties of effective alleviation are so great, that there is an understandable public disposition to suspend discussion of practical or legal constraints on action, and to focus only on how to fashion effective and immediate responses. As has been often observed, legal guidelines developed in relation to moderate circumstances tend to be cast aside in crisis situations. Less often noticed, is the extent to which logistical constraints distort responses by inducing governments and international institutions to take action, more for the sake of doing something than in a manner likely to alleviate human suffering. In fact, under some conditions, doing something is definitely worse for the victim population than doing nothing. Such concerns have surfaced in relation to the deteriorating situations of oppressive violence in both Yugoslavia and Iraq.

The tendency to ignore geopolitics and downplay logistics, while understandable, is unfortunate for several reasons. For one thing, even if not acknowledged, geopolitics is rarely absent from the motivating behavior of leading states. In retrospect, the U.S. government, probably mistakenly, jeopardized democratic prospects in Iraq by failing to set political conditions as the basis for agreeing to a cease-fire in the Gulf War. The largely unacknowledged motive for doing this back in 1990 was a preoccupation with regional stability and moderation. This was understood at the time to mean containing Iran and resisting the further spread of Islamic fundamentalism—that is, factors on the geopolitical level that were consistent with the statist level (thereby respecting traditional notions of Iraqi sovereignty), but that contradicted imperatives on the normative level (ignoring adverse effects on the Kurds and the Shi'ites of leaving Saddam Hussein and the Baath Party in control of a unified Iraqi state; in effect, relinquishing the opportunity to liberate the Iraqi people from brutal oppression either by encouraging separatism by the oppressed groups or by making the democratization of Iraq a war aim of the UN coalition as it had been for the allied powers in relation to Germany and Japan after World War II).

Contrariwise, in relation to Yugoslavia, the U.S. government early on, when it might have been still possible to hold the Yugoslav federation together, was indifferent to the dismemberment of Yugoslavia, partly in deference to Germany's regional ambitions and Croatian separatist sympathies and partly out of dislike of the governing communist elite in Belgrade, and especially of Slobodan Milosevic. In both the Iraqi and Yugoslav instances, the normative dimension was subordinated to the geopolitical. In relation to Iraq, however, the problematic aspect of the U.S. approach was the practice of activist geopolitics in the Middle East, whereas in relation to Yugoslavia it was the practice of passive or laissez-faire geopolitics. To understand the policies acted upon, it is necessary to explicate as well as possible the geopolitical motives, which are both more conjectural and more essential because these motives are rarely acknowledged, and if so, only obliquely. Unlike the statist and normative levels of explanation, the geopolitical tends to remain hidden or obscure because it is not formally legitimated in a manner comparable to the legitimation of statist practice by way of the doctrine of sovereignty or normative justifications by way of human rights and international law.

Geopolitical motivation also operates within regional settings in a manner that often imposes heavy additional burdens on human rights and humanitarian assistance. As a regional actor in the Middle East, Turkey has used its positive links with the United States to avoid support for Kurdish separatism elsewhere in the area, especially in Iraq. Similarly, Thailand, still concerned about the spread of Vietnamese influence in Southeast Asia, has sustained a policy of covert military and economic support for the Khmer Rouge that seriously threatens UN efforts to restore peace and human rights to Cambodia.

Despite these complexities, a more general and coherent orientation seems desirable and possible. This effort is particularly important at this time in the United States, with regard both to public opinion and the policy-making community. The United States, for better and worse, has in the last few years merged its role as geopolitical leader with its championship of a variety of normative causes. This merger reached a climax during the Gulf War, leaving an ambiguous legacy: effectiveness and resolve on one side; insensitivity and inconclusiveness on the other side. One consequence has been to raise suspicions about the capacity of the UN Security Council to act independently of its main geopolitical sponsor. Such a perception of UN independence is extremely important over time in achieving some reconciliation between the statist claims of sovereignty and the normative claims of human rights and humanitarian assistance.

In some respects, the logistical complexities of severe humanitarian crises are equally troubling. If it is correct, as repeatedly reported in the media, that it would require a minimum of 300,000 fully armed troops for an indefinite period to protect the remaining Muslims in Bosnia from Serbian and Croatian attack, the burden of humanitarian intervention seems too high—especially against the background of such long, unresolved internal struggles as have been experienced in Vietnam, Afghanistan, Northern Ireland, and "Palestine." Regarding Iraq, the media carries reports probably not read by most readers, that the "intelligence community" is convinced that the no-fly air zone south of the thirty-second parallel in Iraq will not protect the Shi'ites who have taken refuge in the marshlands, as these insurgent forces are primarily under attack by as many as ten Iraqi army divisions. To engage these forces effectively would require resuming a full ground war against Iraq, with enormous collateral suffering inflicted on the civilian population, or an actual invasion and occupation of Iraq, again an undertaking of great magnitude and uncertain effect. Not only might such an approach fail to relieve the suffering, it might accentuate and prolong it. The same intelligence sources indicate a concern that further encroachments on Iraqi sovereignty would strengthen Saddam Hussein's hold on power both internally and internationally.[2] Of course, responsible international leadership must avoid being pushed into such undertakings, but this may be easier to say than to do. The wavering between action and inaction by both Prime Minister John Major and President George Bush in relation to both crises revealed a tug-of-war, quite literally, between doing something not very helpful and doing nothing while abuse and atrocity persist. In other words, logistical constraints (which include both anxiety about the consequences and scale of military action and about the financing of large, continuing operations) can be formidable even if normative pressures are acknowledged as providing ample legal and moral grounds for overriding deference to sovereign rights. In this regard, all four of the most notable humanitarian crises in 1992 may exemplify this tragic predicament of confronting logistically overwhelming challenges.

The Shifting Weight of Political Discourse

In the last several years, increased support has been given to claims associated with the defense of human rights and the protection of humanitarian assistance at the expense of traditional deference to sovereign rights. Such a shift has resulted *sotto voce* in lowering the barrier on UN involvement in situations where the government in power withheld the consent granted it by Article 2(7) of the UN Charter, which declares off-limits to the UN all matters "essentially within the domestic jurisdiction" of its members. In 1991, Secretary-General Javier Pérez de Cuéllar signaled the new thinking on domestic jurisdiction in his annual report on the work of the UN:

> It is now increasingly felt that the principle of non-interference with the essential domestic jurisdiction of States cannot be regarded as a protective barrier behind which human rights could be massively or systematically violated with impunity. . . . [T]he case for not impinging on the sovereignty, territorial integrity and political independence of States is by itself indubitably strong. But it would only be weakened if it were to carry the implication that sovereignty . . . includes the right of mass slaughter or of launching systematic campaigns of decimation or forced exodus of civilian populations in the name of controlling civil strife or insurrection.[3]

Because this formulation by the secretary-general seemed so calculated to exert influence and has been reflected even more emphatically in subsequent practice, especially during considerations in 1992 regarding Yugoslavia and Somalia, it seems useful to quote again from the same text. Mr. de Cuéllar poses a rhetorical question and then provides a prescriptive answer:

> Has not a balance been established between the rights of States, as confirmed by the Charter, and the rights of the individual, as confirmed by the Universal Declaration? We are clearly witnessing what is probably an irresistible shift in public attitudes towards the belief that the defence of the oppressed in the name of morality should probably prevail over frontiers and legal documents.
> We must now ponder this issue in a manner that is at once prudent and bold. In a prudent manner, because the principles of sovereignty cannot be radically challenged without international chaos quickly ensuing. In a bold manner, because we have probably reached a stage in the ethical and psychological evolution of Western civilization in which the massive and deliberate violations of human rights will no longer be tolerated.[4]

There are several revealing difficulties with this formulation of an undoubted trend in interpretation and practice. To begin with, the former secretary-general's reference to the ascendancy of "the rights of the individual" misses a central point that it is group rights that seem most characteristically at issue in the worst humanitarian crises, which arise from ethnic and/or religious struggles as in Bosnia, Sudan, Somalia, and Iraq. Also, the generality of Mr. de Cuéllar's reference to eroding sovereignty in "defence of the oppressed" is suspect, especially if one contemplates the plight of refugees, most spectacularly, perhaps, in relation to "boat people" from such countries as Vietnam and Haiti. Most surprising of all is his association of this new phase of international relations with "the ethical and psychological evolution of Western civilization." Such a nineteenth-century formulation seems startlingly out of place at the end of the twentieth century!

The most serious oversight in Mr. de Cuéllar's important formulation is its obliviousness to geopolitics. It is correct that if the issues are perceived as sovereign rights versus human rights, then there is a significant shift in favor of human rights both at the level of discourse and practice, and both in the settings of international organizations, especially the United Nations and in relation to leading states. Such a shift is even more pronounced if geopolitical factors fall on the human rights side of the ledger as they do in Yugoslavia, and to a varying extent in Iraq since the 1991 cease-fire. But what if geopolitical factors fall on the sovereign rights side of the ledger, as they do in Kuwait, elsewhere in the Gulf, and in Indonesia? What if the UN, in conjunction with a state, causes severe humanitarian distress while using force to further a geopolitical ambition? (As arguably has been the result of maintaining sanctions in relation to Iraq over the course of the last year or so. A Harvard health survey predicted more than 170,000 deaths of Iraqi children under five from war-related effects.)

The basic conclusion seems clear when related to the conceptual framework described earlier: sovereign rights are definitely giving way to human rights (including a wide range of humanitarian concerns about the relief of civilian suffering, especially famine), but not if geopolitical calculations favor deference to sovereignty. One small confirmatory illustration: during the August 1992 crisis in Iraq involving the establishment of a protective zone for the Shi'ites in the southern part of the country, Turkey refused to allow its air bases to be used for such a mission; no questions were raised about Turkey's sovereign right to withhold support, despite the evident humanitarian urgency and the UN mandate.

Should those who espouse humanitarian concerns welcome this course of development? In general, yes, but with a few caveats, already prefigured. We need to appreciate that geopolitics rules the roost when it comes to the enforcement of human rights and humanitarian intervention. This means, among other things, that the overwhelming number of instances will involve the flow of force from North to South, and that strong states in the North are definitely off-limits. (Can anyone imagine a UN humanitarian intervention in the United States to protect Native Americans against allegations of ethnocide?) It also means *exclusions* for mixed reasons of motivation and capability (it is difficult to construct a plausible scenario that involves helping the Punjab or Kashmir achieve self-determination in the face of India's opposition regardless of the human rights/humanitarian argument), and *double standards* (it is difficult to conceive of any major UN efforts to protect the East Timorese or West Papuan peoples from Indonesian oppression, which has amounted in some past instances to "ethnic cleansing").

There are further grounds for caution. The loudest voices of opposition to this trend come from weak and poor states in the South that continue to regard respect for sovereign rights as integral to their political independence and territorial integrity. Also, many of the champions of this expansion of humanitarian claims come from circles in the North that adhere in their writings and diplomacy to "a realist worldview." One of the prime features of realism as applied to world order thinking is to be scornful of normative constraints on the foreign policy of leading states whether derived from international law or morality. The U.S. repudiation of the World Court's 1986 decision regarding Nicaragua is a dramatic illustration of realism in action.[5] If realist thinking embraces the humanitarian agenda it can be understood in two main, somewhat contradictory, ways—either as a belated acknowledgment, made easier in the aftermath of the Cold War, that normative factors are important even if not all-important,[6] or that in the new world order the humanitarian agenda is a useful geopolitical instrument for projecting power by way of reliance on force (the most cynical reading of President Bush's approach to the Gulf crisis).

International Law

International law is in a state of flux regarding these issues. The encounter between sovereign and human rights has not been authoritatively resolved by either an international codification of rules or through a series of judicial pronouncements issued by a fairly unified World Court. There is a definite trend in diplomatic rhetoric, the practices of states and international organizations, and public opinion to brush aside sovereign rights in the face of humanitarian emergency arising from either political circumstances or natural disaster, but is this trend authoritative? Can one infer in customary international law rules and principles establishing rights (and according to some, duties) of humanitarian assistance on behalf of the organized global or regional communities and of states acting on their own?

There now appears to be a strong consensus among international law experts that the UN can authorize humanitarian intervention, including the use of force, even absent any internal condition that poses a threat to international peace and security. Whether the same scope of authority exists in relation to individual states that act for alleged humanitarian purposes is open to more doubt, and the diplomatic record is more ambiguous. Douglas Hurd has recently argued that Britain and its allies could act in Iraq on behalf of the Shi'ites without the benefit of Security Council Resolution 688 because "(r)ecent international law recognises the right to intervene in the affairs of another state in cases of extreme humanitarian need."[7]

But recall the Western reaction to the Vietnamese intervention in Cambodia to drive the Khmer Rouge from power, thereby saving the Cambodian population from an admittedly genocidal regime, a circumstance of undoubted "extreme humanitarian need." Leading Western states as well as China and Thailand (who for geopolitical reasons, were intent on keeping the Khmer Rouge as a force in being) focused on Vietnamese "aggression" and regional ambitions, demanding immediate Vietnamese withdrawal from Cambodia. Undoubtedly, the Cold War context was an overriding geopolitical factor, as were Vietnam's dubious humanitarian credentials, given its own antidemocratic regime and lamentable human rights record. International law has not established a "clean hands" requirement as a precondition to humanitarian intervention. Indeed, the history of humanitarian intervention over the past two centuries discloses that dirty hands and suspect motives were more common than not.[8]

The mandate of the UN, or in some settings, a regional actor or even an NGO, is an important legitimizing dimension of humanitarian assistance operations undertaken in defiance of the will of the internationally recognized government. International law is shaped in the process of responding to such events, which test the collision of such opposed conceptions as territorial sovereignty and the protection of human rights; that is, the manner in which current humanitarian crises are resolved will provide important precedents that will influence the legal posture toward future crises of a similar kind.[9] The humanitarian law of war as embodied in the Geneva Conventions of 1949 (especially Convention IV on the protection of civilians) and the Geneva Protocols of 1977 provides an indispensable foundation for negotiations and diplomacy in the difficult circumstances of unconventional warfare and massive civilian misery, and are particularly helpful to representatives of international institutions and NGOs.[10] A further effort to elaborate rights and duties of states, international institutions, and nongovernmental relief organizations specifically in relation to humanitarian crises would be of great practical value as a source of guidance in these difficult settings.

Reinforcing Humanitarian Claims

The qualifications addressed previously represent real concerns, but strengthening normative claims relative to sovereign claims is of great historical relevance in this period of heightened ethnic and religious conflict. To raise confidence and diminish skepticism requires a concerted effort to limit to the extent possible the encroachment of geopolitics upon the dynamics of response on behalf of human rights and humanitarian distress. Such an assertion is easy to make. The challenge is to propose tangible steps.

Secretary-General Pérez de Cuéllar set forth some guidelines intended to address this set of concerns in his 1991 annual report:

> First . . . the principle of protection of human rights cannot be invoked in a particular situation and disregarded in a similar one. To apply it selectively is to debase it.
>
> Second, any international action or protecting human rights must be based on a decision taken in accordance with the Charter of the United Nations.
>
> Third . . . the consideration of proportionality is of the utmost importance. . . . Should the scale or manner of international action be out of proportion to the wrong that is reported to have been committed, it is bound to evoke a vehement reaction, which in the long run would jeopardize the very rights that were sought to be defended.[11]

These guidelines are of undoubted importance, but unless interwoven in the political texture of UN operations, they are likely to be of interest only to those scholars and commentators who pay more attention to forms than substance. One need only scrutinize the recent record of the Security Council, especially in relation to the Gulf War and its follow-up, to notice the disregard of such a framework. Secretary-General Boutros Boutros-Ghali made an admirable effort to have similar humanitarian emergencies treated similarly with his plea that the crises in Somalia and Sudan deserve as much attention as the debacle in Yugoslavia, and it seems to have had some effect.

Thus, vigilance and autonomy by the secretariat of the United Nations in relation to these guidelines is one approach. An indispensable step in this direction would be a willingness of geopolitical forces to revalidate the office of secretary-general by encouraging the election of public figures of moral and political stature who would be expected to operate with the sort of independence associated with the tenure of Dag Hammarskjöld and U Thant.

Another approach, as proposed in a peacekeeping context by the secretary-general in his June 1992 report, "An Agenda for Peace," but also applicable to humanitarian claims, is adequate financing and standby capabilities. Without assured logistical capabilities for response, the UN must make a Faustian bargain with its richest and most powerful members, thereby bringing geopolitical factors inevitably, if covertly, to bear on the shape, effectiveness, and legitimacy of the UN response. Even limited financial and logistical capabilities would be important for both confidence-raising and to enable more independent, principled action by the UN, at least in small- and medium-range situations.

A third approach is to augment the disposition already present to shift attention from response to prevention. Surely, one area of effort should center upon restraints on arms trade, both by way of agreement and through policies adopted at the state and regional levels. Here, too, the pieties and the politics are not always mutually reinforcing—to restrict arms trade while not curtailing interventionary diplomacy of geopolitical variety may only aggravate the vulnerability of weak, dissident states in the South.

Such a concern leads naturally to a fourth approach, which may seem utopian to those with a firm realist outlook, but in a formal sense is already legally mandated: namely, to endow citizens with an effective way to challenge foreign policy initiatives in domestic courts as violating international law. Such challenges have been frequently mounted in the United States since the Vietnam War with little success; they are usually brushed aside on procedural grounds, grandly justified by reference to the anachronistic "political questions doctrine." Curtailing geopolitics from below and within is part of an evolving notion of constitutional democracy in an increasingly integrated world. Every person, and certainly every citizen, should be entitled to a determination of whether or not a particular, contested action of the state is consistent with international law. Constitutionalism would be extended to include a commitment to adhere to a lawful foreign policy as determined, when appropriately challenged, by an independent judicial body.

A fifth approach follows from the first four. It summons the world of informal citizens' associations (the NGO dimension of international life) to monitor responses to allegations of human rights violations and in furtherance of humanitarian assistance as rigorously as the violations themselves occurred. For instance, in responding to the horrifying campaign of "ethnic cleansing" in Bosnia, such an approach would publicize the failure to condemn Croatian violations as vigorously as Serbian violations. These independent assessments, emanating from what I have described elsewhere as an emergent "global civil society,"[12] have proved invaluable in exerting pressure on even the most powerful governments when it comes to uncovering patterns of gross violations of human rights or serious instances of environmental deterioration. Such monitoring could also increase pressure to treat similar situations similarly, thereby minimizing the machinations of geopolitics and helping to implement the guidelines advocated in the abstract by Pérez de Cuéllar.

Monitoring is, of course, only the beginning. As it is, many NGOs in the humanitarian context are playing a variety of roles involving the delivery of services and the mitigation of human suffering. There is a useful diversity of NGO perspectives, illustrated by the general insistence of the International Committee of the Red Cross to respect statist guidelines as contrasted to the style of Médecins sans Frontières that stresses the priority of humanitarian considerations and casts aside, to the extent possible, statist and geopolitical constraints. It is not a matter of choosing one style over the other; both are needed, and with due sensitivity can and do complement one another in specific circumstances.

Conclusion

More than ever before, 1992 has focused attention on the humanitarian agenda. The four main cases—Yugoslavia, Somalia, Sudan, and Iraq—are tragedies of immense proportions; each strains both the moral imagination and logistical capabilities to, or beyond, the breaking point. Such prominence has shifted the balance of language and law away from sovereign rights and in the direction of humanitarian assistance. If these tragedies remain unresolved there is a definite threat of political despair and a revival of realist cynicism about humanitarian challenges.

It is important to develop a trustworthy framework of humanitarian response that will alleviate human suffering and victimization in settings in which the logistical challenges are not so overwhelming as they are in Yugoslavia, Iraq, Sudan, and Somalia. It is possible that we are entering an era of recurrent overwhelming challenge—a type of "new world disorder"—but such pessimism is premature, and it is important to do everything possible to avoid it becoming a self-fulfilling prophesy. The political atmosphere is favorable, as never before, to weighting the balance of international law in favor of humanitarian intervention as authorized by the UN and other international institutions. Although such authorization contains the dangers of abuse that have been mentioned, this basic shift of normative emphasis is to be welcomed.

There is one further lesson that can already be learned from the downward spiral of events in Yugoslavia over the course of the last two years: In circumstances of ethnic tension maintain even defective mechanisms of peaceful coexistence, and if these collapse, seek by all feasible means, either their restoration or a negotiated transition to some new, less-than-perfect arrangement that terminates violence and encourages reconciliation.

2

The Contribution of International Humanitarian Law to the Restoration of Peace

MICHEL VEUTHEY

The first purpose of international cooperation is, and should remain, preventing armed conflicts. The second is to preserve humanity in the face of the reality of armed conflicts. This is the primary intention of international humanitarian law.[1] However, international humanitarian law's contribution to peace should not be overlooked. Humanitarian law is a permanent reminder that armed conflict, and enmity between civilians on opposite sides of a conflict, is a temporary, exceptional situation, since civilized life—both within and between communities—is founded on peaceful relations (peace being not the absence of conflict, but harmonious management of conflicts). Additionally, the very nature of humanitarian law shatters the dangerous illusion of unlimited force or total war, creates areas of peace in the very midst of conflicts, imposes the principle of a common humanity, and calls for dialogue (this last aspect being tantamount to recognizing others as one's equals).

The opinions expressed in this chapter are those of the author and do not necessarily reflect the official position of the International Committee of the Red Cross.

Humanitarian law lies at the heart of peace, focusing as much on maintaining peace as on restoring it.

The role of humanitarian law in *maintaining peace* is clear from the fact that many conflicts, both internal and international, have been sparked by serious violations of humanitarian law. Massacres of civilian populations in the Middle East, Latin America, Indochina, and Europe inflamed hatred and passion rather than imposing fear and submission. Furthermore, breaches of humanitarian law have accounted for the spreading of conflicts. For example, refugees, victims of persecution in their homeland, often bring to neighboring or more distant countries the violence to which they were subjected.

The role of humanitarian law in *restoring peace* is twofold: It leaves open the possibility of dialogue, thus averting degradation by excessive violence both between international adversaries and among one's own population. And it aims to solve humanitarian problems (refugees, prisoners, disappeared, missing in action, and so forth) that can become serious political issues.

The Nature of Humanitarian Law

The simplest and most universal definition of humanitarian law is found in the Golden Rule, *"Love thy neighbor as thyself."* The great Rabbi Hillel's response to a question on the Torah was: *"Do not do unto others what you would not want to be done unto you. This is the essence and the rest is commentary."*[2]

The historical sources of humanitarian law are universal and timeless. Throughout the history of humankind, all civilizations have developed rules within the group, tribe, nation, civilization, and religion to ensure its survival—in Asia, Buddhism, Hinduism, Taoism, and Bushido; in the Middle East, Judaism, Christianity,[3] and Islam; in Africa, a multitude of customs valid only within a given tribe; in Europe, the mutual restrictions imposed by chivalry, before the condottieri and lace-clad war generals were supplanted by the humanists (Grotius, Hobbes, Kant, Pufendorf, Rousseau, Vattel, Henry Dunant, and Francis Lieber)[4]—all aiming to avoid excesses that would turn clashes into anarchy and hence make peace more difficult to achieve.

Thus, in article 6 of his *Perpetual Peace*, Kant wrote: *"No State at war with another must allow itself hostilities of a kind which would make reciprocal confidence during future peace."* The legal formulation of humanitarian law again underlines its link with peace. Humanitarian law may be expressed in bilateral agreements, concluded before hostilities begin (cartels), during hostilities (truces, instruments of surrender), or at the end of a conflict (cease-fires, peace treaties), laying down the treatment to be given to civilians, prisoners, sick and wounded, and neutral intermediaries. Or it may take shape in multilateral agreements, frequently concluded in reaction to a bloody conflict. For example, each of the stages of humanitarian law codified in Geneva from 1864 to 1977 followed a war that created a shock wave in public opinion and for governments: the battle of Solferino (1859) between Austrian and French armies was the impetus for the First Convention, in 1864; the naval battle of Tsushima (1905) between Japanese and Russian fleets prompted adjustment of the Convention on war at sea in 1906; World War I brought about the two 1929 Conventions, including a much broader protection for prisoners of war; World War II led to the four 1949 Conventions and an extensive regulation of the treatment of civilians in occupied territories and internment; and decolonization and the Vietnam War preceded the two 1977 additional protocols, which brought written rules for the protection of civilian persons and objects against hostilities. Likewise, most of "Hague Law" stems from the Peace Conferences of 1899 and 1907. And World War II and regional conflicts prompted the drafting of the United Nations instruments on human rights, disarmament, the prohibition of terrorism and mercenaries, protection of the environment, and protection of the rights of children.

The terminology used to refer to these international treaties may vary (humanitarian law, international humanitarian law applicable in armed conflicts, laws of war, law of Geneva, Red Cross Conventions, law of The Hague, human rights in armed conflicts), but all seek the same objective—namely, to limit the use of violence. Some of these instruments, like human rights treaties, are based on a peacetime approach, while others, such as humanitarian law, are normally applicable during armed conflicts. Yet their scope often overlaps, especially as regards the fundamental guarantees they embody.

Humanitarian law may be defined as the principles and rules restricting the use of violence in armed conflicts in order to spare the persons who are not (or are no longer) directly engaged in the hostilities (civilians, wounded and sick, shipwrecked, prisoners of war) and to limit the use of methods and means of warfare of a nature to cause superfluous injury (or excessive suffering, like in the case of "dumdum bullets" or with gas warfare), or which could cause severe damage to the natural environment or betray an adversary's confidence in agreed-upon obligations ("perfidy").

The fundamental rules of humanitarian law are closely linked to the survival of human beings; the safeguarding of cultural objects, places of worship,[5] and objects indispensable to the survival of the civilian population;[6] the protection of medical establishments and units (both civilian and military), public works, and installations containing dangerous forces (like dams, dikes, and nuclear power plants);[7] and the preservation of the natural environment.[8] Even beyond these objectives, the need to maintain a minimum of confidence between adversaries (in other words, the prohibition of perfidy) is one of the pillars of humanitarian law, both customary and written.

By its very nature, humanitarian law aims, through acts of humanity, to preserve the survival of humankind,[9] to maintain the necessary conditions for a return of peace even during a conflict. As one well-known expert on international law, Denise Bindschedler-Robert, writes, "The law of armed conflicts is certainly not a substitute for peace. Nevertheless, in the last analysis it preserves a certain sense of proportion and human solidarity as well as a sense of human values amid the outburst of unchained violence and passions which threaten these values."[10]

FIELDS OF APPLICATION

It is important for the restoration of peace that humanitarian law scopes of application be respected. Whether in material, temporal, or spatial terms, the scope of humanitarian law has always been associated with situations of armed conflict, and hence as standing in opposition to peacetime. However, this theoretical dichotomy does not stand up to scrutiny in practice. It is true, as demonstrated by Professor Dietrich Schindler at the University of Zurich, that since the adoption of the two additional protocols of 1977, there have been four fields of application of humanitarian law: two types of international conflict and two types of non-international conflict.[11] But it is also true, as quite rightly pointed out by Henri Meyrowitz with regard to the Vietnam War, that situations (internal and international conflicts; even so-called peace situations) overlap in time and space, and even the actors involved may change roles.[12]

The commencement of application is sometimes deferred. Perpetuating the illusion of peace, refusing to recognize the state of conflict, and ignoring or concealing victims are not without risks for the application of the law or, indeed, the restoration of peace. As the number of victims grows—individuals are taken prisoner, are tortured and executed, or disappear—and methods and means of warfare degenerate on both sides, it becomes extremely difficult to revert to the legal path. Examples of this are the Algerian War thirty years ago, as well as more recent, even ongoing conflicts. While large-scale military operations are qualified for too long as "operations for the maintenance of order" or even "fraternal assistance," hatred accumulates, and sincere but belated efforts to set reciprocal limits run into enormous problems, with an adverse impact on civilians and prisoners. Thus emerge, somewhat late in the day, the pacifying value of humanitarian restrictions and the bitter taste left by some of the violations of humanitarian law.

The period of application is also subject to change. Often the actual hostilities are brief and a lightning war gives way to a long period that belongs no longer to war but not yet to peace. During this period, which may last several years, victims remain: thousands of prisoners remain in detention (as was the case in the western Sahara, in the Iraq-Iran conflict, even in the conflict between Iraq and Kuwait), and civilian populations come under attack or are continually under military occupation.

At the end of hostilities the accumulation of unsolved humanitarian questions often constitutes an additional obstacle to successful peace negotiations. Humanitarian questions are more and more frequently mentioned in Security Council resolutions. Such was the case in the Arab-Israeli conflicts, in Lebanon, in Yugoslavia, and in Somalia. The question of the repatriation of prisoners of war between Iran and Iraq was referred to on two occasions in Security Council resolutions:

- In paragraph 4 of resolution 582 (1986), which, after an appeal for an immediate cease-fire, reads: "Urges that a comprehensive exchange of prisoners of war be completed within a short period after the cessation of hostilities in cooperation with the International Committee of the Red Cross"
- In paragraph 3 of resolution 598 (1987), which, after paragraphs demanding that a cease-fire be observed and requesting the secretary-general of the United Nations to dispatch a team of observers, reads: "Urges that prisoners of war be released and repatriated without delay after the cessation of active hostilities in accordance with the Third Geneva Convention of 12 August 1949"

Many of those prisoners had not been registered, and the International Committee of the Red Cross (ICRC) was unable to visit them under the arrangements provided for by the Third Convention; a persistent obstacle to their repatriation was the insistence of certain parties on prior settlement of other (military and political) points in the negotiations. ICRC nevertheless considered that the conditions for complete repatriation of all these prisoners were fulfilled, pursuant to article 118 of the Third Convention, the first paragraph of which clearly stipulates: "Prisoners of war shall be repatriated without delay after the cessation of active hostilities."

Pending a full-scale repatriation, humanitarian measures also incumbent on the parties in accordance with their obligations under the Third Geneva Convention—such as the obligations to release the names of prisoners, to authorize ICRC to visit them, to organize the repatriations of wounded and sick prisoners, or even to take voluntary humanitarian measures in favor of prisoners of war who are minors or who have been imprisoned for a long time—are gestures of goodwill that could but promote further gestures of the same kind.

The Contribution of Humanitarian Law to the Restoration of Peace

As noted earlier, breaches of humanitarian law aggravate and prolong conflicts; on the other side of the coin, application of the law appeases and shortens conflicts. Let us consider these two observations.

BREACHES OF LAW LEADING TO CONFLICTS

"Pacification" as a euphemism for genocide is the most extreme example of this, and is not only a question of terminology. History has proven that the idea that a conflict may be shortened by resorting to torture or massacres, bombardments of civilian populations, or terrorist attacks against civilians is a mere illusion. From World War II to this day, violations of humanitarian law have served merely to strengthen the adversary's determination to resist. They also have severely undermined the legitimacy of the party to a conflict condoning inhumanitarian practices. As Albert Camus wrote during the Algerian War, one should be watchful "to fight for a truth without destroying it by the very means used to defend it."

Using the fate of prisoners of war as a pawn in peace negotiations, as was done at the end of the October 1973 war between Israel and Syria (the Yom Kippur War), is a serious abuse that has proven to be counterproductive in both the short and the long term. As ICRC stated in December 1973: "The commitments arising out of the Geneva Conventions are of a binding and absolute nature. Under those commitments, each State unilaterally undertakes, vis-à-vis all other States, without any reciprocal return, to respect in all circumstances the rules and principles they have recognized as vital. These do not involve an interchange of benefits but constitute a fundamental charter that proclaims to the world the essential guarantees to which every human being is entitled."[13]

Breaches of humanitarian law leave lasting and often serious after-effects, which hinder the return to civil and international peace, a fact witnessed during the American Civil War, on the Eastern Front in World War II, between American and Japanese in the Pacific, between Japanese and Chinese, and in the Middle East.

Humanitarian issues that are not resolved during the conflict often handicap the restoration of peace between former adversaries; only when they are settled can normal political and economic relations be resumed, sometimes many years after the cessation of hostilities. The issues of mistreatment of POWs, MIAs, and several thousand Eurasian children, and the case of former "reeducation camp detainees," paralyzed the relations between the United States and Vietnam for nearly twenty years after the end of the war.

APPLICATION OF LAW TO SHORTEN CONFLICTS

Well before the first signs of political negotiation, humanitarian gestures help, informally, to institute a minimum of dialogue between adversaries. Such dialogue may result in cease-fires, often tacit, between enemy positions, to evacuate the dead and wounded; truces to let civilians out or supply them with food and medicines; or contacts to exchange news of the latest captures or even to exchange prisoners. A humanitarian truce may lead to a complete halt in the fighting. In Santo Domingo in 1965, for instance, the joint efforts of the ICRC delegate, the president of the local Red Cross, and representatives of the United Nations and of the Organization of American States succeeded in halting the fighting for twenty-four hours in order to collect the wounded; during that time negotiations were held that put a final end to the armed clashes.

Humanitarian clauses are the first ones adversaries wish to negotiate. For example, the provisional government of Algeria sought first of all to negotiate a "special agreement" with the French government, under article 3 common to the 1949 Geneva Conventions, and then, after Paris refused, initiated the procedure for accession to the four 1949 Geneva Conventions.[14] In 1984, in La Palma, El Salvador, the first item in the negotiations between the government and the guerrillas was "to humanize the war." The first contacts between Soviet representatives and mujahideens in Afghanistan dealt with the plight of prisoners of war. The first talks between various warring factions in former Yugoslavia, held in Geneva in 1991 under the auspices of ICRC, focused on humanitarian issues (exchanges of prisoners and relief supplies to civilians).

The treatment of prisoners plays an important role in the return to peace, as does the treatment of civilian populations. Repatriation of refugees is an essential component in the restoration of peace, but is exceedingly difficult if villages have been razed, and roads and fields strewn with mines. The question is highly relevant today for hundreds of thousands of Afghan, Angolan, Cambodian, and Mozambican civilians.

In noninternational conflicts, amnesty in fact corresponds to an essential feature of prisoner-of-war status—namely, impunity for participation in the hostilities. It also may be a powerful means of relieving antagonism; a measure of national reconciliation following a crisis; or a political solution to a crisis, to encourage partisans of armed struggle to turn (or return) to democratic forms of political struggle.[15] It is, indeed, with this in mind that article 6, paragraph 5, of protocol II of 1977 invites governments "to grant the broadest possible amnesty to persons who have participated in the armed conflict." The object of this provision, according to the ICRC commentary on protocol II, "is to encourage gestures of reconciliation which can contribute to reestablishing normal relations in the life of a nation which has been divided."[16]

The same question also arises at the international level: Should one prolong hatred and punish criminals (on the losing side), or wipe the slate clean and decree, as in the Treaty of Nimeguen of 1678, an official "act of forgetting"?[17]

Today, the question of whether priority should be given to pardon or to criminal prosecution is still a subject of negotiations. When Bangladesh was created after a war between India and Pakistan, criminal proceedings against 195 Pakistani prisoners of war and civilian detainees held for violations of humanitarian law (accusations of genocide) were curtailed: Pakistan made full repatriation of all prisoners, without exception, a condition for peace negotiations. The matter was brought before the International Court of Justice by Pakistan, and later, with the agreement of the parties involved, was struck from the register.[18]

The provisions of the 1949 Geneva Conventions—reaffirmed in 1977—would no doubt be sufficient to punish the violations that still occur in many conflicts. Actual prosecutions have been rare and unilateral events. Nevertheless, governments party to the 1949 Conventions (practically all members of the United Nations) should not too easily escape their responsibility to prosecute violators of humanitarian law: the preventive role of the effective use of the universal jurisdiction provided for in the 1949 Geneva Conventions for all states party could contribute not only to justice but sometimes also to peace.

Conclusion

HUMANITARIAN LAW: A SUM OF EXPERIENCES

Humanitarian law, both customary and treaty law, is a sum of real-life experiences. It is based on warnings against the destructions of war, and advice on how to overcome difficult choices and avoid tragedies that have become increasingly deadly as modern means of destruction have become more powerful and the number of protagonists involved has grown.

One should use the dynamic role of humanitarian action to disarm the adversary, or, in the words of Sun Tzu, "build a golden bridge to the retreating enemy." The military, political, and economic effectiveness of humanitarian behavior—on top of the fact that such behavior is consistent with ethical requirements—should be constantly emphasized, in the hope that we may finally move on from chaos to peace, from internecine strife to dialogue. Octavio Paz writes:

> Hölderlin sees history as a dialogue. Yet that dialogue has always been interrupted by the sound of violence or the monologue of chiefs. Violence exacerbates differences and prevents us from talking and listening. Monologue is the negation of others; dialogue does of course maintain differences, but it provides an area within which alterities [alternatives] coexist and become interleaved. To establish such a dialogue, we have to affirm what we are while at the same time recognizing others and their inherent differences. Dialogue prevents us from denying ourselves and from denying the humanity of our adversaries.[19]

This perspective has much in common with the Dalai Lama's declarations and writings on the vital necessity for compassion in order to cope with today's difficult challenges:

> A leitmotiv: compassion, compassion, compassion, which enables peace to be achieved, both individual and collective. Altruism is the key to universal peace. It is the only option in today's planetary debacle. It is a matter of life and death for humanity.[20]
>
> The problems we face today—violent conflicts, destruction of nature, poverty, hunger, and so on—are mainly problems created by humans. They can be resolved—but only through human effort, understanding and the development of a sense of brotherhood and sisterhood. To do this, we need to cultivate a universal responsibility for one another and for the planet we share, based on good heart and awareness.[21]

THE LETTER AND THE SPIRIT

The letter of humanitarian law is essential. It must, however, be applied in the proper spirit: for the benefit of victims, rather than to serve momentary interests.

Not only legal experts can understand humanitarian law; every human being is capable of grasping its fundamental principles. Pierre Boissier, founder of the Henry-Dunant Institute, trained new ICRC delegates on the Geneva Conventions with this method: he gave his students a blank page and asked them to rewrite in their own words the essence of the four Conventions, placing themselves, in turn, in the position of the wounded (First Convention), the shipwrecked (Second Convention), prisoners of war (Third Convention), civilians in an occupied territory (Fourth Convention), and enemy forces. This powerful maieutic ploy brought out essential provisions of instruments that seem at first sight extremely complex and difficult, but then, as individuals respond to vital requirements, are easily understood.

TOWARD A GLOBAL CONCEPT OF HUMANITARIAN ACTION

Humanitarian law has evolved from a law protecting only certain categories of individuals (from the medieval knights to today's prisoners of war), to a set of provisions ensuring human rights (protecting entire populations).

Humanitarian instruments in force form part of international law and are interlinked with the system of international security, whether for arms control or for peaceful settlement of conflicts. They have still to be placed in the general context of the development of cooperative relations at the political and economic levels.

Humanitarian action cannot be confined to exceptional or emergency situations. Different actors (individuals, organizations, and governments) will be involved in different situations, each most effective in one particular sphere of activity. Nevertheless, no one should lose sight of the problem as a whole and, in particular, of how his actions interrelate with those of others. (For instance, decisions by the International Monetary Fund, a typical "peace" organization, may have caused riots or even civil war in some Third World countries.) At the same time, implementing humanitarian law facilitates a return to peace and reconstruction of a country, and emergency relief organizations (like ICRC) will give way to development organizations (such as the United Nations Development Programme, the World Bank, the WHO, the FAO, and others, including the other components of the International Red Cross and Red Crescent Movement and the increasing role of nongovernmental organizations).

Humanitarian law and its principles thus form part of a chain of solidarity: at the height of a conflict, with the necessary support of other political and economic measures (military peacekeeping and peacemaking measures should normally be kept separate from humanitarian activities—at least humanitarian activities by non-UN organizations, especially from ICRC) and efforts to mobilize public awareness, they often constitute a vital link contributing to the restoration of peace. As President Abraham Lincoln said, *"Do I not destroy my enemies when I make them my friends?"*[22]

3

Obligations
and Responsibilities
of Donor Nations

DAVID OWEN

It is part of the purpose and principles of the United Nations enshrined in article I of the Charter to achieve international cooperation in solving problems of a humanitarian character. In Somalia and in Bosnia in 1992 we have seen humanitarian abuses of a degree and depth that are scarcely conceivable for those of us who live comfortable Westernized lives. In both countries we have seen the need for an armed UN capability to protect and ensure the delivery of food, medicine, and other vital supplies. We have seen nightly on our television sets the linkage between humanitarian and peacekeeping efforts that the UN Charter wisely anticipated.

In the Security Council the Charter has shown itself to be a flexible instrument of policy-making. The absolute doctrine of noninterference in the affairs of a member state, itself a product of the old East-West conflict, has now been replaced, and the Charter is being used as a legitimate instrument for dealing with humanitarian abuses "in extremis" inside a member state. This new interventionist role will, however, have to be very carefully used by the Security Council, or the veto will constrict. In the main it will still be prudent for governments to rely on nongovernmental organizations, like Médecins sans Frontières,

Oxfam, and Save the Children, to cross frontiers when governments fear to tread. The UN must not attempt to become the peacemaker of first resort when internal conflict emerges within member states. Nor can its proven peacekeeping role be expected to easily or always develop into a proactive peacemaking role. The UN has more freedom to develop now in ways that in the Cold War period would have been inconceivable, but it is not capable of policing or providing for the world. The UN has to limit itself to working with the member states in a partnership; it will never replace the member states as a world government. That is an aspiration even more foolish than the dream of a "United States of Europe," acting in all respects as a single country like the United States of America.

What the UN can do is to mobilize its member states to act to uphold the Charter. The decision of UN secretary-general Boutros Boutros-Ghali to establish the Department of Humanitarian Affairs within the UN and the appointment of an emergency relief coordinator to help deal with natural and man-made disasters represent a welcome recognition of the need to place humanitarian principles at the core of all UN activity.

As a member of the Independent Commission on International Humanitarian Issues[1]—which produced, in addition to its final report, many detailed reports on how humanitarian principles should govern our response to famine, indigenous peoples, the encroaching desert, street children, the vanishing forest, refugees, the disappeared, and modern wars—I am convinced that humanitarianism embraces more than just human rights. Human rights was rightly moved higher up the world agenda by President Carter in the late 1970s. But inevitably at that time the very words *human rights* became embroiled in the rhetoric of the East-West confrontation. Also, the definition of what were human rights reflected the Judeo-Christian tradition, itself predominantly Western. What our Humanitarian Commission attempted to do was to bring other great traditions, those derived from the Muslim, Buddhist, and Hindu faiths, into a broader and more international definition of humanitarianism. It was helped in doing this by having Sadruddin Aga Khan and Crown Prince Hassan as its cochairmen.

If, as I hope, UN activity is to be evermore influenced by humanitarian attitudes, then it is essential that they are universally acceptable attitudes. That means that they cannot always reflect the same order of values that dominate in the Western industrialized democracies. Also, international humanitarian attitudes need to be enforced by the more extensive application of international law. Crimes against humanity must be able to be brought before an international court if there is to be any really new international order.

Of all UN humanitarian concerns, health—in the wider World Health Organization (WHO) definition—is the one that provokes the least controversy and receives the maximum cooperation. WHO, within the UN family, has a proud and enlightened record of advancing the cause of humanitarianism. In seeking to further promote humanitarianism, the UN would be wise to reassert the preeminence of better health, for it can still do much to lighten the multiple loads of life. I make no apology for starting with its greatest success, the eradication of smallpox.

I was involved, albeit very much on the margins, in the Smallpox Eradication Programme during my period as U.K. minister of health, starting in March 1974, when one of the first papers presented to me dealt with the program, which had started in 1967. In 1973 the number of recorded cases of smallpox in the world had been 135,904. This was the highest for fifteen years. Nevertheless, I was advised that "target zero" was still felt to be on course, and the Ministry of Health and WHO doctors were optimistic.

In 1975 the eradication of smallpox from Asia was achieved. This was itself a formidable milestone, since it meant the end of transmitting the variola major virus, which had caused the most severe form of smallpox. However, I well remember officials coming to me around this time desperately worried about the future effectiveness of the whole eradication program. Smallpox was spreading rapidly among the hundreds of thousands of people displaced by floods and famine in Bangladesh, proving once again that disease is the all too frequent accompaniment of natural disaster. The number of smallpox outbreaks in Bangladesh had increased from 78 in October 1974 to 1,280 in mid-May of 1975. I was told there were no reserves of money left within WHO to cope with this extra demand. Sweden was contributing more money, and I unhesitatingly found extra money from our own hard-pressed U.K. National Health Service budget for WHO. We did the same in the U.K. the following year, when smallpox, though suspected of being confined in sixty-six villages in Ethiopia, looked likely to break out across the country as Ethiopia was engulfed by civil war. The WHO health teams faced formidable difficulties dealing with the scattered and mobile population in the Ogaden Desert, and they needed more vehicles and personnel. Despite the increased WHO activity, the smallpox virus did spread to adjoining countries. In Djibouti, Kenya, and Somalia some 3,000 cases occurred. Even so, the last case of naturally occurring smallpox was in Somalia in October 1977: ten years, nine months, and twenty-six days from the start of the Intensified Smallpox Eradication Programme.

A tragedy then occurred when two cases of smallpox, resulting in one death, were caused by a laboratory infection in Birmingham, U.K., in August 1978. Fortunately, this did not spread, and on May 8, 1980, the Thirty-third World Health Assembly made the historic announcement that smallpox had been eradicated from the entire world. That was a magnificent result and one of the great successes of international activity.

Eradication of smallpox could never have been achieved without the existence of WHO, nor without the dedication of WHO staff, with their ability to stimulate the interest and commitment of health staff in individual nations. Eradication was not a centrally imposed program; rather, each national program adapted it to fit particular circumstances. There was also an active research program running parallel to the fieldwork. The program gathered momentum from 1967, but even as late as 1976–1977 no one could be certain of a successful conclusion. As we now look to future health challenges, we would be wise to learn some of the lessons from that smallpox program, and the 1,460 pages of *Smallpox and Its Eradication*[2] provide a comprehensive source.

Eradicating other major diseases—whether cholera, dengue hemorrhagic fever, schistosomiasis, AIDS, or malaria—will be harder. Health has no frontiers; nor, unfortunately, has ill health. Hunger and famine still haunt millions of people. Millions survive on far too few calories. Millions barely have access to water and even less often to clean water. It has been estimated that every day, 40,000 children die from illnesses that are made life-threatening because of malnutrition. For many of these diseases, unlike smallpox, there are no vaccines or even curative medicines. Those medicines that are available in developing countries may not be the best, and health care can be rudimentary. Unlike smallpox, many of these diseases are hard to diagnose, to trace, and to control. Also, we cannot hope to manage most of these diseases by relying only on health workers, for all aspects of public health are involved—water supply, sanitation, housing, nutrition, and a host of other factors—necessitating multidisciplinary activity.

AIDS is the global illness that has captured the world's attention. Even though the number of people who are HIV-positive is relatively smaller in the industrialized world than in the developing world, media attention has ensured that massive resources for research have been allocated, and pharmaceutical firms have identified a clear commercial interest. It is estimated that 12–14 million people in the world are HIV-positive, and the latent period means that there are many more who will develop the virus.

Thankfully, AIDS is being tackled in a major way internationally. I would be a happier person if I could see any prospect that a fraction of the effort devoted to AIDS would be devoted to malaria in the coming decade. Today over 2 billion people are exposed to malaria every year. Over 250 million can expect in any one year to be infected by malaria, and over 100 million can be expected to be taken ill by malaria, with over a million dying from it. Malaria is the most dominant and debilitating disease in the world, particularly among children in the endemic regions. A serious humanitarian strategy for relieving global suffering must give malaria a far higher priority than it has at present.

I was fortunate to be of a generation of medical students where tropical medicine was an integral part of our study course. Sadly, that can no longer be said for every medical school in the world. When I began as a medical student in 1956, the eradication of malaria was in full swing. Even during the consolidation period of the 1960s, medical opinion was still optimistic that the disease would become a rarity. Unfortunately, resurgence of malaria took place in the 1970s; even so, when I ceased to be minister of health in 1976, most were hopeful that malaria would soon be eradicated. Unfortunately, that optimism was misplaced. Even more worrying is the way the situation has worsened with the spread of resistance to drugs by the parasite and to insecticides by mosquitoes. A ten-year study in Thailand has confirmed that the parasites are mutating to become resistant. Even quinine, used for over five hundred years against malaria, is failing fast.

Eradication of malaria is no longer a WHO objective, having been replaced by the less-ambitious target of control. It was very appropriate that in October 1992 a conference of all the nations' health ministers specifically discussed the problems of malaria. At present neither our governments nor the pharmaceutical industry devotes anywhere near sufficient funds to research or prevention.

Experts are, however, hopeful of developing a specific peptide as a vaccine for malaria. But the world should not wait for the development of a vaccine or even vaccines before taking substantial steps toward eradication. I hope that the eradication of malaria will be restored as a formal objective of the World Health Organization. Yet for such a pledge to be credible, it will require immediatcly a greatly expanded research effort on both vaccines and new drug therapy. In terms of control, it will need to involve from the outset many other UN agencies in an integrated program. Many techniques—for instance, in China the treatment of bed nets with deltamethrin—have produced encouraging results.[3] But it also has to be admitted that with DDT banned, the substitutes are often not as effective; nor is the discipline of dealing with the breeding grounds. Again control has not been helped in countries where wars and poverty have diminished their public health capacities.

Malaria eradication, starting in the 1990s, could provide the challenge for a new humanitarian effort. It will be far more demanding and include many more scientific disciplines and much greater communal effort than was represented by the challenge of smallpox in the 1960s.

One of the most exciting aspects of the new secretary-general's actions has been his readiness to look at the working of the Administrative Coordination Committee, the body that brings together the leaders of all the UN specialized agencies, including the World Bank, the International Monetary Fund (IMF), and the General Agreement on Tariffs and Trade (GATT). The secretary-general takes the chair, and this could become one of the most important bodies outside the Group of 7 (G-7). A high-level consultant has been asked to report to the secretary-general, and there seems to be widespread acceptance that this is the time to make changes in the structure of international cooperation. Without change we will continue to see overlap, rivalry, and gaps in the activity of the UN family.

Will the donor countries be ready to find special finance for malaria? One reason they might is that it is possible to see a return at least in part for their own citizens. First, the eradication of malaria would end the necessity for preventive drug therapy and for any vaccination. Second, as tourism becomes evermore global, and travel to sub-Saharan Africa and Asia from the European and North American continents becomes evermore popular, the tourist industry has an interest in the program. There is even some indigenous malaria still in the United States of America, which would become more troubling if newspaper stories of tourists' dying from cerebral malaria started to appear in the American press. There is also the future possibility of extensive climatic change.

I do not wish to belabor the point of self-interest, but there is no doubt that in donor countries, it is easier for health ministers or ministers responsible for overseas development funding to persuade their electorate to allocate extra resources when it is possible to demonstrate some connection to them or some return to them from an investment.

It is also important to stress that while there are obligations and responsibilities among donor nations to help promote good health, eradicate disease, protect human rights, emphasize humanitarian principles, and provide humanitarian assistance, these are mirrored by obligations and responsibilities of recipient nations, too. We have seen the end of a world polarized since 1945 between communism and democracy, capitalism and the command economies. We are all, it seems, now ready to accept to a lesser or greater extent the market economy. Even the distinction between developed and developing nations is diminishing. Some nations have characteristics of both within their own territory. What should be the ingredients of any new approach to the dilemma of the growing imbalance between the rich, industrialized nations and some of the poorest nations, particularly on the African continent, and also the contrast between nations with a good and bad health record? The Organization for Economic Cooperation and Development (OECD) and the World Bank are the key institutions on economic relations. The Development Assistance Committee of the OECD is the key Western policy institution. Though there is a case for bringing the UN more into this field, it must not be done by weakening or reducing the credibility of these proven vehicles. Adjustments are needed in the structure of the world economy, but that can happen only by consent and within the framework of an avowedly market-based structure. New relationships can be encouraged to develop on the basis of enlightened self-interest, based on investment and reasonable returns, with the private sector fully participating. There is a need for investment to be properly conducted, and too often in the past in the hands of weak or corrupt governments we have seen new investment go disastrously wrong. But it has gone wrong even more frequently when well-intentioned governments have had an inadequate understanding of market economics.

It would be of mutual advantage for any new structuring of the world economy to be based on an open acceptance of different though often complementary commitments from both donor and recipient nations. Thankfully, the world is moving toward such a new contractual approach between nations, based on mutual obligations and responsibilities in many fields.

We have seen contractual relationships develop in their most structured form in the European Community of twelve member states. The Association of Southeast Asian Nations (ASEAN) countries have developed their own distinctive pattern. The North Atlantic Free Trade Agreement among Mexico, Canada, and the United States is but a most recent example, and there are others. We are seeing a recrudescence in the authority of the Organization of American States, and there are many who believe that the massive and often unique problems of the African continent could be helped by an increase in the authority and effectiveness of the Organization of African Unity. The Conference on Security and Cooperation in Europe grouping, which essentially links the North Atlantic Treaty Organization and the old Warsaw Pact countries, is young, and its economic development is as yet in its infancy; but I would expect this aspect of its development to be particularly rapid.

Politics and economics are inseparable. Where organizations start by aiming for a common market and dealing predominantly with trade and economics, experience shows, this inexorably leads to wider political activity. But the same is not true when politics is put first. As the terms of membership become more demanding of the member states, they develop the concept of contractual obligations freely undertaken, and often legally binding. Nations can contribute in different ways and at times unequally, and the best structures are designed to provide for give and take. Bargains are struck in which there are different gains and different losses, but the outcome aims at overall fairness, albeit over time. These relationships are not characterized by the description of recipients or donors. Some nations may be net financial contributors, others net gainers, but the relationship is still that of partners. It is high time for the UN to now consciously turn away from the very concept of donors and recipients, and fashion deliberately a relationship of partners.

In addressing the future of our planet, the 1992 United Nations Conference on Environment and Development (UNCED), held in Brazil, tried to marry obligations and responsibilities on the environment. One point soon became apparent: that progress could not be made on an environmental relationship hitherto polarized rather inappropriately as donor and recipient nations. Cynics have said that UNCED was a triumph of politics over economics and of exaggeration over science. Though there was perhaps inevitably a lot of this, there was also the start of a true understanding of the necessity to consider as part of sustainable development market adjustments to reduce environmental damage.

Sustainable—which means environmentally sound—growth will not be achieved without a complex interplay between former donor and recipient nations. There is a sound economic case for increasing direct aid from the developed to the developing nations. This was the essential message of the Brandt Commission report, which said that "above all, . . . a large scale transfer of resources to the South can make a major impact on growth in both the South and the North and help revive the flagging world economy."[4] Now even the North-South divide is otiose. There are developing nations now clearly within Eastern Europe, and there is a danger that they are attracting preferentially more aid than, for example, the poorest nations in Africa.

One of the great problems for the world economy is the debt overhang and the fact that some of the poorer countries return their whole aid support program in interest charges. A greater readiness on behalf of the rich nations to write off debt to the very poor is essential. But if such action is to be undertaken by developed nations, then developing nations will have to be readier to accept responsibilities in fields like public health, narcotic production and sales, forest management, and pollution controls. They will have to absorb some of these costs and be ready to contribute, with the payback coming in different forms. They might contribute through conservation—for example, with tropical reforestation schemes—or through UN peacekeeping.

Another area for reciprocal action involves the rapid population expansion in parts of the developing world. Population growth places enormous stress on developing countries' capacity to provide sufficient food and improve standards of living. It also makes many in the richer countries feel that the problems of the developing world are insoluble. The world population presently totals 5.5 billion people; it is expected to reach 10 billion within sixty years, and the World Bank has estimated it could exceed 12 billion if the birthrate in the Third World does not fall. We all know that it is not enough just to provide for birth control. The high rate of infant mortality, poor prenatal health care, and the lack of education for women have all to be addressed. These programs need not only funding by the richer countries with low birthrates; they need commitment from within the poorer nations with high birthrates. The programs need to be managed and given the high priority they deserve. Population control is just as important an ingredient for sustainable development as protection of the environment. It has become, unfortunately, emotionally linked with internal political debates about abortion and the right to life, whereas international population programs have wisely excluded any support for abortion and steered clear of the fundamentalist debate.

In summary, I do not see the donor nations enlarging foreign aid substantially if there is no obvious sign that the recipients in the developing world will accept responsibilities that contribute to international objectives beyond the confines of their nation-state.

Take pollution. The U.S. government's estimates for the cost of reducing industrial production sufficiently to reduce emissions to levels discussed in Rio was 1–3 percent of annual GNP, or as much as $3 trillion over the next twenty years. This may be an exaggeration, but at least it draws attention to the fact that there is, by any standards, a substantial cost. If traditional donor nations are to accept such reduced pollution targets as some traditional recipient nations advocate, then the recipient nations would be wise to face up to the risk that the donors will be less generous in other areas where they contribute to development in recipient nations. It is no use talking about "political will" the whole time when too often those who bleat have never faced an election in their life and seem oblivious to voter attitudes.

The reluctance to contribute more among donor nations is already very marked. With the collapse of the Soviet Union and the dire economic problems of the many new countries in Eastern Europe, a heavier load is bound to fall on the G-7 countries—the United States, Germany, Japan, the U.K., France, Italy, and Canada. There is abundant evidence that the United States is going to expect Japan and the European Community to increasingly match their contribution to international projects, not unreasonable, given that there is broad equivalence between the three nations' GDPs.

The U.S. Congress is becoming evermore blasé about moral arguments for increasing the foreign aid budget. That budget currently amounts to less than 0.2 percent of GDP, which is the smallest proportion since the Second World War and the smallest proportion among all industrialized countries.[5] In the United Kingdom over the last decade our aid budget as a proportion of GNP has been substantially reduced—and, I regret to say, without any obvious political backlash.

Already the U.S. aid budget is heavily skewed toward Israel and Egypt, where political factors weigh heavier than poverty. The U.K. and France skew their aid program toward former colonies, and the ability of the Japanese to tie their aid to the purchase of Japanese goods is quietly envied by many other industrialized nations. The old liberal belief that tied aid has a special value has been surreptitiously ditched by many nations even if they continue to espouse its virtues.

The United States has a treaty obligation to pay 25 percent of the UN budget and 30 percent of the regular UN peacekeeping budget. There is no case for the United States to take such a high share of the peacekeeping budget, and Japan and Europe should offer to shoulder at least 5 percent of that contribution. Some other Western European countries may, too, have to shoulder some of the costs formerly carried by the Soviet Union. In the future all nations should fund UN peacekeeping from defense budgets. It is absurd that defense departments all over the world charge their foreign ministries extortionate amounts for peacekeeping operations. The public justification for maintaining defense spending in future years will increasingly be that it is making an indirect or direct contribution to UN peacekeeping. The ridiculous attempt to regard UN assignment as a separate element from national security must end. Fortunately, the concept of "common security,"[6] which we developed in the Palme Commission, is now commonplace. Bring peace to Zimbabwe, and it becomes easier to deal with the tsetse fly and malaria. Let the fighting continue in Mozambique, and the disease spreads. Had there been even a small UN force on the Kuwait-Iraq border in the summer of 1990, there could well have been no military action like Desert Storm. Poor nations that maintain grotesquely large defense forces, sometimes for no other reason than to prop up discredited dictatorships, must not get as upset as they have in the past if donor nations demand reduced expenditure. The promotion and sale of evermore sophisticated defense equipment to poor nations by rich nations has to be curbed. Attempts to do so in the 1990s are less likely than earlier efforts to be seen as a perpetuation of colonial attitudes. Politicians in donor nations are well aware of the anger of their electorates when asked to increase aid contributions or contribute to peacekeeping operations for countries that spend large sums of money on arms, on grandiose spending on palaces, and on government offices and international airports.

Part of a new contractual world order is a more open and honest understanding of mutual obligations and responsibilities. Compassion, concern, and altruism, as well as the concept of international citizenship, are far better nurtured in a world order where value for money is not a concept to be ashamed of; where investment can be seen to produce a return; where debt write-off can be expected to benefit the poorest, not those who rule; where peacekeeping and peacemaking are not constantly undermined by arm sales; where national boundaries cannot be changed by force of arms; and where humanitarian principles, attitudes, and actions are underpinned by the sanctions of international law.

4

The Concerns of Recipient Nations

KOFI N. AWOONOR

The firsthand experiences of those of us from developing countries, where almost all humanitarian relief work has been concentrated over the past two decades, provide us with a unique opportunity to reflect on the subject in the hope that the end result will advance our knowledge of the entire humanitarian relief enterprise, as well as provoke suggestions as to new initiatives and corrective measures for this important aspect of international work, particularly in the areas of organization, administration, and the perception of relief aid to developing nations. Humanitarian aid in our times springs from the universal acceptance of the principle of international cooperation, as a necessary component and expression of our common humanity. The idea of the interdependence of states has become a major fixture of our global reality. The need to help one another is a cornerstone of the philanthropy that has accompanied all religions and cultures since time began. Though built into it is an enlightened self-interest, which includes the euphoria, well-being, and self-congratulation that accompanies philanthropy, there is also the accompanying human feeling that in the face of the unfortunate our own good luck becomes writ large, and we thank whatever God who sent us for it.

But humanitarian aid has come more and more to be perceived as the responsibility of the rich to the poor, the affluent to the indigent. It is this perception which becomes confused with many other issues that are part of the global political and power realities. Our world is still dominated by power politics in international relations. The statistics are stark and revealing: a few well-endowed industrialized nations, 15 percent of the world's population, control 70 percent of the world's trade returns.

On the other side of the coin, 30,000 children will die today mainly from intestinal disorder; 10 million will die this decade in developing countries, as a result of a combination of causes including malnutrition and preventable diarrheal ailments. Two million children will die this year from vaccine-preventable illnesses. There are 1.3 billion people worldwide who have no access to safe drinking water; 2.3 billion people have no access to sanitation services; 135 million people live in desert areas where virtually nothing grows. One child out of every five children dies at birth.

In a world dominated by the self-interest of the powerful, sometimes the concerns of the poor and the nonpowerful become palpable irritants. In a UN negotiation session to align the interests of the poor countries with those of the rich, one European ambassador was loudly heard to say that the game has changed and only the important ones must now play.

Sometimes, humanitarian aid is constructed into intimidating and even primitive foreign policy objectives. The United States publishes an annual register of countries that did not vote with it on all issues. This register is distributed dutifully and unashamedly every year to remind every state of their sins of commission and omission, with loud hints as to possible punishments or rewards to be meted out. During the Persian Gulf debate in the Security Council, Yemen was threatened after it cast a vote opposing the wishes of the United States. The threats were later carried out, and a small package of assistance for educational work in Yemen was withdrawn. Such are the ways of democracies.

Advances in electronic technology have made it much easier for every disaster to be brought dramatically into the living rooms of almost every home in the advanced nations. Spectacles of human suffering and misery have become the daily fare of the television industry. We come into regular and close encounter with death and tragedy, even when they occur in a far distant corner of the globe. Definitely, the world has come to respond more quickly to human tragedy across the globe as a result of this crucial development. But we must also admit that the farther away the tragedy, and the less familiar the victims are to us, the more remote, unreal, and even boring it all may seem.

The media have become specialists in the projection of the gory details. The more bloody, traumatic, and spectacularly devastating or sensational the tragedy, the better for the corporate profits that will accrue to the owners of the networks. So to those of us from the poor nations, the heroic efforts of those intrepid journalists have become deadening experiences, as our cynicism vies with their seeming callousness when these reports seem to be palpably colored with blatant racial and cultural prejudices. It is as if the only news worth reporting from those benighted parts of the world are human tragedy and suffering, vividly depicting colossal miseries and never-ending disasters.

But the real tragedy and suffering of developing countries are not readily available for the cameras because they are eternally cyclical, undramatic, and relentless, and of almost biblical proportions. This is the compound of recurrent human misery, acutely stamped by the most abject conditions of poverty and degradation. In almost every nation of the so-called Third World—whether in the *favelas* of Rio de Janeiro or the slums of Abidjan, in Accra's Nima, or Lagos' Agege or the garbage dump communities of Lima and Manila, or in the desperate slums of Port-au-Prince—we are confronted by a merciless picture of human misery that defies the cynicism of any television in the comfortable homes of middle-class viewers in BellTerre or in the hills of Hollywood.

Such unremitting misery may escape the attention of humanitarian relief experts both within and outside the UN, but it represents the grim face of underdevelopment—the absence of economic and social opportunities, the sad harvest of illiteracy and its consequent joblessness. It accounts for the widening disparity of statistical data with which we are now fairly familiar. It is the direct result of a global economic regime that virtually confiscates the fruits of the toils of these nations to satisfy debt payments, a lack of access to foreign markets, a lack of access to rudimentary technology for such simple sectors as water treatment, and the scarcity of regular vaccines for curable ailments. Often, it is the result of venal politicians who rob the coffers of the state with the full connivance of powerful foreign governments who need thieving and murderous thugs to further their own foreign policy agendas.

The end result is that the human condition in the poor nations does not capture the imagination of those who live in the advanced countries; the remorseless truth does not inspire spectacular and heroic efforts on the part of the world community. So it is more than ironic when an American administration claims credit for toppling Marcos, or disavows any responsibility for Mobutu, or chastises nations burdened by debt and denied access to market for not following free market economic principles.

Let us return to the drama of disasters. During our protracted negotiations on the issue of appointing a coordinator for UN humanitarian relief, it was quite evident that some of our partners of the North are locked in the arrogance of those who are always supposed to give. This was dramatized by the reaction to our proposal to look more closely at cyclical disasters, such as the droughts of the Sahel and the Horn of Africa or the recurrent floods of Bangladesh. We asked that the developed world help the UN initiate major water production and reforestation programs in the desert countries of Africa as a long-term solution to African drought. It was as if we were asking for a ten-mile canal to be dug on the moon. The response was stone-faced amazement at this piece of audacious nonsense. We also proposed examining engineering possibilities that might assist India, Nepal, and Bangladesh in organizing construction on a system of dykes and canals to control for all time the raging waters that cause regular havoc in the low-lying lands inhabited by over the 100 million people on the shores of the Bay of Bengal. A few years ago, 200,000 people lost their lives in one of the worst floods to hit the area. The drama was impressive, breathtaking, absorbing, and riveting. The planes flew in food and medicine. Other life support equipment was dropped. A few days later the waters subsided, leaving behind bloated corpses of man and beast. The drama was over. The donors from far away in their magic machines and their well-ironed and expensive tropical clothes, vaccinated against all the known Third World diseases, had gone. Next year or the next, this frightening visitation shall occur again with the venomous predictability of a biblical plague prophesied by a saintly if half-demented prophet. The silence that met our proposals was deafening.

It is a fact that disasters afflicting developing countries produce more devastating effects on their population than the same disasters when they occur in advanced nations. An earthquake of 6.5 on the Richter scale in California will, by some perverse logic, produce fewer victims than a quake of 3.5 in Nicaragua or the remote hills of Turkey. A flood in the Tennessee basin or in the Mississippi delta will kill fewer people than a flood of lesser ferocity in the lower Ganges or upper Nile areas around Khartoum.

The fact is the nations in the South have neither the infrastructure to minimize the effect of such disasters nor the means to evacuate the affected people, evaluate the phenomenon, or adequately alert their citizens. The zones occupied by the poor suffer most during these afflictions, as their tin and cardboard houses or flimsy palm frond dwellings are swept along like paper toys being crushed by a giant bully let loose among the fragile edifices. The first thirty minutes to an hour is the most crucial time for saving lives in any natural disaster. For the poor nations, particularly in the vast portions inhabited by the very poor, this half hour should be reduced to ten or fifteen minutes, whether it is in the case of an earthquake that attacks in the still of the night or a placid, slow-flowing river that rises on a stormy night and by early light carries all before it.

This relentless human tragedy is grounded in one grim and merciless reality—underdevelopment. No matter what euphemism you use for it, underdevelopment has a strong historical basis in many of the nations of the South. Its roots lie in relentless colonial programs based not only on naked and brutal exploitation of their natural resources but on the equally brutal and systematic marginalization of their people and the pitiless neglect of their social advancement. Colonialism, many tend to forget today, left many people gasping on the edge of an arrested and denuded history, and ruled by the imposed foreign machinery of debilitating, dehumanizing, and oppressive regimes. None of them was benevolent. Rather, each fulfilled the most ancient of imperial agendas wherein conquered peoples provided the labor, the markets, and at times the cannon fodder for thriving empires, some of which would later blossom so gloriously into wonderful expressions of the democratic ideal. The slaves who toiled in the fields and kept the Athenian democrats in victuals and raiment have never enjoyed recognition as contributors to human civilization.

Their fate was repeated over a thousand years later in the fate of the colonial and subject peoples. Nineteenth-century European anthropology assigned to them an intrinsically inferior status; the Roman Catholic hierarchy debated for centuries whether some of them had souls. Their nations, peoples, and lands and rivers were discovered by intrepid explorers and missionaries, who braved the abominable climates in which they lived to bring them the startling facts of the names of the main features of their landscapes and to redeem them from their dark, satanic ways. As the imperial flags fluttered in the wind, the sons and daughters of the subjected peoples were exported in chains in a profitable human trade. The foundations of the underdevelopment of

Africa were laid in this iniquitous trade. In a perceptively seminal book entitled *How Europe Underdeveloped Africa*, the late Guyanese social scientist, historian, and political activist Walter Rodney advanced the thesis, earlier promulgated by Eric Williams, the late prime minister of Trinidad—hardly a black power militant—that the foundations of European and American industrialization and development were predicated on the massive profits that accrued from the slave trade.[1]

The details of this phenomenal piece of historical data are depressing. Underdevelopment in countries such as ours is neither God-ordained nor self-willed. The advanced nations have yet to come to terms with their responsibility. It is the fundamental outcome of a massive historical injustice for whose redress the word "reparation" is utterly inadequate.

One would have thought that once the liberal democratic ideology triumphed in the aftermath of two horrendous world wars, and the colonial subjects had, by dint of their own energy, thrown off the yoke of foreign domination, that a fair and equitable global economic order would emerge from the old prewar order to redress the historic exploitation. No. It is as if by some divinely instituted arrangement, those who hewed wood for four hundred or more years must continue to hew wood. The marvelous perceptions that launched Bretton Woods obviously did not include those long-held exploited territories of Africa, Asia, or Latin America. The victors over fascism and nazism, in a war fought to make the world safe for democracy, constructed an impeccably efficient trade system based on the most refined mercantile ideas, liberally appropriated from the nineteenth century. The heirs of Adam Smith understood the firm link between economic power and military power. The refinement consisted of a wonderful recipe for European reconstruction under General Marshall, and the concerted work of restoration on behalf of the foes that had recently been thrashed on the battlefield. The former colonies, emerging from years of virtual servitude, received literally nothing for their pain. It is said repeatedly that the slaveowners always get compensated for losing their chattel.

In almost all the postcolonial countries, national reconstruction—the building of schools, clinics, universities, and basic socioeconomic infrastructure that benign colonialism forgot to provide—became the responsibility of the independent governments. Strive as they might, they could not meet the needs and the expectations of their people, since the prices for the commodities they had been programed to produce under colonialism were subjected to the ferocious laws of the marketplace in which they did not have a say. Development for the former colonies therefore did not feature in the dictionary of the colonial powers in their relationship with their former subject peoples.

But a new war broke out—the Cold War. And we, the newly independent nations, were drawn into this war on the basis of our legitimate desire to leap-frog into the twentieth century. The superpowers with their elaborate war games sacrificed us in order to score ideological points. The Soviet Union, born of a dream that keeps man's hope for freedom eternally alive, dissipated its energies in a senseless arms race, and neglected to give its people freedom and bread. The purity of the Marxist paradigm was sullied by the construction of a bureaucratic leviathan distinguished by massive corruption and mindless brutality. Its paradise, complete with locks on the gates, extended neither development nor humanitarian help to the former colonies, with the self-serving excuse that Marxists did not plunder, had no colonies, and did not sell slaves. In our naïveté we expected so much from our socialist, anti-imperialist comrades, but with a few spectacular exceptions, such as the Aswan Dam, and despite well-planned geopolitical considerations, not many clinics, schools, libraries, or pipe-borne water systems were built for us. In many instances they gave us guns—efficient killing implements, of which the AK-47 has become more than a nightmarish metaphor.

The huge sums spent in wars of liberation against forces equally well equipped by the other side provide neat corresponding fiscal data for the numerous graves, single and mass, that litter our various nations. Over our carcasses, the ideological giants locked horns. Not much clean water, or vaccines, or books accompanied enterprises of such historic moment.

Development is the only instrument that will remove the stigma of charity that accompanies all humanitarian relief efforts. It is the only means by which all nations of the South shall escape the horrors of cyclical droughts, death by flood, and devastating earthquakes. Our demands remain simple and direct: fair prices for our commodities; an international economic system that provides a safety net for each country to earn its way by the fruits of its labor through a fair exchange mechanism that protects every currency, not only those of the G-7; access to markets where we can sell our products; transfer of technology that will enable us to develop water resources, grow our food, clothe our children, and educate our people.

In the last twenty years, the UN adopted development programs with declarations meant to provide international support for economic growth and development in our parts of the world. But the basic economic growth that will spur development eludes us precisely because our friends, members of our human family in the rich North, refuse to heed our call for an equitable global economic and trading system. In recent years, a number of countries have undertaken structural adjustment reforms stridently insisted upon by our friends. Enormous sacrifices have been made. In some countries, riots rocked fragile governments as the price of corn rose overnight and workers' wages stagnated. Some of us were told the way to succeed was to export more of the already depressed luxury agricultural produce which we had been organized to produce under colonialism at the expense of food production. So we grew more coffee, more cocoa, more sisal. We cut more timber, dug more bauxite and manganese. We borrowed heavily to do all this. Meanwhile, our debts soared as we struggled to service their exorbitant interest rates and as the prices for these commodities were subjected to the voracious greed machine that propels the commodity markets run by cabals of speculators. The fruits of our labor were confiscated in the daily movement of the stock market indices. The anonymous farmers of Bolivia, Ghana, Ethiopia, Uganda, many of whom are malnourished, without access to health facilities, whose barefoot children have no schools—ten million of whom will die of preventable diseases before they are five—are the direct victims of this vicious, cruel, and inhuman economic system.

Today, the underdeveloped countries subsidize the affluence of the advantaged economies of the world through the transfer of their paltry earnings to service their foreign debts. The international financial institutions and their support bases of donor nations do not want to address this vexatious and terrible issue. Even feeble efforts made through either the United Nations Development Programme (UNDP) or the United Nations Conference on Trade and Development (UNCTAD) are quickly subverted by conspiracies manufactured in the Bretton Woods institutions, which are dominated by the rich nations. So the UN, born in the hope of providing a peace predicated on the total eradication of poverty, is rendered impotent to carry out the objective that will prop up the edifices of peace. Instead, its Security Council is being slowly turned into a war cabinet which will mandate the use of military force to police the world in the name of preventive diplomacy, peacekeeping, and peacemaking. What about the peace that derives its first energy from a full stomach, ample health, education, adequate shelter, and protection from capricious nature itself?

Humanitarian assistance, laudable as it is, cannot be an end in itself.

Behind it must be a true desire to help the poor escape poverty for all time. Spectacular food drops and dramatic stunts by accomplished airmen alone cannot solve the problem. The real stunt is to accept the humanity of those who inhabit the poor nations and to marshal the energy to eliminate the incubus of their underdevelopment. None of those nations had the advantage of empires or colonies, nor spectacularly heroic wars of conquest of land and resources, in the cause of which many aboriginal peoples were virtually wiped out. It is precisely because they are victims of these historic degradations that they ask for more than a basic redress.

One hears a great deal these days of donor fatigue. There is also something called recipient fatigue. Next time, look straight into the eyes of your regular corner panhandler. He may be a beggar, but, more often than not, he has not lost his sense of dignity or self-worth. It is with these things that he confronts you anytime you drop a dime into his paper cup; it is with these things that he challenges your humanity in that silent, instant clash of wills—that he is no less a person than you are. There is an Akan-Ashanti saying, *Obira Ye Onipa,* "everyone is a human being," trite and commonplace, but profoundly reflective of the singularly binding philosophy of the African peoples who placed man at the center of the universe and constructed everything else around him—family, food, shelter, the gods, and the afterworld—all revolve around this central entity, living, undying, eternal.

Today, we hear voluble hymns of praise to democracy, multipartisan politics, and the free market. These, we are told, are inextricably linked. It is our humble opinion, however, that democracy—true democracy—cannot thrive in conditions of poverty. Haiti, that heroic little country that was the first to throw off the chains of slavery, remains the poorest republic in the Americas even though it breathes in the shadow of the greatest democracy of modern times. When Father Bertrand Aristide was overthrown, howls went up in every capital of the world, with the loudest heard in the chambers of the UN. It takes very little imagination to come to the conclusion that Haiti's democracy, like democracy elsewhere in the underdeveloped nations, cannot thrive unless Haiti's $3 billion debt is cancelled, and adequate fiscal opportunity for development is given. A democracy that cannot guarantee jobs, safe drinking water, and secure streets for its people is a hopelessly flawed democracy. So we witness the feeble antics of sanctions against Haiti, while many merchants of the same countries that sponsored the resolution continue to defy it every day.

Democracy is linked with development, the absence of poverty, and the availability of food, health, and education facilities; development defines stability and social equilibrium. Poverty breeds dictatorship, just as social well-being, well spread, breeds a truly democratic order. Political democracy is meaningless without social democracy.

Many of our nations, in accepting the proposition that our earlier governments mismanaged our economies, are now implementing structural adjustment programs under the direction of the International Monetary Fund (IMF) and the World Bank. One of the most painful features of these programs is the condition that our governments withdraw entirely from the task of providing social services. The modest and rudimentary social infrastructures we constructed after independence, since colonialism did not deem it fit to provide them, have long since collapsed during the decades of acute economic crisis. The withdrawal of the state from its social responsibility, designed, some say, to keep inflation low and balance the budget, has led to a serious crisis in such basic social services as health and education. The persistent threats and actual occurrence of social unrest are major components of the civil unrest that plagues our nations, leading to the creation of conditions that are not conducive to humanitarian efforts. It seems that the great era of the monetarists has no accompanying humanitarian philosophy, hence the despair that exists even in the inner cities of the great, market-driven democracies, where the problems of the urban poor, the homeless, and the unemployed are left to fester into regular riotous eruptions, whether in Los Angeles, Bristol, or Paris.

The disengagement from the social sector that is being forced upon all developing countries undergoing structural adjustment for receiving aid, and under the rubric of balancing their budgets and eliminating deficits, is downright brutal and inhuman. We who have not had advantages of adequate social sector investment either before or after independence are being prevented from making the very investments that constitute the basis of our people's survival.

There is a link between the central core of Darwinism—the concept of the survival of the fittest—and the more outrageous ideas of Reverend Malthus. Darwin, to our mind, was not aware of the disenabling and incapacitating conditions which historical imperialism, slavery, and colonialism imposed upon many peoples of the world. According to Darwin's severely objective scientific law, those who do not survive because of disabilities imposed upon them fall into the category of those who should not be born at all. Malthus went further: Help should not be extended to these unfit specimens through charity lest they reproduce their own kind, peopling the world with inferior beings that threaten the survival of the entire species.

These concepts have manifested themselves through the conduct of European politics over thousands of years, from the Greek and Roman efforts to civilize others through conquest, miscegenation, or annihilation, to the various excesses of more recent European imperial enterprises. Nazism, whose pedigree derives from some of the best thinkers, including Darwin, Malthus, and Nietzsche, resulted in gas chambers and concentration camps. Apartheid, the Bantustans or so-called homelands of South Africa, and the most recent horrors of ethnic cleansing in the former Yugoslavia are other examples of racist excess.

Lords of Poverty by Graham Hancock is a book that is said to have drawn angry reactions from both official UN spokesmen and representatives of charitable organizations, but represents an exciting and truthful, if at times overstated, account of the entire humanitarian industry. In a hilarious prefatory poem by Ross Coggins, we are presented a wonderfully honed ballad that ridicules some of the obvious insensitivities of the industry, just as it correctly provides an underlying link between the issue of charity and development.

> *Excuse me, friends, I must catch my jet—*
> *I am off to join the Development Set.*
> *My bags are packed, and I have had my shots*
> *I have travellers' cheques and pills for the trots.*
> . . . .
> *We discuss malnutrition over steaks*
> *And plan hunger talks during coffee breaks.*
> . . . .
> *Just pray to God the biblical promise is true*
> *The poor ye shall always have with you.*[2]

This book's basic thesis, which coincides with ours, is that many people in the rich countries, especially those who run governments, though ready to send food and medicine to the poor abroad, are not prepared to support long-term development programs for these nations. As Hancock puts it, "The emotional demand of mass suffering is strong and direct. It compels us to reach for our cheque books in response to disaster appeals. . . . It influences the behaviour of elected governments [who] impose political ban on countries but yet are generous with humanitarian assistance."[3]

Humanitarian assistance is guided by moral virtue, a sense of anticipated well-being that the gesture of giving is sure to bestow on the giver. Not to give can be seen as immoral. A mild degree of self-righteousness propels the gesture, the feeling of "but for the Grace of God, there go I" that refuses adamantly to be transmutted into the reality that it *is* I who go without. In the end, what exactly, as Hancock asks, are the recipients expected to be grateful for?

The regular tardiness of relief assistance sometimes renders a great deal of it totally useless to the victims of disaster. A case in point was the Sudan floods in 1988. One million people became homeless as a result of the flooding of the Nile. The victims' precarious condition was compounded by their original state of destitution. The rich nations responded with great fervor, but two weeks after the floods, there were no signs of any relief effort on the ground except a few tents, a dozen or so plastic sheets, some blankets, twelve sacks of floor, and a large container of fresh meat which had begun to rot in the sweltering heat of the Sudan.[4]

Some of the aid agencies, we are told, spend a disproportionate amount of their funds on enrollment and committee activities, communication, information and education services, publications, management, and fund-raising. In 1984, one agency in Britain was said to have sent only 7,000 pounds of the 193,000 pounds it raised from the public to the poor nations! Another organization in Dallas was said to have sent overseas only eighteen cents out of every dollar it received in donations. One famous charity organization was accused by both the UN and the State Department of failing to send a single cent out of the $18 million it raised expressly for famine relief in Ethiopia in 1985.

A major failure of relief organizations working in poor countries is their inexplicable refusal to use expertise already existing in those countries. Instead, huge sums are spent importing experts from the United States and Europe. So operational logistics and other costs become enormous. One report claims that in Phnom Penh, the food of the expatriate experts was imported from Europe. In Thailand, UN officials complained that the Swiss relief team spent its days in air-conditioned cars and their weekends on the beach. One WHO official was said to have insisted on a fee of $50,000, a generous per diem, and a ticket for his wife before he put in a stint in Phnom Penh. The level of consumption of relief aid personnel has become a scandal, more disgraceful than the scandal that accompanies the life-style of UN representatives and international bank and development experts in poor countries. The immorality of this life-style is made more unacceptable when placed against not only the standard of living in those poor nations but also the very conditions of disaster and its accompanying acute indigence these good merchants of charity are supposed to relieve. Many disaster experts turn out to be beachcombers and adventurers out to make a quick buck with doubtful credentials as relief aid administrators. As one commentator on African relief situations puts it, "During an emergency, whatever their background, almost any white face which arrives on the scene has the chance of a job."[5]

Hancock makes a startlingly revealing yet credible point that many of the Christian relief organizations use relief work as a means for evangelizing. Ted Engstrom, the former president of World Vision, was quoted as saying, "We analyse every project, every programme, we undertake to make sure that within that programme evangelism is a significant component. We cannot feed individuals and let them go to hell."[6] The hungry can be consoled that at least they will enter heaven on a full stomach.

The charge of using humanitarian assistance to force people to become members of a particular religion or denomination was leveled against World Vision in Honduras where it operated relief work in the refugee camps of that country between 1980 and 1981 under the direction of UNHCR. Threats of withholding food supplies were allegedly used to coerce Salvadorean Catholic refugees into attending Protestant services. The charge was also made that World Vision allowed the Honduran military, which had close ties with the right-wing Salvadorean death squads, access to the camps. Two refugees who were handed over on May 22, 1981, were found dead on the border. World Vision denied any involvement.

A UN relief organization that has persistently come under serious criticism over the years is its High Commissioner for Refugees (UNHCR). Not an implementing agency, UNHCR's function has been relegated to raising funds and passing them on to private relief organizations that undertake relief work in the field. It is believed in many quarters that UNHCR's field supervision has been poor, leading to many abuses over the years. One recent audit exposed a markup of 300 percent on purchases of tents, beds, blankets, and sheets through fictitious companies. Auditors discovered that in many cases "the quantities purchased were considerably more than the number of refugees, and there were substantial differences between the quantities paid for and those actually received."[7] One U.S. voluntary agency working in East Africa received almost half a million dollars entirely in the United States as "relief staff support costs."[8]

The refusal to use local expertise has been pronounced in UNHCR-supported relief efforts especially in Africa. Even qualified Africans who live in the countries where some of the relief work originates have been bypassed for field appointments in favor of non-Africans with neither the knowledge nor the fundamental empathy requisite for work among desperately needy people on the continent.

Waste seems to accompany a great deal of humanitarian work in poor countries. The story is told of a $1 million all-purpose health center in Somalia finally costing $2 million because two flush toilets instead of one were added, even though there was neither plumbing nor water source to which the health center could be connected.[9] Hancock writes, "The folly, irrelevance—and sometimes dangerous idiocy—of much that passes as humanitarian assistance is not publicised by the aid agencies . . . for understandable reasons. On the contrary, their press releases paint a rosy picture."[10]

There have been occasions when food considered unwholesome was cynically shipped to poor nations under humanitarian assistance. After the Chernobyl nuclear disaster in 1986, a great quantity of contaminated food from the European Economic Community (EEC), already declared unwholesome and illegal in Europe, turned up in aid shipments. In 1988, a number of African countries, including Ghana, were forced to reject meat and milk from the EEC because they were radioactive. What was sad in this ghoulish affair was the repeated assertions by a number of European spokesmen that the food was good. Hancock reports another incident when, under the auspices of Food for Hungry Inc., nineteen tons of "Survival Food and Drugs" were shipped to Cambodia during the famine there in 1979 and 1980. The food was so old that San Francisco zookeepers had stopped feeding it to their animals, and the life of some of the drugs had expired fifteen years earlier. After Djibouti rejected 974 tons of EEC wheat in 1982 on the grounds that it was unfit for human consumption, the Community succeeded in getting the same shipment to Zaire two years later. It was undoubtedly enthusiastically received by the corrupt and immoral Mobutu regime with a great fanfare. EEC butter oil containing a very high level of aerobic germs ended up in a soap factory in Morocco. EEC's humanitarian aid record has been described by auditors as a "catalogue of disasters" "with bureaucratic errors and inefficiencies, wastefulness, inappropriateness and unforgivable lateness."

Moving from the grotesque to the comic, one British charity's response to an African emergency was to send a relief package made up of packs of tea, tissues, and tampons, while a West German voluntary agency sent 1,000 polysterne igloos which proved too hot to live in, and since they could not be dismantled, they had to be burnt. One health official in Nicaragua spoke sadly of how donations of medicine seem to be preponderantly milk of magnesia. Laxative and anti-indi-gestion remedies are hardly the most appropriate remedies for starving people.

Sometimes, humanitarian food aid poured indiscriminately into a poor country creates major problems for that country's farmers, who inevitably are driven into bankruptcy. USAID once gave Guatemala 41,000 tons of corn after a devastating earthquake. Because much of the country's food supplies were intact, this massive generosity wiped out a large percentage of Guatemala's farmers, who had worked hard to bring in a good harvest that year, by collapsing domestic prices for grain. A little research into Guatemala's own food capacity and some external financial assistance to support the small percentage of the population affected by the earthquake could have averted this obvious disaster for the farmers.

The most controversial feature of the charity industry lies in the area of fund-raising. It is very much like the classical collection of pennies by Christians to send missionaries into darkest Africa in the nineteenth and early twentieth centuries. Loud appeals centered around multiple images of starving children and dazed refugees have constituted the pattern for what one commentator called the "capitalism of mercy," in which aid organizations compete to boost the size of their take along-side their media image, with little or no reference to those for whom their charity is meant. As worthy as the causes behind these charities may be, a feeling of deep sorrow and apprehension overwhelms any sensitive soul, particularly from the poor nations, who witnesses the grandstand mega-media events that have come to be associated with relief appeals for funds, whether it is Bob Geldof and his spectacular concerts, or a group of well-heeled superstars singing "We Are the World." One hears also of ugly struggles for turf as media organiza-tions and big business with decided commercial interests in poor na-tions are manipulated into parting with huge sums of money which are then written off as corporate tax reliefs.

Sometimes, our disasters are exaggerated or understated. In 1987, the incipient Somali drought was written off by the USAID representa-tive as exaggerated by the government in Mogadishu in an obvious attempt to take advantage of donors overseas. In the same vein, World Vision has gained the reputation for gross overexaggeration of disas-ters in poor nations. *The National Catholic Reporter* claimed on Octo-ber 2, 1981, that twelve million people in East Africa were on the "verge of death" in the "greatest human need crisis of our time." The statement, it was later established, was not true. Even pictures of old disasters are sometimes used to ring alarm bells for incipient disasters that never occur; it is good for fund-raising.

At times, the tearfully mawkish appeals represent obvious overkill. Do these types of appeals in their excessive sentimentalism not humiliate the poor and the would-be beneficiaries as passive victims incapable of doing anything for themselves? Are we the peoples of the so-called Third World so helpless that we can only be portrayed as eternal objects of pity? What of those pictures of men, women, and children frozen in time, flies buzzing around their facial orifices, their hands eternally outstretched? The psychological effect of these images upon many of us is deep and unsettling. Steve Bonnist of the Intermediate Technology Development Group has written about the perpetual negative mechanism at work in the constant barrage of images of the South perfected by the Western media. Bonnist writes of an infamous promotional video that showed rats crawling around the feet of actors, portraying starving natives scrabbling in the dust for grains of corn. These disaster appeals on behalf of nameless victims of disasters reinforce the stereotype of underdeveloped nations who can do nothing for themselves unless the rich and the powerful intervene. Nothing positive happens in our parts of the world—nothing. We have not worked for ourselves; we have not achieved anything; we do not amount to anything.

At the outbreak of the Liberia crisis, West African nations sent out an appeal to the United States and other rich nations for humanitarian intervention. Master Sergeant Doe, a classic creation of the U.S. military machine, had begun a systematic massacre of the members of those tribes considered opposed to him. But the fact is during the ten years of Doe's rule, the United States poured $500 million in arms alone into Liberia. After Doe rigged the elections in 1986, Assistant Secretary of State for Africa Chester Crocker stated openly that the United States could live with the victory. Between 1986 and 1991 more than 200,000 Liberians were massacred. Refugees poured over the frontiers into the neighboring states as far as Ghana. The Americans sent in warships to evacuate their nationals and left all the others to be finished off by another set of pathological killers named Taylor and Johnson. The volume of humanitarian assistance extended to Liberian refugees by the West African nations of Ghana, Guinea, Sierra Leone, and Nigeria, beyond the lives lost by their peacekeeping troops, is yet to be computed. I was confronted at the time by an irate Western European ambassador about an incident of Ghanaian planes bombing Taylor's position. According to the ambassador, this was reprehensible conduct. I recall that encounter especially these days as the atrocities of Bosnia and Sarajevo are daily fares on the news, and the democracies are about to send in troops.

The time has come for efforts made by disaster-struck countries and their neighbors to be recognized as a valuable and laudable component of global humanitarian relief work. It is not true that only the rich help the poor in those desperate times. The poor also help the poor and the needy.

The Liberian refugees are still in Ghana. The friends of Liberia and the architects and accomplices of the disastrous foreign policy that led to Doe and Taylor are still mouthing voluble alibis. We take consolation in the fact that as a small country, even if we were propelled by the need to protect and save the lives of our nationals, we went into Liberia and took out more than 100,000 people on our ships and planes. We have set up camps where food, clothing, education, and health are being dispensed with some help from abroad. That is a glowing example what regional efforts can mean, when neighbors help neighbors in crisis situations. The capacity of poor nations to help themselves must not be ignored by the international community. It is still an intrinsic part of the task of saving lives worldwide. Ethiopia, Sudan, Somalia, Honduras, Guatemala are examples of countries that not only helped themselves but also helped their afflicted neighbors.

Perhaps a few pieces of advice to our would-be benefactors will not be out of place at this juncture:

1. Let the donor countries be more discriminatory about whom they give the authority to dispense charity to disaster victims in the poor nations. Some screening of the personnel, work habits, fund-raising machinery, and basic cultural attitudes of these organizations will help to weed out the charlatans, the racists, the religious bigots, and the agents of dubious political causes.
2. Let the poor nations be spared the proliferation of charity organizations in their midst. The unseemly jealousies accompanying these organizations in the field does no good to the name and reputation of the serious ones.
3. It will be of great value if, as much as possible, the victims of disasters are consulted as to their most urgent needs.
4. Aid cannot and should not be seen as something the rich, out of some troubling guilt complex, bestow upon the unfortunate. Therein lies the humiliation and the degrading paternalism that have accompanied aid work for many years.

5. Recognize the humanity, the resilience, and the boundless courage of the victims of disasters, many of whom live below all imaginable standards of survival, eke out precarious existence from harsh, unfriendly terrain—volatile mountainsides and flood-prone riverbeds.
6. Abjure the arrogance and patronizing self-aggrandizement summed up in Margaret Thatcher's statement about Ethiopian peasant farmers: "We have to teach them the basics of long-term husbandry."
7. Let us work to remove from the aid and charity industry the malevolent notions of ethnocentrism, bordering on stupidity, that denigrate and abuse the cultures and ways of nations of the poor South—the attitude that allows a European nurse to run a medical relief program in Uganda while a fully qualified Ugandan doctor is assigned menial duties in the same camp. The inbred superiority complex that has characterized Europe's and America's dealing with all of us seems to permeate even humanitarian relief work. The victims of disasters or the poor of the world are no less human than the organizers of relief agencies and the exalted representatives of the donor nations.
8. Finally, let each humanitarian relief agency in the West work to persuade its government that development is at the core of the search for a better life for the millions in the poor nations. The ignorance of or refusal to confront this basic fact found among aid workers reinforces the paternalistic attitude on which repetitive humanitarian work is predicated. It is as if the desperate conditions of underdevelopment are necessary for humanitarian relief work to perpetuate itself.

During the discussions of UN resolution 46/182 on strengthening the coordination of relief efforts, there was ample evidence that although the developed countries believe that humanitarian assistance is an effort deserving support, as soon as the word development is mentioned, they go into a fit of fear and trembling. Could it be that this fear is because the object of the great acts of charity of the developed nations would be removed by the final solutions that could be provided in the construction of dams, provision of water and irrigation facilities, the realignment of regularly flooding rivers, the provision of better housing, and the guarantee of an overall global economic system that will bestow economic rights on peoples who have been the world's beasts of burden for many centuries?

Once I stated that humanitarian relief cannot be delivered at the point of a gun, nor should the UN be commandeered into performing this role. My position was received with mild amusement. A *New York*

Times's correspondent at the UN actually believed my position stemmed from remnants of the Cold War rhetoric. Bosnia Herzegovina for a time proved me right, when even a mighty and unified continent that fought two horrendous wars in recent memory, and participated in armed intervention on all the continents of the earth could not protect the lives of a small minority in the very heart of Europe. How then can they claim to be the defenders of the human rights of obscure tribes in far away countries?

The news of the emergence of concentration camps in Central Europe has more than a sense of deja vu about it. We are keen students of history, long-standing victims of some of its horrendous perpetration.

In the final analysis, the moral undergrid that makes us each our brother's keeper must be constructed on true commitment to all our fellow men. The crusade for human rights must be stripped of its double standard, for these are rights that begin only when we recognize the rights that are fundamentals to life itself. Freedom and liberty become distant abstractions for a person who is homeless, sick, or hungry. As recipients of humanitarian aid, we have an uncomfortable feeling when we know you in the advanced countries also have sick, homeless, and uncared-for people. In the name of our common humanity, our appeal to you is to put your own houses in order: feed your poor, house your homeless, cure your sick. It will strengthen your claim to be our economic and social mentors.

In a world where some nations feed and house their dogs and cats at costs greater than the combined receipts of many nations of the South for the fruits of their labor; in a world where the cost of one bomber is the budget of a multiple set of nations; in a world where large numbers remain locked in living conditions that beggar the human imagination; in a world where underground springs are pumped to water golf courses; and in the epoch of great space travels and terrestrial explorations, perhaps the day has come when another revolution must take place. This time, it will occur in the conscience of man, especially Christian man, who, in spite of the breathtaking amplitude of the Christian message sent daily through a church founded by a Nazarene carpenter and a group of simple fishermen and artisans two thousand years ago, has so much to answer for, particularly when today the Christian nations claim a preeminence in the comity of nations. Leadership comes with responsibilities; it is time for these nations to discharge them to the full. It is time for the Christianity of these nations to become a living reality for all peoples on our common earth-home.

5

The Economics
of Neglect

PARTHA DASGUPTA

The subject of political economy is concerned with the circumstances in which people are born, and the manner in which they are able to live and die. Since life involves the use of resources, economics, a somewhat more specialized subject of inquiry, studies the strengths and weaknesses of various methods of allocating those resources.

Of all resource allocation mechanisms, the *market mechanism* has undergone the greatest scrutiny in the literature of economics. Although it is rarely defined in formal terms, its outlines are familiar. A market mechanism is a means of allocating resources in which the state restricts its activities in the socioeconomic sphere to facilitating the operation of private markets by developing and enforcing commercial laws, protecting private property rights, and so forth. The *competitive market mechanism* is a special example in which all commodities have markets, and all parties are price takers in these markets.

Even the competitive market mechanism, however, cannot be relied

This chapter is based in part on the author's book, *An Inquiry into Well-Being and Destitution* (Oxford: Clarendon Press, forthcoming, Spring 1993).

upon to protect and promote human well-being. The reasons are many and varied, including the fact that markets are not a propitious set of institutions for producing public goods (such as immunization, public sanitation, and courts) and merit goods (such as primary and secondary education). One obvious though often overlooked reason is that for the competitive market mechanism to function efficiently, everyone must have resource endowments to bargain with; in other words, each person must have something to bring to the market if he is to take anything back home from it.

One may suggest that even when a person owns no physical assets, he owns one inalienable asset—namely, labor power—but the science of nutrition has shown that this presumption is false.[1] The only thing an assetless person owns is *potential* labor power. Conversion of potential into actual labor power can be realized only if the individual finds the means of making the conversion. Nutrition and health care are a necessary means for conversion, as are primary and secondary education. For this reason these commodities are often called basic needs. The "economics of neglect" deals with the circumstances in which the conversion of potential into actual labor power is not possible because basic needs are not met for a large proportion of the population.

One of the most impressive and pleasing achievements of modern economic analysis has been the demonstration, through both analytical and empirical means, that a central responsibility of governments is to ensure that the basic needs of their populations are met. All too often since World War II, however, governments of developing nations have been encouraged to spend time and resources on matters at which they have proven singularly inept and intrusive (for example, in the production of private goods, such as steel and motor cars), and have not been charged with performing vital functions (the supply of public goods and food security). Shibboleths such as "public ownership of the means of production" have proven enduring even while people have remained uneducated, and gone malnourished and diseased. Health, education, the gathering and dissemination of knowledge, the establishment and enforcement of laws of property and contracts, the central role of political and civil liberties, and, more broadly, the motivational forces necessary for the promotion of well-being have not exactly held sway in most poor countries. Nor have they attained the high ground in development economics, even though they constitute the proper domain of government activity. The market mechanism, as I have defined it, is particularly inept in South Asia, Africa, and Latin

America, largely because their rural populations have very few resource endowments at their command.

In this chapter I will provide an account of the possible economic consequences of a failure to meet basic needs. Surprisingly, we have little quantitative feel for such an important question; in particular, about the loss of productivity owing to low nutritional status. The science of nutrition and public health has advanced considerably over the years, but economists have not taken advantage of its findings. I have, for example, been unable to find any good estimates of rates of return on investment in primary health care and nutritional guarantees. For this reason, my account will in the main be qualitative, and I will squeeze out the occasional quantitative estimate only when I am able to. Along the way, I will also provide evidence of the extent to which governments of poor countries have systematically neglected their responsibilities to provide basic needs for their populations. The two basic needs I will address are the commodities required for health and education. Nutrition and primary health care are the two chief inputs in the "production" of health. The role of education in economic life will be addressed, and I will also examine corresponding issues raised by the differences between the two genders. Finally, I will argue, by looking at data on expenditure in warfare, that the lack of provision of basic needs in poor countries cannot have been due to a paucity of funds.

Health: Mortality Indices

Table 1 presents a list of countries (mostly in Asia and sub-Saharan Africa) that, in 1970, enjoyed a per capita income of less than $2,500 in 1980 international dollars. The idea is to look at a snapshot of the standard of living in each country by noting four social indices: life expectancy at birth, per capita income, infant mortality rate, and adult literacy rate.

Life expectancy at birth is the number of years a random newborn can expect to live, on the assumption that current age-specific mortality rates will persist. In the sample of countries in Table 1, national *per capita income* is positively and significantly correlated with life expectancy at birth.[2] That the two seem to go together may suggest that growth in income is the sole means of achieving greater life expectancy, but it would be wrong to make this inference. A number of countries, such as Mauritius, Sri Lanka, and China, are striking outliers.

TABLE 1. *Indicators of Living Standards, 1980*

	Per Capita Income*	Life Expectancy at Birth (Yrs.)	Infant Mortality Rate (per 1,000)	Adult Literacy Rate (%)
Bangladesh	540	48.0	140.0	26
Benin	534	47.0	124.0	28
Bolivia	1,529	50.0	130.0	63
Botswana	1,477	55.0	78.0	35
Burundi	333	46.0	126.0	25
Central African Republic	487	47.0	143.0	33
Chad	353	42.0	147.0	15
China	1,619	67.0	41.0	69
Ecuador	2,607	63.0	75.0	81
Egypt	995	58.0	108.0	44
Ethiopia	325	44.0	155.0	15
Gambia	556	40.0	159.0	15
Haiti	696	52.0	132.0	23
Honduras	1,075	60.0	87.0	60
India	614	54.0	107.0	36
Indonesia	1,063	53.0	105.0	62
Jordan	1,885	62.0	58.0	70
Kenya	662	55.0	83.0	47
Korea	2,369	67.0	32.0	93
Lesotho	694	52.0	116.0	52
Liberia	680	52.0	100.0	25
Madagascar	589	51.0	146.0	50
Malawi	417	44.0	169.0	25
Mali	356	44.0	184.0	10
Mauritania	576	43.0	142.0	17
Mauritius	1,484	65.4	45.2	85
Morocco	1,199	57.0	102.0	28
Nepal	490	45.1	142.2	19
Niger	441	42.0	150.0	10
Nigeria	824	48.0	118.0	34
Pakistan	989	49.0	124.0	24
Paraguay	1,979	66.0	47.0	84
Philippines	1,551	61.0	52.0	75
Rwanda	379	45.0	127.0	50

TABLE 1 *(continued)*. *Indicators of Living Standards, 1980*

	Per Capita Income*	Life Expectancy at Birth (Yrs.)	Infant Mortality Rate (per 1,000)	Adult Literacy Rate (%)
Senegal	744	45.0	147.0	10
Sierra Leone	512	38.0	172.0	15
Somalia	415	44.0	145.0	60
Sri Lanka	1,199	68.0	34.0	85
Sudan	652	46.0	123.0	32
Swaziland	1,079	51.7	133.4	65
Tanzania	353	50.0	119.0	79
Thailand	1,694	62.0	51.0	86
Tunisia	1,845	60.4	91.8	62
Uganda	257	46.0	113.0	52
Yemen	957	42.9	163.7	21
Zaire	224	49.0	111.0	55
Zambia	716	50.1	90.4	44
Zimbabwe	930	55.0	82.4	69

*1980 purchasing power parity.

Differences in life expectancy at birth between rich and poor nations is large. In sub-Saharan Africa life expectancy at birth today is approximately fifty years; in Western industrial democracies the figure is about seventy-six years. There are also large gaps in the infant mortality rate and literacy. The *infant mortality rate* is the number of live-born infants out of every thousand who die during their first year. In Western industrial democracies the infant mortality rate is down to something like ten per thousand, and primary and secondary education have a universal reach. The infant survival rate is one thousand minus the infant mortality rate. Plainly, it is not unrelated to life expectancy at birth, but it focuses on something quite different: nutrition and hygiene at the earliest stage of life. It is also related closely to the health of the mother, the duration of lactation, and the mother's educational attainment.

Table 2 shows the extent of undernourishment among children under five years of age and among women, in the three regions where undernourishment is pervasive. For children the indices shown are anthropometric; for women the index reflects the prevalence of nutritional anemia. Life expectancy at birth tells us something quite different from anthropometric indices. For example, newborns and children under five are less wasted in sub-Saharan Africa than they are in Asia. Within Asia the worst figures are in the Indian subcontinent. But life expectancy at birth in the Indian subcontinent is higher than in sub-Saharan Africa: it is fifty-four years, as compared with fifty years. This illustrates the limitations of the index, which is the expectation of longevity at birth. Ideally we would be interested in longevity at different stages of life, or age-specific mortality rates, which reflect the threats a class or gender faces at various stages of life. Today, across countries the variation in life expectancy at age five is much less than the variation at birth. For example, a five-year-old girl in Western industrial democracies can expect to live another seventy-four years, whereas her counterpart in sub-Saharan Africa can expect to live an additional sixty years or thereabouts. This is what we would expect. The impact of food, sanitation, and health care deprivation is felt dramatically during early childhood. In hostile environments large groups of people get weeded out in the early years of their lives. In fact, some of the weeding gets done at the household level by the parents' practicing differential child care.

TABLE 2. *Indicators of Undernourishment in Poor Countries*

	Africa	Asia	Latin America*
Under-5 malnutrition			
Low weight for age†			
No. in millions	22	115	9
%	26	54	18
Low weight for height†			
No. in millions	4	33	2
%	7	16	4
Low birth weight‡ (%)	14	19	10
Anemia in women (%)	40	58	17

Source: Food and Agriculture Association, *The Fifth World Food Survey* (Rome: FAO, 1987).
*Excluding Argentina and Uruguay.
†More than two standard deviations below median value for reference growth patterns adopted by the World Health Organization.
‡Below 2.5 kilograms.

Between genders, life expectancy at birth differs in almost all countries. (A current exception is India, where the figure is approximately fifty-seven years for both.) Differences have changed over time because of evolving technological possibilities and altered life-styles. For example, in the first half of the nineteenth century in England, female life expectancy at birth exceeded that of males, but mortality rates for females in the age range ten to thirty-nine years were greater than those of males. Today, female mortality rates in Western Europe and the United States are lower than those of males at all age levels.[3]

Unless conditions improve for a person, there is a sense in which the first three years of life are crucial; they tend to leave a marked imprint on future capacities. A longitudinal study in Guatemala that controlled for differences in nutrition in early childhood revealed that the absolute difference in the average heights of two poor populations (a control group and a group that was provided with food supplements) remained approximately constant from about age three. Moreover, the intellectual performance of the control group in later years was significantly worse. Growth failure in early childhood, according to the data, predicts functional impairment in adults (for example, in stature, strength, intelligence, numeracy, literacy, lean body mass, and, for women, obstetric risks).[4] The finding suggests that unless conditions improve for a deprived group, the absolute gap in final heights due to nutritional differences between two populations is reached by age three. The issue, therefore, is not whether one can be a stunted but healthy adult, but whether one becomes a stunted adult because of periodic nutrition, sanitation, and health care deprivation during childhood.

We should note as well that a determinant of prenatal and infant mortality rates is the mother's size and health; for example, birth weight is influenced by the mother's condition.[5] It was thought for some time that the condition of the placenta is to a large extent impervious to the mother's health status, but this is not so.[6] This is one way in which the effect of food and health care deprivation in early childhood is passed on to the succeeding generations. But a person is subject to different mixes of risks as she passes through infancy to early childhood. For many purposes, even the first year is too large an interval to work with, since the risks an infant is vulnerable to in the first month are different from those she faces in subsequent months. A good portion of infants who die in the first month (the neonatal period) is composed not only of those suffering from congenital defects, but also of those who were born prematurely or who experienced fetal growth retardation. Therefore, for certain purposes it makes sense to distinguish neonatal mortality rates from postneonatal mortality rates. Such data are not easy to come by in many countries, but as a pithy summary of the earliest set of risks to which a person is vulnerable, the infant mortality rate has much to commend it.[7]

Nutrition and Infection

Nutrition is not the sole determinant of good health; food adequacy standards depend to an extent upon other factors, as well, including potable water, immunization and general medical care, sanitation, and personal hygiene. Waterborne diseases (such as cholera, typhoid, and hepatitis) and water-based diseases (such as guinea worm) are immediate examples of why nutrition alone is not sufficient for good health. While diarrheal infections (a central cause of infant and child deaths in poor countries) are not usually transmitted by contaminated water, they are spread by contact, and this can be contained by washing in clean water. Unhappily, over a billion people in Africa, Asia, and Latin America have no reliable access to drinking water.[8] Thus, it is not unusual for children in poor countries to suffer from six to eight episodes of diarrhea per year, on average, which adds up to some two months' diarrheal illness each year. This pattern systematically retards growth.

One well-known study compared weight, as a function of an infant's age in weeks, with frequency of illness.[9] It showed a direct, negative relationship between the number of days an infant suffers from diarrheal illness and the infant's growth. Airborne diseases (such as influenza, pneumonia, and whooping cough) also continue to be prominent causes of infant and child deaths in poor countries, responsible for a quarter to a third of child mortality there. But although infections produce short-term faltering in growth, they cannot explain the long-term deficits in growth observed among the poor in poor countries. A diet has to be very marginal if it cannot cover the relatively modest quantities of additional nutrients required for catching up during childhood and adolescence. This is a prime reason governments should be concerned with food needs when developing the notions of nutritional status and the capacity to do work.

There is synergism among diseases, in that reducing deaths from one disease helps reduce deaths due to other forms of illnesses. A wide-ranging empirical study on infant and child mortality rates in poor countries found that there is a threshold level for the under-five mortality rate (about 150 per thousand), such that progress in reducing the rate is slow when the number is above it, whereas it is fairly rapid when the number falls below it.[10]

There is a similar link between malnutrition and diarrheal infection. A study of data on children in the age group six to thirty-six months in the Matlab Thana experiment in Bangladesh reports on the relative risk of death from diarrhea among the severely malnourished, as compared with the risk among those who were not suffering from severe malnutrition.[11] About 60 percent of all deaths in this age range occurred in the five months following the monsoons, when infections are rampant. Children with no previous diarrhea indicated a positive association between malnutrition and subsequent diarrhea. Furthermore, diarrheal illness in one period was found to increase the likelihood of its occurring in some subsequent period.[12]

The complementary needs of nutrition and freedom from infections are also synergistic in cases of tuberculosis, measles, cholera, and most respiratory infections. This means that a person's nutrition requirements up to a point diminish as his environment improves, which in turn implies that there is some possibility of substitution among them. Severe or repeated infections are a common cause of malnutrition, and there are several paths along which this happens, including both supply and demand factors.[13]

On the demand side, infections create an additional need for nutrients, by increasing a person's metabolic rate and the rate of breakdown of tissues. They also indirectly reduce the supply of nutrients. This they do for a variety of reasons. First, infections often reduce a person's appetite. Second, they lower a person's ability to absorb nutrients, by affecting the functioning of the gastrointestinal tract. Third, they entail increased loss of major macronutrients, vitamins, and minerals through the feces because of the increased speed of transit of the food that is eaten. Finally, infections result in the direct loss of nutrients into the gut. Malnutrition is frequently precipitated by outbreaks of infectious diseases, such as gastroenteritis.

The debilitating effects of infectious diseases go beyond undernourishment. Infections can lead to an increase in the excretion of micronutrients; deficiencies in any of these is damaging. For example, in Asia some five million people suffer from noncorneal xerophthalmias, a disease linked to vitamin A deficiency. In sub-Saharan Africa, over thirty million people are estimated to suffer from goiter, caused by iodine deficiency, and half of all children under twelve years are thought to suffer from iron-deficiency anemia.

The relationship between nutrition and infection seems to work the other way, as well. Reviewing an extensive literature, one study concluded that malnutrition predisposes one to diarrhea.[14] Moreover, a person's ability to fight an infection once he has caught it is reduced under conditions of moderate to severe malnutrition; his immune system is affected. There are exceptions, however: nutritional status has negligible impact on morbidity and mortality associated with the plague, smallpox, typhoid, yellow fever, tetanus, and AIDS. It is even possible that mildly undernourished hosts enjoy survival advantages over their well-fed counterparts for some of these infectious diseases. For example, someone suffering from iron-deficiency anemia would enjoy this perverse effect were the invading pathogen unable to obtain enough free iron to multiply as rapidly in the bloodstream as it would in a well-nourished person. This remains a matter of speculation, but historically it may have been important. Of the infectious diseases identified as leading causes of deaths during the eighteenth and nineteenth centuries, those whose relationship with nutritional status could be "perverse" accounted for about one-third of deaths. Fortunately, so far as public policy goes, it is not a matter of any great moment that we do not know if such "perverse" effects are at all significant. Today it is possible to have our food and eat it, too: modern public health measures can prevent the spread of many such life-threatening pathogens.

Growth and Development

Unless the circumstances of life improve, the first three years of life have a pronounced effect on a person's mature body stature. Early nutrition and the extent of freedom from infections leave deep imprints. Failure in growth amounts to wasting (low body weight) and stunting (low height), and there is now much epidemiological evidence that both increase the chance of morbidity and mortality.[15] By the end of the first year, a child's growth rate becomes quite small, and physical activities assume great importance. The energy cost of growth has two components: the energy stored and the energy used. One way a child can economize energy expenditure is by reducing physical activities. Mild to moderately wasted preschool children under free-living conditions have been observed to spend more time in sedentary and light activities than their healthy counterparts. They have been found to rest longer and to play more often in a horizontal position.[16] A Jamaican study found stunted children in the age group twelve to twenty-four months to be significantly less active than their nonstunted counterparts. The energy thus saved was comparable to the energy cost of growth at that age.[17] At an extreme, when we observe little children in poor countries lying expressionless on roadsides and refraining from brushing the flies off their faces, we should infer that they are conserving energy.

Marked differences in activity levels have been reported among a sample of infants from poor households in rural Mexico, between those who received nutritional supplements and a control group.[18] The former made greater contact with the floor, slept less during the day, spent more time outdoors, began playing almost six months earlier, and so forth. The thesis here is that low nutritional intake depresses activity, which isolates the child from contact with the environment and from important sources of stimuli to both cognitive and motor development. It is significant that the control group in the study was not clearly undernourished.[19]

Motor development is the process by which a child acquires basic movement patterns and skills, such as walking, running, jumping, hopping, throwing, kicking, and holding something in her grip. In normal circumstances children develop these fundamental motor patterns by the age of six or seven years. It is through such movement patterns and skills that many childhood experiences, especially learning and interpersonal experiences, are mediated. During infancy and early childhood, interactions between the mother and child are of critical importance in this development. This is a hidden cost of anemia and low energy intake on the part of mothers. Since housework and production activity are mandatory, reductions in discretionary and child-rearing activities offer the mother a way of maintaining her energy balance. To be sure, societies differ in the way people other than the mother are involved in a child's upbringing. Nevertheless, the mother is an important figure in a child's cognitive and motor development in all societies.

Long-term malnutrition would appear to be particularly associated with mental development; the presence or absence of current malnutrition has a less pronounced effect. Under conditions of severe undernourishment (for example, marasmus or marasmic kwashiorkor), retardation of psychomotor development in young children has physiological reasons, as well. Some of the damages are extremely difficult to reverse and may indeed be irreversible. In one study, for example, even after six months of nutritional rehabilitation of a sample of infants hospitalized for severe malnutrition, no recovery was observed in their motor development.[20] It may be that severe malnutrition affects development of the brain, whose growth starts rapidly at around ten weeks of pregnancy and continues in spurts to about three to four years of age. (Fetal iodine deficiency is well known to damage the central nervous system.) However, there is evidence that malnutrition has an effect on brain development only when it coincides with a period of rapid growth and differentiation.[21] Equilibrium reactions (otherwise called righting reflexes) are functions of the cerebellum and play an important role in the development of motor control.[22] It is, of course, possible that even such anatomical changes as have been observed are results of retardation rather than permanent injury, but this is not known with any certainty.[23]

Among schoolchildren the matter is somewhat different, in that peer group pressure tends to counter the instinct for reducing physical activities. This is likely to be especially so among boys. To be sure, even for them decreased activity is a line of defense.[24] However, some studies indicate that in school-aged children the low energy expenditure associated with nutritional deficiency can be traced to low body weight: basal metabolic rates of underweight children are low. The development of lean body mass among undernourished children is retarded. This has a detrimental effect on their capacity to work when adults.

On a wider front, malnutrition and infection have been found to have a pronounced detrimental effect among schoolchildren on such cognitive processes as attention and concentration. There is abundant evidence that children who suffer from nutritional deficiencies and infections perform badly on aptitude tests.[25] As noted earlier, in extreme cases nutritional deficiencies affect the central nervous system. In less-than-extreme cases the matter is not one of brain function; frequent absence and attrition affect learning, as well.

The studies with which I am familiar did not explore the extent to which it is possible for a person to catch up in height during adolescence if she had suffered from deprivation when young, but it is possible to make up past deficits, although the process is slow.[26] In order to catch up, a stunted adolescent needs more protein and energy than would be required by a normal adolescent. If the person was deprived when young, however, the presumable reason was poverty, in which case she will hardly be in a position to command more than is required for normal growth during adolescence.

Pregnancy and Lactation

Earlier, we observed that maternal malnutrition results in low birthweight and high prenatal and neonatal mortality. During pregnancy

well-nourished women in Western industrial societies acquire something like 7.5 kilograms of extra weight. (The median infant birth
weight there is 3.3 kilograms.) This translates into an energy cost of a
bit more than 80,000 kilocalories over the nine-month period. The cost
is not distributed evenly over the three trimesters of pregnancy. Nevertheless, for practical purposes it makes sense to recommend a uniform
addition to energy intake for the duration. It works out to about 285
kilocalories per day.[27]

The energy cost of lactation is the energy content of the milk se-
creted plus the energy required in converting food intake into milk. For
healthy women in Western industrial societies this additional energy
requirement is roughly 700 kilocalories per day. If requirements during
pregnancy have been met, a woman will start lactating with about
36,000 kilocalories of additional reserve of fat. This is a source of
approximately 200 kilocalories per day if the reserve is to be drawn
down over six months. It follows that she needs an additional 500
kilocalories per day.[28]

To what extent is the health cost of nutritional deprivation shared
between a pregnant woman and her fetus? The evidence is mixed. A
Gambian study has shown that it is shared during the lean season:
women lose weight during pregnancy, and the proportion of low-birth-
weight babies increases. This is a finding among people who would
presumably have adapted to an annual food cycle. Nutritional supplementation programs pick up something else, since they are not
habitual. One study found energy supplementation to have no effect
on lactation performance. On the other hand, average birth weight in
the wet season responded to energy supplementation. (There was no
response during the dry season.)[29]

A similar finding has been reported from a field study of nutritional
intervention among marginally undernourished women in west-central
Taiwan.[30] While a combined energy-protein supplementation had a
significant effect on prenatal growth of the offspring, the study did not
discover any effect on maternal anthropometry (for example, skin-fold
thicknesses). Additional food was usurped by the fetus.

Adult Stature and Physical Productivity

When nutritionists talk of physical work capacity, they mean the maximum power (that is, maximum work per unit of time) a person is
capable of offering. It transpires that the most compelling index of a

person's physical work capacity is his *maximal oxygen uptake,* which is the highest rate of oxygen uptake a person is capable of attaining while engaged in physical work at sea level. The reason maximal oxygen uptake provides us with the measure we need is that it is dependent on the body's capacity for a linked series of oxygen transfers (diffusion through tissues, circulation of hemoglobin, pulmonary ventilation, and so on). It also measures cardiorespiratory fitness: the higher its value, the greater the capacity of the body to convert energy in the tissues into work. Broadly speaking, taller and heavier, nonobese people have greater physical work capacity. Unskilled laborers in poor countries are often slight and weak, but they are seldom out of shape; it is sedentary workers who often are. As a very rough approximation we may distinguish people's capacity for physical activities solely by their physical work capacity.

Much international attention has been given to saving lives in times of collective crisis within poor countries. International agencies have also given attention to keeping children alive in normal times through public health measures, such as family planning counseling, immunization, and oral rehydration. This is as it should be. That many poor countries fail to do either is not evidence that the problems are especially hard to solve. In fact, these are among the easier social problems: they can be fielded even while no major modification is made to the prevailing resource allocation mechanism. The harder problem, in intellectual design, political commitment, and administration, is to ensure that those who remain alive are healthy. It is also a problem whose solution brings no easily visible benefit. But the stunting of both cognitive and motor capacity is a prime hidden cost of energy deficiency and anemia among children and, at one step removed, among mothers. It affects learning and skill formation, and thereby future productivity. The price is paid in later years, but it is paid.

Education and Productivity

The output of education (knowledge, skills, and so forth) is a durable capital asset. A society's formal education system (schools, colleges, and other centers of learning) offers the means by which people are able to acquire this asset. Other sources of education are the family, friends, and the community at large. In this section I will deal with the instrumental value of education in general, and of numeracy and literacy in particular. I will also address improvements in labor productivity brought about by education.

That primary education has a considerable effect on industrial labor productivity has been widely documented. A study in the state of Punjab in India showed that primary education is important even for the cultivation of traditional varieties of wheat. Agricultural laborers who had been through primary education made more effective use of labor, and made better choice of production inputs. The study also showed that the impact of secondary education increased significantly between 1961 and 1972, suggesting that returns from secondary education increase with the coming of new technology of the kind embodied in the Green Revolution.[31]

There are now a number of cross-country estimates of social rates of returns on various levels of education. Table 3 provides estimates for three regions: sub-Saharan Africa, Asia, and Latin America (including the Caribbean). The aggregation involved is heroic, but the figures are telling. In each region, among different levels of education the primary level has the highest productive value (a rate of return of about 26 percent), secondary education much less so (about 15 percent), and higher education least so (about 13 percent). One cannot escape the thought that poor countries have consistently underinvested in primary education relative to education's higher reaches.

TABLE 3. *Social Rate of Return on Education, by Level of Schooling (Percent Per Year)*

Region	Primary	Secondary	Higher
Sub-Saharan Africa	26	17	13
Asia	27	15	13
Latin America and the Caribbean	26	18	16

Source: G. Psacharopoulos, "Returns to Education: A Further International Update and Implications," *Journal of Human Resources* 20 (1985).

The effect of parents' education on their children has been investigated, and has been found to be beneficial. For the most part, the studies have explored the effect of some six to seven years of schooling, but they have differed over the measurement of well-being. Some have looked at household consumption of nutrients and the use of contraceptives; others have looked at child health in general, at infant and child survival rates, and at children's height.[32] These studies confirm that education helps mothers to process information more effectively, and enables them to use available social and community services more intensively. Education also appears to impart a degree of self-confidence that enables a person to make use of whatever new facilities are available. This is an invaluable asset for rural populations living through changing circumstances. Female education, especially secondary education, also has a pervasive and significant effect on female reproductive behavior.[33] Although the links here are complex,[34] female education as a general rule appears to lead to a reduction in fertility rates.

There is a strong complementarity between social and community services and literacy and numeracy. Among the most important examples of the former are agricultural extension services, trade facilities with the rest of the world, provisions for health care, and advice on health care. Remove these services, and rates of return on primary education are likely to decrease. Literacy and numeracy are unlikely to be of much use if they have nothing to act upon. One study used data from Bangladesh to argue that maternal education has little effect on child mortality rates because health services in rural Bangladesh are negligible.[35] By the same token, literacy is of little use to people who remain unemployed and are unable to make use of their literacy.

Calculations of rates of return on primary education are based on highly aggregated data, and they cannot reveal a central reason for recalcitrance on the part of poor families in acquiring education. A fine early empirical study noted the large costs poor families must bear when they send their children to school.[36] Poverty forces parents to send children out to work at an early age. Child labor (employing both girls and boys) in the marketplace, including bonded labor, is common. Children are an early source of income, of much value to impoverished parents. By the age of six children in poor families in the Indian subcontinent tend cattle, goats, and younger siblings; fetch water; and collect firewood. Therefore, even when primary education is subsidized, schooling is costly for poor households, as the poor have limited access to credit, and so the benefits flowing from these subsidies are captured disproportionately by well-off families. In the case of rural India, to the extent wealth is correlated with caste hierarchy, education subsidies are captured mostly by the higher castes. There is also a gender bias in educational attainment. In patrilineal societies, the benefits derived from sending a daughter to school are less than those from sending a son. An educated girl may also be perceived as less pliable than an uneducated one, and hence will be at a disadvantage in the marriage market.

Across households within a country, poverty and illiteracy usually go hand in hand; each reinforces the other. Across countries the matter is different, since countries differ in their social ethos and political design. In an earlier work, I showed that among poor countries there was no systematic relationship between real national income per head and improvements in adult literacy during the 1970s.[37] I also discovered that there is a positive correlation between countries with a bad record in political and civil rights and those with a good record in improvements in literacy. I have no compelling explanation for this statistical fact. What is incontrovertible is that it is possible for a poor country to break away quickly from the grip of illiteracy. It requires concerted effort from several parties: the household, local organizations, the village community, religious organizations, and the government. It involves government engagement in the form of free primary and secondary education, free midday school meals, and so forth. These factors are required to bring private returns on education closer to social returns.

Is female education socially cost-effective in poor countries? A rough calculation based on World Bank data on Pakistan indicates that female education is an excellent form of social investment.[38] In 1990 educating an additional thousand girls in Pakistan would have cost $40,000. Each year of schooling there has been estimated to reduce the under-five mortality rate by 10 percent; this translates to a saving of sixty deaths of children under five. Saving sixty lives with health care interventions would have cost around $48,000. But this is not all. Educated women typically have fewer children than average; an extra year of schooling reduces female fertility by 10 percent. Given Pakistan's astonishingly high total fertility rate of 6.6 births per woman, a $40,000 investment in educating a thousand women would avert 660 births. The alternative route of family planning expenditure for achieving the same result would have cost around $43,000.

Wars and Strife and the Funding of Basic Needs

No discussion of basic needs is complete without at least a reference to political and civil liberties, but they, too, have been systematically neglected in the economics of development. Space forbids me to enter into these issues in any detail here, but recent findings suggest that during the 1970s, poor countries with better political and civil rights records performed, on average, better in terms of growth in national income per head, and improvements in life expectancy at birth and the infant survival rate.[39] There is some evidence that civil and political liberties are necessary (though not sufficient) for protection of the environmental resource base of rural communities. What are popularly called human rights not only are of fundamental value, they would appear to have instrumental worth, as well. For me this has been one of the few agreeable findings in what is an unusually depressing field of research.

All too often, human rights have been systematically and strenuously violated in the majority of poor countries.[40] Government violence against citizens is also a commonplace occurrence in most poor countries. Political instability is often allied to such violence. Over 50 of the approximately 115 so-called developing countries are run by military-controlled governments. From 1958 through the end of 1981, there were more than fifty successful coups in 25 sub-Saharan countries, and more than fifty major attempts that proved unsuccessful. The coercive powers of the state are enhanced by the accumulation of machinery for warfare. Excluding India and China, among those classified by the World Bank as "low-income countries" (having a gross national product of less than $480 per head in 1988), military spending represented about 11 percent of government spending in 1988. This should be contrasted with the corresponding figures for health and education, which were 3 percent and 9 percent, respectively (see Table 4).

TABLE 4. *Government Expenditures on the Military, Health, and Education as Percentage of Total Government Expenditures, 1988*

	Military	Health	Education
India	21.5	1.8	2.9
Pakistan	29.5	0.9	2.6
Low-income countries (excluding India and China)	10.5	2.8	9.0

Source: World Bank, *World Development Report* (New York: Oxford University Press, 1990), Table 11.

Excessive armaments expenditure is not the monopoly of military dictatorships. The Indian subcontinent is a telling case. In the late 1980s government expenditure as a proportion of gross national product was 18 percent in India and 22 percent in Pakistan. Table 4 shows the stark contrast between military spending and the sums allocated to health and education—the contrast being particularly stark when we consider the status of these countries in levels of life expectancy at birth, infant survival, and literacy (see Table 1). India and Pakistan have fought three wars against each other, and each country's military accumulation has been dominated by a display of paranoia about the other. Neither country can afford its armaments expenditures, and yet there are no signs of a breakthrough in this long, drawn-out stalemate: there are no regional trade agreements in the offing, no collaborative ventures, and no serious cultural exchanges. That in earlier times each was supported by a rival superpower is on occasion offered as an excuse on their behalf, but it is no excuse. Each is a sovereign nation. If their political and civil leaders had displayed the required courage and vision, the governments of India and Pakistan would have entered into negotiations long ago, and kept the superpowers at bay.

Table 5 contrasts military expenditure among poor countries in the mid-1980s with expenditures in health and education. The bias is self-evident and was not unique to the period. The evidence is incontrovertible: if the allocation of public expenditure had been systematically directed at basic needs, the quality of life in poor countries would have been vastly different from what it is today. It is not low income that keeps the rural populations of poor countries in such wretched shape: the problem lies elsewhere, and it can be located easily if one cares to look for it.

TABLE 5. *Government Expenditures on the Military, Health, and Education as Percentage of Gross National Product*

	Military*	Health†	Education†
World	5.0	4.1	4.9
Industrial economies	5.2	4.7	5.2
Poor economies	4.3	1.6	3.8

Source: R. S. McNamara, "The Post-Cold War World: Implications for Military Expenditure in the Developing Countries," *Proceedings of the World Bank Annual Conference on Development Economics 1991* (New York: World Bank, 1992).
*1988.
†1986.

II

HEALTH ISSUES

Concern for innocent victims of war and soul-wrenching images of famine-stricken women and children are the rationales most frequently invoked in justifying international intervention in areas of conflict and disaster. Then, as if it were a predetermined role, statesmen and soldiers, lawyers and economists, politicians and academicians, invariably formulate foreign policies and offer solutions that are often more relevant to their own interests and cultural sensibilities than to the realities of the situations they seek to address. Their efforts seem, with incredible regularity, to provoke a recurrent cycle of tragedies. Rarely do these leaders seek the views or benefit from the experiences of those who must deal with the terrible carnage that inevitably follows military maneuvers or natural catastrophes.

Health workers know, most intimately, the pain and waste of battle. They also have the privilege of healing wounds and relieving the pangs of starvation; occasionally, and uniquely, they can secure the trust and cooperation of adversaries. Their role in conflict resolution offers an innovative direction in a global diplomacy searching for new approaches.

In this section five physicians with extensive field experience in disasters bear witness to the suffering masses they have served, and offer both facts and observations that should help improve our ability to respond to predictable crises. Three of the contributors address the clinical and epidemiological aspects of refugee medicine, while another focuses more specifically on the perverse consequences of mine warfare on civilian populations. The fifth contribution documents the embarrassingly anemic response of the American medical establishment to global health crises.

6

When the System Doesn't Work: Somalia 1992

JENNIFER LEANING

Relief efforts in Somalia in 1992 constitute a searing case study of failure. Failure on a scale as grand and miserable as this has been determined by cumulative inadequacies on many fronts. This essay focuses on the role of the international community in attempting to provide relief to a society trapped in a vicious downward spiral of famine and anarchic internal war. Faced with the new intersection of violent disorder and massive food deprivation, the international community has only most belatedly and at enormous cost to the Somali people recognized that it is confronting a new kind of challenge: the problem of delivering relief where there is no order; the problem of distributing food and medicine where there is no neutral status protecting those who would help.

Expectations for System Performance

In the last forty years, the international community through its international agencies has increasingly assumed responsibility for providing relief to disaster-stricken areas. This responsibility is pursued through two interrelated main tracks: threat assessment and response. The general theoretical outlines of disaster relief have been hammered out with experience and extended critical evaluation.[1]

Threat assessment, the process by which international agencies identify areas of impending food crises or vulnerability to natural disaster, is a function of surveillance, a steady-state observational and analytic activity undertaken by experts and officials in local areas, summed up in a hierarchy of information and leadership to general levels of evaluation and prediction for given geographical areas. It is also a function of focus, whereby areas that appear problematic as the result of surveys or routine reports become the targets of more in-depth investigations, in an effort to gain knowledge about the true dimensions of risk at hand. The knowledge gained becomes the basis for planning and delivering the needed response. Disaster response, in which the provision of relief to populations is a key element, is supported by informed anticipatory planning efforts and sustained by a complex process of leadership, coordination, and communication—all vigorously directed towards the supply and transport of personnel and goods to the affected areas.

Despite criticism from within agencies and from the public during and after the response phase to particular disasters, years of effort in responding to famine and natural disasters have honed these aspects of threat assessment and response to commendable levels of effectiveness in many of the UN and nongovernmental organization (NGO) agencies. The world has come to expect that in any given instance of portending or actual disaster a set of actions will take place, regardless of political or geographic difficulties: The continual monitoring of threat potential will result in expert assessment of the risk at hand. The threat will be communicated to international agencies and the larger international community. These agencies will engage in timely analysis and decision-making. Needed resources will be identified and mobilized. The strategy and logistics for delivery and distribution of these resources will be defined and agreed upon. The agencies will embark within the appropriate time frame dictated by the disaster on the coordinated implementation of the logistical plan. These agencies will continue the tasks of analysis and communication in order to maintain the required level of international interest and marshaling of resources.

Conduct of Forces during War or Civil Conflict

A minimum level of civil order is a prerequisite for this system of disaster relief to be able to function. Local or regional observers and officials must be able to stay on site to act as sources of information and foci of coordination; medical workers and relief personnel have to be able to reach people in need. Deliveries of people and goods assume relatively safe passage and transport. The existing relief system has not been linked, conceptually or logistically, to a cadre of armed forces deployed to create or maintain secure corridors or bastions. It is possible to maintain this minimum level of civil order in settings of armed conflict. The codes defined by international humanitarian law permit the transport and delivery of civilian relief in all conditions of war or armed unrest.[2] To the extent that the armed combatants understand and observe these codes, the neutral noncombatant status afforded medical and relief workers will protect and enable the relief effort. There have been many instances in the last decades when the international community has provided disaster relief in the midst of war, civil strife, armed unrest, or rebellion.

The agency charged with responsibility for establishing and monitoring adherence to international humanitarian law is the International Committee of the Red Cross (ICRC). The work of the ICRC is legendary, yet legal experts caution that it takes far more than the specific efforts of the ICRC to ensure the application of the tenets of international humanitarian law. Within the context of war and civil conflict as it has usually played out, two other conditions are essential: a general recognition on the part of the warring factions that this body of law exists and each individual combatant is subject to it; and a more detailed understanding and commitment to enforce these principles on the part of the senior officers on all sides.[3]

The bloody conflicts in Somalia and Yugoslavia have identified two other underlying preconditions for the application of international humanitarian law: the warring factions must adhere to some semblance of a chain of command and communications in order for the senior officers to exert any control, and the warring factions must be constrained in their cost-benefit analysis of war by certain Clauzwitzian notions of means ultimately supporting ends. Chaotic violence fueled by an apparent thirst for mutual annihilation subverts any attempts to introduce the principles enshrined in the Fourth Geneva Convention. The fundamental challenge posed by Somalia (and to some extent Yugoslavia) is this: how to provide disaster relief in the setting of savage anarchy.

The Crisis in Somalia

Somalia is a nomadic and pastoral society of approximately six million people whose agricultural economy has always been characterized by a precarious balance between rain and food supply. Drought and intermittent famine are chronic scourges.[4] Formed as a republic in 1960 with the merger of the British and Italian colonial territories, Somalia's native clan structure was held in the oppressive grip of Siad Barre from 1969 until his dictatorship of corruption and intermittently bloody suppression of dissent[5] was violently overthrown in January 1991.

Under Barre, Somalia served as an ideological playground for East-West ambitions in the Horn of Africa and the Mideast and, thanks to this rivalry, became the recipient of large amounts of military aid.[6] Until 1978, Moscow held sway; in the last decade of Barre's rule, the United States was the dominant force. The overthrow of Barre in January 1991 led to months of inconclusive political struggle among the leadership of the several clans that surfaced to claim ascendancy. Much of Somalia was in a state of upheaval, with open armed conflict among clans particularly evident in the north, where a secessionist battle was being waged by the Somali National Movement (SNM) and its Isak clan supporters; and in central Somalia, where several clans were in hot pursuit of the remnants of Barre's clan and supporters.

In January 1991, within days of the overthrow of Barre, Mohammed Ali Mahdi, a businessman and leader of the Abgal, a subclan of the Hawiye clan, declared himself President of Somalia. General Mohammed Aidid, the leader of the Habr Gidir, another subclan of the Hawiye, challenged this declaration. Against a backdrop of simmering conflict and social disruption throughout the countryside, open war erupted between these two subclans in the fall of 1991. This war was waged within and in the environs of Mogadishu, where most members of the Hawiye clan lived.

In early September, during a flare in hostilities between these two factions, a UN team, consisting of several UN officials and armed Somali guards, was held up at gunpoint. The Somali guards were executed in front of the UN officials, who were stripped, robbed of all effects, and forced to find their way back to their offices.[7] Within days, the UN, which had just restored a skeleton staff in Mogadishu in July, pulled all personnel out of Mogadishu.

On November 17, 1991, the hostilities between the forces of Aidid and Ali Mahdi exploded across the city, escalating to a massive artillery bombardment of one side of the city against another. For the next six weeks, Aidid's forces pushed Ali Mahdi from the southern sector of the city to a northern stronghold, which Ali Mahdi maintained against all-out assault. As of February 1992, heavy night-time artillery barrages and more sporadic daytime engagements maintained an ugly stalemate: Aidid controlled the southern two-thirds of the city, including the air field and the deep-water port; Ali Mahdi controlled the northern third of the city, including the hills overlooking the harbor.

The November explosion in hostilities caused consternation in the international community in Mogadishu. Although many in the diplomatic corps (including the U.S. consulate) had left the city in the month after Barre was overthrown, several NGO agencies had still maintained offices, their numbers augmented by the several teams of foreign medical workers who had arrived in October 1992 to help the Somali medical establishment cope with the casualties caused by the fighting. The November attack by Aidid against Ali Mahdi turned the entire city into a war zone. Each day for the next several weeks, hospitals reported receiving on average approximately 100 casualties per day, per hospital. Any vestige of civil order evaporated.

The latter weeks of November and all of December saw high levels of carnage. Casualties were produced day and night, but because of difficulties in transport, most (civilian and military) were brought into the hospitals during the day. Many of those who died outright from their wounds were not brought to the hospital, and many who made it to the hospitals died in the casualty area. During periods of most bitter fighting, soldiers would swarm the hospitals, their jeeps screeching into the courtyards, men piling out with wounded companions. They would order physicians and nurses at gunpoint to take immediate care of these victims, to the exclusion of those already in the process of evaluation and treatment, regardless of priority of need.

Mogadishu became a place of death, destruction, and chaos. Heavily armed bands of men and boys roamed the city. Even with armed guards, travel in the open during the day was hazardous to anyone. Food scarcity began to surface as a serious issue. After almost a year of civil unrest, agricultural production in the countryside had been reduced to a fraction of pre-1991 levels. Commercial markets no longer existed; food supplies, to the extent they came in from the surrounding regions, were appropriated by the warring factions and distributed to the soldiers in lieu of money. No food had been imported into the country in months. Aidid's forces patrolled the airport and seaport; guns on the hills were controlled by Ali Mahdi's men and aimed at the harbor.

On December 11, 1991, a Belgian worker for the ICRC was shot and fatally injured while engaged in distributing food in a sector of the city that constituted the no-man's zone between the forces of Aidid and Ali Mahdi. Also killed was an elderly Somalia clansman who threw himself in the path of the bullet in an attempt to protect the ICRC worker. The circumstances of these deaths underscored the dilemma facing relief workers in Mogadishu: efforts by neutral noncombatants to distribute relief to members of the civilian population were seen by the armed bands of one side or the other only as actions of favoritism in the distribution of most valued commodities. In early January 1992, a Bulgarian physician working for UNICEF was killed in northeastern Somalia.

Word of what was happening in Mogadishu, and elsewhere in Somalia, trickled out only intermittently to the international community. Press coverage depended upon the resourcefulness of journalists in obtaining transport into and out of Mogadishu. The ICRC, the only relief agency with regular flights into and out of the city, did not permit journalists to stay overnight. More official communication depended upon bulletins from the ICRC, since representatives of all other international agencies, with the exception of a few medical and relief teams, had left the city.

Medical Need and Resources

In February 1992, Africa Watch and Physicians for Human Rights cooperated in sending two separate missions to Somalia. The intent was to describe and communicate the medical and food relief situation in the country, with particular focus on Mogadishu. Information gained from these missions has been detailed in a recent report[8] and forms the basis for the following firsthand account of the situation in Mogadishu during this period.

Based on site visits to the hospitals, reviews of medical admission logs, interviews with medical personnel, and surveys of hospitalized patients, it is estimated that in the city of Mogadishu between mid-November 1991 and the end of February 1992 approximately 1,200 people per week were killed outright or died of their injuries, and another 2,500 were surviving wounded, with casualties totalling 41,000 for this eleven-week period. These estimates attempt to account for systematic underreporting in casualty area logs and the fact that a proportion of those who were injured and who were killed did not reach the hospitals.

As in all traumatic casualties of war waged with high velocity conventional weapons, the deaths resulted from massive head or abdominal injuries, or from exsanguinating traumatic amputations of limbs. The high proportion of numbers killed to numbers wounded reflects several factors: the lethality of the weapons used and the close range at which they were fired; the absence of emergency field medical response; the absence of emergency transport; and the austere conditions at the hospitals for emergency and follow-up care. The surviving injured were those with superficial wounds, for whom medical care would have only marginal affect on survival, or those who required and received life-saving medical intervention: amputations, abdominal explorations and repair, fluid resuscitation, transfusions, antibiotics, and splinting and stabilization of limb injuries.

The resources available to manage this burden of traumatic casualties were meager. Three hospitals, variously damaged and looted by the war, provided care for the southern region of the city. These three, Benadir, Digfer, and Medina, had a total inpatient capacity of approximately 1,700 beds but a census probably twice that level. Prior to October 1991, none of these hospitals had a specific casualty ward, separate from the ambulatory clinics, and none of the staff, Somali or expatriate, were emergency or trauma specialists. In the northern sector of the city, controlled by Ali Mahdi, the November events had forced Somali physicians to contrive a hospital out of a string of forty-five private villas. Two large villas facing the ocean, used as operating theaters, and twenty-seven other converted villas constituted what was called the Karaan Hospital. Another sixteen villas had been converted for postoperative and convalescent care, permitting a total of 5,000–6,000 patients to be hospitalized in these sites at any one time.

The task of caring for the casualties of war prevented any possibility of treating routine or nontraumatic illness. Occasionally people in extremis from untreated diabetes or heart disease would present to the hospitals, but the conditions were sufficiently stressed that most medical conditions went unseen and unattended. To the extent that regular medical care was still delivered at all in the city, it took place out of the homes of those few private physicians who had not either left the country entirely or gone to the hospitals to participate in the emergency effort.

Medical supplies to hospitals on both sides of the divide were flown in by ICRC planes out of Nairobi six days a week. Shortages of tetanus toxoid and antibiotics were acute during February. Blood was obtained from relatives who accompanied the injured; only ABO typing was available. The operating rooms had access to a few hours of electricity from diesel powered generators; running water was unpredictable and unclean. No gas anesthesia was available in the city; operations were performed on patients under intravenous anesthesia with ketamine. Drapes of any kind were scarce and rarely used; equipment was sterilized at best only once in twenty-four hours. Elsewhere in the hospitals conditions were grossly unsanitary. Inpatient rooms, corridors, and stairways in interior sections of the hospitals (particularly Digfer) were dark and oppressive with stench and debris.

Under these austere conditions, the hospital staff in the casualty and operating areas performed triage, stabilization, and, as needed and as could be accomplished, emergency surgery on all arriving casualties. Accuracy and completeness of record-keeping was inversely related to numbers of casualties seen in a given period, as those responsible for maintaining logs were drawn into the medical effort. At Digfer and Benadir there were insufficient staff and resources to provide postoperative rounds or nursing care except very intermittently; at Medina, where the staff from Médicins sans Frontières had established their own unit, rounds were afforded those recovering from abdominal and orthopedic operations. For most of the patients at Digfer and Benadir in the south, and at the Karaan Hospital in the north, patients depended on their families to provide whatever medical and personal care they required after the first or second day of admission.

Joint review of records with hospital physicians, nurses, and administrators yielded agreement on the following death rates at each site of hospital care:

casualty ward	10%
observation ward	10%
operating theater	5-10%
inpatient ward	5-10%

Hunger stalked patients and staff alike. The ICRC brought in enough food to afford the Somali staff one meal a day, which was not sufficient to maintain nutritional balance. A slow loss of weight and energy was manifest among the staff, and reported by foreign workers, whose own separate sources of food were consumed at their guarded villas, distant from the hospitals and hospital compounds where the Somali staff lived.

No food was available for patients, whose families were the only source of supply. The saying was common—"if you have no family, you die." As the carnage in the city wore on, an increasing number of casualties brought to the hospitals were in this orphaned or abandoned state. Even those with families were in states of moderate to serious malnutrition, impairing wound healing and overall recovery. Based on hospital surveys conducted in February, about 1 to 2 percent of the inpatients in the south were actually dying from starvation. Individual foreign staff workers confided in private that they would try to sneak food to one or more of the Somali workers, and occasionally to patients. The stakes were high, however: antagonism from those staff who were not so favored; threats or worse from those patients or their relatives who were not given gifts. In a few cases (an orphaned child on an adult ward), it was possible for foreign staff to provide small amounts of food on a more routine basis. The need so vastly outstripped supply, however, that the risk of creating serious disruption kept acts of generosity to a minimum.

LONGER-TERM ISSUES: MEDICAL, PSYCHOLOGICAL, AND PUBLIC HEALTH

Thousands of the injured survive in Mogadishu as amputees and perhaps hundreds are partially paralyzed. (It is highly unlikely, given the care conditions, that those who initially survived as quadriplegics would have persisted long.) Many more have relatively useless limbs, the result of incomplete knitting of shattered fragments of bone. There are no facilities for making prosthetic devices in Mogadishu. Rehabilitation of this large population of disabled survivors will require a great investment of time and resources in the postwar setting. The psychological scars of this experience will produce many cases of pathological grief and post-traumatic stress disorder (PTSD). The situation is currently too harsh and dangerous to permit much overt expression of psychological issues, since all available mental energy is focused on surviving, but whenever the conflict and famine can be eased, the psychological needs of thousands of people may surface and contribute to the complex difficulties of the recovery effort.

Although Mogadishu is a coastal city, its relatively arid conditions make malaria less a problem than elsewhere in the country, where it is prevalent. The lack of food and sanitation and the widespread disruption in living quarters contribute to epidemic levels of respiratory, enteric, and skin diseases, particularly among those hundreds of thousands who have fled to the outskirts of the city, gathering in refugee clusters, with virtually no shelter.

Violations of International Humanitarian Law

International humanitarian law, the body of law governing the conduct of combatants towards civilians and neutral personnel in time of war, has developed into a robust and effective net of constraints on military behavior. Although it is still the case that violations of international humanitarian law routinely occur in all wars and civil conflicts, these violations, when observed and reported, usually result in some reimposition of discipline and change in procedure. The ICRC and the international community have had some success in getting warring parties to heed the provisions of the Geneva Conventions and Protocols that prohibit the indiscriminate use of weapons against civilians and guarantee protection of medical personnel, facilities, and patients in all settings of armed conflict. Specific violations include all forms of interference in the delivery of medical care, the transport of patients, the supply of medical resources and equipment, and the movement and actions of health care personnel. Firing into hospitals, invasion of hospital premises, interference with medical triage and treatment, and intimidation of health care workers constitute gross violations. Moreover, in settings where food shortages have become acute and the supply of food to civilian populations is considered life-saving, interference with such delivery is considered a violation of international humanitarian law.

In Mogadishu, violations of international humanitarian law were the norm, rather than the exception. Virtually no one with a weapon had heard of the Geneva Conventions, from the most senior officers down to the lawless bands of heavily armed men and boys who constituted the two armies and myriad subsidiary factions. The sophisticated heavy artillery that had fallen into the hands of both sides came with detailed technical manuals, instructing the user in how to aim the weapon, assess accuracy of hit, and readjust settings to ensure more accurate hits on subsequent volleys. The Somali men and boys, many of them unschooled, fired these weapons in the general direction of a target, moved the weapons frequently, and made no systematic effort at accuracy. Their targets, in any case, were private villas and homes in Mogadishu, since the city had become the battleground. Consequently, civilians were inexorably and intimately entrained in the war. Protection of civilians and noncombatants was an absolutely illusory concept.

Violations of medical neutrality took place with regularity in the first two months after the onslaught of fighting in November. In the absence of any knowledge that international conventions existed, and without strong discipline from a centralized command system, individual groups of soldiers carried their hostilities and their concern for their comrades past the gates of the hospitals and into the casualty areas and wards. The most serious violation was the intimidation of hospital workers by heavily armed men into caring for patients out of order of medical triage. No instance of specific deliberate physical injury to a medical worker has been reported, but the presence and threatening demeanor of soldiers with machine guns created a tense and volatile atmosphere in which to take care of casualties.

In January 1992, the Médicins sans Frontières medical staff at Medina organized all medical staff on the south to plead with General Aidid to prohibit armed personnel from entering the hospital compounds in the sectors of the city he controlled. This effort was successful, and large signs in Somali and English were posted at all gates, requiring soldiers and the armed guards of medical personnel to leave their weapons with the hospital guards before permission would be granted to enter the compounds. Although these measures resulted in a substantial decrease in the frequency by which armed soldiers invaded the compounds, there were still reports in late January and February of armed men, in the heat of battle, careening with jeeps of wounded past the guards and into the hospital compounds.

In addition, throughout this five-month period from November to February, there were many reported instances of heavy but apparently indeliberate artillery bombardment of hospitals. These barrages, and occasional "sky shots" (random firings into the air, resulting in bullets falling from a height) caused substantial physical damage to hospitals on both sides of the city and deaths and injuries of patients and hospital personnel.

The most dramatic instance of a violation of medical neutrality occurred on February 13, 1992, when armed men who claimed allegiance to Ali Mahdi's army entered Keysaney Hospital, the ICRC hospital in the northern sector of Mogadishu, and forced its closure. During the previous two months, at a cost of $200,000, the ICRC had created this hospital on the grounds of an old fort, and it had been up and running for about ten days prior to the armed invasion of the premises. Flying several Red Cross flags from various parapets, staffed with medical personnel who were all clearly wearing Red Cross identification, and filled with approximately forty-five patients, there was no possible ambiguity about the status of the building or the mission of its staff. The Somali staff were ordered to disperse at once; the ICRC staff were herded into jeeps and summarily ordered to fly out of the city that evening. Under heavy threat, they were forced to abandon the patients. (It was later learned that these patients were taken to beds in the Karaan Hospital complex.) The incident was not explained, although it appeared from indirect communications that Ali Mahdi disavowed responsibility for this event, stating that the armed men were acting without his authority.

The Problem of Famine

It was evident to the relief community in Mogadishu in February 1992 that a famine of epic proportions was likely to hit Somalia by late spring or early summer of 1992. Local sources of food, from agricultural production in Bay and in the Juba and Shebelle river regions, had been widely disrupted by civil conflict waged there in spring and summer of 1991. The unrest had also severely limited food imports and virtually halted deliveries of food aid, other important sources in prior times. The drought throughout eastern Africa had also played a role.

Estimates of 1991 food production for Somalia were only 30 percent[9] of normal levels. Production issues were only part of the problem, since the normal channels for distribution no longer existed and market forces could not be relied upon. Because of the widespread unrest, it was also impossible to arrive at an accurate assessment of need. Local surveys in late 1991 and early 1992, conducted by the ICRC and Save the Children-UK in the Gedo region and the displaced persons camps around Mogadishu, suggested very high child malnutrition rates. In March 1992, the ICRC reported "horrifying" levels of 90 percent moderate to severe malnutrition in the populations around Belet Huen and Merca.[10] As in all situations of impending famine, the most vulnerable populations are the displaced; all children, especially those under five years of age; the elderly; and pregnant and lactating women.[11]

The ICRC estimated in March 1992 that food needs were approximately 7,000 metric tonnes per month to feed greater Mogadishu and 35,000 tonnes per month for the country as a whole.[12] Nothing approaching that level of delivery was then taking place, or in the pipeline. Food supplied by the ICRC, the UN, and the NGO community was reaching Mogadishu only by daily flights of the small ICRC plane. The ICRC was also attempting to deliver about 7,000 tonnes per month by sea to the southern and central regions of the country.

In February 1992, the ICRC updated its food surveys from the summer of 1991. Forecasts for 1992 were grim. Lack of seed, agricultural equipment, and ongoing insecurity meant that the 1992 harvest, even if the spring rains came in abundance, would be less than the meager harvest of 1991. The population had already consumed its food and livestock reserves in getting through 1991. Wherever surveys could be attempted throughout the country, high levels of severe malnutrition were found. The February draft document prepared by the ICRC predicted that of the 4.5 million people in Somalia south of the disputed region of Somaliland, one-third, or 1.5 million people, were at serious risk of death from starvation over the next six months. In its March 1992 bulletin the ICRC made this announcement public.

Summary Assessment, February 1992

Medical and food relief workers in Mogadishu shared a common assessment of the situation and what sort of intervention would be necessary to avert the famine that threatened to dwarf the numbers of casualties already incurred in the bitter factional fighting. These relief workers had labored on site for months, enduring the chronic tension and fear imposed by living in the midst of war. Most of them had known the ICRC relief worker who had been killed; many knew about the other aid worker who had been slain in the north. They had watched and negotiated with the two leaders of the factions and understood to some extent the limits of the agreements these men could and would commit to. They had witnessed and analyzed the politics of food shortage and distribution in the city and the surrounding countryside. They were also in touch with the few relief workers who had made forays by plane into the interior of the country. As the ones delivering medical care and supplying food to the few feeding stations that could be maintained in the insecure setting, they were well informed about the declining nutritional state of the population. In their assessment, the problem was a tightly linked question of food and security. An enormous increase in food aid was needed, logarithmically greater than current influx, if famine was to be avoided during the summer of 1992. The security situation in Mogadishu and throughout the countryside made delivery and distribution of food very dangerous. The shortage of food aggravated the danger in distributing it: the more desperate the need, the greater the value placed on food as a commodity, and the more it would provide the focus for attack.

Consequently, a radically new approach to the distribution of food to famine-affected areas was needed. The strategy usually employed by the international relief community, consisting of incremental and sequential steps of delivery and central storage, aimed towards creating and filling a pipeline of distribution, would serve only to escalate the frenzy of violence at those initial delivery and storage sites and do little to alleviate the food crisis. Only a massive food program, delivering thousands of tons a week at many key points in the country, would saturate the markets, fill the trucks of looters and military bandits, and through organized and informal routes, reach the majority of those in need. The need was so severe over such a vast area that the old deliberate processes, used with moderate success in previous famine settings, would not work in a country where violence posed such a barrier to the establishment of formal and sequential chains of supply and distribution.

Many local aid experts in Mogadishu during this period did not feel that the international aid agencies could carry out this massive airlift and ground transport of food without sustained and substantial armed protection, at least during the first several months before the relief efforts began to ease the need and reduce the intrinsic and barter value of food. Men and boys throughout the country were heavily armed and only nominally at best under any kind of local control. The risks of hijack, looting, and pillage were so great that aid workers who risked their lives daily in the constrained and moderately well-fathomed threat environment of Mogadishu considered it impossible to expand food relief to other areas without heavy armed guard, on the order of 5,000–10,000 armed troops for the entire country.

There was a difference of opinion among local relief workers between those who thought the armed presence, perhaps a police force supplied by the UN, could or should be deployed in advance of negotiating a cease-fire between Aidid and Ali Mahdi, and those who thought such a force would have to await the accomplishment of a cease-fire agreement. The latter group conceded that a cease-fire was unlikely in the near future, and thus attempts to mount a realistic food aid program were doomed to delay.

Those in the first group believed that since the situation in Somalia required a new approach to food delivery, a new stance on the part of the international community's use of armed force in support of humanitarian relief was also required. Historically, and by international agreement, UN forces have only been deployed in peacekeeping modes, after a negotiated cease-fire agreement has been reached. In the view of people familiar with Somalia in 1992, however, the deployment of UN peacemaking forces authorized to use force to create safe corridors for the transport of humanitarian aid in advance of a cease-fire required an expanded definition of mission that was absolutely essential for the delivery of aid. It was also recognized that even if a cease-fire were accomplished, it was unlikely the relief workers could depend upon protection from the forces of Aidid and Ali Mahdi. Cease-fire or not, thousands of UN armed troops would probably be needed to define and support safe corridors.

These views and their attendant controversies were already under active debate in February 1992 among the relief workers familiar with the situation in Somalia. Why did a similar debate not surface at this time in the UN, in the pages of the international press, or within and among governments? Why has it taken so long for fragments of this assessment to appear in public declarations? Only at the end of July 1992 did officials of the U.S. Office of Foreign Disaster Assistance conclude, after a five-hour visit to Mogadishu, that "ways had to be found to saturate Somalia with food so that the incentive for the fighting would be reduced."[13] In early September relief officials moved into rural areas of Somalia and reported that "the country's famine is far worse than previously believed and that present efforts, including an American airlift, are falling far short of what is needed to ease the crisis."[14]

The Response of the International Community

The reason for the delay in assessment and response to the disaster in Somalia is complex in detail but simple in outline: only the UN or the United States and European Community had the standing to create an international consensus on these issues, and none, for an unconscionably long period, chose to do so. The challenge was significant—new ways to deliver food and a new use of force to protect that delivery. To define and meet that challenge required a sense of urgent responsibility, which for months no one wanted to own. In the post–Cold War era, Somalia was a distant and fractured country, whose problems, provided they remained within local borders, did not command high-level attention.

Among the international relief agencies, the ICRC had acquired a particularly deep understanding of the food crisis. The ICRC could not endorse, for reasons of political neutrality, the need for a substantial armed UN military presence to support the necessary massive food program.[15] Other agencies with deep understanding of the food crisis had limited resources and were preoccupied with delivering care on the ground. They were not equipped to engage in the debate in the international arena.

The UN, the one agency aside from the ICRC with the authority and resources to shape the international debate, had pulled out of Mogadishu in the early winter of 1991 and maintained a low-profile stance in Nairobi, communicating via relatively junior staff to UN headquarters in New York. Until the appointment in May 1992 of Mohammed Sahnoun as senior UN representative in Somalia, no high-ranking UN staff person from headquarters had been assigned responsibility for Somalia. Mr. Sahnoun has since become one of the UN's harshest critics, charging in early September 1992 that much of the relief failure was due to "an overwhelming United Nations bureaucracy that, in contrast to the Red Cross, is made up of civil servants more interested in careers and perquisites than in the job at hand."[16]

For most of the winter and spring, the efforts of the UN and the United States with regard to Somalia were focused on attempting to arrange a cease-fire in Mogadishu. These efforts were moderately successful, in that a shaky agreement negotiated in March has for the most part held in the city. In the same period, however, famine and armed anarchy, unattended to, secured a stranglehold on the country.

Three factors converged in July and August of 1992 to cause the international community to swing into some form of active response to the deteriorating situation in Somalia. First, the vicious ethnic fighting in Bosnia created such a clamor in Western societies for the UN to intervene—even in a setting where a cease-fire could not be accomplished—that the parallels to Somalia became impossible to ignore. Given the scale of need in Somalia (at least five and perhaps ten times the estimated 200,000 to 300,000 people at risk in Bosnia[17]), if the United States and UN were seriously compelled to consider sending in 40,000[18] to 120,000[19] armed international peacemaking forces to provide protection to relief convoys and to Sarajevo proper, nestled in the mountains of Bosnia, how could they ignore the relatively simple logistic task of deploying 5,000 to 10,000 UN armed troops in the flat open terrain of Somalia?

Second, the presence in East Africa of the new UN special ambassador to Somalia, Mr. Mohammed Sahnoun, provided abundant fresh information about the calamity and the occasion for intensified and detailed updates on Somalia in the national and international press.[20] Third, U.N. secretary-general Boutros Boutros-Ghali began to speak more openly about his personal sense that the UN had failed to maintain a sense of fairness in weighing relative deployment of resources for relief in areas of former Yugoslavia versus Somalia. His public statements of dissent galvanized a more sustained and informed debate in the press and in the UN about the threat in the Horn of Africa, as well as in Europe.[21]

To have a substantial mitigating effect on the epidemic of famine now afflicting Somalia requires the international community to move quickly to craft a realistic and comprehensive strategy that links the delivery of food to the provision of adequate security. Very little time is left. People are dying at a rate of over one thousand per day, and those still alive are sinking into a state of inanition where ordinary food aid will be of no use to stave off terminal decline.

Recommendations

Elements of this strategy should include:

1. Integration of UN and U.S. efforts with ICRC staff and expertise;
2. Deployment of armed UN and U.S. military forces in sufficient numbers to deter, and where necessary, successfully ward off violent attack;
3. Commitment to hold the gains, and not withdraw but augment armed force if violence escalates;
4. Commitment to reach all areas of great need, regardless of distance or political factionalization;
5. Procurement and delivery of at least 60,000 tons[22] of food aid per month for as long as necessary.

To accomplish this strategy will require a level of creative energy and cooperation that has rarely been reached in the international community. Speaking of Bosnia, and the need to move toward a policy in which the UN might have to intervene in violent internal situations, John Steinbruner, defense and foreign policy analyst at the Brookings Institute, has said, "Inevitably, we are going to be shaping new doctrine . . . Both the principles and the mechanisms are going to have to be invented here."[23]

A step towards this discussion of new doctrine has been taken with the release of the UN report, "Agenda for Peace," prepared by Boutros Boutros-Ghali in June 1992 calling for a dramatic expansion of the UN peacemaking role in ways not currently defined in the UN charter.[24] In this last decade of the twentieth century, without the constraints imposed by rival superpowers, regional war, civil conflict, and communal violence may become more frequent and bitter, portending death, misery, and dislocation for millions of people. As these events arise, the UN will be asked with increasing urgency to restore order and uphold current principles of humanitarian law and human rights, including the right to food, medical care, peace, and security, as enshrined in the Universal Declaration of Human Rights.

The key unresolved issue is that to act effectively in areas of the world where government is either nonexistent or has run amok, the UN may have to intervene against the wishes of whatever authorities claim to be in control. To send UN peacemaking forces into such areas, national sovereignty (or its locally proclaimed variant) might have to yield to the overriding interest of the international community in protecting the welfare of the people caught within the borders of violence. To provide humanitarian relief in areas of widespread violence will require major changes in the way the UN views itself and its scope of authority and in the way the nation-states of the world are willing to cede to the UN the capacity to keep the peace. To pretend that the challenges of the new world order can be faced without such changes—including revised or expanded membership in the UN Security Council, more secure financial arrangements with member states, the creation of a standing international force, an expansion of the UN charter, and revisions in current international law—is to persist in the illusion that institutions do not have to accommodate to events. Yugoslavia and Somalia are desperate tugs on the sleeve of humanity, and, unheeded, they are also harbingers of things worse to come.

7

Casualties of Conflicts and Mine Warfare

RÉMI RUSSBACH

While international political negotiations and arbitration have made it possible to prevent and solve numerous conflicts, war nevertheless remains a reality in many regions of the world, in spite of the widely held conviction that it should be eradicated. The physical and emotional suffering it creates is affecting more and more civilians, in spite of the provisions of international humanitarian law (IHL), which specifically protect all those who do not play an active role in the fighting.

The International Committee of the Red Cross (ICRC), in its efforts to come to the aid of the victims of armed conflicts, either by direct action or by developing and enforcing the application of IHL, is in urgent need of the support of the states party to the Geneva Conventions in order to tackle this enormous problem. Although the situation is a tragic one, we should not lose courage; on the contrary, it should inspire us and give us the necessary energy to mobilize all those who wish to make a positive contribution to the peaceful solution of

The author acknowledges Louise Doswald-Beck and Robin Gray for their assistance in the preparation of this paper.

conflicts, to the development of IHL, and to a more effective application of existing law.

Being responsible for the ICRC's medical activities, we come into constant contact with the suffering of war victims in over forty countries. We will not elaborate here upon the fate of the millions of civilians who face starvation and disease because of warfare, nor on the fate of the prisoners—of which we are all so painfully aware—since these staggering problems do not belong to the specific subject covered here. Rather, we will deal with the ICRC's experience in work for the war-wounded in general. We will first focus on those who have been wounded by mines and then describe the provisions of IHL that are applicable to them, and the actions that can be undertaken to reduce the number and sufferings of the victims.

Action of the ICRC on Behalf of the War-Wounded

It often occurs that the war-wounded cannot be taken care of by local surgical structures, either because these structures are insufficient or because access to them is closed to certain groups of victims, for political reasons. The ICRC first attempts to solve the problem either by providing material support to the local structures or by negotiating with the authorities for access to surgical care for all the wounded, in accordance with the principles of the Geneva Conventions.

The ICRC does not open its own surgical units until it is clear that these measures are unable to provide care for all the wounded. Therefore, the ICRC's statistics do not reflect the total number of those wounded as a result of a given conflict, since they do not reflect the actions carried out by official structures. Nevertheless, they are indicative of the proportions of given categories of wound victims in terms of the groups the ICRC attends to. In 1992 the ICRC ran ten surgical units in seven countries (Table 1). Between 1982 and 1991 the number of surgical admissions in ICRC hospitals rose from 2,000 to 20,000 patients per year (Figure 1).

Caring for war-wounded directly is a practical measure, and ICRC personnel require orientation and preparation for working in this context. For surgeons there is also the problem that civilian practice does not prepare them for the special requirements and understanding needed to deal with war injury, especially mine injury. The ICRC is increasingly active in sharing and propagating its special experience with war injury. To this end the ICRC has made available the booklets

Amputations for War Wounds and *The Red Cross Classification of War Wounds.* A sixty-five minute film, *War Surgery: An Introduction,* and the book *Surgery for Victims of War,* in addition to some thirty articles in medical journals, also help this process. The approach by which the ICRC assists in training medical personnel, both civilian and military, for war surgery is still being developed.

Antipersonnel mines were first used in World War II to prevent

TABLE 1. *Locations of ICRC Surgical Units for War-Wounded, 1992*

City	Country	
Lokichokio	Kenya	For Sudanese wounded
Naopares	Iraq	For Iraqi wounded
Kabul	Afghanistan	
Peshawar	Pakistan	For Afghan wounded
Quetta	Pakistan	
Khao-I-Dang	Thailand	
Pursat	Cambodia	For Khmer wounded
Kampot	Cambodia	
Mongol Borei	Cambodia	
Mogadishu	Somalia	For Somali wounded

FIGURE 1.
Number of War-Wounded Admitted to ICRC Hospitals, 1982–1991

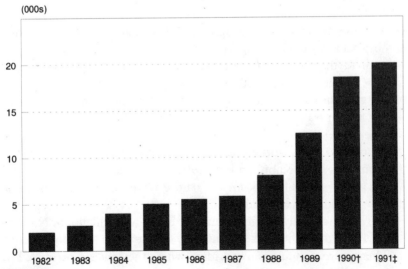

(000s)

* Two hospitals
† Thirteen hospitals
‡ Twelve hospitals

enemy soldiers from removing antitank mines. They are now also employed to protect defended localities and to delay and demoralize advancing infantry, a use referred to as "nuisance mining." Southeast Asia and Afghanistan are the areas most infested by antipersonnel mines—which, deplorably, are often called "eternal sentinels" because they continue to kill and maim long after the war is over.

The use of antipersonnel mines in present-day warfare extends beyond the purely military, to the vicious purposes of psychological, rather than defensive, warfare. This is most graphically illustrated by the use of "butterfly" mines, which are scattered by aircraft at random over wide areas and strike, in an indiscriminate and cowardly fashion, the first passerby, whether or not that person is involved in the war. One can only wonder if it is possible for the men who use such mines to do so without feeling any form of remorse. Perhaps a better knowledge of the psychological mechanism that leads men to kill innocent people at random, without taking risks themselves, and without even witnessing the explosion—which, indeed, may take place years later— might make it possible to find a way of touching the minds of these mine spreaders.

CASE STUDIES

Here are a few examples from among the thousands of victims we have cared for:

- A girl of thirteen was brought to the Mongol Borei (Cambodia) hospital late one morning in 1992. Her family had recently moved back to their village, about twenty-five kilometers from Mongol Borei, which had previously been in a fighting area. She had been out gathering firewood at dawn. Fortunately, her family was able to pay for her transportation, and she was brought to the hospital quite quickly.
- A boy had been working on farmland at a village some forty-five kilometers from Kabul, in June 1992. Something came up with the spade and exploded. From the nature of the injury, it appears to have been a butterfly mine PEM-1.
- During one family's flight from Cambodia to Thailand, in November 1992, the father was wounded by a mine and a little boy injured. There were difficulties in deciding where they should be sent. The father died before reaching hospital; the wounded boy, his mother, and a sibling were admitted to an ICRC hospital.

  • In separate incidents, a boy of fourteen and a boy of eleven were
    wounded while tending their families' cattle in Kabul, in June 1992,
    after stepping on antipersonnel mines.

Four other types of antipersonnel mines blight innocent populations. Foot-triggered mines are laid on or just below the ground and
damage principally the lower limbs by blast. Stake mines explode in a
360-degree range from a position ten to thirty centimeters above the
ground and produce damage by the lateral projection of metal fragments of the outer casing. Bounding mines jump into the air to variable
heights before exploding. Individuals within their range die from the
effects of blast and fragments, and peripherally placed persons are
wounded by fragments. Directional mines are positioned above
ground on pods, on stakes, or in trees, and project metal fragments or
spheres in a predetermined arc for distances of up to 150 meters.

Mines may be classified as metallic, minimal metallic, or nonmetal-
lic. Hidden foot-triggered and bounding mines represent the biggest
problem for de-miners. Those containing metallic parts, however
small, are detectable; but plastic renders detection virtually impossible.
Designers use much ingenuity in making mines nondetectable and
irremovable. Paint can prevent detection by infrared equipment, and
electronic antiremoval devices can be built in to mines.

Jane's *Yearbooks* refer to nearly twenty countries that have developed over forty designs of antipersonnel mine; the 1992–1993 edition
describes well over a hundred varieties. Many other countries produce
mines under license. There are certainly more designs and manufac-
turers; for obvious reasons, expertise and technology are not openly
shared. Much thought goes into making mines undetectable, and special construction considerations are required for delivery by mortar,
artillery shell, or rocket, or for distribution from aircraft and helicopters. Of seven remotely delivered mines it describes, Jane mentions
only one as having a self-destruct mechanism. To quote on the butterfly mine: "The device is designed to maim rather than kill and has no
self-destruct or neutralising capability."[1]

Mines produce injury either by blast or by penetration of metallic
fragments. The problem for the surgeon faced with wounds from
foot-triggered hidden mines is that, as well as blowing away a variable
part of the leg, the explosion drives mud, dirt, and debris up and into
the tissues of the leg; this calls for amputation more often than is
apparent to inexperienced personnel. These mines also frequently
damage the other leg, genitals, chest, arms, and face. The surgery for

those who survive bounding, stake, and directional mines involves a deep understanding of fragment injury.

Of the 14,221 wounded who were treated at four of the ICRC hospitals, 23 percent were admitted for mine injuries (Figure 2). However, the proportion differs according to the specific context (Figure 3).

It reaches its peak (62 percent) in the hospital of Khao-i-Dang, on the border between Thailand and Cambodia, because the people from the surrounding camps live in a heavily mine-infested area in which there is currently little military activity. The proportion is lower in Kabul (17 percent), because mines are used less in towns and because the city's inhabitants are exposed mainly to street fighting and artillery attacks.

In the hospitals of Peshawar and Quetta, where the wounded from the same conflict are being treated, the proportion of mine victims is larger than in Kabul, since the entire border area between Afghanistan and Pakistan is heavily infested. From April to July 1992 the proportion of mine-wound victims increased sharply on the Afghanistan border in comparison to the proportion from January 1991 to July 1992 (Peshawar, from 26 percent to 51 percent; Quetta, from 20

FIGURE 2.
Distribution of War-Wounded, by Cause of Injury,
January 1991–July 1992*

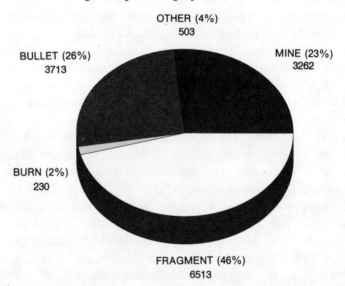

OTHER (4%)
503

BULLET (26%)
3713

MINE (23%)
3262

BURN (2%)
230

FRAGMENT (46%)
6513

*Total of 14,221 wounded treated at five ICRC hospitals

FIGURE 3.
Mine-Wound Cases as Percentage of Wounded

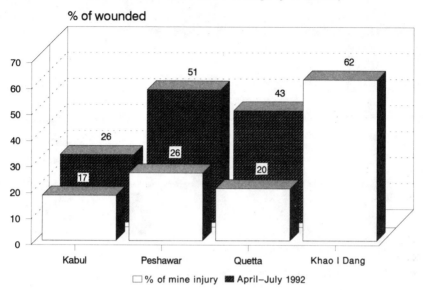

% of wounded

☐ % of mine injury ▨ April–July 1992

percent to 43 percent), owing to the partial return of refugees to Afghanistan.

Of the 3,262 mine-injury cases studied, 21 percent were women and children, and 79 percent were men; it is not known what percentage of the men were not involved in the fighting (Figure 4). The ratio of women and children to men varies from one hospital to another. It is especially high in Kabul (33 percent) because the shepherds tending the herds on the outskirts of this city, which are heavily infested with mines, are mainly children. In the border areas of Afghanistan and Cambodia, the proportion of cases who are women and children is lower because the proportion of men circulating in the mined zones is higher.

Action to Help the War-Disabled

Since 1977, the ICRC has made a great effort to help those who have undergone the amputation of lower limbs, who are for the most part mine-wound victims. Indeed, after an amputation, it becomes necessary

FIGURE 4.
Percentage of Mine-Wound Cases Who Were Children and Women

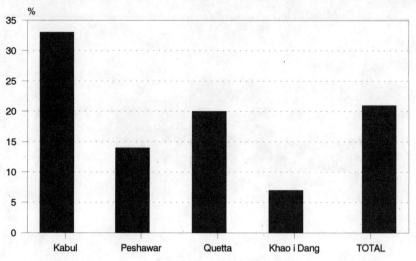

to provide the victim with a decent way of surviving and a chance to be reintegrated into his social milieu. Given the almost total lack of means in countries where warfare has been rife, this calls for rehabilitation—provision of artificial limbs and reeducation—that is simple, inexpensive, and compatible with the country's standard of living and resources. A vast number of experiments have been carried out all over the world to develop acceptable ways of doing this with a minimum of external funds, by training local personnel and using—according to the country's resources—wood, iron, aluminum, leather, polyester, and even polypropylene. While this last is a synthetic material that must be imported, it often provides the best solution because of the ease with which it can be shaped, its relatively low price, and its durability. In spite of our attempts to standardize these techniques, the widely varying conditions that exist in each country make it impossible, for the time being, to establish a uniform international technical procedure.

In 1991 the ICRC operated twelve orthopedic centers in different countries (Figure 5), where it manufactured 11,116 prostheses and provided artificial limbs for 7,876 leg amputation victims, of whom about 5 percent had had both legs removed. Women and children represented, on average, 26 percent of all patients in the centers.

Fifty-one foreign technical experts, assisted by nine hundred local

FIGURE 5.
Locations of ICRC Orthopedic Centers, 1991

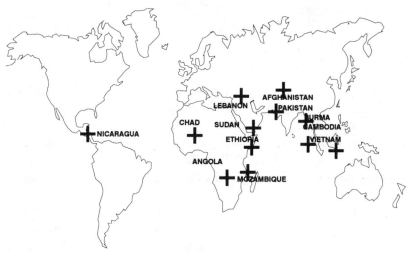

employees, manufacture the artificial limbs and fit them to the victims. About three hundred local technicians have received training, and about fifty of these have been awarded government diplomas. Some U.S. $9.6 million were spent in 1991 to create these centers and train personnel. The ICRC's goal is to gradually transfer these centers to the country's health ministry, which should take over activities in the long term.

It is obvious that the ICRC centers cover only a small part of the needs of mine-wound victims, and that many of those who live in war zones have no way of reaching the centers. It is difficult to calculate the exact number of amputation victims of a country at war, where data gathering is hampered by chaos and the resulting isolation of remote areas, which explains why, even when we are installed in a country, it is usually impossible for us to count all the amputation victims. This is especially so for the civilian victims, who are not as easy to categorize as the military ones.

It should be stressed that action in favor of amputation victims should not be confined to emergency treatment, since artificial limbs, even when they are of high quality, suffer from wear and tear, and must be changed. Children's artificial limbs must be altered to accommodate body growth. It is therefore obvious that any action in favor of amputation victims must be followed up by long-term support. Other organizations are also active in providing artificial limbs to amputation victims, but the total result still falls far short of existing needs.

International Law Governing the Use of Mines

The respect of existing international law provisions would go a long way toward preventing the kind of widespread mine casualties that we are witnessing. We will now briefly review the law that can already be taken advantage of and the steps that need to be taken to assure a reasonable respect of this law. We will then look at some of the ways in which the law could be supplemented to better deal with the present situation.

One of the most fundamental rules of international humanitarian law is that during military operations a distinction is to be made between the civilian population and military objectives so that attacks are limited to military objectives. This customary rule has frequently suffered in practice, but it has been reaffirmed by treaty in the 1977 protocols additional to the Geneva Conventions in the following terms:

PROTOCOL I (INTERNATIONAL ARMED CONFLICTS), ARTICLE 48:

In order to ensure respect for and protection of the civilian population and civilian objects, the Parties to the conflict shall at all times distinguish between the civilian population and combatants and between civilian objects and military objectives and accordingly shall direct their operations only against military objectives.

PROTOCOL II (NONINTERNATIONAL ARMED CONFLICTS), ARTICLE 13:

1. The civilian population and individual civilians shall enjoy general protection against the dangers arising from military operations. To give effect to this protection, the following rules shall be observed in all circumstances.
2. The civilian population as such, as well as individual civilians, shall not be the object of attack. Acts or threats of violence the primary purpose of which is to spread terror among the civilian population are prohibited.
3. Civilians shall enjoy the protection afforded by this Part, unless and for such time as they take a direct part in hostilities.

From this it follows that indiscriminate attacks are prohibited; indeed, protocol I deals in some length with the prohibition of indiscriminate attacks and with the precautions to be taken to avoid these (articles 51 and 57). It is noteworthy that protocol I now has 113 states parties, including the majority of North Atlantic Treaty Organization members, and protocol II has 103.

Another general rule of importance, also customary in nature and reaffirmed in protocol I, is the prohibition of the use of weapons that cause unnecessary suffering. Article 35 (2) prohibits the use of "weapons, projectiles and material and methods of warfare of a nature to cause superfluous injury or unnecessary suffering." This means that the use of weapons whose damaging effects are disproportionate to their military purpose are prohibited, and this rule is relevant to the design of mines: we have seen, in particular, that some mines cause far worse injury than others, even when the military purpose of the mines is identical.

In addition to these basic rules, there is a treaty that specifically regulates the use of land mines: Protocol II to the 1980 "Convention on Prohibitions or Restrictions on the Use of Certain Conventional Weapons Which May Be Deemed to Be Excessively Injurious or to Have Indiscriminate Effects," commonly referred to at the United Nations as the "Inhumane Weapons Convention." Protocol II ("Protocol on Prohibitions or Restrictions on the Use of Mines, Booby-Traps and Other Devices") is fairly complex; we summarize its principal provisions here and reproduce the most relevant articles in appendix 1. The treaty repeats the general rule that mines may be directed only at military objectives, prohibits indiscriminate use, and provides that all feasible precautions are to be taken to protect civilians (articles 3 and 4).

This protocol also establishes particular restrictions on the use of remotely delivered mines—namely, that they may not be used unless either their location is accurately recorded or they are fitted with an effective neutralizing mechanism (article 5). Such mechanisms can be either automatic or activated by a remotely controlled device. As far as recording of mine fields is concerned, a distinction is made between mine fields that are preplanned and those that are improvised during hostilities. The treaty requires that parties record all preplanned mine fields (whether remotely delivered or manually placed), whereas it requires only that they "endeavor to ensure" the recording of others. However, as we have already mentioned, improvised mine fields made of remotely delivered mines have to be recorded unless they incorporate neutralizing mechanisms.

After the end of active hostilities, the parties to the conflict are to give to each other and to the secretary-general of the United Nations information on the location of mine fields, based on these records. However, in the case where hostilities have ended with one party still in occupation of another party's territory, the release of such information is not compulsory, but is encouraged (article 7 [3]).

Finally, the treaty requires the parties to the conflict to try to reach agreement between themselves and, where appropriate, with other states and international organizations in order to take the necessary measures to clear mine fields (article 9).

Although these legal provisions are not ideal, their respect would substantially reduce the numbers of mine victims. With regard to the general rules, it is heartening that the 1977 protocols have obtained a large number of ratifications, and it is to be hoped that their further ratification, particularly by all the major powers, will take place so as to add to their moral weight. On the other hand, the 1980 Convention so far has only thirty-two states parties, and major states, including the United States, have not yet ratified it.

A first major and important step that must be taken is a much wider ratification of this treaty, in order to show the importance that states attach to limitations on mine use. Such a step is a minimum prerequisite to improving the extremely serious situation that we are now faced with as a result of the widespread indiscriminate use of mines. The next stage is to ensure that these provisions are actually carried out, and for this purpose training in the use of mines needs to incorporate the requirements of the law.

In this respect we may mention that developed countries train not only their own armies but also a number of military personnel from the Third World, and they therefore have a special responsibility to stress the importance of the law, in particular, the recording of mine fields and how this is done. On a diplomatic level, major states can underline the importance of restraint in mine use and encourage the respect of these legal provisions in all conflicts, including internal ones, although the 1980 Convention technically applies only to international conflicts.

Although these steps would be very positive ones, the current dramatic situation shows that some further measures are in fact called for to more effectively deal with the problem. Short of banning all mines, which is the suggestion of an increasing number of nongovernmental organizations and personalities, several possibilities deserve serious thought.

First of all, the legal provisions of the 1980 Convention are not as all-encompassing as they could be; the original draft, which had been presented by the United Kingdom, contained more substantial limitations and requirements. Thus, it is a pity that the recording of manually placed mines during hostilities (which cannot be classed as preplanned) is not compulsory but only hortatory.

Second, it should perhaps be provided that all mines be fitted with automatic self-destruct mechanisms so as to avoid the absurd situation of mines' killing people many years after the end of hostilities. The wisdom of manufacturing mines that are virtually undetectable also warrants consideration. The military value of these mines needs to be weighed against the human and environmental tragedy that they cause, and a sensible solution must be found. It is also unfortunate that the provisions on mine clearance are relatively weak, and these could benefit from more stringent and realistic requirements.

Finally, extending the rules of the 1980 Convention to noninternational armed conflicts merits thought. Although protocol II of 1977 additional to the Geneva Convention does provide basic limitations for the protection of the civilian population, detailed regulations on the use of mines would clearly be of more value than are such general rules on their own.

The most perfect legal provisions, however, will be of no benefit if they are not accompanied by the necessary diplomatic and political pressure to carry them out, as well as practical programs for their implementation. They will also be more effective if they are implemented together with controls on manufacture and sales, so as to take into account the type of indiscriminate use that is likely to persist, especially by nonstate entities and those less influenced by legal and diplomatic pressures.

Conclusion

We observe, in the light of our field experience, that the use of mines in current warfare is generally planned without any regard for existing regulations. In fact, the scattering of antipersonnel mines by aircraft and the random placing of land mines take place solely in order to terrorize local inhabitants. These practices serve no military purpose and constitute a serious violation of international law.

The result is disastrous from the humanitarian standpoint, since these mines not only cause the death of many of their victims but also result in major handicaps, which are particularly devastating to children. The war-disabled represent a long-term burden that war-impoverished communities are simply unable to bear.

These observations have led us to place a high priority on the problem of antipersonnel mines, and to send out an appeal to all those who have already begun to act in favor of mine-wound victims and who might be able to help alleviate the enormous suffering caused by the wicked use of antipersonnel mines.

These actions should take place on various levels, involving physicians, army personnel, politicians, and individuals on every point of the scale, from those who are directly responsible for caring for the victims to those active at the highest level of the prevention effort —namely, international law.

The existing courses of action can be classified as follows:

- Fostering the adherence of states to IHL
- Enforcing observance of IHL
- Developing IHL
- Making IHL known to military authorities
- Making potential mine users aware of their responsibility
- Detecting the manufacture and sale of forbidden weapons
- Keeping local populations informed of dangerous areas
- Striving to de-mine infested zones by all possible means
- Transporting the wounded to hospitals
- Rehabilitating amputation victims

All these actions are complementary and should be undertaken simultaneously, in order to be effective in the long term.

This is a problem that concerns all of us. Each of us should do what we can to bring pressure to bear as decisively as possible, while also encouraging others to do what they can in their specific areas. Nothing short of concrete action will have any effect in improving the fate of the victims of antipersonnel mines.

Appendix 1.
Protocol on Prohibitions or Restrictions on the Use of Mines, Booby-Traps, and Other Devices

Article 3—General restrictions of the use of mines, booby-traps and other devices
  1. This Article applies to:

(a) mines;

(b) booby-traps; and

(c) other devices.

2. It is prohibited in all circumstances to direct weapons to which this Article applies, either in offence, defence or by way of reprisals, against the civilian population as such or against individual civilians.

3. The indiscriminate use of weapons to which this Article applies is prohibited. Indiscriminate use is any placement of such weapons:

(a) which is not on, or directed at, a military objective; or

(b) which employs a method or means of delivery which cannot be directed at a specific military objective; or

(c) which may be expected to cause incidental loss of civilian life, injury to civilians, damage to civilian objects, or a combination thereof, which would be excessive in relation to the concrete and direct military advantage anticipated.

4. All feasible precautions shall be taken to protect civilians from the effects of weapons to which this Article applies. Feasible precautions are those precautions which are practicable or practically possible taking into account all circumstances ruling at the time, including humanitarian and military considerations.

Article 4—Restrictions on the use of mines other than remotely delivered mines, booby-traps and other devices in populated areas

1. This Article applies to:

(a) mines other than remotely delivered mines;

(b) booby-traps; and

(c) other devices.

2. It is prohibited to use weapons to which this Article applies in any city, town, village or other area containing a similar concentration of civilians in which combat between ground forces is not taking place or does not appear to be imminent, unless either:

(a) they are placed on or in the close vicinity of a military objective belonging to or under the control of an adverse party; or

(b) measures are taken to protect civilians from their effects, for example, the posting of warning signs, the posting of sentries, the issue of warnings or the provision of fences.

Article 5—Restrictions on the use of remotely delivered mines

1. The use of remotely delivered mines is prohibited unless such mines are only used within an area which is itself a military objective or which contains military objectives, and unless:

(a) their location can be accurately recorded in accordance with Article 7(1)(a); or

(b) an effective neutralizing mechanism is used on each such mine, that is to say, a self-actuating mechanism which is designed to render a mine harmless or cause it to destroy itself when it is anticipated that the mine will no longer serve the military purpose for which it was placed in position, or a remotely-controlled mechanism which is designed to render harmless or destroy a mine when the mine no longer serves the military purpose for which it was placed in position.

2. Effective advance warning shall be given of any delivery or dropping of remotely delivered mines which may affect the civilian population, unless circumstances do not permit.

Article 7—Recording and publication of the location of minefields, mines and booby-traps

1. The parties to a conflict shall record the location of:
    (a) all pre-planned minefields laid by them; and
    (b) all areas in which they have made large-scale and pre-planned use of booby-traps.

2. The parties shall endeavour to ensure the recording of the location of all other minefields, mines and booby-traps which they have laid or placed in position.

3. All such records shall be retained by the parties who shall:
    (a) immediately after the cessation of active hostilities:
       (i) take all necessary and appropriate measures, including the use of such records, to protect civilians from the effects of minefields, mines and booby-traps; and either
       (ii) in cases where the forces of neither party are in the territory of the adverse party, make available to each other and to the Secretary-General of the United Nations all information in their possession concerning the location of minefields, mines and booby-traps in the territory of the adverse party; or
       (iii) once complete withdrawal of the forces of the parties from the territory of the adverse party has taken place, make available to the adverse party and to the Secretary-General of the United Nations all information in their possession concerning the location of minefields, mines and booby-traps in the territory of the adverse party;
    (b) when a United Nations force or mission performs functions in any area, make available to the authority mentioned in Article 8 such information as is required by that Article;
    (c) whenever possible, by mutual agreement, provide for the release of information concerning the location of minefields, mines and booby-traps, particularly in agreements governing the cessation of hostilities.

Article 9—International co-operation in the removal of minefields, mines and booby-traps

After the cessation of active hostilities, the parties shall endeavour to reach agreement, both among themselves and, where appropriate, with other States and with international organizations, on the provision of information and technical and material assistance—including, in appropriate circumstances, joint operations—necessary to remove or otherwise render ineffective minefields, mines and booby-traps placed in position during the conflict.

8

The Clinical Face of Famine

KEVIN M. CAHILL

T he majority of the world's population survive with hunger and
infections as constant companions, and live in "accident-
prone" nations where famine and epidemic diseases often
complicate the civil conflicts and natural disasters that are, unfortunately, regular events. Television pictures of the skeletal starving are
the tragic, terminal images in a complex cycle of progressive malnutrition, especially in victims already burdened by an incredible array of
dangerous parasitic, bacterial, and viral organisms. Since widespread
hunger and the existence—or even threat—of contagions are the most
common reasons offered to justify international humanitarian interventions, it is important that all involved in determining and effecting
foreign policy be familiar with the evolving clinical face of famine.

Famines have occurred in all areas of the globe and in every period
of recorded history, but our era has the odious distinction of being the
period when more people will die of famine than in any previous
century. To fully appreciate this indictment it is necessary to realize
that today mass death by starvation is rarely due to the vagaries of
nature alone but reflects, rather, human decisions. Today's famines are
man-made, for we have the ability to control short-term food deficits.[1]

Many factors can cause a local crop failure—droughts, floods, locusts, the spread of the desert, toxins, the erosion or exhaustion of soil—but in our modern world of instant communications and rapid transport there must be an almost calculated effort for famine to flourish. Political decisions—or indecisions—ignorance, neglect, and economic and cultural conflicts cause famines today. During periods of peace, corruption and mismanagement may lead to famine. The need for foreign exchange may force food-rich nations to export essential nutrients, leaving the indigenous populations to waste away. Wars, however, are the major man-made cause of famines, disrupting populations and the patterns of planting and harvesting essential for fruitful agriculture. Food stores are looted and hoarded, and supply lines are cut.

The developed nations of the world control the critical surplus of food supplies and have the capacity to both make and resolve, or, as is too often the case, simply ignore famines. Throughout the developing world, famines develop on a fragile nutritional foundation where dietary intake is usually woefully inadequate and parasites, such as blood sucking hookworms, drain their human hosts of protein, vitamin, and iron stores. The physical effects of malnutrition can be readily measured; low weights, stunted growth, frail bone structure, high infant and child morbidity and mortality rates, decreased work capacity and intellectual performance. Acute prolonged malnutrition also impairs mental development, leading to tragedies that last for generations. The ultimate irony is that the vulnerable poor who are most often affected are the ones who need both their maximum physical and mental health to survive with their meager resources and harsh environmental challenges.

Although I had managed isolated outbreaks of acute malnutrition in Somalia for over a decade, the Sahel famine in the mid-1970s was my introduction to the chaos that stalks large-scale starvation. The traditional supportive nomad society seemed to disintegrate as over one million refugees overwhelmed the land. Confusion reigned as neither the government nor clan structures could sustain the flood of utterly dependent persons. Most families had become separated, and the individual daily search for food and water dominated the escalating desperation. Infants, children, pregnant women, and the elderly died in disproportionate numbers while the stronger adults prevailed. The apathy and lethargy of a refugee camp contribute to the impression of imminent disaster.[2]

Those people most severely affected can present a clinical picture of great variety. At one end of the spectrum are the walking ghosts with marasmus, the victims of rapid, extensive caloric deficiency or, in a single word, starvation. At the opposite end are those suffering from chronic protein deficiency, or kwashiorkor. As in most disease states, the majority fall between these classic poles; the clinical picture is further complicated by almost universal infection with multiple parasites.

The child with marasmus leaves the impression of an old man's face on an infant's body. There is obvious wasting of muscles with total loss of subcutaneous fat. The buttocks disappear and the skin is loose and wrinkled. Scrawny limbs seem incapable of supporting the typical swollen body. The bony skull appears disproportionately large, and the knees stand out as awkward knobs. Eye lesions and skin rashes, with infected "tropical ulcers" are frequent. Diarrhea is the rule, and complete rectal prolapse from weakness of the anal orifice is not uncommon. A simple measurement of height and weight on a growth chart

FIGURE 1.

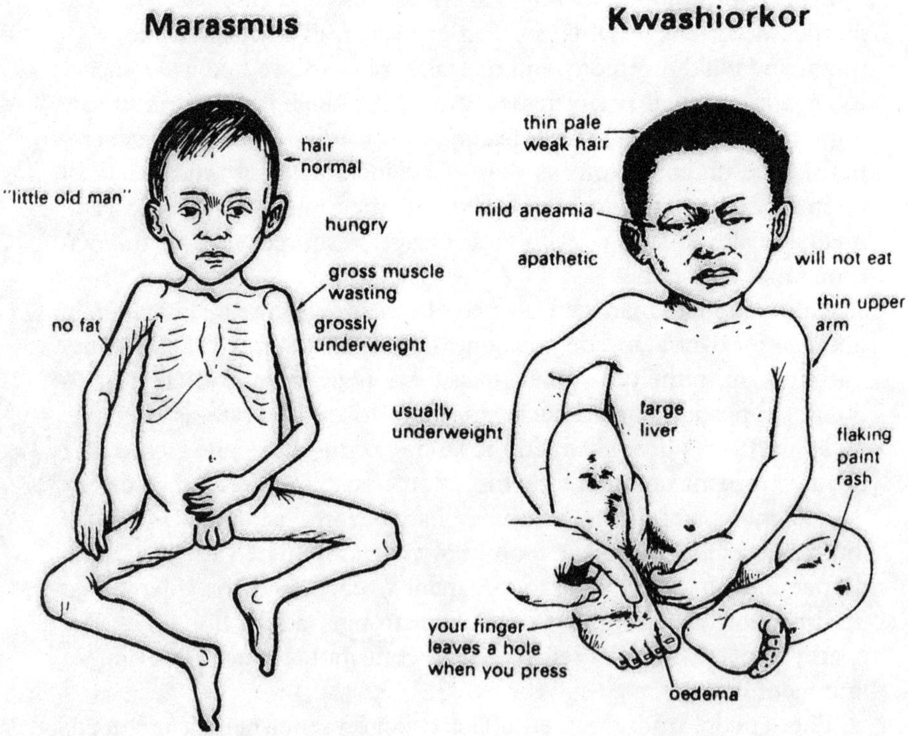

Marasmus

"little old man"
no fat

hair normal
hungry
gross muscle wasting
grossly underweight
usually underweight
your finger leaves a hole when you press

Kwashiorkor

thin pale weak hair
mild aneamia
apathetic
will not eat
thin upper arm
large liver
flaking paint rash
oedema

will document marked stunting. Nevertheless, the marasmic child is almost surprisingly alert, showing constant indications of hunger such as sucking and grasping movements. They are, however, patently weak and rapidly tire, becoming short of breath after the slightest exertion.

Kwashiorkor is the other major protein deficiency disease. It was almost unknown to the Somali nomads because their customary diet of camel's milk and occasional goat meat is very rich in protein. I cannot recall seeing a single case of kwashiorkor in Somalia before the Sahelian drought of 1976, and there is surely nothing subtle about the striking features of kwashiorkor in the black African.[3]

The hair turns a soft red or white and becomes straight and limp. The moon faces and swollen bodies do not have the texture of a healthy, cherubic child, but rather are pitted with edematous fluid. These children are apathetic or constantly whining. Skin rashes range from a dry, scaly, dark, "crazy pavement" pattern to almost total desquamation and severe ulcerations. The skin is often cold, and many children die of hypothermia when they are moved from the warmth of the mother's body. Obvious heart failure is the usual terminal event.

Micronutrient deficiencies also contribute to the clinical spectrum of famine. Ancient scourges such as scurvy, pellagra, and beriberi—due to lack of vitamin C, niacin, and thiamine, respectively—are common problems in the severely malnourished. Inadequate vitamin A is recognized as a frequent cause of serious eye problems in refugee camps. Iron deficient diets can produce profound anemias, especially in the most vulnerable groups, pregnant women and young children.

There were no laboratories in the Somali refugee camps I directed. Fortunately, there was little need for scientific confirmation to permit a working diagnosis for either marasmus or kwashiorkor. Therapy can be extremely challenging and deaths can be caused by inappropriate actions as well as neglect. Forced feeding can precipitate both diarrhea and aspiration pneumonia. Washing a child can exacerbate hypothermia, and it is better to have a dirty child than a dead one. The careful replacement of fluids, calories, and specific nutrients must be coordinated with the therapy for concurrent infections. The clinical picture is rarely due solely to starvation but reflects the added burden of multiple parasitic infestations and respiratory infections. Malaria is extremely common and measles and tuberculosis are rife.

Tuberculosis is a rampant problem and establishing isolation tents must be a priority since dissemination of contagious diseases among the immunocompromised malnourished is a lethal combination. The usual benign course of measles, for example, becomes a deadly scourge in the setting of a refugee camp; the greatest tragedy is to watch children who have managed to survive starvation and long treks to the relative security of a feeding station then succumb in epidemic numbers to an infection such as measles which could have been prevented by simple vaccine costing less than ten cents.

There is, however, evidence that the relationship of malnutrition and infection is not always synergistic; an appreciation of this phenomenon is essential for those charged with food relief programs. There have been many documented outbreaks of diseases only *after* food supplies are restored. Malaria, for example, appears to decline among those strong enough to survive starvation and then reaches fatal epidemic levels only after intensive refeeding efforts begin. Relief workers have long been aware that their well-meaning efforts may actually be causing unnecessary deaths, thereby defeating the whole purpose of international humanitarian intervention. Recent scientific studies offer an explanation for the transient protective effect of malnutrition against malaria. As essential nutrients, such as para amino benzoic acid (PABA) and vitamin E, decline, the malaria parasite cannot develop in the deficient human red cell.[4] As refeeding programs correct these imbalances, fatal malaria outbreaks occur. PABA and vitamin E are high in grain and low in milk and meat products. The implications for those charged with nutrition planning in famine situations such as in Somalia are obvious. The Hippocratic oath begins with the phrase *primum non nocere*—the first thing is to do no harm. Poorly conceived refeeding programs after famines can kill; the vast mountains of surplus grain may prove fatal if not integrated with appropriate supplemental antimalarial efforts.

Even in optimal circumstances—which hardly describe a Somali refugee camp—the period of rehabilitation for a patient with marasmus is judged in terms of months, rather than days, and the pressure of new problems for an overworked health team frequently results in inadequate attention during recovery, inevitably ending in a rapid deterioration and death.

The role of a physician in managing a catastrophic famine is not limited to the traditional diagnostic and therapeutic approach of the profession. He or she must learn to organize truck convoys, establish basic camps, and develop a team that will enable the foods donated or purchased to reach the hungry masses. The physician-leader, in this situation, must emphasize hope rather than disease, offering a future to those who have lost their past.

Medical school training rarely prepares one for such challenges.

The essential qualities required to effectively serve in such situations are not built on technical details that can be memorized, but must be based rather on the broad traditions that once made medicine a noble and learned profession.

The clinical faces of famine in Somalia are seared in my mind. The picture of marasmus or kwashiorkor tells a tale that few can evade, for it stares into our souls.

9

The Public Health Consequences of Inaction: Lessons Learned in Responding to Sudden Population Displacements

MICHAEL J. TOOLE

During the past two decades the world has witnessed a demographic epidemic of unprecedented proportions—an epidemic of forced migrations that has had grave public health consequences. These mass migrations have resulted in large part from the wars, civil strife, and violence that have plagued so many parts of the developing world. Now, in the 1990s, the same phenomena have returned to Europe, with major refugee populations being generated by ethnic-based wars in former Yugoslavia, Armenia, Azerbaijan, and Georgia. In this paper I will summarize our knowledge of the public health impact of mass population displacement; look at the essential elements of an effective public health response to emergencies involving refugee and displaced populations; and attempt to analyze the reasons for the relative failure of the international community to act

The author thanks the following organizations and individuals for having shared information gathered in the various displaced and refugee emergencies referred to in this paper: Epicentre; International Rescue Committee; Médecins sans Frontières; Save the Children Fund (U.K.); UNHCR; UNICEF; the governments of Bangladesh, Ethiopia, Guinea, Kenya, Malawi, Nepal, Somalia, Sudan, and Thailand; and his colleagues at the Centers for Disease Control.

decisively and consistently to prevent the most serious adverse consequences of these crises on the affected populations.

In 1980 refugees dependent on international assistance numbered only about five million; by 1985 this number had jumped to eight million, and today there are approximately eighteen and a half million such people dependent upon the world's generosity for their survival (Figure 1).[1] By definition, a refugee is an individual who has crossed from one country to another; in addition, there may be up to twenty million people who have been abruptly displaced from their homes and have fled to other, more secure regions within their own countries. These "internally displaced" persons do not automatically qualify for international assistance. With limited access to relief and without legal rights to the protection accorded refugees by international law, the internally displaced are frequently in a particularly desperate situation.

Most refugees and internally displaced persons have suddenly fled the violence that has engulfed their homes, leaving most of their belongings behind. They risk further violence, starvation, and exposure during their sometimes protracted flight to safety. Most refugees have fled poor, developing countries for safe haven in equally impoverished

FIGURE 1.
Countries with Major Refugee Populations, 1992

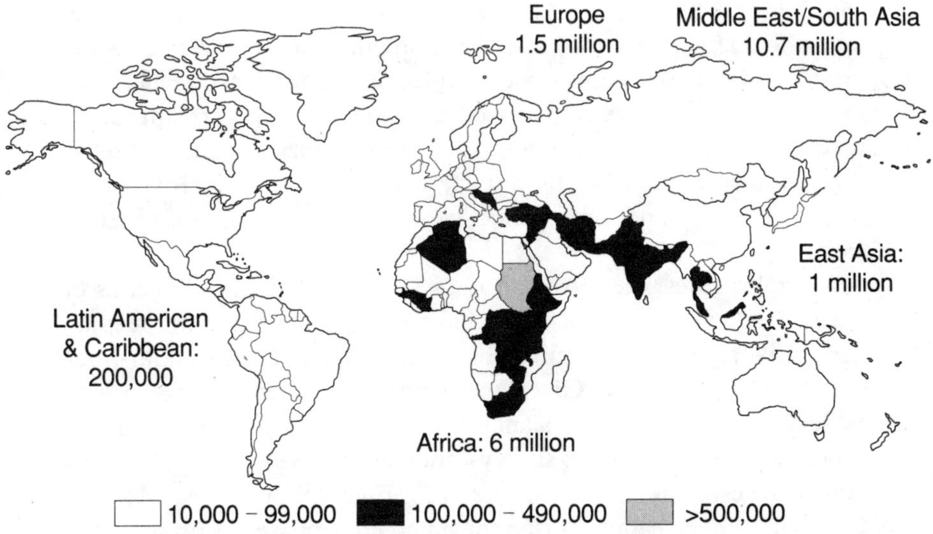

Note: The global total was 18.5 million refugees in 1992.

neighboring countries that struggle to support their indigenous populations. When refugees arrive, they are often placed in crowded, unsanitary camps in remote, harsh environments where their inability to earn an income, their total dependency on the generosity of others, and their unhealthy living conditions can lead to loss of dignity, helplessness, and despair. When the response to these emergencies is slow, inadequate, or inappropriate, the human cost can be exceedingly high; it is this cost that I shall attempt to describe in epidemiologic terms.

The public health consequences of mass population displacement have been extensively documented since about 1980. On some occasions, these migrations have resulted in extremely high rates of mortality, morbidity, and malnutrition. The most severe consequences of population displacement have occurred during the acute emergency phase, in the early stage of relief efforts, and have been characterized by extremely high death rates—in some cases up to twenty-five times the crude death rate (CDR) of the population in the country of origin.[2] Although the quality of the international community's disaster response efforts has steadily improved, death rates associated with forced migration remain high, as demonstrated by several such emergencies during 1992.

Since the early 1960s, the international community's response to the health needs of refugee and displaced populations has at times been inappropriate, relying on teams of foreign medical personnel, many of whom have had little or no training or experience in the developing world. Hospitals, clinics, and feeding centers have sometimes been set up without any preliminary needs assessment, and essential prevention programs have sometimes been neglected. More recent relief programs, however, have emphasized a primary health care approach, focusing on preventive programs such as immunization and oral rehydration, involvement by the refugee community in the provision of health services, and more effective coordination and information gathering.

Mortality rates, the most specific indicators of the health status of emergency-affected populations, have been estimated from hospital and burial records, community-based surveys, and twenty-four-hour burial site surveillance. Given the general underreporting of deaths associated with these surveillance systems and the problems of recall experienced in population surveys, the data presented here represent minimum estimates of death rates in refugee populations. Monthly CDRs in refugee camps during the emergency phase are presented in Table 1; these rates are up to fifteen times the death rates in the countries of origin of the refugees.[3] Table 2 lists CDRs reported from various internally displaced populations; in these situations death rates have been as high as forty-five times the local, baseline rates.[4]

TABLE 1. *Monthly Crude Death Rates (CDRs) among Selected Refugee Populations, and Baseline CDRs from Countries of Origin, 1978–1992*

Month and Year	Host Country	Country of Origin (baseline CDR)		Refugee CDR
June–Dec. 1978	Bangladesh	Burma	(1.0)	6.3
Oct. 1979	Thailand	Cambodia	(2.5)	31.9
Aug. 1980	Somalia	Ethiopia	(2.0)	30.4
Jan.–Mar. 1985	Sudan	Ethiopia	(2.0)	16.2
Sept. 1985	Sudan	Chad	(1.6)	24.0
Jan.–June 1987	Malawi	Mozambique	(1.5)	1.0
Sept. 1988–Aug. 1989	Ethiopia	Somalia	(1.8)	3.8
July 1990	Ethiopia	Sudan	(1.7)	6.9
April 1991	Turkish border	Iraq	(0.7)	12.6
June 1991	Ethiopia	Somalia	(1.8)	14.0
March 1992	Kenya	Somalia	(1.9)	22.2
May 1992	Bangladesh	Myanmar	(1.0)	8.1
May 1992	Nepal	Bhutan	(1.4)	16.5

Note: The CDR is the number of deaths occurring per 1,000 population.

TABLE 2. *Monthly CDRs among Selected Internally Displaced Populations, and Baseline CDRs, 1982–1992*

Month and Year	Country	Baseline CDR	Displaced Population CDR
Nov. 1982–Oct. 1983	Mozambique	1.4	8.0
Oct.–Dec. 1984	Ethiopia (Korem)	2.0	60–90
Oct. 1984–Jan. 1985	Ethiopia (Harbu)	2.0	40
July 1988	Sudan	1.7	90
Jan.–Dec. 1990	Liberia	1.1	7.1
April 1991–April 1992	Somalia	2.0	13.7

Note: The CDR is the number of deaths occurring per 1,000 population.

Figure 2, showing trends in death rates over time, indicates that only in Thailand (1979–1980) and Iraq (1991) did improvements occur relatively quickly as assistance programs were mounted promptly by

FIGURE 2.
CDR by Month after Arrival of Refugee Populations,
1979–1991

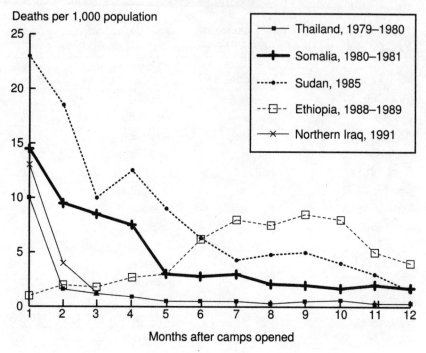

Deaths per 1,000 population

Thailand, 1979–1980
Somalia, 1980–1981
Sudan, 1985
Ethiopia, 1988–1989
Northern Iraq, 1991

Months after camps opened

the international community. The death rates shown for Somalia (1980–1981) and Sudan (1985) six to nine months after the influx of refugees occurred were still well above baseline rates (1.5 to 2.0 per 1,000).[5] In the case of 170,000 Somali refugees in Ethiopia in 1988–1989, death rates actually increased significantly six months after the influx. This increase was associated with elevated malnutrition prevalence rates, inadequate food rations, and high incidence rates of certain communicable diseases.

Most deaths in refugee camps occur among children under five years of age. For example, according to results of a population survey of Kurdish refugees, an estimated 64 percent of deaths in this population during April and May 1991 occurred among children less than five years of age, who represented only 18 percent of the population.[6] In most reports from refugee camps, mortality rates have not been stratified by gender; however, the surveillance system for Burmese refugees currently in Bangladesh did estimate sex-specific death rates, demonstrating considerably higher rates in females at most ages (Figure 3).[7]

The main causes of death have been those same diseases that cause most deaths among nonrefugee children in developing countries, as shown clearly by data from Somalia and Sudan: measles, diarrheal diseases, acute respiratory infections, and malaria (Figure 4).[8] Cause-specific mortality data from most other refugee populations show the same basic pattern, although in recent years major outbreaks of measles have been successfully prevented by immunization in most refugee emergencies. Nevertheless, measles—although easily prevent-

FIGURE 3.
Deaths by Age and Sex, Burmese Refugees, Gundhum II Camp, Bangladesh, May–June 1992

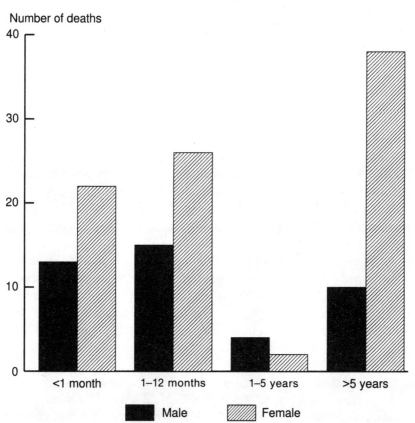

FIGURE 4.
Major Causes of Death, All Ages,
Refugee Populations, Sudan and Somalia

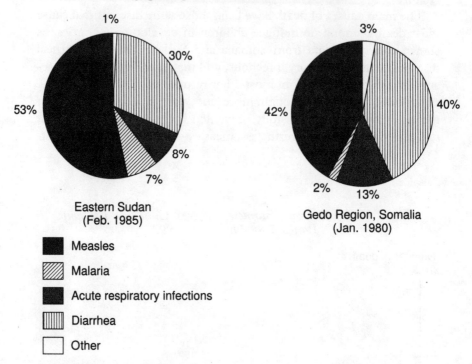

Eastern Sudan
(Feb. 1985)

Gedo Region, Somalia
(Jan. 1980)

■ Measles

▨ Malaria

■ Acute respiratory infections

▥ Diarrhea

□ Other

able—has been a major cause of death in some instances. For example, in 1985 more than 2,000 children died of measles during a three-month period in the Wad Kowli camp of eastern Sudan.[9] Figure 5 shows measles deaths as a proportion of all deaths in this camp during a four-month period.

Refugees and displaced persons living in crowded and unsanitary camps have been at high risk of epidemics of communicable diseases, including cholera, meningitis, hepatitis, typhoid fever, and typhus. Cholera has occurred in refugee camps in the Horn of Africa, west and southern Africa, Asia, and the Middle East. In Malawi there have been at least twelve cholera outbreaks among Mozambican refugees since 1988.[10]

In most cholera outbreaks in refugee settings, case-fatality ratios (CFRs) have been around 3 percent. The CFR was 21 percent in the camp of Gannet in northern Somalia, where water and sanitation were

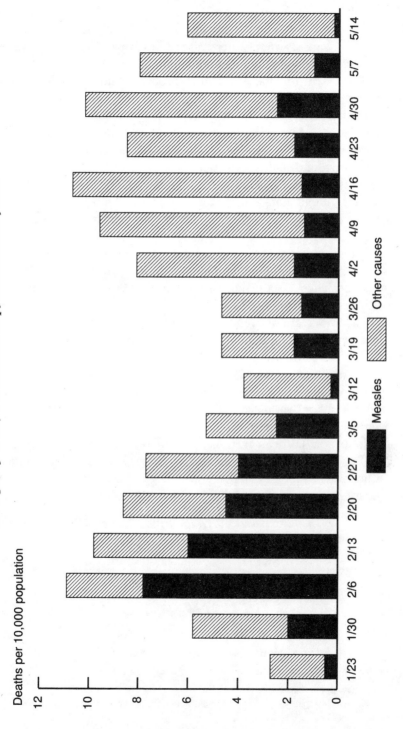

FIGURE 5.
Death Rates Associated with Measles and Other Causes,
All Ages, by Week, Wad Kowli Camp, Eastern Sudan, 1985

grossly inadequate and no community health program existed. In contrast, the CFR was only 2 percent in seven more established northern Somalia camps, where water and sanitation were adequate and community health workers had been trained.

The extent to which AIDS is a problem among refugees and displaced populations is largely undocumented; however, human immunodeficiency virus transmission is likely a problem in some populations, such as Mozambicans in Malawi, Liberians in Côte d'Ivoire, and Cambodians in Thailand. A recent assessment of Sudanese refugees in Ethiopia found high prevalence rates of several sexually transmitted diseases (STDs), including infection with HIV.[11] Increasingly, STD and HIV prevention should be a component of most, if not all, refugee relief programs, although it is probably not a high priority during the emergency phase.

An important underlying risk factor for high death rates in most of these situations has been energy-protein malnutrition. Figure 6 shows the prevalence of acute malnutrition in children under five years of age during the emergency phase of relief operations in nine refugee populations;[12] data are derived from cluster sample population surveys. In refugee camps prevalence rates between 15 percent and 50 percent have been common. It may be significant that the two populations where malnutrition prevalence rates were low—Malawi and Guinea—were in countries where refugees were largely integrated into local villages rather than placed in crowded, unsanitary, and unmanageable camps. In many internally displaced populations, the rate of acute malnutrition has been even higher than in refugee populations (Table 3). Surveys by Médecins sans Frontières have recorded acute malnutrition rates as high as 76 percent among Somali children in camps for the internally displaced.[13]

TABLE 3. *Prevalence of Acute Malnutrition* among Children under Five in Internally Displaced Populations, 1983–1992*

Date	Country or Region	Population Affected	Prevalence (%)
1983	Mozambique	na	12–28
1985	Ethiopia (Korem)	800,000	70
1988	Sudan (Khartoum)	750,000	23
1988	Sudan (South Darfur)	>80,000	36
1990	Liberia (Monrovia)	500,000	35
1992	Somalia (Qorioley)	100,000	46–76

Note: na = not available.
*Defined as less than 80 percent of median weight for height.

In addition to energy-protein malnutrition, severe outbreaks of various rare micronutrient deficiency diseases, such as scurvy and pellagra, have affected tens of thousands of refugees, especially in Africa. Major outbreaks of these deficiency diseases are listed in Table 4.

TABLE 4. *Micronutrient Deficiency Disease Outbreaks in Refugee Camps, 1984–1990*

Disease	Year	Location	Prevalence
Scurvy	1984	Sudan	22.0
	1985	Somalia	6.9–44.0
	1989	Ethiopia	1.0–2.0
	1991	Sudan	na
	1992	Kenya	na
Xerophthalmia	1985	Sudan	na
Beriberi	1985	Thailand	na
Pellagra	1989	Malawi (11 camps)	0.5
	1990	Malawi (11 camps)	6.3
Iron-deficiency anemia	1990	Syria, Jordan, West Bank, and Gaza	54.5–73.9 (children) 12.5–62.5 (women)
	1990	Ethiopia	10.0–13.0

Note: na = not available.

Experience to date, therefore, indicates that the high incidence of childhood communicable diseases and the high prevalence of malnutrition are the major causes of high excess death rates among displaced and refugee populations. The vulnerability of these populations may also be partly explained by the high rate of relatively rare micronutrient deficiencies.

Consequently, the interventions that will prevent most excess mortality are as follows: sufficient food rations, providing at least 1,900 kilocalories of energy per person per day, as well as other essential nutrients, especially vitamins A and C; sufficient quantities of clean water (the United Nations High Commissioner for Refugees recommends fifteen to twenty liters per person per day[14]); and adequate shelter and sanitation facilities. Other essential components of a public health program are a simple, flexible, and accurate health information system; measles immunization for all children between six months and five years of age; a diarrheal disease control program focusing on the treatment of dehydration with oral rehydration salts; epidemic pre-

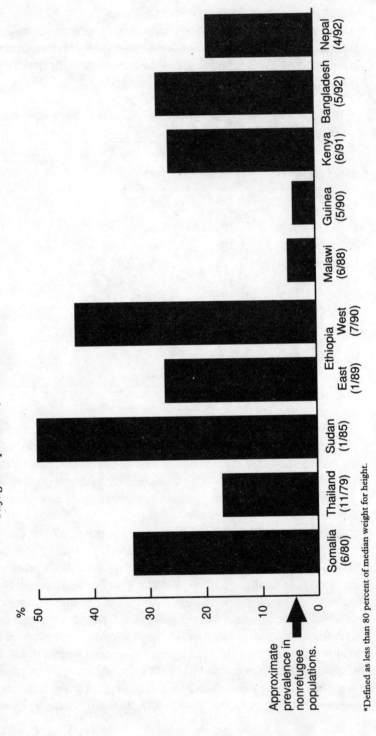

FIGURE 6.
Prevalence of Acute Malnutrition★ Among Children Under Five in Refugee Populations, Nine Countries, 1979–1992

%

50

40

30

20

10

0

Somalia
(6/80)

Thailand
(11/79)

Sudan
(1/85)

Ethiopia
East   West
(1/89)   (7/90)

Malawi
(6/88)

Guinea
(5/90)

Kenya
(6/91)

Bangladesh
(5/92)

Nepal
(4/92)

Approximate
prevalence in
nonrefugee
populations.

★Defined as less than 80 percent of median weight for height.

paredness plans; and appropriate curative care focusing on standard case management protocols, essential drugs, a referral system, and community health worker training, and targeted particularly at malaria and acute respiratory infections. In some cases selective feeding programs are also indicated.

Unfortunately, several international relief programs have failed to provide the basic elements described here. The international relief operation on the Turkey-Iraq border in 1991 provides an example of both the achievements and the problems associated with recent refugee assistance programs. When an estimated 400,000 Kurdish refugees fled northern Iraq into the mountains on the Turkish border, they ended up in several large camps where barbed-wire fences and armed soldiers prevented most of them from entering Turkish territory.

Although the international response was not immediate, air drops of food that were organized after several days' delay by the military forces of several countries (including the United States) probably saved many lives. This impressive use of military power to address a major humanitarian crisis offered an exciting glimpse of the potential role of the military in future relief operations. We need to realize, however, that the military resources of most countries will always be under partisan political control and cannot be consistently relied upon to respond to humanitarian emergencies. The failure of Western military forces to ensure an adequate humanitarian response to recent tragedies in Liberia and Somalia and their relatively slow response to events in Bosnia illustrate this point.

Back to the Turkish border in April 1991. Apart from food deliveries, very few of the priority programs listed earlier in this paper were established on the ground within the first four to six weeks. The only water sources available to refugees rapidly became polluted; sanitation facilities were either absent or inappropriate; and adequate supplies of oral rehydration salts did not arrive until four weeks after the influx. In addition, the rate of breast-feeding among the Kurds was quite low, and many infants were given milk powder or infant formula mixed with unclean water.

Not surprisingly, diarrhea was the most common health problem affecting all ages, especially children. Up to 70 percent of patients presenting at clinics in the early stages had diarrhea; cholera occurred in at least two camps.[15] Supplies of measles vaccine sufficient to launch a mass vaccination campaign were not obtained until six weeks after the influx; however, epidemics of measles did not occur, probably because immunization coverage rates in Iraq had been relatively high.

In addition, medical kits sent from Europe did not contain certain essential items, such as vitamin A.

Mortality rates among the Kurds during their period of displacement were estimated by a population survey conducted in May 1991 (Figure 7).[16] Death rates increased dramatically during the second two-week period (April 13–26), the time when the incidence of diarrheal diseases was highest, and when relief efforts were still rudimentary.

Although some nongovernmental organizations (NGOs) and U.S. Special Forces teams did eventually provide appropriate community-based health care, other agencies set up field hospitals and provided inappropriate inpatient treatment, while neglecting to implement basic public health programs. The overall lack of focus on the most critical

FIGURE 7.
*Daily Crude and Under-Five Mortality Rates,
Kurdish Refugees, March–May 1991
Turkey and Northern Iraq*

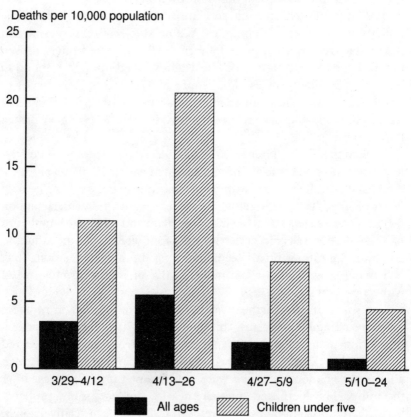

Deaths per 10,000 population

public health problems was due to the lack of central coordination and poor technical leadership. Since Turkey did not offer asylum to most of the Kurdish refugees, the Office of the United Nations High Commissioner for Refugees was not invited to implement its traditional mandate of protection and assistance.

The UN system, as it is currently organized, was incapable of responding promptly to circumvent this obstacle and to obtain prompt access to the refugees on the border. The UN may operate only with the concurrence of the sovereign governments of the territory where refugees are located (in this case Iraq and Turkey). Consequently, Western governments decided that the only effective solution to the crisis was to repatriate refugees to their towns and villages of origin in northern Iraq under the protection of Western military forces. Even when the UN response was mounted in late April 1991, scant attention was given to technical issues. The emphasis given to the repatriation effort diverted attention and resources from the immediate needs of refugees in the border camps.

In general the constraints to mounting an adequate international response to refugee emergencies can be categorized as political, organizational, and technical. In my experience the technical constraints are the least problematic. The remaining challenges to improving technical knowledge include the refinement of rapid assessment and surveillance techniques; development of effective strategies to prevent micronutrient deficiencies (although a good diet would be sufficient); evaluation of the impact of various water systems on morbidity and mortality; and adaptation of diagnostic techniques and cold chain equipment to field conditions. In addition, further research on the effective prevention of certain diseases that commonly affect refugees (e.g., cholera, measles, hepatitis E, and malaria) would be beneficial.

More critical is the challenge to improve the management of public health programs. Experienced technical personnel should be given a greater role in decision-making early in emergency programs. During the Kurdish relief operation, it was apparent that certain basic skills were lacking among many relief workers—for example, in the management of diarrhea and dehydration and of maternal and child nutritional problems. NGOs need to invest more heavily in the training and technical orientation of their personnel. International rosters of experienced personnel need to be developed and perhaps shared between agencies and nations. In the United States, the mandate of government technical agencies needs to be clarified to allow more directed training and preparation for emergency work.

A further lesson from the Kurdish crisis is the vulnerability of populations from relatively developed countries to the more severe public health consequences of mass migration. Well-nourished and relatively affluent populations, such as those in former Yugoslavia, Armenia, and Azerbaijan, are at risk of the same high death rates experienced by refugees and displaced persons in the developing world if their basic needs—in particular, food and water—are not promptly and effectively met.

It is critical that the international community respond to each emergency in a systematic and consistent manner, irrespective of the political implications of the particular crisis. To implement the essential programs outlined earlier, the United Nations and its technical agencies must be empowered to gain access to all populations in urgent need of humanitarian assistance, even in areas of contested sovereignty. The role of military logistics support should be seriously examined; however, it will be useful only if the military response is depoliticized and consistently mounted for each emergency.

Once access to affected populations is achieved, however, international relief agencies should be held more accountable for the impact of their interventions. Standardized information systems should be put in place early in each emergency to ensure effective monitoring and evaluation of relief programs. Monitoring should not focus merely on the process of relief assistance (e.g., tons of food delivered, numbers of vaccine provided); impact indicators, such as malnutrition and mortality rates, should also be routine components of such information systems. Relief managers, therefore, need to be adequately trained in both the implementation of technically sound relief programs and the accurate monitoring of their impact.

Excessively high death rates continue to be reported from some of the refugee emergencies of 1992 (Kenya, Bangladesh, and Nepal). No single agency or government can be held responsible for this situation; collective international action is urgently needed to ensure that civilian populations worldwide are promptly and effectively protected from both the direct and the indirect public health consequences of organized violence. The idea of *protection* of refugees should be extended to include protection from *preventable* diseases and death.

10

The American Medical Establishment: An Absent Partner

H. JACK GEIGER

This morning's headlines—every day's headlines—announce ongoing disasters: the massive health, human rights, and refugee problems of the new world order in Somalia, Yugoslavia, Haiti, Afghanistan, Indonesia, as well as Armenia, Azerbijan, Georgia, and other warring splinters of the former Soviet Union. Other new world order disasters, less dramatic, receive only intermittent attention. These include such items as the effect of sanctions on medical care, nutrition, and infant mortality in Iraq; the daily toll, in death and dismemberment, of land mines in Cambodia, Angola, Mozambique, Afghanistan, and elsewhere; the ongoing effects of radioactive contamination from Chernobyl and Chelyabinsk, and of deadly pollution of air, soil, and groundwater by lead, other toxic metals, and organic toxins in much of Eastern Europe. Dwarfing all of these is the implacable daily toll of poverty and its health consequences in the Third World; to cite the best-known statistic, the 40,000 children who die each day.

The political configurations have shifted and some of the suffering locales, in consequence, are new. In most respects, however, from the point of view of international health and human rights workers, the new world order looks much like the old world order. It presents us with the same agendas, challenges, and needs. There is nothing new about civil wars and regional wars, except that now they are less likely to be surrogates in superpower struggles and more likely to have been unleashed by the end of superpower confrontation. There is nothing new about deliberate disruptions of medical care, violations of medical neutrality, torture, and other blatant human rights violations; nothing new about the use of poison gas, cluster and fragmentation bombs, napalm or land mines, and nothing new—since Guernica and certainly since World War II—about the deliberate destruction of civilian populations. Similarly, there is nothing new about famines, earthquakes, floods, hurricanes, and volcanic eruptions; nothing new about pandemics, whether of "new" organisms such as HIV or "old" organisms like the tubercle bacillus and cholera vibrio. Most of all, there is nothing new about poverty, unemployment, staggering population increases, absent or collapsing infrastructures, and inequity in resource allocation and trade relationships, except perhaps that they have worsened. Half of the less developed countries are poorer today than they were a decade ago,[1] in part due to structural adjustments and drastic reductions of investment in social programs, courtesy of the International Monetary Fund and the World Bank.

Americans have long viewed themselves—with considerable justification—as extraordinarily generous, humanitarian, and responsive to these miseries. Most U.S. citizens have supported, and believe (with less justification) that their government has adequately supported, the humanitarian efforts of the United Nations, the World Health Organization (WHO), UNICEF, the UN High Commissioner for Refugees, the International Committee of the Red Cross (ICRC), and many other international mechanisms of response. Almost all are proud of U.S. contributions of food, medical care, and other forms of disaster relief in acute overseas emergencies. Many are aware of our substantial role in the eradication of smallpox, the international work of such government agencies as the Agency for International Development (AID), the Centers for Disease Control, and the Fogarty Center at the National Institutes of Health, and of both research and material contributions to Third World immunization campaigns and to the struggles against AIDS, malaria, schistosomiasis, and other plagues.

The most impressive evidence, however, is the extraordinary American creation and support of private voluntary organizations, both church-related and secular. The proliferation and individual donor support of organizations such as CARE, Save the Children, Project

HOPE, Project CONCERN, the International Medical Corps, Oxfam America, and the like, is the dominant mode of U.S. involvement in international health efforts. The National Council for International Health 1992 Directory of U.S. International Health Organizations lists more than 700 of them.[2] They range from large foundations—Rockefeller, Carnegie, Pew, and Kellogg, investing in institutional and organizational development in less developed countries—to the myriad small service and consulting organizations comprising the growth industry of recipients of AID and other government contracts. The largest number, however, are devoted to providing food, medical care, and other forms of hands-on assistance and direct material relief to those who are suffering overseas. To these must be added the voices of conscience—the international defense of health and human rights by such organizations as Physicians for Human Rights, Human Rights Watch, the Lawyers Committee for Human Rights, the medical network of Amnesty International, the Committee for Health in Southern Africa, and others.

There is, however, another side to the ledger of our international contributions, and it provides no cause for national self-congratulations. In relation to the size and depth of our health professional riches, and the strength of our medical establishment, our international health contributions are inexcusably limited. Given our resources, it is not an overstatement to describe this as a moral failure. The relative absence of the American medical establishment from international health efforts is at once a cause and a symptom of that failure.

Although the United States in 1990 had an estimated surplus of 70,000 physicians and one of the highest physician/population ratios in the industrialized world,[3] we have for decades *imported* tens of thousands of physicians from developing countries, the brain drain that has been more aptly described as a hemorrhage from nations which have as few as one physician for 4,500 people—or 45,000 in rural areas.[4] At the same time, almost without restraint, we have exported millions of tons of tobacco,[5] tens of millions of potentially dangerous prescription drugs improperly promoted and lacking appropriate warnings,[6] millions of tons of toxic wastes, and—more recently—thousands of U.S. manufacturing operations seeking not only low wages but the freedom to create occupational and environmental health hazards without fear of effective regulation or penalty. We have also aggressively sold lethal arms of almost every description to Third World nations, siphoning billions of dollars away from their most urgent domestic needs for health care, food, housing, and social support services. These contributions do not arrive in packages neatly labeled "Gift of the American people."

In the postcolonial decades following World War II, with the eager support of American foundations and the best intentions of fostering excellence, we also exported a model of medical education and training: tertiary-care-based, high-technology, bench-research-focused medical schools and teaching hospitals that were wildly inappropriate to the needs of developing countries often did more to deepen their social inequities in health care than to correct them, and devastated their health care economies. During those same decades, inexcusably, some Third World populations were used, without full informed consent, for clinical trials of experimental contraceptive and other pharmaceuticals.

What one observer has called our "rich heritage of past contributions to international health"[7] presents, in fact, a very mixed record. Our international record on human rights over the past half-century, and particularly during the past two decades, is equally mixed. We can, however, draw some lessons from both sides of the ledger if we are to do more for international survival, health, and human rights in a new world order. We will need at least two things that we do not now have.

The first requirement is a coherent, proactive, integrated, and sustained U.S. policy on international health to replace the essentially uncoordinated and often inconsistent mixture of public and private sector efforts that now make our interventions seem so fragmented, spasmodic, and reactive. A defined and consistent governmental policy on international health would permit coordination of the public and private sectors. It would inform domestic health manpower and agricultural policies and provide a consistent rationale for our relationships with, and contributions to, WHO and the health-related, refugee, and relief agencies of the UN. It would permit intelligent linkage of international health efforts to economic assistance aimed at building infrastructure and reducing poverty—the root cause of so many of the health problems. It should be expressed in adequately funded long-term programs, free from political biases and right-wing ideological and religious constraints.

The second requirement is a far greater effort and contribution from the American medical establishment, particularly from its academic sector: the institutions training new cohorts of physicians, dentists, nurses, public health workers, health educators, health administrators, and planners—the essential and primary resource for any expanded U.S. efforts in international health and human rights. Given the dependence of American health professional education on government support, a significant increase is not likely to occur without the development of a consistent international health policy.

U.S. Health Professionals in International Health

It is the academic sector—the production of people with a commitment to international health—that is likeliest to initiate real change. What has that sector done? There is little current data on the magnitude and specifics of the current involvement of American physicians and other health professionals in international health work. Even policymakers lack precise information on the numbers, the types of organizations involved, and the kinds of work being done. A 1984 survey[8] by the Johns Hopkins University Department of International Health and the National Council for International Health estimated that some 8,700 U.S. health professionals were thus engaged, including at least 1,488 nurses, 1,417 physicians, and nearly 900 health and hospital administrators, managers, and planners, and some 2,700 trainers and educators, dentists, environmental health specialists, social workers, nutritionists, and technicians.

Those figures represent less than one-half of 1 percent of all U.S. physicians and barely more than one-tenth of 1 percent of all U.S. nurses. Given the depth and richness of American health resources, that contribution is shamefully low. Contrast the American statistics with the more than 2,000 physicians, 13 percent of its total supply, sent to Third World nations during the 1970s and 1980s by Cuba, a nation one-twentieth the size of the United States.[9] More to the point, the U.S. figures compare poorly with those of other Western industrialized nations—France, for example—that encourage and reward international health service as a matter of government policy.

Nevertheless, the 1984 survey showed a 63 percent increase over figures assembled in 1969, and the numbers are probably somewhat higher today. By no means all of the overseas personnel, however, are engaged in humanitarian work. The authors of the 1984 survey noted: "Church-related organizations still employ the largest number of health professionals, but private voluntary organizations, corporations and universities have almost caught up."[10] The importance of corporations reflected the market for U.S. health manpower in oil-rich nations; the rise in NGO employment reflected the rapid increase of small consulting firms working for the U.S. government.

Less than half of the U.S. health professionals, furthermore, were long-term (salaried and working for one year or more); one-third of all physicians were volunteers, and most were in clinical work with limited long-term impact on health services development—"their service areas often relatively small, based in hospitals whose levels of technology and staffing increase the cost of care, thereby limiting access and community participation."[11] Compared to the average for all organizations combined, physicians and nurses were overrepresented in church-related organizations; nurses were underrepresented in universities; physicians were underrepresented in governmental agencies; administrators, managers, and planners were concentrated in corporations.

The bottom line represented by these 1984 figures is that supply—the recruitment and involvement of U.S. health professionals in international work—fell significantly short of the demand. There were more than 241 budgeted vacancies—that is, those for which secure funding was available—in international health programs for physicians alone, and budgeted positions do not begin to reflect the real unmet need.

U.S. Health Professional Schools and International Health

The United States has more than 127 medical schools, close to thirty schools of public health, and hundreds of schools of nursing, dentistry, pharmacy, and other health-related professional disciplines. A relatively recent survey[12] counted 494 international health programs or projects at these institutions, but they involved only 69 percent of the medical schools and 50 percent of the schools of public health. Most of the projects in developing countries (the People's Republic of China and Mexico had the largest number) were short-term and tenuously funded. In medicine, more than 90 percent of the projects were classified as "training" and "research"—in all probability, representing the assignment of a small number of visiting faculty at overseas medical schools—and only 7 percent were devoted to institutional development. In contrast, while training and research were also major emphases in school of public health projects, almost half were devoted to institutional development for overseas medical schools, health science centers, and universities.

Perhaps the most important figures in this study are those involving American medical students. More than 90 percent of U.S. medical schools permit overseas electives for students, most of them limited to two months or less. In the 1987–88 year, Asper estimates, approximately 1,235 U.S. medical students, mostly juniors and seniors, studied abroad (and by no means all of them were in less developed countries). That represented only 4 percent of all U.S. medical students in the junior and senior classes in that year. In 1989, according to a survey by the Association of American Medical Colleges,[13] approximately 2,400 of the graduating medical students—15.3 percent of the total cohort of new American physicians in that year—reported participating in an overseas clinical elective, most in developing countries, at some point in their four years of training. That represents a 247 percent increase since 1984, when a similar AAMC survey[14] found only 6.2 percent had participated.

Again, international comparisons show that these figures, representing students at all U.S. medical schools, are shamefully low. Between 1978 and 1990, at *one* Irish medical school, a total of 1,588 students chose international health electives at rural hospitals and health projects—including 809 in Africa, 334 in Asia, and 238 in Southeast Asia.[15]

Students: The Driving Force for Change

This relatively poor showing reflects lack of support, not lack of interest. Appeals for international health training and experience, and the practical steps required to facilitate them, have come from American medical students with increasing urgency for more than a decade. In 1985, Dr. Helen Burstin, then the president of the American Medical Student Association (AMSA), argued for a U.S. international health service corps relying on loan forgiveness in exchange for service in less developed countries to help "young physicians to give of themselves in a needy world."[16] A year earlier, Dr. David Kindig and Dr. George Lythcott called for an international health service corps of "a carefully selected group of doctors with skills emphasizing public health, prevention, a knowledge of appropriate technology and the organization and management of health services . . . there is ample evidence that many American medical students have interests in careers in such international humanitarian service, but the opportunities are limited and fragmented."[17] Victor Sidel pointed out that American physicians "are among the most isolated from in-depth knowledge of health problems and of health services outside their own country" and argued that

U.S. medical schools "should consider international work an indispensable part of a core medical education."[18] J. E. Banta, testifying before a Senate subcommittee in support of one of the several failed congressional efforts[19] to create an international health service corps, noted that "there has not been an established, clear and coherent pattern for international health workers; efforts have been ad hoc, fragmented, obscure, and devoid of the possibility of long-term career planning."[20]

THE AMSA PROGRAMS

No group has responded more vigorously to these challenges than AMSA. Since the early 1980s, AMSA has published five editions of "International Health Electives for Medical Students," a listing of faculty contacts and curriculum information on international health at U.S. medical schools, and an international health funding guide for U.S. medical students and residents.[21]

From 1986 to 1990, AMSA sponsored an International Health Fellowship Program in which twenty-six medical students and residents from nineteen U.S. medical schools completed an eight-month rotation in Ghana and Nigeria. They were assigned to five medical schools for clinical rotations and community health assignments together with Ghanian and Nigerian medical students in both urban and rural settings under the supervision of a faculty preceptor in the Department of Community Health. Then four African medical students participated in a ten-week program of community-oriented primary care activities in the United States. AMSA's stated goals were

> to prepare medical students and residents for leadership roles among U.S. health professionals working with the medically underserved at home and abroad; to offer opportunities for aspiring young physicians to learn about health problems and delivery systems in developing countries, and to enable medical students to examine appropriate roles for U.S. physicians in international health.[22]

More recently, AMSA (with funding from the Pew Charitable Trusts) created an "International Health Partnership Program in Community-Based Medical Education," linking the University of Rochester Medical School with the Universidad Autonoma de Chiapas, in Mexico; the University of Colorado School of Medicine with

the Universidad del Valle, in Colombia; and the University of Massa-
chusetts Medical School with the Universidad Autonoma Nacional de
Honduras. Two post–third-year medical students from each school—
U.S. and Latin American—will work in community health projects in
their partner schools for three to four months, and faculty members
from each will participate in a two- to three-week exchange.

AMSA is now seeking support for a similar collaborative program
to link the University of California at Davis with the University of
Ghana Medical School, the University of Wisconsin with the University of Ilorin, Nigeria, and Cornell University Medical College with the
University of Ibadan, Nigeria, in a three-year effort in which thirty-six
medical students and residents and six faculty preceptors will rotate.

It is important to note that international health exchanges and rotations are not limited to undergraduate medical students. Since 1982,
Yale University School of Medicine has regularly sent residents and
fellows to Haiti and Tanzania.[23] The University of North Carolina at
Chapel Hill has similar programs,[24] and the University of New Mexico
Medical School is deeply involved in bilateral faculty exchanges for
curriculum development with Xian Medical University in China—an
effort in which the Chinese Ministry of Public Health, Project HOPE,
and WHO are also involved.[25]

PREPARING STUDENTS FOR INTERNATIONAL HEALTH WORK

Only 9 to 15 percent of the estimated 2,400 U.S. medical students
who had done international health work, however, had participated
in formal medical school courses covering the clinical aspects of the
diseases students were likely to encounter and the social, economic,
and environmental aspects of the community and health system in
which they worked.[26] A national survey of U.S. medical schools identified only twenty-six schools—22 percent of the U.S. total—that
offered training programs in international health. Though the availability of training is increased somewhat by regionalization and by
medical school access to appropriate courses in some schools of public health, the authors concluded that "medical schools in general do
not appear to train students adequately for their international health
care rotations."[27]

The combined effect of appropriate training and the international
health experience itself is illustrated by a study at the University of
Arizona, which since 1982 has offered an intensive three-week orientation course, a "core curriculum for international health," each year for

twenty-four selected U.S. medical students. Of 154 course graduates surveyed in 1991, 81 percent said they planned some form of international health work as part of their future careers.[28]

These limitations in the appropriate training are likely to improve, however, with the recent formation of the U.S. International Health Medical Education Consortium (IHMEC), with members representing more than fifty American medical schools. IHMEC will promote international health medical education in four program areas—curriculum, clinical training, career development, and international health education policy. IHMEC proposes to establish a network of clinical sites overseas and standards for selection of both trainees and sites; develop stronger career tracks for potential certification of students, residents, and faculty involved in international health training and programs; and facilitate collaborative training relationships with students and faculty in foreign medical schools.[29]

Relevance and Reward: International Health and U.S. Problems

"For medical students and residents," one study notes, "a two-month elective in a developing country can be a profound experience . . . can dramatically alter their perceptions of health, health care, and societal and personal responsibility . . . [and] can lead to permanent changes in career direction."[30] Almost invariably, students return with fresh eyes for American society and American health care, recognizing the profound similarities between what they have just experienced in developing nations and the problems of underserved and poverty-stricken urban and rural American populations—the Third World in the United States. Not infrequently, they find that they can adapt and use here what they have learned from their international colleagues and mentors. International health experience has become a two-way street—not *for* but *with* less developed countries—and its rewards are not merely the growth of a corps of professional international health workers but also the enrichment of American medicine and public health.

Here, like Northrup and many others, I speak from personal and career-determining experience. As a senior medical student in 1957 I was fortunate to spend six months in South Africa's rural homelands and urban townships, working and studying in novel institutions called community health centers practicing community-oriented primary care (COPC). It seemed clear to me then that my life's work would be international health, and I prepared myself accordingly: training in internal medicine, infectious disease, epidemiology, and social science. At the completion of that process, in the bitter summer of 1964, I found myself in rural Mississippi, organizing health care for civil rights workers in a population staggering under the burdens of poverty, racism, and inequity and their health consequences. The parallels were inescapable, and it occurred to me that what worked in South Africa— community health centers and community-oriented primary care— might be adapted to our needs. The first OEO-funded community health center opened at Boston's Columbia Point housing project— not so different from a township—six months later; the second, a year later in rural Bolivar County, Mississippi. Today there are almost six hundred such community health centers across the United States, the primary source of care for some six million low-income Americans. They are a modest but permanent part of the U.S. health care system with an enviable record of effectiveness.[31] There is a wonderful bilateral footnote to this small story: today, thirty-five years later, as South Africa prepares for liberation, I have been returning there to describe the U.S. experience and to help reintroduce the community health center/COPC concepts as models for the development of their new health care system.

In the evolution of international health work, what was once unidirectional (and often, as "technical assistance," openly paternalistic) has become bilateral, and what was bilateral has, in turn, become a network in which developing country institutions in Asia, Africa, Latin America, and the Caribbean collaborate with each other as well as with schools and programs in the industrialized world.[32] More than fifty institutions from all sectors are now joined in the Network of Community-Oriented Educational Institutions for Health Sciences, with headquarters in the Netherlands; its First International Symposium on Student Assessent (with special emphasis on assessment in community settings) will be held in Malaysia in 1993.

At a time when the United States is struggling mightily to emphasize primary care, health care teams, preventive medicine, and community-based interventions, we have as much to learn from developing countries as we did almost a century ago when we sent our students, residents, and young faculty to Europe to learn the secrets of bacteriology, biochemistry, and the electrocardiogram. A significant expansion of international experience for U.S. health professionals is neither a gift nor a drain on our resources; it is, instead, in our own domestic interest, and could contribute significantly to our own efforts at health care reform.

Schools of Public Health and Other Omissions

This brief review, of necessity, slights the central role and importance of the U.S. schools of public health, both as trainers, researchers, and collaborators in international health and as primary loci of research and training in tropical medicine. (More than one in four of the Arizona course graduates indicated that they planned to obtain an MPH degree; more than 15 percent of the students at U.S. schools of public health come from overseas; the Ministries of Health in a score of developing nations are headed—and staffed—by our graduates.) Schools of public health are surely not the "absent" sector of our medical establishment.

The details of such programs as Johns Hopkins' Health and Child Survival Fellows, or Harvard's work on diarrheal diseases, though relevant, are also beyond the scope of this discussion. If this omission is justified at all, it is because applicants to schools of public health are those who are already committed, either to international health or to public health work in the United States. If the field of international health is to grow, the recruits must be found at an earlier stage, in schools of medicine, nursing, dentistry, and other professional and technical disciplines.

The medical establishment surely includes the American Medical Association (AMA), but here the record is much more sparse. The AMA helped establish the World Medical Association and supports the work of WHO; it was a contributor to the formation of the National Council for International Health, and it publishes intermittent reports on American physicians in international health work.[33] Its journal reports on international health activities and has spoken out courageously on the U.S. responsibility to export health workers. Beyond that, however, AMA efforts in international health have been limited.

Similarly, the Association of American Medical Colleges has other and more urgent priorities. Several decades ago it sponsored the production of a five-volume international health curriculum[34]; more recently, in collaboration with the Educational Commission for Foreign Medical Graduates, it has explored the development of innovative programs in international medical education,[35] and it surveys U.S. medical schools intermittently on their international health activities.

Finally, any complete account of the medical establishment's role in international health would include a detailed report on the work of U.S. philanthropic foundations, great and small, not merely as funders but as catalysts for change and innovation. They most assuredly are not absent partners—particularly the W. K. Kellogg, Henry J. Kaiser, Rockefeller, Carnegie, and Pew foundations—and their present importance in support of international health will grow as government support, in a time of recession, recedes.

Health and Human Rights

During the past two decades, perhaps the fastest-growing curricular development in undergraduate and graduate medical (and other health professional) education has been the proliferation of courses in medical ethics. Yet there has been almost no effort to teach human rights, or to explore the unique roles and responsibilities of medicine in the protection of human rights—including the rights of refugees—and in the documentation of violations and abuses. Perhaps the closest we have come, sadly, is in the development of a new medical specialty—the treatment of torture victims. This development illustrates the blurring of the distinctions between "international" and "domestic" health concerns, and the obsolescence of such terms as "tropical medicine." With large and ever-growing immigrant populations of Cambodians, Vietnamese, Haitians, Salvadoreans, Guatemalans and others, and the frequency of overseas travel, international health problems and the need for relevant expertise have become domestic concerns.

Two pioneering exceptions to the prevailing medical silence on human rights should be noted. At Columbia College of Physicians and Surgeons, Professors Sheila and David Rothman have created a fellowship program in which carefully selected medical students and residents are offered elective human rights placements around the world, in organizations as varied as the National Medical and Dental Association of South Africa and the Israeli-Palestinian Physicians' Committee for Human Rights. At the postgraduate level, Physicians for Human Rights, in collaboration with Harvard Medical School, recently conducted an intensive three-day continuing medical education course on human rights, the first in a proposed national series.

Conclusion

Increasing the U.S. contribution in collaboration with the health institutions of other nations is in our own best interest and certain to yield returns of substantial relevance to our own health problems. The United States needs an international health corps, the equivalent of the National Health Service Corps, with scholarships and loan forgiveness to facilitate overseas work for debt-burdened medical and other health professional graduates. We must establish and reward professional and academic career lines in international health, and develop and expand the international health curricula in all health professional schools and residency programs.

Beyond such specifics, we need a coherent international health and human rights policy, a sustained governmental commitment, without which none of these increased efforts are likely to occur. The American medical establishment can and should contribute to the formulation and implementation of such a policy, from which it would surely benefit. A young American serving as a medical officer in Nigeria put it best a few years ago. She wrote: "We would do better to believe that we are all in it together, that the problem belongs to us all. We must believe that privilege implies responsibility, that education implies the power to change."[36]

III

PRIVATE VOLUNTARY RESPONSE

The quality of mercy can certainly be strained in disasters. Long ago individuals realized that even their most well intended efforts had a very limited impact amidst the chaos of war or epidemics, famine, or floods. Highly motivated private groups, often influenced by profound religious convictions, were formed to improve relief programs. Their humanitarian philosophy, their pragmatic approaches to problems, and their seemingly limitless energies unfettered by the burdens of bureaucracy combined to make them welcome partners in distress.

Some of these nongovernmental organizations (NGOs) gradually expanded their efforts and can now offer a highly professional response in multiple disasters in different countries. Furthermore, many governmental donors, concerned about corruption and inefficiency, now prefer to channel relief aid through these NGOs. There are dangers, however, in this expansion.

Only governments, through bilateral or multilateral efforts, have the capacity to offer the vast and costly supplies needed to cope with major disasters. No amount of personal goodwill can substitute for the hundreds of thousands of tons of surplus food, or the airplanes or helicopters, or the security forces that may be required to effectively relieve hunger among the displaced starving in a war situation. Yet somehow the private NGOs must be allowed to preserve their unique role without becoming political fronts for superpowers; it is in everyone's best interest to nurture the NGO community and encourage collaboration for the sake of the suffering victims that all agencies are supposed to be helping. It is also clear that NGOs must learn to function more cooperatively with host governments, indigenous NGOs, and international agencies or the plight of the dispossessed can be made worse by petty conflicts caused by ignorance, arrogance, or a combination of both.

In this section the leaders of three major international NGOs consider such questions; the founder of the largest NGO in the developing world offers his reflections on these and related topics. An academically oriented expert on refugee relief then presents his analysis of the strengths and weaknesses of the current approach.

11

The Changing Roles of Voluntary Organizations

AENGUS FINUCANE

I was the parish priest in Uli, Nigeria, in 1967 for much of the Nigera-Biafra civil war. It was there, twenty-five years ago, that I had my first experience in the delivery of humanitarian aid and health services under conflict conditions. The eastern region of Nigeria had seceded as Biafra and the federal Nigerian government was sparing no effort to reintegrate the oil-rich breakaway region. Uli, a rural townland deep in Biafra, became the epicenter of a massive relief operation. The road just outside my parish residence was widened to make an airstrip. All flying was at night and planes had to run the gauntlet of the federal Nigerian forces, who with vastly superior firepower, were steadily squeezing and reducing Biafran-held territory. "Uli Airport" found a place on the world map. By October 1968 it had become the busiest airport in Africa! On some nights it handled as many as fifty planes. My parish church became a feeding center. Sermons were exhortations to eat mice, cockroaches, and cassava leaves. Parish duties gave way to airport duties.

In the latter months of the conflict I was based in Libreville, Gabon, organizing an airlift of relief supplies for the newly formed organization Africa CONCERN. Having unloaded their relief cargoes, the returning flights brought thousands of near-dead children to be cared for by nongovernmental organizations (NGOs) in camps set up for them in neighboring countries.

Twenty-five years later, in August 1992, I flew into Baidoa, a town of 60,000 people in Somalia, on board a cargo plane carrying sixteen tons of supplies for a CONCERN relief team. In Somalia, on the opposite side of Africa from Biafra, another chapter of misery, tragedy, and famine was unfolding. Prior to this famine, Baidoa had been as little-known to the outside world as Uli had been. In August 1992, television, radio, and print media in Baidoa catapulted the town into the center of the world stage. In the few days I was there, the satellite dishes and elaborate equipment of two television groups beamed the misery and dying of Baidoa live into drawing rooms around the world.

During my time in Baidoa, an average of two hundred deaths were recorded daily. On one day, trucks collected 176 corpses for burial. These were the bodies of people with no friends to bury them. Most often the near-dead buried their dead in shallow graves. The population swelled as starving people were drawn to the town. In the first ten days of September 1992, the trucks collected 2,353 bodies from the streets of Baidoa, and 70 percent of them were children. By September 16, the grim tally had reached 3,520!

NGO Origins and Growth

Uli to Baidoa; Biafra to Somalia; 1967 to 1992. A huge proliferation and wide diversification of NGOs took place during this twenty-five year period. It is little short of obscene that two such gruesome landmarks as Uli and Baidoa stand as the parameters for this paper. There were NGOs before Biafra, but NGOs in the sense we know them today—as accepted players with a major role in the transfer of resources from rich to poor countries—only became an identifiable force on the international Third World aid stage in the past twenty-five years. The whole concept of international development through the transfer of resources from richer to poorer countries belongs to the postcolonial era of the second half of this century. The Third World NGOs we now know are in a few instances a development of older organizations: Save the Children, U.K., has roots going back to 1919 and a shattered post–World War I Europe; Oxfam was formed in Britain in 1943 in an attempt to help children in Belgium and Greece during World War II; CARE was formed in the United States to send relief parcels to post–World War II Europe.

Early NGOs were driven by a Western philosophy of caring for the needy. Specifically church-founded or "confessional" NGOs only came on stream from the 1950s onwards. Their core constituency consists of their church membership. Although they run parallel to church structures, they are, almost without exception, at great pains to disassociate their development and relief work from their religious or evangelistic work. They make considerable efforts to ensure that their work is targeted on the most needy, regardless of religious affiliation, and in ways calculated to benefit the population in general.

The past twenty-five years have also seen the emergence of many nonaligned NGOs on the international stage. While the majority of them are nondenominational and secular, they are still inspired by the same Western philosophy of caring that motivated the earlier NGOs.

There are countless nonprofit organizations and groups that justifiably describe themselves as NGOs. This paper, however, is concerned only with NGOs that exist only to help right the imbalance between rich and poor countries by promoting the transfer of resources in some way. Some NGOs deal only with children, or only with crisis interventions, or only with health or agriculture or water resources. Others deal only with fund-raising, development education, or lobbying. Some adopt a wide mix of approaches, and even the most specialized sometimes make forays outside their plotted routes. A major distinction exists between operational NGOs, meaning those that actually implement and manage operations in the Third World, and those which are not.

The Effect of Biafra on NGOs

Third World NGOs came into their own during their involvement in Biafra. Biafra created a new level of awareness of Third World famine and disaster in the West. It was the first major disaster that was brought to the living rooms of the world by television, which, with its visual immediacy, challenged indifference to faraway suffering.

The Biafrans fought a good propaganda war. They engaged Markpress, a Geneva-based public relations firm, to present their case to the world. This was done to great effect. In his memoirs Harold Wilson, whose Labour government in Britain had supported Nigeria, described Biafra's public relations exercise as "a success unparalleled in the history of communications in modern societies."[1] People around the world were moved by the plight of Biafra, but most governments reacted reluctantly and covertly to demands from their people. For governments Nigeria's sovereignty outweighed Biafra's agony.

In Biafra, the many NGOs involved learned the power of the media, a lesson that has stood them in good stead in winning support for their work ever since. The response to Biafra demonstrated that people do care; obtaining support is a question of getting the message to them. Since Biafra, NGOs are very conscious of their responsibility to inform the world of disasters and suffering so that the problems may be addressed.

The confessional NGOs were the most active in Biafra. The Protestant organizations were grouped under The World Council of Churches (WCC) and the Catholic NGOs were grouped under Caritas. Together they formed a strong and influential operational body, Joint Church Aid (JCA), which was also substantially funded by the American Jewish Committee. It was an unprecedented example of cooperation between world religious bodies. Dozens of private agencies from twenty countries grouped together under the JCA banner. JCA funded and ran a huge airlift to beleaguered Biafra—a lifeline that linked into the extensive church networks on the ground and became a highly effective distribution system.

The Christian churches in Biafra had a particularly well-developed infrastructure of schools, churches, and hospitals, which became feeding centers, refugee shelters, and additional hospitals. Eastern Nigeria, which had become Biafra, was in step with the most advanced development trends of the time in Africa, all of which proved useful in setting up systems to receive and distribute support being airlifted to the country by international NGOs and other donors. Older NGOs that were not operational inside Biafra were active in mobilizing opinion and sending supplies. New organizations were founded in response to the needs of Biafra. CONCERN and Médicins sans Frontièrs are two organizations founded for Biafra which continue to exist. Others, such as Canair Relief, were operational during the crisis and then wound up. (In the mid-1980s Band Aid made a similar appearance for a few years to help Ethiopia and Sudan before winding up.)

The new and extraordinary role of NGOs in Biafra proved that there was indeed a niche and role for NGOs on the international stage. In Biafra, NGOs discovered that they had particular strengths in emergency situations, and ever since they have played a prominent role in virtually every disaster relief operation in the Third World. The basic thrust of NGOs in conflicts and disasters has changed little in the intervening years. They are still totally committed to getting assistance to the victims in these situations. However, NGOs have changed a great deal in themselves. They have become a great deal more sophisticated and professional. They have chosen or settled for different ways of carrying out their missions. Their international clout as a group, or even individually, has greatly increased. Many of the organizations that are now operational in disaster relief situations have become more effective in delivering health services and humanitarian assistance. Some of these organizations have also built up an infrastructure to make them effective in delivering health services and humanitarian assistance even when other systems have broken down or are greatly weakened.

Changes to NGOs Since Biafra

The first major change that has strung out the NGOs in the past two decades is one of scale. Even the smaller organizations among those most frequently active in conflict and disaster situations often have budgets of $40–$50 million a year. Some NGOs have vastly greater budgets, and of course there are many that run on much smaller budgets, although it is difficult to be operational in disaster and conflict situations on a small budget except in a very select way. When government has broken down, when UN or other multilaterals are not functioning, it is nearly impossible for an NGO that has not built up its own systems to mount an effective operation.

Inevitably, some erosion of idealism goes hand in hand with growth in scale. Although the general public still looks on the operatives in the NGOs as ill-paid or even unpaid, and highly idealistic, most people might be somewhat shocked if they saw the salary and operating budgets of major, and even smaller, NGOs. While most NGOs are very cost conscious they are repeatedly confronted with the " 'pay peanuts and get monkeys' dilemma." To get the kind of high-level, professionally qualified personnel necessary to handle the complexities of large organizations costs money. Being entrusted with huge resources by the public and by governments and institutions imposes great responsibilities.

Invariably NGOs start out with an extremely high degree of idealism and commitment. As scale increases so too does the difficulty of maintaining these very things that give special strength and credibility to NGOs as personalized conduits of caring. "Small is beautiful" is an attractive concept, but it is difficult to uphold in the real world in face of the enormity of needs. Nowhere more than in conflict and disaster situations is there call for self-sacrificing commitment and the type of personalized care that NGOs can best contribute.

In Biafra, NGOs were effective and highly successful largely because there was an extensive network of professional, committed personnel already in place. No disaster, especially no disaster in a conflict situation, has since enjoyed that luxury. In Somalia, twenty-five years later, there were virtually no ready-made feed-in points with which NGOs could connect. Among the operational agencies, those with their own backup systems stood by far the best chance of doing extensive and effective work. It was distressing to see NGOs abounding in goodwill floundering because of lack of support systems.

The JCA airlift into Biafra has never been fully recognized for what it was. Recalling it now helps put the belated and pathetic efforts to get assistance to Somalia in perspective. Although there was a cease-fire in Somalia in April 1992, and Baidoa has a very good existing airstrip, the first UN relief flight did not arrive in Baidoa until August! It was not until September that the first U.S. plane landed in Baidoa from Mombasa. French flights brought a few hundred tons of supplies to Baidoa in August with considerable fanfare. In early September two large U.S. air force planes were each making one trip a day from Mombasa to Baidoa and each carrying but nine tons of supplies. Twenty-five years earlier, however, many of the JCA planes carried fifteen tons per flight to Uli, and it was a major disappointment if each plane did not manage two flights each night.

As many as fifty flights a night flew into Uli. Not all were JCA flights, but, for example, on the night of November 19, 1969, JCA landed 376 tons of relief supplies at Uli! The nightly average in April 1969 was 70 metric tons (mts), in August, 150 mts, and in December, 250 mts. WCC and Caritas received JCA supplies on alternate nights, thus allowing each system a day to distribute. Attached to the Caritas central stores there were 145 truck drivers and seventy-five mechanics to staff the fleet, and WCC had a like number. Fuel, tires, and spare parts were also flown in during the hours of darkness and under fire. It was a marvelous ecumenical cooperative effort.

Where there is a will, there is a way. There was a will in Biafra. Twenty-five years later, there wasn't a will in Somalia until very late in the game, and even then it was lukewarm for too long. One can only be cynical about the uncoordinated efforts of the superpowers and supersystems in Somalia. In the twenty-five years since Biafra, we have launched satellites into space, put people on the moon, and made all manner of technological advances. At the end of July 1992, there were twenty-five million mts of cereal in European intervention stores alone. Given these facts, how did the world community cope with the shame of watching hundreds of thousands of people die of starvation? It was not that we did not know.

There is an ever-present danger that NGOs may become overconfident because of their undoubted success in small undertakings. They often overstretch themselves, but they *should* stretch themselves. They can also annoy other actors on the stage by raising strident voices and finger-pointing, by exaggerating their own expertise and capabilities, by seeming to lay claim to a monopoly on caring. Such actions can build up unreal expectations, and by so doing, to some extent they allow other actors off the hook. Often because of their own frustration and inability to deliver, bigger actors have lured NGOs out of their depth. The NGOs can be like small fishing trawlers tempted into deep waters to service large factory ships. Usually they respond with alacrity. When the factory ships fail to function, the smaller vessels are in dire trouble.

NGOs are but one actor, and usually a relatively small one, on the international aid stage. This should be borne in mind especially in conflict situations. They must function in an awareness of and with respect for bilateral or government donors, multilateral donors, host governments and, where they are present, local NGOs. Whether in conflict, disaster, or long-term work situations, NGOs should respect local institutions, culture, and customs. Far too often many NGO personnel display a staggering lack of sensitivity and respect for their host environment.

Bilateral Aid

During the last twenty-five years there has been a growing disillusionment among bilateral donors with regard to recipient Third World partner governments. Romantic expectations have been replaced by often bitter recriminations. Often, donor governments have sought to help Third World countries out of self-interest, political, commercial, or strategic motives. The motivation has seldom been humanitarian or genuinely altruistic. This should not occasion too much surprise. Democratic governments are elected to look after the interests of those who elect them, not to practice international altruism. When they do so, they must answer to their electorates. In every government, however, there are people who will strongly and sincerely support international humanitarian causes for all the best reasons.

Increasingly the bilateral donors send a greater, though still small, portion of the resources they wish to supply to Third World nations through NGO channels, since NGOs are often perceived as being more capable of delivering this aid. Third World recipient governments can become resentful at being bypassed and seemingly not trusted. I have experienced such reactions in Ethiopia, in Sudan, and in Bangladesh in recent years. They will often vent their frustrations on the NGOs, placing almost unbelievable constraints on their operations. Indeed the NGOs sometimes, because of their insensitivity, arrogance, and even incompetence, deserve any backlash they receive.

NGO Roles

The sometimes startling growth in size of NGOs is largely attributable to government funding. Growth in size may not only entail an erosion of ethos and a replacement of committed volunteerism by costly professionalism, but may also lead to a lessening of independence. This is, of course, particularly likely if an NGO becomes heavily dependent on a single government source. NGOs must be careful not to become the tools or simply the contractors of donor governments. At the same time, NGOs are committed to exploiting to the fullest all resource possibilities on behalf of their clients, and government resources offer the greatest possibility. Availing of government resources to the full while retaining independence and remaining true to ethos can be very difficult.

The scale of fund-raising necessary to maintain the larger NGO has begotten many well-oiled NGO publicity and lobbying machines. Sadly the growth and increased efficiency on the public relations and fund-raising side of NGOs has too often not been matched by a proportionately improved performance, and has been accompanied by some sacrificing of independence. Bigger is by no means necessarily better.

Contrary to widely shared public perceptions, many, perhaps even most, international NGOs are not directly operational. This means they often play support or backstage roles rather than hands-on roles in times of emergency. The choice of different ways in which to serve poor countries has been one of the major developments among NGOs in the last two decades. Many NGOs that were initially operational are no longer operational or only marginally so. They support local Third World partners or other NGOs, or provide technical resources to multilaterals. Some devote virtually all their energies to fund-raising, to campaigning on Third World issues, to development education and awareness-raising.

Lobbying is a vitally important role that some NGOs specialize in and all NGOs exercise at times. For a year, while Somalia drifted ever faster toward anarchy, the country was not on the world agenda. Individual NGOs and NGO networks, which now exist in considerable numbers, worked hard to publicize Somalia's plight. Media personnel were encouraged to visit Somalia and were facilitated in every way. Once interest is nurtured to a certain point, it snowballs, feeding on itself.

Politicians and governments were lobbied at the same time as the public. As the wave of public concern for Somalia grew, so too did politicians' awareness. Many, somewhat belatedly, showed an interest. In major disasters and conflict situations the intervention of governments is critical in addressing the large-scale needs. Involving governments is a role NGOs can play. NGOs can blaze an action trail on the ground, but their resources, even when augmented by bilateral and multilateral inputs, cannot cope with disasters on a grand scale. The sooner governments become openly interested the better. Governments, however, can move very slowly.

Bilaterals in Somalia

The slowness of governments in responding to nonstrategic tragedies was illustrated in Somalia. The British foreign secretary, Douglas Hurd, at a press conference in Mogadishu on September 4, 1992, after visiting Somalia with the Danish foreign minister and the Portuguese state secretary put the matter succinctly in saying "we were all collectively slow." The U.S. government, the biggest actor on the international resource transfer stage, played a somewhat coy role backstage for quite a while. Then, coinciding with increased publicity, and despite preoccupation with the presidential election campaign, there was a major increase of U.S. interest in Somalia. At a press briefing in mid-August 1992 in Washington, D.C., Andrew Natsios, President Bush's special coordinator for Somalia, told the world that "The

United States has been in the forefront of the humanitarian relief effort for Somalia since the crisis began eighteen months ago. To date we have provided over $85 million in relief assistance, including the delivery of 80,000 tons of food. . . . The strategy the U.S. government initiated in the summer of 1991 was to mobilize the International Committee of the Red Cross (ICRC) to do a massive feeding program . . . something it has never done before. . . ."[2] At the same time, President Bush announced an additional 145,000 tons of food aid and the mounting of a massive airlift. Although these announcements gave great encouragement to NGOs on the ground, they were surprised to hear that the U.S. air force would fly in the supplies and hand them over to the NGOs for distribution; the NGOs had not been consulted and had no capacity for such a massive distribution. It is unfortunate that the U.S. government interest in Somalia was not more widely publicized earlier; it might have encouraged other governments to grant more assistance and take public stances earlier. But perhaps they too were active behind the scenes and not claiming any credit for their good works!

In August 1992, the Irish foreign minister, David Andrews, became the first foreign minister to visit famine-ravished Somalia. He went at the invitation of NGOs and was shocked into action by what he saw. He immediately contacted all European Community foreign ministers and the UN. The British, Dutch, and Germans responded immediately with increased aid. The U.S. initiative followed shortly thereafter. Also about this time Boutros Boutros-Ghali, secretary-general of the United Nations, ruffled many feathers by accusing the world community of neglecting the poor man's plight in Africa while paying great attention to the rich man's war in the former Yugoslavia.

Some governments, notably the British, had been supportive of NGOs before this, but it was only when other governments became more openly involved that things really began to move. For many, however, it was too late. It should be remembered that the tragedy of Somalia was enacted against the backdrop of Rio de Janeiro and accompanied by an international chorus singing about the new world order.

Funding relationships between donor governments and NGOs are highly important and useful to both parties in the delivery of services in disasters. Acting through NGOs enables donor governments to follow their consciences in transferring resources, even if they have grave reservations about the local government and do not wish to support it. They can bypass (to an extent) governments of which they disapprove and reach the "deserving poor."

For all kinds of reasons, governments may be less forthcoming for some recipient countries than for others. There can be very definite political discrimination in the distribution of aid. This was particularly so during the Cold War. Ethiopia and Cambodia were ruled out by many Western countries for development aid. Now there is much stress on the human rights record of the recipient country. Sudan is very prominent on the negative listing. This criterion is, however, applied rather selectively. The tyrant Siad Barre was supported for years in Somalia for strategic reasons. If a clean human rights record was made an essential criterion for receiving aid, there would be a very short recipient list.

Humanitarian aid, however, is treated differently than so-called development aid by donors. There is vastly less self-interest or hidden political agendas attaching. Donor governments may channel such aid through NGOs to movements they do not officially recognize as having legal status while they still continue to recognize the de facto government. Eritrea and Tigray within Mengistu's Ethiopia are good examples of this.

The Multilateral Organizations

The multilaterals—such as the UN, acting through its specialized agencies, and the European Community (EC)—are another major group with whom the NGOs share the stage in addressing needs in disasters and conflict situations. It is no revelation that the UN received very bad press for its poor showing in the Somalia situation. It was castigated from within and without. Speaking of the Somalia situation in mid-August 1992, a senior UN official said, "It is so bad because we've let things simmer without paying proper attention . . . we've had inexperienced people who don't know what they are seeing, who don't know what the implications are and didn't blow the whistle. . . . Because of the disorganization in the United Nations, less than a third of the food that is needed was delivered."[3] After a visit to Somalia in August, the overseas director of Save the Children Fund/U.K., the oldest of the NGOs and one that had been present in Somalia throughout the turmoil, scathingly attacked the UN. The BBC quoted him as describing the UN operation as pathetic, ill-informed, and ill-equipped. He spoke of the shameful degree of political infighting and lack of coordination. The SCF director-general added a further blow by describing the UN relief efforts as a shambles that had cost thousands of Somali lives. He said, "The UN's leadership and coordination was so lacking that it was in fact obstructing the relief effort."[4]

Bilateral and multilateral aid agencies can function very well in peaceful conditions, but it is extremely difficult for them to function in conflict situations. The bilaterals are at a loss in situations such as Somalia, no matter how much goodwill they have. To whom could they accredit their representative when there is no government? The basic role of UN specialized agencies is to support governments in member states. Again, how do they function when there is no government?

United Nations specialized agencies tend to present themselves as representing some independent world power. They tend to fly the UN flag as if it were a national rather than a world flag. Thus, they frequently create unreal expectations and cannot deliver. They have all the conceits of the NGOs developed to a higher degree. Because they have access to great resources they have the possibility, in certain conditions, of a level of performance that cannot be achieved by NGOs. They are important bodies, but as with bilaterals and NGOs, their weaknesses were glaringly exposed in the Somali crisis. All that has been said of the UN specialized agencies also applies to the EC emergency sector. They were conspicuous for the absence of representation or operatives on the spot, and by a disproportionate preoccupation with more sexy disasters elsewhere.

Despite their shortcomings, the multilaterals, especially the UN specialized agencies and the EC, are close and supportive forces for NGOs in Third World activities. In normal operating circumstances they are geared to longer-term work, and they can be slow off the mark in disaster situations. Many field offices become comfortable and complacent. Like many others—bilaterals and NGOs included—they are loathe to move from development to relief or emergency work.

There are two dangers in analyzing the performance of any of the actors on the stage in disaster situations. One is to flail out and condemn the people on the ground doing the work, which is a bit like shooting the messenger. The other danger is of closing ranks and covering up—sweeping the death statistics under the carpet. An agency's operations are only as good as they are allowed to be by those who direct them. Operatives of UN agencies tend to be smothered by bureaucratic requirements; their flexibility is stifled; they cannot indulge the kind of gut reactions that are necessary to save lives in disasters. To a lesser extent this is also true of many NGOs, who can lose flexibility and spontaneity in growing and end up aping the UN agencies they criticize. They should learn from what happened to bigger actors in Somalia. A permanent UN coordinating agency with the muscle to be effective is certainly needed. This body should include teams which can be deployed to disasters on the ground. Visiting Nairobi in August 1992 at the height of the Somali crisis was like visiting Cape Canaveral. Somalia was very remote from the twenty-fourth floor conference chamber where I counted fifty-five heads discussing Somalia. A few had been in Somalia for substantial periods. A greater number had had brief exposure. More had read reports. But the controls were there in Nairobi, or if they weren't they could be referred back to in distant locations.

One of the great tragedies of disaster situations is that experienced relief workers have moved up the ladder or left Third World relief activity. A new generation is left to reinvent the wheel at the expense of the unfortunate disaster victims.

Local Relief Structures

Normally, national and local government must be the principal actors in disaster situations. There are exceptions such as Somalia, where there was literally no government through 1992, but in most disaster situations there is some developed services structure. While some such structures are quite sophisticated, in most countries in the Third World, health and humanitarian services are altogether inadequate even in normal times. There is no way they can cope alone with the massively expanded demands that arise in a major disaster. Neither is it likely that they will have the capacity to utilize quickly and effectively the resources handed over to them. Local governments are highly unlikely to accept this reality. They are generally, and understandably, slow to admit to any weakness.

Lack of sensitivity, arrogance, high-handedness, and issues of sovereignty are the issues that cause the loss of lives at times of disasters. The position of the host government must be respected, but there comes a time when ways around sovereignty must be found. If such ways cannot be found then humanitarian needs dictate that sovereignty be ignored. This situation will most often arise where a government is holding sway with the gun or has a dubious mandate from the people.

LOCAL NGOs

In the twenty-five-year period that saw the development of the international NGOs, there was also a growth of local NGOs in Third World countries. Some international NGOs devoted most of their efforts to fostering the growth of local NGOs. Others supported the growth in lesser ways. Quite often partner NGOs are set up or sponsored by international NGOs. Confessional NGOs have made particular use of this method. Parent churches had earlier developed local counterparts, now the confessional NGOs encouraged the formation of local counterpart NGOs.

Some countries (I can speak especially of Bangladesh and India) have many strong, home-grown NGOs. Many of these NGOs modeled their organizations on Western NGOs. Some generate an independent income and have developed structures capable of partnering bilateral and multilateral donors. Local NGOs focus primarily on development. Few of them wish to be dragged into relief situations except in a developmental way. They will, however, usually play an active role in emergencies or disasters. In Bangladesh, local NGOs have sadly had too many opportunities to develop their disaster skills. They were much more competent in addressing the Rohingya refugee influx from Burma in 1992 than they had been during a similar episode in 1978.

Unfortunately, what is true of Bangladesh is not true of many other countries. Local NGOs hardly exist, or exist only in name. Many are localized and rather loosely structured groups. Often they exist only to promote the interests of their members. Others—particularly in countries where there is a military or one-party government—are largely tools of government; they are not the kind of NGOs dealt with in this paper, although they can play a useful local role in times of disaster. There is a desperate desire on the part of some international NGOs, encouraged by funders and theorists, to demonstrate a great deal of local NGO participation. The international development literature portrays an enormously inflated image of local NGOs. In most Third World countries they are largely nonexistent or extremely weak. The same is true of the local Red Cross or Red Crescent; they can play useful roles but they are not NGOs.

The reality is that NGOs require a climate of some affluence to thrive. Even more critical to the growth of an NGO is freedom of action and association, and freedom is limited in almost every Third World country. Genuine local NGOs are more likely to be subjected to even greater harassment by their government than the foreign NGOs. In spite of the difficulties, some NGOs manage to form, survive, and operate in even the most adverse circumstances. The reality, however unpalatable, is that there isn't a great body of independent and genuine local NGOs in the Third World, and they are unlikely to be major players on the stage in disaster or conflict situations.

The foregoing is not meant to imply that there is not a great reservoir of local talent, skill, and commitment in every country in the Third World. Every year the number of highly educated and trained personnel increases. This availability of qualified local staff has greatly changed a major aspect of the role of international NGOs in disasters: nowadays their operations will largely be staffed by locally recruited personnel.

NGO Personnel

The people on the ground—the operatives of the NGO in a disaster situation—are the single most critical factor in the role played by the NGOs. They are also the factor that most often distinguishes NGOs from other actors on the stage. Indeed, they distinguish NGOs from one another by the level of their commitment, self-sacrifice, enthusiasm, and competence. The abundance of these qualities in NGO personnel is partly attributable to their youthfulness and partly to their organizational ethos and sense of mission. They are like sprinters joining a more jaded marathon field for a few laps.

The Third World and disaster situations have no need for cowboys and misfits. Disasters inevitably attract a number of them. NGOs have serious obligations to screen and train the people they recruit to work in disasters. They must then support them, back them up, and insist on standards. The desperate need for pairs of hands can lead to inadequate screening. There are far too many adventurers let loose in disaster situations by NGOs.

Organizations that do not have the necessary capacity to supervise their field operatives should refrain from practicing on disaster victims. There is a particular danger of Western operatives doing so in a Third World situation: double standards are very readily applied. Common sense and scarcities frequently demand improvisation, but this should not become an excuse for lowering standards or indulging in practices that infringe on the rights and dignity of those being helped.

Conclusion: Then and Now

In looking at the changing roles of NGOs in disaster and conflict situations, the change in the scale and complexity of operations is striking. The position and clout of NGOs has drastically increased. There is an acceptance of NGOs as having a very definite role to play. If anything there is an exaggerated expectation for NGOs by other actors, and NGOs are often inclined to bask in the warmth of that perception.

As NGOs become more professional, handle vastly increased budgets, manage enormously bigger and more far-flung organizations, and support heavier structures and bureaucracies, their real strengths have been severely eroded. These strengths include commitment, ethos, mission, caring, flexibility, spontaneity. I fear that much of what was distinctive and valuable has been sacrificed on the altar of progress. NGOs should not allow success to go to their heads nor settle for becoming junior members of the major international league. They must regularly go back to their roots and renew their commitment to serve those most in need.

12

Relief and Reality

PHILIP JOHNSTON

The key to shaping effective relief responses to disasters and conflicts is understanding how current relief situations are vastly different from those encountered in years past. Recent and dramatic changes in geopolitics and the environmental realities of today dictate a need to change relief work. Major changes are necessary in how relief work is coordinated and how the mandate for intervention is crafted and delivered.

The experiences of humanitarian organizations are helpful in understanding the reality of relief operations today. CARE, one of the largest development and relief organizations, first began sending relief in the form of "CARE packages" in 1946 to Europeans who had been left destitute by World War II. The founders of CARE felt deeply about the need to demonstrate a moral and humanitarian commitment to helping those who required help. CARE's dramatic growth as an organization reflected the desire of Westerners to participate in reaching out to others. CARE packages became a popular symbol of those

Dr. Johnston gratefully acknowledges the research contributed by Steven Gray.

who cared for those in need and created goodwill toward the United States, earning the lifelong appreciation of millions who had been helped by these efforts.

After assisting the victims of World War II, CARE shifted to undertaking development work and responding to emergencies in the developing world. The organization responded to earthquakes, typhoons, and large cross-border civilian movements in civil wars. Often, these were transient emergencies, lasting only a few months.[1] The task was to come in, help feed and provide basic health care to the affected, and help them get back on their feet. Then CARE would leave, and people would get on with their lives.

Today such tragedies are exacerbated by several trends that have emerged over recent years and are redefining relief work. To begin with, some emergencies are now long-term, and many are man-made. CARE is now immersed in several situations involving long-term droughts and long, drawn-out civil wars. In certain countries drought is becoming endemic because of the progressive degradation of arable land. Northwestern Sudan is an example where emergencies are likely to be continuous. The land has continually been degraded, and its capability to produce enough to feed families or sustain cattle is questionable. The long, heinous, and ruinous war in Mozambique is another example of an emergency lasting many years, in which provision of emergency assistance has become continuous.

The same services are still needed—namely, food and health care. In addition, though, safe drinking water is an increasing concern. Water has been a major relief commodity during the Cambodian refugee crisis in Thailand since the early 1980s. In Ethiopia over 400,000 gallons of water per day are being transported to refugee Somalis who are victims of the war and drought. It is a phenomenally expensive undertaking. CARE spends several million dollars a year on transporting water in Ethiopia alone.

Even if the current conflicts and disasters ended quickly, there is one big difference between today's relief situations and those of the past. In most of the countries affected today, the basic elements of a quality life were tenuous or nonexistent prior to the emergency. More often than not, the conditions of human life have no tolerance for deterioration, and an emergency crowds people out of the narrow margins of life they live on. Farmers in Ethiopia, Somalia, Bangladesh, Mozambique, Cambodia, Haiti, or any one of a dozen other countries are living so close to the edge that a dramatic political or climatic shift is enough to change their lives permanently for the worse.

Overpopulation and lack of access to quality land are doing more than anything else to undermine the ability of people to feed themselves. Typically, the poorest farmers live on the most marginal land and have the highest birthrates. The poor farmer has learned to survive by intensively working this marginal land and by having plenty of children, who will help out now and will provide a safety net when the farmer is too old to work. The farmer is caught in a no-win situation. The land does not produce enough food for him to save any in reserve. If war or drought disrupts the planting cycle, the family goes hungry, and once the crop cycle fails, the farmer resorts to selling major assets, such as cattle, just to survive. This scenario has been played out in Ethiopia, Sudan, Somalia, Mozambique, and many other of the least developed countries.

Conflicts and disasters force people to move from their homelands; usually they do not return for many years. The combination of civil war, drought, and mass movements of whole communities creates disasters beyond the scope of any one humanitarian agency's ability to alleviate. As a result, relief responses must increasingly stress collaboration among the entire world humanitarian community.

Another major trend of the past several years affecting relief work is the increase in "economic" refugees. Western countries, leery of being overwhelmed by new immigrants, are defining major refugee movements as economic, not political, flights. In 1992 the U.S. government took the extraordinary step of intercepting fleeing Haitians at sea so it could technically comply with United Nations refugee conventions by turning them away before they reached U.S. territory.[2] While the economic prospects for Haitians are not rosy, their refugee status cannot be judged summarily. The nearby shores of the United States are appealing to people whose per capita income is less than $400 per year. Yet the flow of Haitians dramatically increased after the coup that deposed Jean Bertrand Aristide, and an estimated 200,000 people are "in hiding" within the country, fearful of being persecuted because of their political beliefs.[3]

Germany is also concerned and is making efforts to alter its constitution to make settlement within its borders more difficult for economic immigrants. The political changes in Eastern Europe and the former Soviet Union have produced the largest number of European refugees since World War II. Many Russians, Romanians, Turks, Bulgarians, and Soviet Jews see Germany as the economic promised land.[4]

The truth is that most disaster situations, whether climatic or political, produce economic refugees. People are fleeing a tenuous life and need money to rebuild their life, whether it is back in their home or in another country. The most basic problem facing the world today is how to increase people's standard of living no matter where they live.

Long-term Relief Situations

Unfortunately, a long list of countries could serve as examples illustrating the above points and highlighting why responses to emergencies need to reflect current realities. The list includes Sudan, Mozambique, Cambodia, Ethiopia, Afghanistan, Angola, Haiti, Somalia, and a dozen other countries affected by conflicts that have political, environmental, and social dimensions beyond the norm. Let us examine the first three of these.

SUDAN

For more than twenty years Sudan has been a major refugee-hosting and refugee-producing country.[5] Currently, an estimated 4.7 million Sudanese are displaced, or internal refugees; of these, 1.8 million are living in and around Khartoum. Another 200,000 Sudanese are external refugees. Close to one-fifth of the total population of the country is displaced. Add to this another 700,000 refugees from Ethiopia, and there are close to 5 million refugees within the country living a temporary existence, without their own land and often without food, water, or decent shelter from the harsh desert weather.

While a long and persistent drought is a major cause of the food shortage that threatens more than one-third of the country, the severity of the crisis is man-made. The ongoing civil war between the Muslim, mostly Arab north and the Christian, animist, and mostly African south has severely exacerbated the problem. Even when food aid was flowing, each side diverted it or withheld food or seeds from those of a different race or religious persuasion. A succession of openly corrupt and cynical military governments have purposely avoided confronting the humanitarian crisis and have so alienated the few countries and nongovernmental organizations willing to care about the crisis that the people of Sudan are almost without anyone to help them.

If the crisis in Sudan were to end today, if the government suddenly reformed itself, if peace between the north and south were achieved, and if relief efforts were again begun in earnest, it is still likely that the crisis would go on for years. Almost every Sudanese family has been affected, and the country suffers from a trauma that will not easily go away. The environmental degradation from the drought, war, and neglect is so severe that it will take years of sustained development efforts to help the Sudanese people rebuild their country and their lives.

MOZAMBIQUE

Mozambique has been locked into a civil war that has totally disrupted its fragile infrastructure. The opposition group, RENAMO, has effectively disrupted the country's agricultural and economic system. This war has produced 1.5 million external and 2 million internal refugees.[6]

Terrible droughts are aggravating an already tragic situation. Food production and distribution have been so disrupted by the war that only 5 percent of the arable land within the country is under cultivation.[7] Many Mozambicans are suffering from malnutrition, and starvation is evident.

The war crimes of RENAMO have been well documented elsewhere.[8] The organization's widespread kidnapping of children and forcing them to shoot neighbors and family members are reminiscent of Khmer Rouge tactics. These atrocities may have irreparably ripped the moral fabric of the country.

If the crisis were to end today, if RENAMO suddenly discovered a political agenda beyond terror, and if people were allowed to return to their homes, it would take years to get the country back to sustained economic growth. While Mozambique does have a government interested in democratic freedoms and protecting basic human rights, the country has been so devastated and the effects of the drought are so severe that it will take tons of short-term and long-term assistance to feed, shelter, and empower the population to take care of itself.

CAMBODIA

Cambodia illustrates that the dilemma of long-term, persistent relief work is not confined to the African continent. The case of Cambodia is well known. The holocaust perpetuated by the Khmer Rouge led to a quarter of the population's being killed. The resultant invasion by the Vietnamese stopped the killing fields but led to a long, protracted civil war and the seemingly permanent displacement of hundreds of thousands of Cambodians.

A solution to the crisis has been negotiated, but as of late 1992, the Khmer Rouge are breaking promises that allowed them to take part in that brokered solution. If the Khmer Rouge had not broken their promises, the development task ahead would still be long and arduous. The removal of land mines, the rebuilding of an infrastructure designed to support life, and the reeducation of a population traumatized and devastated by the holocaust will take several years.

COMMON CHARACTERISTICS

What do these above examples have in common? First, each has a government or an insurgent movement that does not recognize internationally accepted rules of behavior, including those governing humanitarian assistance. The governments of certain East African countries, as well as the Khmer Rouge of Cambodia and RENAMO of Mozambique, have denied aid to those not in their group and have sought to gain or retain power through illegitimate means.

Second, large proportions of the populations in each of the countries have been uprooted and disempowered. In each of the countries mentioned, between one-fifth and one-fourth of the population have been internally or externally displaced, and large numbers of people have been killed outright. In past wars most victims were combatants. Today most victims are civilians, largely women and children.

Third, each country, with the possible exception of Cambodia, has a fragile environment that has been altered to an extent that complicates long-term development prospects. Often the land has been so neglected or degraded that food production cannot be maintained at levels needed to feed the refugee and host populations. Additional burdens are felt because of high birthrates. The proportion of people who lack food security is high, increasing the need for both short-term and long-term food aid.

Fourth, these populations lack the kinds of skills needed to rebuild their societies. Engineers, managers, midwives, and others needed to provide the basic human needs of food, water, organization, and health care are not available. Often these types of professionals were killed or were the first to flee.

Factors Inhibiting Effective Responses

Some problematic factors inhibit the ability of humanitarian organizations to respond to the current relief situations. The biggest problem is lack of money. The fact that relief efforts are long-term and affect millions instead of thousands of people means costs are high. The office of the United Nations High Commissioner for Refugees has been overwhelmed by the demand for its services as the worldwide refugee population has doubled since 1980. Unfortunately, its budget has not risen accordingly, and many countries are in arrears. Donations to CARE, from the American public in particular, are not keeping pace with the demand. This deficiency is partly due to the recession, but an important part is that Western people are getting burned out on providing emergency assistance. They have seen too many disasters that do not have easy solutions.

United States foreign aid priorities are changing, too. In the 1970s humanitarian aid focused on helping the neediest of the needy. In the 1980s U.S. humanitarian aid was increasingly used as an extension of short-term foreign policy objectives.[9] In the early 1990s there appears to be a shift to providing aid where it is most likely to "have an impact."[10] Eastern Europe and the former Soviet republics will receive large increases in aid, while African countries will see decreases or stagnant levels. The current political focus in the United States on "domestic" issues is also a factor.

The proliferation of brutal demagogues hostile to their own people and a world community unable to secure unfettered relief help to explain why so many situations defy solution. In addition, various Western nations have different criteria for providing aid when host governments are at odds with their own people, as is the case, for example, in Sudan, Ethiopia, Somalia, and former Yugoslavia. The Scandinavian countries seem to be more tolerant than the United States; they will continue to work with governments the United States has "given up on." As a result, Sudan, with close to five million refugees, has only a handful of humanitarian agencies remaining in the country. This has reduced important commodity lifelines and links to the world media capable of mobilizing efforts to help displaced Sudanese and other refugees.

Positive Developments

On a more positive note, in some ways the humanitarian community is better prepared to deal with the realities of relief work than it used to be. A great deal has been learned about how to provide efficient relief. The capability to respond faster and get more aid to more people is available. Success in mitigating disasters in Turkey with the Kurds and in Bangladesh helped reduce the numbers of those who died and suffered. The world can be proud of those efforts.

In addition, the partnerships between the military and nongovernmental organizations in Turkey, Bangladesh, and Kenya have been truly enlightening. The military establishments have done a good job of providing the logistical capacity NGOs lacked. Envisioning a role for the military in relief work is a major breakthrough that could provide dramatic improvements in the ability of the humanitarian community to respond.

The realization that relief work has to have a developmental focus has also been a big plus. Almost every disaster response now has a training component for refugees or involves more integrated coordination with host country agencies. These efforts help build longer-lasting capacity in host countries and empower refugees in otherwise helpless situations.

Another major positive development is that a number of drawn-out relief situations are starting to see some movement toward resolution. Ethiopia, Angola, and Cambodia are a few of the situations that could not be solved in the 1980s, but now appear headed toward settlement.

Humanitarian Intervention

Most of the disaster situations mentioned above have one other important factor in common. In retrospect, it is clear that some outside humanitarian intervention should have taken place to stop the violations of human rights occurring within the borders of each country. Even though this type of intervention is fraught with political land mines, it is clear that until recently, the world lacked the political will to prevent atrocities and violations of people's rights even though we knew what was happening.[11]

The end of the Cold War has begun to strengthen the UN's ability to thrust humanitarian assistance into countries where sovereign governments are violating basic human rights of their population. Widespread violations of human rights and the deliberate endangerment of vast numbers of people can no longer be tolerated. Despotic rulers have got to be consistently put on notice to clean up their act. The end of the Cold War allows definitions of what is acceptable, based not on ideological terms, but on internationally recognized humanitarian principles.

There is a great need to continue to build political institutions that make it impossible for demagogues and despots to have any legitimacy. The United Nations has made incredible strides in this direction during the past few years. The evolving concept of humanitarian intervention is gaining hold in the UN. Several years ago UN secretary-general Pérez de Cuéllar set the tone when he publicly reminded those violating human rights that they could not hide behind the veil of sovereignty. He observed that "the Universal Declaration of Human Rights has universal applicability. It is now accepted in practice that infringements, wherever they may be, are of common concern."[12] The world needs that kind of forceful leadership on an ongoing basis. The UN can lead the way in actively promoting the principle that throughout the world, all people, no matter which sovereign nation they reside in, are protected by an agreed-upon set of rights. All nations should be strongly persuaded to sign the Human Rights Convention and Protocol. The UN has taken some years to act, but it appears ready to take on the difficult role of mitigating human rights disasters.

A major part of ensuring that despots do not feel free to violate people's human rights is the multilateral ability to intercede with humanitarian aid even without the approval of the local government. While nonforcible methods of humanitarian intervention must first be fully explored and exhausted, there will be times when bold action will be needed to adequately protect populations suffering human rights abuses. We have had enough mass killings to learn the lessons of Ukraine, Nazi Europe, Cambodia, Ethiopia, and other clearly heinous examples of man's inhumanity toward man. Iraq, former Yugoslavia, and Somalia have drawn or are now drawing enough attention to warrant such a response from the United Nations. We need to further develop this capacity so we can collectively respond forcefully and quickly when it is clearly warranted.

There is enough evidence in the case of Somalia that the UN was not prepared to act in a situation with no government in charge. The new reality of relief is that the world must be prepared to provide humanitarian assistance to those caught in the middle of tribal or other internal struggles. The UN might have delayed too long to save the hundreds of thousands of Somalis trapped in this war.

Food Aid

A major component of all relief responses will continue to be food aid. More and more food (and nutritious food) will have to be provided. Short-term food aid has always been part of the humanitarian repertoire. Serious long-term food aid will have to be part of the response, as well. In essence, long-term food aid has been provided, but it has been always framed in successive short-term food aid contracts. Short-term survival food, such as provided by the World Food Programme, is not enough in a long-term situation. The relief situations today require long-term commitments of nutritionally balanced foodstuffs. While this kind of food aid costs more to provide, it is vital to keeping people alert and healthy enough to take a major role in helping themselves. Money spent up front on nutritionally healthy diets will be saved in reduced health care costs later on.

Other challenges include providing long-term food aid in a manner that does not undermine the ability of the people to produce their own food; storing, securing, and transporting food to remote locations; and redoubling efforts to research new high-yielding varieties of crops that can be indigenously grown without harmful impacts on the environment.

Involvement of U.S. Citizens

Developing a collective political will to stand up to and defeat those who perpetuate human rights violations must include actively involving the American public in relief and development organizations. It is important to continuously involve the citizens of the United States to show how these situations directly affect the quality of life in their country. Citizens have to see how being more active in world politics is advantageous. We have to do a better job of promoting the concept of interdependency, especially as it pertains to environmental degradation, battling human rights abuses, and development. We need to provide study groups, task forces, and other vehicles that help organize a political movement that reenergizes the American public and adds meaning to development and emergency relief issues.

U.S. citizens can play a key role in building the capacity of NGOs. First, they can respond with financial support not just to emergencies but also to the long-term fight to end the kind of poverty that makes disasters in the developing world so devastating. Second, they can advocate continued government spending on Third World relief and development by contacting their local representatives and expressing their support of the work that NGOs are trying to do.

Final Thoughts

The complexity and large-scale nature of current relief situations necessitates responses that are multidimensional and well coordinated. There is a need to begin planning for potential disasters before they occur. There may be a need to intervene in countries to neutralize internal threats precipitating large-scale migrations.

While there are environmental and technical hurdles to overcome, the most difficult task is marshaling the political will to create governance systems that are "rights-protective." We need to be vigilant in creating systems that make protection of human rights a central element of their mission. We need to actively help all citizens of every nation understand they are part of one world with certain inalienable rights, such as adequate nutrition and security. The rights mandated at the 1990 World Summit for Children were a good start. These rights must be extended to all people, and the UN must take an active role in ensuring that nations afford these rights to all their citizens. Creating rights-protective regimes will not eliminate disasters and conflicts, and will not drive CARE out of business (although we all would be glad to not be needed), but it will ease the difficult task of ensuring that people do not go hungry, and that they live full and productive lives.

13

The Médecins sans Frontières Experience

R O N Y   B R A U M A N

The 1971 creation of Médecins sans Frontières brought about a small revolution in the world of humanitarianism. The purpose of this paper is to record how that revolution came about and how it continues today, twenty years later.

MSF Today

With a budget of $187 million and a total of two thousand people in the field each year, Médecins sans Frontières has become one of the world's leading private medical emergency assistance organizations. It is widely known throughout the world as MSF and, in English-speaking countries, as both MSF and Doctors without Borders.

Much of MSF's recognition derives from its missions in Afghanistan, Ethiopia, and Iraqi Kurdistan, which were widely reported in the English, American, and French press. MSF today also enjoys the confidence of leading institutional financiers: MSF is privileged to be a partner of the United Nations High Commissioner for Refugees (UNHCR); the European Economic Community (EEC); and, as of more recently, the United States Agency for International Development and the United States Bureau for Refugee Programs.

How MSF Began

As I will describe in more detail below, MSF was founded on December 20, 1971, by two groups of doctors. The first group had become recognized for its work in Biafra, where it operated from 1968 to 1970 on behalf of the French Red Cross. The second group had become known for having volunteered in 1970 to treat the victims of a tidal wave in eastern Pakistan (the future Bangladesh).

Independently, these groups each discovered—the first during a war, the second during the aftermath of a natural disaster—the shortcomings of international aid: it offered too little medical assistance and was too deferential to international law to be effective in crisis situations.

Thus, by forming MSF, this core group of doctors intended to begin a humanitarian aid revolution both by providing more medical assistance more rapidly and by being less deterred by national borders at times of crisis. As such, MSF was the first nonmilitary nongovernmental organization to specialize in emergency medicine.

RED CROSS ROOTS

MSF's creation was actually the culmination of a trend initiated ten years before by the International Committee of the Red Cross (ICRC). That trend was developed by ICRC partly in response to American aid practices.

After World War II, American aid had been mostly targeted for development projects that were designed to promote the financial and material reconstruction of the European countries. Later, such aid was used to raise the economic level of Third World countries in an effort to protect them against communist contagion.

Given this focus by the Americans, humanitarian emergency aid was provided primarily by the Red Cross movement. Red Cross Leagues have in fact coordinated the assistance provided after each natural catastrophe since World War I. But the effectiveness of their actions has been reduced considerably by slow transport facilities and cumbersome administrative and diplomatic formalities.

In times of war ICRC intervened. Its main role was to make sure that the belligerent nations complied with the Geneva Conventions providing for the protection of and assistance to prisoners and civilians in time of war. Until the beginning of the 1960s, the Geneva-based ICRC carried out its duties without sending medical units to battle sites or even to the lines behind the front.

ICRC was not encouraged to send out medical units because most conflicts in the past century involved either industrialized nations opposing each other or industrialized nations opposing their colonies. In both types of conflicts medical care was provided by the military of the countries involved. In the first type of conflict most victims were soldiers. The armies facing each other were medically well equipped: each had its own medical unit to treat its own wounded. Military doctors were assisted by nurses and stretcher bearers from the Red Cross sections of only their own countries. In the second type of conflict the colonial powers used the principle of noninterference to outlaw any foreign medical assistance to nationalist guerrillas. Here, too, war medicine was limited to military medicine.

It took the multiplication of civil wars in the Third World after the decolonization era (Katanga in 1960, Yemen in 1962, Biafra in 1967) to prompt ICRC to add medical assistance to its roster of help. These new conflicts were much harder on the civilian population than earlier wars because, for example, of food blockades, and because guerrilla and counterguerrilla strategies caused massive flows of refugees under very precarious circumstances. Most of these conflicts tore apart countries already lacking doctors and therefore limited in their capability to deal with the public health problems with which they were abruptly confronted through the confluence of underdevelopment and war.

THE CONSEQUENCES OF BIAFRA

ICRC began its emergency medicine efforts by sending out a few doctors, whom it hired temporarily for renewable three-month terms. These doctors were recruited by the national Red Cross Societies. During the summer of 1968 ICRC offered the French Red Cross (FRC) the opportunity to run its own independent medical mission in Biafra. FRC accepted readily, particularly since its acceptance enabled the French government to support the Biafra secession without too much compromise.

From September 1968 until January 1970, under extremely dangerous circumstances, FRC managed to send some fifty doctors to Biafra. These doctors were a mixture of people driven by their religious convictions and of adventurers driven by the search for sensations and exotic places. They included the future founders of MSF, including Bernard Kouchner.

For many, Biafra meant the discovery of the Third World, of little-known conflict, and of the inability of humanitarian action to find effective solutions. The Biafra war, ending in 1970 with the Nigerian victory and the death of one million people, clearly revealed the short-comings of the Red Cross in emergency medicine. Of those shortcomings, the most important was the defect in ICRC regulations that forbade Red Cross staff from publicly denouncing an ethnic genocide. ICRC was not entitled to intervene in a country without the approval of the country's authorities. It had to accept the sovereignty of any state that accepted its assistance; thus, ICRC personnel had to maintain a reserved attitude toward the events they witnessed during a mission.

Several FRC doctors defied this prohibition by organizing a "com-mittee against the Biafran genocide" as soon as they were back in France—less to make the public aware of the plight of the Biafran population than to denounce the political sources of this conflict, which were too often hidden by the papers covering the war. The committee argued that medical action should not be turned into a blind and dumb instrument. These French doctors also criticized the Red Cross intervention techniques as being obsolete.

This activity attracted a group of approximately fifty people who were persuaded that conflicts such as Biafra would happen again and needed to be anticipated. Thus, the Biafra veterans (the "Biafrans") began meeting once a month to share and refresh their memories. In 1970 they organized the Groupe d'Intervention Médical et Chirurgical d'Urgence (GIMCU), in the hope of setting up an independent associ-ation specializing in providing medical emergency assistance free from the administrative and legal constraints facing ICRC.

At the same time, a second group of doctors was formed in France at the initiative of the medical journal *Tonus*. In 1970 *Tonus*'s editor, Raymond Borel, spoke on television about the distress of the Ban-gladesh tidal wave victims and the lack of French doctors at the site of the disaster. On November 23, 1970, he published an appeal in the columns of his journal to establish an association: Secours Médical Français (SMF). Doctors responded to Borel's call to action for many reasons: a bad conscience in the wake of the disturbing television images; the feeling that France, because of its history, had a duty to cooperate with Third World countries; or simply the desire to get away from routine medicine and "imaginary illness" in order to practice presumably more useful medicine under more stimulating conditions.

On December 20, 1971, MSF was born from the merger of GIMCU and SMF.

THE "FRENCH DOCTORS" MOVEMENT

It is no accident that MSF was set up at this time and in France. MSF could only have been organized in a country still preoccupied with its colonial past, at a time when the first Services d'Aide Médicale d'Urgence units emerged in the region of Paris. MSF's creation further coincided with the democratization of air transport and information, with the era of electronics and satellites, and with the shrinking of the world into a global village. These factors, in combination, made it possible to intervene increasingly rapidly at disaster sites. The instantaneous visibility of disasters and conflicts on television made it less and less acceptable either to do nothing or to offer only a confused effort at emergency assistance.

From its inception MSF hoped to benefit from the experience of its "Biafran" firebrands and the infrastructures (offices and secretariat) of its "Tonus" group. But the first steps were difficult. From 1971 to 1976 MSF was more like a pool of doctors at the disposal of large Third World development aid organizations than a truly independent medical emergency organization. Its budget was limited to a few hundred thousand francs, and its missions, with a few exceptions—such as in Nicaragua after the 1972 earthquake and Honduras after the 1974 hurricane—were not independent. For lack of resources and experience, these early and limited interventions were highly ineffective. In Nicaragua, for example, American assistance arrived well ahead of MSF.

MSF in the 1970s

MSF remained a very small organization in the 1970s for several reasons. First, it consisted exclusively of volunteers, each of whom was employed outside MSF. In the circles of established international organizations, the MSF volunteers were considered amateurs, tourists, or "medical hippies." Second, MSF relied on outdated financing techniques because its members refused to ask for charity from the public or to "sell" humanitarian services like a commercial product. Third, the worldwide clamor for emergency medical assistance without any parallel fund-raising effort was not conducive to growth.

MSF flourished for the first time from 1976 to 1979. A 1976 war mission in Lebanon in a Shiite neighborhood encircled by Christian militia, and a free advertising campaign offered in 1977 by a Havas subsidiary, gave MSF an identity (an organization that dealt with dangerous emergencies) and its first public recognition. MSF was of interest not only in France but also in the United States, because the American press reported on the courage of the French doctors in Lebanon.

But the expansion of MSF is not the incidental result of a widely reported war or the fruit of an advertising campaign. In 1978 there remained a large gap between the association's reputation in France and its actual interventions. At the time, MSF had a symbolic and media existence rather than a real operational existence. It sent out only a few dozen doctors per year.

THE REFUGEE CAMP FACTOR

The formidable growth of MSF after 1978 was fueled by one factor: the multiplication of refugee camps in the Third World at the end of the 1970s. This single situation defined for MSF its main fields of intervention. While the global refugee population remained stable between 1970 and 1976, it doubled between 1976 and 1979, from 2.7 million to 5.7 million. It doubled once again between 1979 and 1982, settling at 11 million persons until 1985.

This increase was due to the sharp growth in the number of conflicts in the Southern Hemisphere since 1975. These conflicts were caused largely by the reemergence, after the decolonization era, of the old national antagonisms and ethnic rivalries, as well as the fact that the East-West confrontation moved out of Europe.

At the same time, the Soviet Union began to increase its influence in several Third World countries, profiting from 1975 onward from the U.S. withdrawal after the Vietnam defeat and the instability brought about in southern and eastern Africa because of the Portuguese decolonization and the fall of the Ethiopian Negus. The Soviet expansion fueled a number of conflicts in Angola and Mozambique between pro-Soviet regimes and counterrevolutionary guerrillas, as well as in the African Horn. There, Somalia and Ethiopia, communist countries that ranked their national rivalries higher than their ideological solidarity, began to fight in 1977 over the control of the Ogaden region, an Ethiopian territory peopled mostly with Somalis. The 1975 communist takeover of Indochina led to the exodus of hundreds of thousands of boat and land people in Thailand, Malaysia, and Indonesia. Meanwhile, ethnic and religious minorities in Eritrea and Lebanon began or continued civil wars to obtain their independence or more power. Millions of people were packed in camps along the borders of these warring countries, often under very poor sanitary and hygienic conditions. Although UNHCR assumed responsibility for these refugees, and built and supplied camps, it had tremendous difficulty in finding medical personnel willing to work in these areas.

MSF saw the increasing number of refugees in the world as a fertile field of action. In contrast to the UNHCR, MSF did not lack doctors. In the second half of the 1960s the French job market was flooded by doctors from the baby-boom generation who did not have to repay their study grants (as in the United States) and who often had had their first taste of the Third World during their military service. Many general practitioners of this generation were experiencing an identity crisis. Faced in their daily practice with benign pathologies that did not interest them and unsolvable problems that they could only refer to specialists, many of them were tempted by a "more authentic" medical practice in the Third World.

From 1976 to 1979 MSF sprang to the aid of Angolan refugees in Zaire; Somali refugees in Djibouti; Saharan refugees in Algeria and Eritrea; and, above all, Vietnamese, Cambodian, and Laotian refugees in Thailand. Initially MSF offered modest help to the American humanitarian organizations that had already been on the scene for over a year (International Rescue Committee and World Vision). French doctors sometimes questioned the motivations of the organizations for which they were working, suspecting them of acting as much for political objectives (anticommunism) and religious reasons (proselytizing) as for humanitarian goals.

Between 1976 and 1979 MSF gradually expanded its operations in Thailand, slowly replacing the American organizations, which began to withdraw from the refugee camps as the memory of the Vietnam War began to fade. In December 1979 MSF also sent 100 doctors and nurses to the Cambodian border, one-fourth of the medical staff sent out to Thailand.

The Tension of Growth

The multiplication of its missions in refugee camps at the end of the 1970s forced MSF to accept a more professional approach (a paid coordinator in Bangkok, allowances for doctors sent out for six-month periods). This trend, far from being welcomed by every MSF member, began to divide those who longed for the days of voluntary emergency medicine (including the "Biafrans") from the new generation of doctors looking for longer terms in refugee camps and more demanding medical services. In 1979 these long-submerged tensions led to a split within MSF.

Until 1977 Bernard Kouchner had been the organization's undisputed leader. But his power was challenged in 1978 by the new generation of refugee camp doctors and by his most brilliant disciple, Claude Malhuret. The baby-boomers, Malhuret's generation, were more numerous than Kouchner's followers, but they were also more pragmatic. Because of personal frustrations, Malhuret and his generation were more aware of the technical insufficiency of MSF interventions in refugee camps. Foremost among technical problems were logistical difficulties, including communications between Paris and the field and delivery of medical supplies for the field and of food for the staff. Advocates of short, independent, voluntary missions, the "Biafrans" were afraid that MSF would be turned into a bureaucracy if it addressed these problems.

The second disagreement between the two groups focused on MSF's media posture. Until 1977 the MSF charter forbade its members to talk about what they had witnessed during their missions. During their interventions the doctors were obliged to respect the Hippocratic Oath, which governed their medical practices in France. Silence was a symbol of MSF's apolitical stance, as well as a condition for "border-free" operations, since it was thought that no state would accept the presence of overly garrulous doctors on its territory.

The revelations of Alexander Solzhenitsyn, the Helsinki conference, the proliferation of dictatorships in Latin America, the crisis in revolutionary ideologies after the failure of the socialist experiments in the Third World, and the 1977 award of the Nobel Peace Prize to Amnesty International all created a widespread agreement in French society on the primacy of human rights. After 1978 some members of MSF attempted to speak to the press, in the belief that testimony in MSF's name would shake the public from indifference.

When Bernard Kouchner chartered a ship to rescue Vietnamese refugees in the Chinese Sea, he triggered the crisis that led to the 1979 split. Two hundred thousand boat people had fled communist Vietnam since 1975. Those who survived assaults by pirates and storms (only half) went to Thailand, Indonesia, or Malaysia. In 1978 the capacity of these three countries became saturated by the sudden arrival of massive numbers of refugees. In order to put a spectacular end to international indifference to its problem, Malaysia decided on November 15 to close its Hai Kong coast to a drifting coaster carrying 2,564 Vietnamese refugees. The maneuver succeeded, and along with reports of the intolerable sanitary and hygienic conditions on the vessel, it aroused the indignation of the world press and international public opinion. On November 22 a group of French intellectuals, moved by the Hai Kong tragedy, founded the Ship for Vietnam Committee, whose purpose was to charter a vessel to receive refugees off the Vietnamese coast and to transport them to a host country. For the first time in thirty years, this project brought together Jean-Paul Sartre and Raymond Aron.

The committee soon asked MSF to take medical responsibility for the refugees received on the ship, which MSF agreed to do. But several MSF members accused Bernard Kouchner, who was personally acquainted with most of the committee members, of playing an overly active role in this operation without always consulting other MSF managers. Although they did not underestimate the media and symbolic interest of this initiative, both for the refugees and for MSF, Claude Malhuret and MSF cofounder Xavier Emmanuelli nevertheless disputed its technical legitimacy: they considered a single ship insufficient to receive the host of refugees whom its presence encouraged to flee.

The correctness of this criticism, prompting MSF to withdraw from the operation, was confirmed by the new objective the committee assigned the ship, *L'Île de Lumière* (Island of Light), in April 1979. The vessel was no longer destined to receive boat people in the Chinese Sea, but was to become a hospital ship designed to treat the forty thousand Vietnamese refugees on Poulo Boudong island. This controversy led to the final split between the majority of MSF founders (except Xavier Emmanuelli and Raymond Borel) and the new generation in power. In 1979 Bernard Kouchner left MSF to found Médecins du Monde. He is now France's minister for humanitarian affairs.

Focus on Funding Stability

From 1979 to 1986 the budget and activities of MSF expanded at a galloping pace. This growth was partly due to the "favorable" international context in the beginning of the 1980s and to the right technical and strategic choices made by the new association managers. Three men held the reins after Bernard Kouchner's departure: Claude Malhuret, Francis Charhon, and myself. We three faced grass-roots MSF members who were still full of reservations toward what they considered a denial of MSF's original values of volunteerism and democratic association. Our task was to convince these members that structural changes could ensure MSF's survival and growth. Those changes included adoption of a salaried administrative system and the organization of marketing (public relations and fund-raising), logistics, and medical departments. These we considered necessary to turn MSF into a powerful and effective organization.

To begin with, the association needed substantial and dependable financial resources. Although its funds had been increasing steadily since 1980, its financial structure remained extremely fragile, depending mainly on the international economic situation—that is, isolated and spontaneous donations from institutions (EEC, UNHCR) or private individuals who had become aware of MSF's work as a result of events covered by the media (for example, the influx of Indochinese refugees in Thailand, the Soviet invasion of Afghanistan, the famine in Uganda, the Polish siege, and the Lebanese war).

MSF France roughly tripled its income between 1979 and 1980 (from $1.5 to $4.3 million) as a result of media-generated voluntary donations. But this financing method, which is actually anything but a method, has its limits. In 1981 income remained at $4.3 million. In 1982 Claude Malhuret began to introduce direct-mail fund-raising techniques based on observations of the success of these methods in American presidential elections. These techniques, at the time unknown in France, for the first time gave MSF regular income (private donations account for two-thirds of MSF's receipts), making it less dependent on political changes and institutional donors (who account for one-third of MSF's income). These fund-raising techniques, combined with the international solidarity shown in 1984 to fight the Ethiopian famine, boosted MSF's budget from $4.2 million in 1981 to $33.7 million in 1985. Between 1986 and 1991, this figure roughly doubled again, to $64.4 million.

From the mid-1980s funding for nearly all emergency missions of MSF was donated by the EEC Emergency Aid Fund. While crucial, this assistance did not lessen the need for MSF to raise money privately, since private funds enabled MSF to launch emergency missions without having to wait for the EEC to release the promised sums. While MSF accepts EEC and UNHCR financing, it refuses grants from the French government in order to preserve its independence.

Transition to the Technical

Upgraded by increasing financial resources, MSF's interventions also improved in effectiveness by the in-depth overhaul of its technical structures. First, MSF decided that its doctors should no longer be asked to work without compensation, both at headquarters, where full-time doctors had been active since 1979 to direct MSF missions, and in the field, where members became entitled to receive a travel allowance and a token salary allowance of $700 per month. Second, the salaried staff at the Paris-based headquarters was expanded (to approximately twenty employees in 1985) as technical units grew. Third, the recruitment efforts were better organized to include more screening and better orientation training; in the early 1980s the number of doctors and nurses sent out increased considerably, to 400–600 departures per year.

MSF has developed a standardized recruitment process designed to match qualified health care professionals with appropriate projects. The organization seeks general practitioners; specialists such as surgeons, anesthesiologists, obstetrician-gynecologists, and ophthalmologists; registered nurses; midwives; and public health and nutrition experts. MSF does not actively recruit participants, but instead chooses from among those who express interest and apply. Candidates submit a written application detailing medical training, professional experience (especially expertise with tropical medicine), foreign language ability, and availability and flexibility. Applicants are then interviewed by MSF recruiters with field experience, who evaluate the candidates' motivation and ability to function and live with a MSF team. Once selected, candidates are placed on a recruitment reserve list.

As MSF staff identifies open field positions, they select candidates from the reserve list for particular missions. If a candidate agrees to go on a mission, he or she is sent the appropriate MSF medical guidelines, as well as information about, for example, inoculations, clothing, and insurance. Finally, the volunteer is encouraged to use the MSF library to gather additional information and attends a briefing session in Paris before departing on the mission.

The Logistics Revolution

The expansion of MSF's logistics department marked an important intellectual and technical revolution for the organization's future. From the refugee camps in Thailand and Somalia, where supplies had to be provided for very large units (up to forty persons), came the awareness that nonmedical activities are frequently needed to ensure the effective provision of medical services.

In 1981 logistics problems had grown to the point of paralyzing medical activity in the field. To solve this crisis, MSF appointed a full-time logistics manager in Paris, who was assisted by a few logistics experts in the field. The logistics managers in turn created the system of rapid response and support for which MSF has gained so much attention.

In summary, this logistics revolution has three central components: communications, transportation, and prepackaged kits for immediate response. The communications logistics gave rise to the establishment of radio links between Paris and the field. Now satellite transmission dishes arrive in the field with staff so that they will not be without instant access to the Mother Ship, MSF's Paris headquarters, and to the outside world. The transportation logistics were developed in collaboration with the French organization Aviation sans Frontières (ASF), thereby creating priority transport capability. For the ground, MSF bought cars and coordinated more efficiently its staff travel arrangements.

Finally, the logistics experts worked with medical experts to develop a sophisticated inventory of arranged medical and field supplies. MSF faces competing challenges to respond quickly to emergency situations while adapting each response to specific and dramatically different conditions, locations, and types of medical problems. Often the nature and extent of the situation can be known only after an exploratory team has been dispatched or the volunteers have arrived to begin work at a mission site.

As a result, MSF has developed kits—ready-to-be-dispatched packages containing the hundreds of medical and nonmedical supplies that are necessary to accomplish specific tasks but are so time-consuming to gather from scratch (witness the time lost in responding to Hurricane Andrew). Upon evaluating conditions and needs in the face of an emergency, MSF personnel determine the types and quantity of kits to be deployed from a ready selection of some fifty kits that includes a basic medical kit, an emergency health kit, a vaccination kit, and a surgical kit. Kits are composed of modules, or groups of basic supplies, such as bandages, that can be restocked as needed during operation at a field location. Since the kits are stocked in advance, all materials in them have been selected and tested, and are ready for use; and the cost, weight, and size of specific kits are known. By using standard kits in combination, supplemented as needed by additional modules, MSF is able to adapt quickly to new or changing situations.

The size and completeness of the kits sometimes surprise observers who are unfamiliar with MSF. For example, to furnish medical assistance to a displaced population of thirty thousand persons in an isolated area, MSF might elect to deploy three emergency health kits capable of serving ten thousand persons each for a period of three months, as well as various kits providing energy sources, all-terrain vehicles, office supplies, satellite communications equipment, and other equipment and tools. Each emergency health kit would include modules of medicines, selected in accordance with MSF's medical protocols, and other basic medical supplies, such as bandages, rubber gloves, thermometers, and syringes. Then, if an MSF exploratory team were to identify the risk of, say, a cholera epidemic in the population, MSF would be prepared to deploy immediately an additional kit containing the medicines and supplies necessary to combat cholera. In 1987 MSF set up a logistics base in Lézignan, in the south of France, responsible for buying, storing, preparing, and testing kits designed for missions.

The progress made by MSF with its kits projects enabled it in the spring of 1991, within the space of ten days, to send seventy-five airplanes loaded with 2,500 tons of equipment to help the hundreds of thousands of Kurdish refugees who had fled Iraq. This progress also increased the effectiveness of MSF's interventions after certain natural disasters. Its missions after the earthquakes in Nicaragua, Algeria, and Mexico had been useful for its image but somewhat ineffective for the victims. MSF emergency units frequently arrived too late at the sites of the earthquakes, which were by then saturated by too much aid. Individuals who had been seriously wounded were already dead, and the others had been taken care of by local medical structures. After the

1986 earthquake in El Salvador and the 1988 earthquake in Armenia, MSF decided no longer to provide earthquake victims with direct medical aid but to operate in the background by treating benign pathologies, in order to leave local hospitals space for truly serious cases, and by using new kits to build shelters, drinking-water reservoirs, or sanitary facilities, in order to offer temporary replacements for infrastructures destroyed by the disaster.

The New Accountability

The period from 1979 until 1986 was for MSF marked by spectacular interventions, which were useful for their symbolic impact, more than by technically irreproachable interventions, even though MSF's effectiveness improved gradually. The reverse occurred between 1986 and 1992: while MSF stepped up its intervention capacity, it had more and more difficulty in attracting media coverage to the wrenching humanitarian problems it witnessed.

While increasing MSF's financial strength, the Ethiopian mission in 1984 revealed certain new technical weaknesses. Awareness of this situation was hastened by the arrival of a generation of doctors who were less politically oriented and more technically minded than the previous generation. These doctors expected to have more technical resources at their disposal.

In response MSF drafted medical guidelines containing standard procedures and protocols. Approximately forty books of guidelines exist, covering basic medical practice, as well as specialties such as surgery and ophthalmology. In addition, MSF organized specialized nutrition, vaccination, and sanitation departments. For example, medical actions in refugee camps must always deal with sanitary problems (well purification, construction of latrines, waste-water discharge) to prevent typhus or cholera epidemics. In recognition of these requirements, MSF in 1986 created Epicentre, a group of epidemiological experts charged with evaluating and improving MSF's work in the field, and with disseminating the results of its research. The creation of Epicentre also gave MSF the means to retain doctors whose experience and skills were much in demand and who would otherwise leave MSF for better-paying jobs at other international organizations.

Aggressive Concepts

From 1979 to 1986 wars and refugee camps became more than ever the preserve of MSF. The conflicts started at the end of the 1970s were followed by wars in Chad and Uganda and the war between Iran and Iraq. The end of the decade was marked by the largest communist expansion in Third World history, including the Sandinista revolution in Nicaragua, the Vietnamese invasion of Cambodia, and, above all, the Soviet invasion of Afghanistan. In the early 1980s the United States decided to react to the Soviet advance. Ronald Reagan, the newly elected U.S. president, led a crusade against communism, supporting several counterrevolutionary guerrilla movements. Regional conflicts, the center of the U.S.-Soviet struggle, continued and compounded the problem of refugees along the borders of warring nations.

MSF intervened mainly in five world regions where the East-West antagonism was at its worst: Central America (MSF worked in Nicaragua and with the Salvadoran refugees in Honduras), southern Africa (MSF worked in Angola, together with UNITA, and in Mozambique, together with the government), the African Horn (MSF had missions in Sudan, Somalia, and Ethiopia, as well as Chad and Uganda), the Middle East (it worked in Iranian Kurdistan; Afghanistan; and Lebanon, successively with the Christians, the Palestinians, the Druze, and the pro-Syrians), and in Southeast Asia (MSF worked in Thailand, for the Indochinese and Karen refugees).

As it continued its interventions, MSF strengthened its position as an original player in international relations, thanks to its aggressive concept of humanitarian action. To enforce application of the principles guiding its action (right of access to victims, inspection of application of aid, and protection of humanitarian workers), MSF was ready to violate the two intangible principles imposed on ICRC workers: respect for national sovereignty and the duty to remain silent. These duties MSF violated by speaking out (in Cambodia, Afghanistan, and Ethiopia) and by conducting clandestine missions (in Afghanistan, Kurdistan, El Salvador, and Eritrea).

In 1980 MSF organized the March for the Survival of Cambodia in order to denounce, for all to see, the looting of Cambodia's economy by its Vietnamese invaders, and the inability of MSF workers to enter the country, even though the nutritional and medical condition of refugees received in Thailand showed that the situation was extreme.

In Afghanistan, where MSF intervened clandestinely just a few months after the Soviet invasion, the organization undertook one of the most dangerous assignments in its history. Here, more than in any other country or conflict, MSF made incarnate the right of all victims to be treated. MSF's stance in Afghanistan set it apart, alone, from American relief organizations and ICRC. For many years, together with the teams of other French organizations, the 550 MSF doctors and nurses who relayed each other for ten years on Afghan territory were the only foreign humanitarians assisting the Afghan resistance fighters. Because of its rarity, the medical assistance offered by MSF gave the Afghans valuable psychological and political support. French doctors were their link with the West to make the international community aware of their struggle, especially from the fall of 1981 onward, when the Red Army began to bomb the hospitals in which MSF was working. At the time, MSF decided to denounce the Soviet exactions and to encourage journalists to visit Afghanistan. MSF even pressured the U.S. Congress to vote for the delivery of Stinger missiles to the resistance fighters.

The Expulsion Lesson

In Ethiopia, MSF continued its outspoken attitude, achieving a precise objective. In the spring of 1984 the organization began to send medical units to this country to help fight the famine. At the end of that year the Ethiopian government began to move the northern population victimized by the drought to fertile regions in the south. When MSF assisted with the first transfers, it saw no reason for criticism. After all, what was more logical than to move people from arid regions to fertile ones? The violence observed at times by MSF members was attributed to isolated problems rather than to deliberate policy. In order to continue their humanitarian work, the doctors decided to remain silent.

The transfers became more authoritarian in early 1985, and the "problems" more and more frequent. MSF members witnessed roundups of hospitalized persons, noticing that no efforts were made to keep families together. Many persons died in transfer. The zone where those being transferred were settled was frequently without adequate facilities or assistance, and the Ethiopian authorities established food quotas in Addis Ababa. Furthermore, the transfers diverted many resources from the MSF rescue operations.

By autumn I became aware of the political and ideological logic behind the transfers, carried out with the twofold aim of weakening the guerrilla movements in the north (in Eritrea and Tigre) by removing their grass-roots supporters and of putting these populations in villages in order to bring them ideologically in line with government policy. Under this fiendish plan, humanitarian aid was used to attract candidates and blackmail them into going along with the program. After lodging many fruitless protests with the Ethiopian authorities, MSF decided in November 1985 that, regardless of the consequences to itself, the organization could no longer remain silent. If it did so, MSF could appear to be condoning the brutality of these transfers, already responsible for more deaths than the famine (100,000 victims, according to MSF reports).

The presence of a host of NGOs in Ethiopia made it less difficult for MSF to denounce the transfer practices in public and enabled MSF to take the risk of expulsion. A few days after officially requesting the discontinuance of the transfers, MSF was expelled from Ethiopia. MSF immediately briefed the media on the diversion of aid, used to oppress instead of help. A few days after MSF's expulsion, the EEC and the United States decided to make further aid conditional on the discontinuance of these forced population transfers. Thus pressured, the Ethiopian government announced in early 1986 that it would cease its resettlement program.

Since the departure of Bernard Kouchner, the leaders of MSF have limited their public declarations. MSF now speaks out only when it is the sole witness of an exaction or when its testimony is the last recourse, as when its medical aid is stopped (Cambodia), attacked (Afghanistan), or diverted for other purposes (Ethiopia). MSF does not systematically denounce all countries violating human rights, but only those that prevent MSF from exercising its right of access to victims.

The Internationalization of MSF

The growth of MSF also led to its internationalization in the early 1980s. The MSF movement, while born in France, was enriched by the organization of Belgian, Dutch, and Swiss chapters in 1980 and 1984. Between 1986 and 1990, this expansion continued with the creation of chapters in Spain, Luxembourg, and Greece, and then the United States, Canada, and Japan. After serious competitive tensions between French, Belgian, and Dutch members in the period from 1984 until 1988, MSF's international structure has finally matured. Today many emergency missions are coordinated at the European level. The chapter managers meet regularly to decide on main lines and organization. In 1990 an international secretariat was created to ensure coordination between all MSF chapters and offices. This international-ization enables MSF to exercise wide and more diversified influence. For example, after the 1982 intervention of the French Army in Chad, the French MSF chapter assigned its mission in Chad to the Belgian chapter, in order to stress the independence of the latter's work.

In 1990, Médecins sans Frontières USA/Doctors without Borders was introduced in the United States. Based in New York City, its purpose is to raise funds for relief projects conducted in the field by MSF, to recruit American medical professionals to volunteer in the field, and to increase public awareness of MSF's work. As a nonprofit charitable corporation, MSF USA focuses its fund-raising activities on contributions from foundations, corporations, individuals, and institu-tions in the United States. MSF USA has awarded grants in support of several MSF missions, including aid to Kurdish and Somali refugees and to Romanian orphans. A Los Angeles office opened in 1991.

MSF Tomorrow

While the structure of MSF has changed over the years, the location of its missions has hardly changed at all: eastern Africa (Uganda, Sudan, Somalia), southern Africa (Angola, Mozambique, Malawi), Southeast Asia (Thailand, Indochina, Sri Lanka, Bangladesh), the Middle East (Afghanistan, Pakistan, Iraqi Kurdistan), and Central America (Honduras, El Salvador, Guatemala).

All of these areas still confront the problem of refugees. This issue was complicated in the 1980s by the downgrade of the status of refu-gees and the peaceful settlement of a number of conflicts, as well as the forced repatriation of populations to their original countries (Cam-bodia, Vietnam, Sri Lanka). MSF made every effort to check the conditions in which such actions were carried out.

The only geographic novelty in this period was MSF's discovery of humanitarian needs on its own continent. With the collapse of commu-nism in Eastern Europe and the continuing economic crisis in Western Europe, MSF began to participate in the effort to restore the public health systems in Romania, Bulgaria, and certain republics of the former USSR. To achieve this aim, it opened dispensaries in France and Belgium in order to provide medical treatment for the steadily increasing number of people who did not qualify for the public health systems of these countries.

On October 19, 1991, MSF sent a humanitarian convoy to evacuate casualties from the besieged Croatian city of Vukovar. Several previous rescue attempts had failed, and the convoy was allowed to proceed only after protracted negotiations with the Yugoslav Army and Croatian authorities. The twelve-vehicle convoy successfully evacuated an estimated 109 wounded soldiers and civilians. As it headed out of the city, however, one of the trucks struck a mine, and two MSF nurses sustained serious injuries.

This incident occurred despite the strictly humanitarian nature of the operation and despite assurances of safe passage from both sides of the conflict. Concern for the safety of volunteers placed MSF in the difficult position of having to rule out any attempts to rescue the remaining wounded in Vukovar's hospital.

The end of the Cold War has multiplied the number of conflicts in which the universal values underlying humanitarian action are less and less respected. In 1989 a missile destroyed an ASF airplane in Sudan, killing two MSF members on board. In 1990 an MSF logistics expert was assassinated in Afghanistan. MSF is also facing serious violence and safety problems in Iraq, former Yugoslavia, Somalia (where its units are protected by armed militia), Liberia, Mozambique, and Sri Lanka.

These ethnic conflicts and the populations victimized by them are increasingly ignored by the international community. MSF has great difficulty in arousing interest for the extremely worrisome scourges threatening southern Africa and the African Horn today. These problems and MSF's evolving response to them will form the basis of the MSF experience of the next twenty years.

14

Coping with Disasters: From Diarrhea to Cyclones

FAZLE H. ABED

B angladesh does not appear very often in international news coverage. But when it does, it usually captures world headlines because of some environmental or natural disaster. In reporting the stories of tragedy, human misery, and suffering that befall our country, the media do not always tell the whole story. We hardly ever come across reports of the many successes that take place in Bangladesh, or the indomitable courage and resoluteness that its people show in facing difficult odds. The story of Bangladesh does include a saga of actions by its people, a saga of hope for a better and more respectable future. In this paper we wish to bring to your attention two such stories—an account of how the people have learned to deal with the everyday problem (disaster) of diarrheal disease, which kills thousands of Bangladeshi children every year, and the sudden violent disasters caused by cyclones that strike our coastal areas.

Coping with Diarrhea

As in most other developing countries, diarrhea is an important cause of mortality and morbidity in Bangladesh.[1] It is a major factor in the low nutritional level of the population. Over 250,000 people, mostly children, are estimated to die from diarrhea annually.[2] Among children under five years of age, nearly a third of deaths are due to this disease. Bangladesh is, incidentally, the country where oral rehydration therapy (ORT) was developed and perfected in the late 1960s. Little attempt was made, however, until the early 1980s to make this wonder therapy, which one medical journal called the most significant medical advance of this century, widely available to the people.

The Bangladesh Rural Advancement Committee (BRAC), which has been working with the rural poor of Bangladesh since 1972, identified diarrhea as a major health problem right from the start. The International Year of the Child in 1979 provided BRAC with an impetus to think about programs that would significantly contribute to children's survival. Field-testing of ORT by the International Centre for Diarrhoeal Disease Research, Bangladesh (ICDDR,B) had shown its potential. Also, work with ORT among Bangladeshi refugees in the Calcutta area during the 1971 Liberation War had shown what ORT could do in epidemic situations. All these considerations led BRAC to embark on a nationwide ORT program. The decision to undertake this large-scale program forced BRAC to choose carefully between distributing oral rehydration salt (ORS) packets and teaching mothers how to mix and use a homemade solution. Research at BRAC and ICDDR,B had found that a pinch of salt and a fistful of unrefined sugar mixed in half a liter of water produced a solution with most of the qualities of the packets. BRAC had found that it was possible to teach village women how to make the solution and at the same time teach them a short, seven-point message about diarrhea prevention and treatment. Furthermore, BRAC felt strongly that even if sufficient quantities of ORS could be produced, packaged, and marketed, poor people, particularly in remote areas, would not have either physical or economic access to it. Thus, BRAC decided that its nationwide effort would focus on teaching mothers to make the solution it had developed. In the early months of 1979 BRAC started to work with thirty thousand families at Sulla, the organization's first field project site. This became the testing ground for effective teaching methods and for working out the management and logistics necessary to scale up the program and maintain quality control. In early 1980 BRAC launched its nationwide effort to teach oral rehydration therapy to every one of the thirteen million village households in the country.

Backed by an experienced group of managers and a well-developed management information system, teams of female workers trained by BRAC (called oral replacement workers, or ORWs) went house to house, teaching village women how to make the solution properly and how to give it to their children. The teaching method and materials were carefully structured and based on an intelligent use of local belief systems; the ORWs were recruited from villages in the same regions of the country where they worked. Under an incentive salary plan, the ORWs were paid according to the quality of their teaching. Monitoring teams followed them into villages a fortnight later, interviewing a random sample of 5 percent of village women to find out how well they had understood and learned the messages, and collecting samples of solutions mixed by the women, which they would send to laboratories for testing of the electrolyte contents. A worker's pay was determined by how correctly the sampled mothers could prepare the solution and the number of messages they could recall spontaneously from the basic seven. Supervision of the ORWs as they moved from village to village was strict but supportive.[3] An active management information system remained in place throughout, and an able evaluation division studied the program as it progressed. The latter provided feedback to management on aspects of the program that needed further research or improvement in implementation. Teaching materials and training were modified and improved constantly. One month after the first fifty thousand mothers had been trained, surveys found that although over 90 percent displayed adequate message retention and mixing skills, the oral rehydration solution was used in only 5 percent of diarrheal episodes. Analysis of the situation revealed a major deficiency in the implementation strategy: the program had focused on women alone, but since men were important decision-makers in the family, it was difficult for the women to administer ORT without the concurrence of their husbands, their fathers, or other men in the family. Accordingly, the program was modified to include male teachers whose job was to hold meetings and seminars with men in mosques, marketplaces, and schools. The inclusion of men in the target group very quickly increased ORS use to 20 percent.

Anthropological research studies revealed further problems. In some parts of rural Bangladesh, people recognized four types of diarrhea, for which they had different names and treatments. Only one of these types—a severe, watery diarrhea—was known to the women by the Bengali equivalent of "diarrhea." Since the classification into four types had been unknown to the ORWs, in the initial teaching they had used the Bangladeshi equivalent of the term "diarrhea." As a result, the mothers thought the solution was for that type only.[4] In the early stages of the program ORS was being used for 52 percent of that type of diarrhea, but not for the other types (see Table 1). This discovery led to a change in terminology and a major change in the seven points to remember.[5]

TABLE 1. *Percentage of Reported Diarrheal Episodes Treated with BRAC Solution, by Type of Diarrhea, Three Program Areas*

	Program Area		
Diarrhea Type	1	2	3
Dud haga	2.0	12.2	12.3
Ajirno	4.0	7.9	9.8
Amasa	1.6	2.9	4.0
Daeria	25.6	31.6	52.2
All diarrhea	4.1	8.2	9.9

Source: A. M. R. Chowdhury and J. P. Vaughan, "Perception of Diarrhoea and the Use of a Homemade ORS in Rural Bangladesh," *Journal of Diarrhoeal Disease Research*, vol. 6 (1988), pp. 6–14.
Note: Dud haga is a diarrhea in infants believed (by mothers) to be caused by "polluted" breast milk. *Ajirno* is a diarrhea caused by indigestion. *Amasa* is a mucoid diarrhea (dysentery). *Daeria* is severe watery diarrhea or cholera.

Despite the promising initial results, surveys conducted up to twelve months after women learned about ORT found a decline from over 90 percent to 70 percent in the mothers' ability to prepare a safe and effective solution.[6] Three factors accounted for this decline: a reduced emphasis by ORWs on the danger of using too much salt; a rapid expansion of the program, leading to a shortage of experienced managers; and mothers' forgetfulness because of the infrequent use of ORS.[7] BRAC responded to this by retraining ORWs, reemphasizing the seven points, and initiating an expanded media campaign through radio and television. Later studies revealed an improved picture; retention after twelve months increased to 90 percent.[8]

In November 1990, more than a decade after the nationwide ORT teaching effort began, BRAC completed teaching the therapy to the last of the thirteen million village households. ORT is now an accepted part of the treatment of diarrhea throughout the country; in fact, it is now becoming a part of the country's folk culture.[9] A recent study of 11–12-year-olds' knowledge of important "life skills" found that 70 percent of participants knew how to prepare oral rehydration salts. Most of these children had not been born or had been very young at the time their mothers were taught about ORT.[10]

BRAC has not been alone in promoting ORT. The government has started a national program, and many nongovernmental organizations have come forward to promote the method. A number of pharmaceutical companies now sell their own ORS brands, and the sales are shooting up. During the disastrous floods and cyclones of 1991 and 1992, when numerous relief operations were carried out, ORS was the most commonly used relief item. Many voluntary groups started makeshift ORS production centers and produced millions of packets of ORS that were distributed to affected people. Whereas the pre-1980 floods or cyclones invariably resulted in many deaths due to outbreaks of diarrhea, the diarrhea epidemics following the recent floods and cyclones had far less impact on the people's health, largely because of the widespread knowledge of diarrhea prevention and knowledge of ORS and its availability.

This ORT program provided several important lessons for Bangladesh, for BRAC, for donors, and for health professionals. The program exploded the myth that poor village women cannot be taught basic health messages. It also dispelled the perception that NGOs are capable of only small, localized activities of little consequence nationally. Furthermore, it dispelled any notions that health programs are necessarily less effective if implemented on a large scale. It taught BRAC managers to think nationally, and inspired confidence to "go to scale" in other programs. Finally, the program confirmed the potential of lay workers to convey useful health information and change health behavior.

Coping with Cyclones

The Bay of Bengal is a natural breeding place for tropical cyclones. Of all the earth's tropical cyclones, 10 percent are formed in there.[11] The bay's geography—its tropical location, the shape of the landmass that forms Bangladesh, the Himalayas lying to the north, and the funnel-shaped coastline touching the bay—makes it all the more susceptible to such disasters.[12] On average, five tropical storms are formed every year in the bay;[13] half of them turn into cyclones, and at least one cyclone every two years gathers strength and takes a path that makes it potentially dangerous for Bangladesh.

The land that is now called Bangladesh has historically been prey to these cyclones. The first recorded cyclone hit a village in the Chittagong area during the sixteenth century, killing a large number of people and destroying all the buildings except a temple.[14] The cyclone of June 1775 destroyed all the buildings in Chittagong town except five. A description of a cyclone in 1876 is available from the account of a British civil servant:

> 31st October was a night of the full moon. Sea level was naturally higher than usual high tide levels. Severe wind was blowing from 10 PM to 3 AM and it prevented the normal discharge of Meghna river into the Bay. By 8 AM on 1st November the wind grew fiercer and hit the coastal area of Chittagong, Feni, Laxmipur, Bhola, Patuakhali, Barisal, Jhalakati and Khulna Districts. The accompanying tidal surge ranged from 18.29 to 9.14 metres in various places. It hit Chittagong with a surge 3.66 metres high. 12,000 people died in Chittagong due to this cyclone. An epidemic that followed the tidal bore killed 14,778 persons. In other affected areas 100,000 people died of the cyclone and the tidal surge, and the subsequent epidemics took a toll of 200,000 people. In Chittagong area alone more than 60,000 boats and ships were sunk, battered or destroyed by the cyclone.[15]

Over the last thirty years, thirty-five severe cyclones hit the coasts of Bangladesh; at least seventeen led to human casualties. The 1970 cyclone in which 500,000 people perished was the most disastrous in terms of human losses. But much was learned from that terrible event, as described below.

THE CYCLONE OF APRIL 1991

On the night of April 29–30, 1991, the coastal areas of Bangladesh were struck by a severe cyclone accompanied by a tidal surge from the Bay of Bengal. Nearly five million people in eight of sixty-four districts were affected. In terms of human losses, this cyclone was the worst since the cyclone of 1970. According to government estimates, over 130,000 people perished,[16] and property worth $2.4 billion, equivalent to the national annual development expenditures for two years, was destroyed.[17]

Although the wind speed and the height of the tidal surge were similar in the cyclones of 1970 and 1991, the later one caused far fewer casualties. Several reasons may explain this. Following the cyclones of the early 1960s, the government constructed a number of concrete buildings to serve as places of refuge at the time of an impending cyclone. A total of sixty double-story coastal community centers and forty single-story subcoastal community centers were constructed. This was clearly not enough, and the structures were not appropriately placed. Following the cyclone of 1970, the government, with support from the World Bank, constructed 238 multipurpose "cyclone shelters" in coastal areas, the areas historically most affected by cyclones. In the 1980s the Bangladesh Red Crescent Society (BRCS) and a local NGO called Caritas built an additional seventy-four cyclone shelters.[18] The government also constructed over 150 *killas* (artificial hills), mainly to protect household animals. Following the 1985 cyclone at Urirchar,[19] the government, in collaboration with the governments of India and Pakistan, built 260 nucleus houses for rehabilitating survivors. India also built a central cyclone shelter, and Pakistan a big mosque (which was used as shelter during the 1991 cyclone). Although the number of shelters available was insignificant compared to the need, they saved many lives. One study on the 1991 cyclone estimated that at least 20 percent more deaths would have occurred if these shelters had not been present.[20]

The cyclone warning system in Bangladesh has undergone tremendous development since the cyclone of 1970. A tropical depression is first detected from the satellite network by the Space Research and Remote Sensing Organization, based in Dhaka. This information is then forwarded to the meteorological department, which tracks the cyclone and issues regular bulletins on its location, its wind speed, and the areas it is likely to strike. These bulletins are circulated through the press, radio, and television. There are eleven cyclone warning signals. The number of a signal indicates the distance, speed, and direction of the wind. The different signals, however, are intended more as warnings for ships and ports than for the inhabitants of the coastal region.

Cyclone preparedness has taken off commendably. BRCS has over twenty thousand village-based volunteers, all located in coastal areas. The Cyclone Preparedness Program of BRCS transmits the danger warnings to these volunteers through its network of district and subdistrict control offices. The volunteers, in turn, alert people through megaphones and house-to-house contact, and encourage them to head for nearby shelters (if available) or safer places.

Last, embankments have been constructed in most areas along the coastline to resist the initial thrust of the cyclone. Though the 1991 cyclone destroyed the embankment in many places, the embankments were able to weaken the initial onslaught.[21]

THE POSTCYCLONE SITUATION

Contrary to popular expectations, the situation during the postcyclone period was well under control. The whole nation rallied to provide succor to the survivors. Consequently, there were no major postcyclone disasters such as epidemic disease or food shortage. In contrast to the situation of previous cyclones, related deaths occurred only during the storm and the surge, not in the postcyclone period.

The Public-sector Response. The response from the public sector was immediate and firm. The newly elected democratic government had just taken over. The prime minister established, and chaired, a relief and rehabilitation coordination committee. All the available resources were placed under the committee, which met daily. Two appointed zonal relief coordinators, with the rank of secretary to the government, coordinated the relief and rehabilitation activities in the field. Senior government officers were deputized to the district and subdistrict levels to oversee the relief and rehabilitation activities. In each tier—the district, subdistrict, or below—relief coordination committees were set up. All the local resources were placed under the direction of these committees. Local elected representatives, public-sector departments, and NGOs worked in close coordination. Everything was mobilized very quickly. For example, electricity in the city of Chittagong was restored within three days of the disaster.

The survival relief phase, aimed at saving the people from hunger and disease and providing immediate medical care and shelter,[22] continued for eleven days, until May 10. Supplies—mainly food items and clothes—were air-dropped, and fast-moving naval vessels were used to ship relief supplies to inaccessible areas.

At the same time, the government appealed for support to friendly governments and international agencies, and received very positive responses. Relief materials and transport vehicles such as helicopters and naval ships from friendly countries arrived in the affected areas within a few days. A joint Bangladesh-U.S. task force, code-named Operation Sea Angel, with helicopters, Hovercraft, and other fast-moving vehicles, provided timely support in lifting food and other essential items, such as tubewells for drinking water and generators for electricity, to the affected areas.

The emergency relief phase, which was also designed to help people get back to normal life, continued until June 30. This phase continued the supply of food, clothing, and emergency medicine, and
the restoration of drinking water, electricity supply, transportation,
and agriculture.

The NGO Response. The large NGO community maintained its
tradition of quickly responding to a disaster situation. BRAC's response is one such example. After receiving the news from a radio
broadcast that the coastal area was hit by a cyclone and that communication with the area was snapped, we at BRAC met at eleven o'clock
on the morning of April 30 to take stock of the situation. Since not
much information was reaching Dhaka, we sent a senior manager to
Chittagong the same day. On the following day, I, along with senior
colleagues from BRAC and the Dhaka representative of the Ford
Foundation, went to Chittagong. Several teams of BRAC workers
were already fielded in the area for an immunization program, and we
mobilized them for relief work. A central relief control office was set up
in Chittagong, with a senior director of BRAC as its coordinator. We
were able to mobilize nearly $1 million from within and outside the
country, and provided relief to nearly 200,000 who had been affected
by the cyclone. The rehabilitation phase concentrated on continuing
supply of food, clothing, medical, and housing assistance, as well as
creating jobs to rehabilitate the people in their own environment and
situation. (See appendix 1 for a chronology of BRAC activities in
cyclone relief.) In one of the subdistricts, with a population of 100,000,
BRAC later initiated a long-term development project for the poor that
includes education, health, institution building, and poverty alleviation. This project also includes building sixteen concrete structures
that will be used as schools during normal times and as shelters during
a cyclone.[23]

NGOs did not stop at providing relief and rehabilitation services.
Researchers were commissioned to study the epidemiology of cyclone
deaths, people's perceptions about the warning system, the effectiveness of the cyclone shelters, and the nutrition impact and morbidity
effects of the cyclone.[24]

It was not only BRAC that was involved in this task. Almost all
national-level NGOs participated, and the coordination role was provided by the Association of Development Agencies in Bangladesh, the
central coordinating body of NGOs in Bangladesh. The coastal area
was new to many of these organizations. NGO staff who had been
working in the area provided orientation to their new colleagues.[25]

The Bureau of NGO Affairs, a government body designated to oversee NGO interest in the government, was effective in facilitating emergency relief operations of the NGOs. Waiving its usual requirements, the bureau allowed NGOs to work without receiving prior permission.

The Public's Response. People from all walks of life reacted to the news of the cyclone with shock. They clearly became united at the time of national emergency and gave overwhelming and enthusiastic support to the relief effort.

Individuals, political parties, cultural groups, student organizations, women's groups, and trade unions were all active in providing relief and succor. Many groups and individuals went to the cyclone-affected areas with relief materials, while others provided whatever they could afford in cash, clothes, food, utensils, and medicine. In Kutubdia, a small island with a population of 100,000, eighteen medical teams worked to take care of the injured and the diseased. A similar response was witnessed in 1988, when more than half of the country went underwater following a devastating flood.

THE AFTEREFFECTS

The above discussion shows how Bangladesh faced the 1991 cyclone—a massive disaster by any proportion. Contrary to popular expectations, there was hardly any postcyclone disaster. There were no postcyclone deaths from epidemic or food shortage. The government and NGOs, with logistical support from within and outside the country, transported the required amount of foodstuffs to the affected areas. The distribution system was much better organized than previous ones, and very well coordinated. There was no report of any major misappropriation of relief goods.

Studies on postcyclone morbidity found little evidence of any major epidemics. The prevalence of diarrhea in children during the third week of June (the cyclone struck on April 29–30) was 10 percent, an expected figure for that time of year.[26]

Observations on the use of ORS in the field were much more encouraging than survey reports in nonemergency situations. People's knowledge of ORT undoubtedly contributed to lower diarrhea mortality levels in the postcyclone period.

In Bangladesh more than 80 percent of the population have access to tubewell water. The cyclone and the tidal surge contaminated and damaged most of the tubewells. Because of the efforts made by the government, NGOs, and the people, the tubewells were ready for use within a few days. Use of tubewell water for drinking and washing utensils, in fact, increased during the postcyclone period. Children and women were seen walking long distances with pots to fetch water from tubewells not damaged by the cyclone. An international team studying the postcyclone water and sanitation sector was impressed by the functioning of the tubewell program, and found that the tubewell water was free from coliforms.[27]

The reason Bangladesh managed so well can be traced to a number of developments that occurred during the 1970s and 1980s. First, the unity of the entire nation provided the needed moral support to the distressed. Second, the new, democratic government received sympathy and support from the people and foreign donors. Third, the infrastructural development in terms of railways, roads, waterways, and air transport has grown impressively, making it easier to speedily provide relief and rehabilitation services to the affected areas. Fourth, the improvement in communications through inland telegraphic, telephonic, and satellite systems has helped immensely in coordinating postcyclone relief. Fifth, the huge network of health facilities and manpower, which has been in place for some time, has helped provide immediate medical support to the injured and the diseased. The spectacular success of the immunization program should be mentioned here. Between 1985 and 1990 the country's immunization coverage rose from 2 percent to 70 percent. Similarly, access to safe water has increased to 80 percent of the population, and the story on ORT has already been mentioned. Sixth, the capacity of the government to procure food and other materials has increased. This has been made possible because of the nation's increased foreign currency earnings through export and remittances. Government food grain stock went from 0.6–0.8 million tons in the 1970s to over 1.2 million tons during the late 1980s.[28] Seventh, the growth of the NGO sector has had a tremendous impact on the whole situation. With their base at the grass-roots level, enhanced management capacities, ability to act quickly, and improved credibility among donors, NGOs have proven to be an important and effective force. Last, the slow but important efforts to strengthen the economic base of the rural poor by NGOs such as Grameen Bank and BRAC have resulted in improved capacity of individual households to cope with natural disasters. The expansion of the irrigation facilities led to increased agricultural production throughout the year. The diversification of the rural employment sector has created employment opportunities for the poor in nonfarm sectors. Poorer households are now better prepared to face a disaster situation.[29]

Conclusion

Bangladesh, more than most societies, is affected with disastrous conditions caused by its environment. Two such problems are diarrheal disease and cyclones. Diarrheal disease, which traditionally has led to over 250,000 deaths annually, is an ongoing problem. Cyclones, which are born in the Bay of Bengal, periodically ravage coastal areas. But far from giving in to these conditions, the country has developed creative and innovative means of coping so as to significantly reduce illness and death. Two such approaches have been described: the Oral Therapy Extension Program of the Bangladesh Rural Advancement Committee, which has reached over thirteen million households to effectively treat and prevent diarrhea; and a national strategy to reduce the effects of cyclones. In both these instances, the Bangladesh community—citizens, NGOs, and government—responded with creative, adaptive, and effective approaches. Those experiences have much to offer others by demonstrating how local solutions to local problems can benefit not only one's own society but the world community.

Appendix 1.
BRAC 1991 Cyclone Relief Program:
Chronology of Events

April 30   BRAC's Chittagong office secures initial funds to commission relief activities.

Executive meeting takes place at BRAC headquarters in Dhaka to discuss extent of damage.

BRAC commissions 50,000 takas for victims of cyclone disaster.

May 1   Program chiefs meet to plan approaches for relief and rehabilitation.

May 2   Executive director, accompanied by BRAC's senior members, visits affected areas and holds program meeting with staff representatives from affected areas.

Relief operations are intensified in worst-hit areas.

May 3	Cyclone Relief Program (CRP) team is formed.
May 4	BRAC allocates 10 million takas for survival, emergency, and rehabilitation work.
	Relief reaches offshore islands, supported by Bangladesh Navy.
May 5	CRP team arrives at Chittagong to coordinate relief activities.
May 6	Bulk relief material—food, medicines, clothing—arrives at Chittagong for distribution among affected people.
	Relief purse is increased to 31 million takas.
May 10	Director of programs visits CRP operations.
May 14	Research work is initiated.
May 18	CRP reviews relief operations and develops rehabilitation plan.
May 24	CRP conducts performance review.
June 1	Rehabilitation plan is reviewed.
July 5	Rehabilitation planners meet.
	Decision is taken to rehabilitate the island Kutubdia.
August 3	Meeting on CRP progress takes place; decision is taken to close emergency relief and rehabilitation phase.
August 20	CRP concludes.
August 21	Post Cyclone Rehabilitation and Development Program is initiated.

Source: Bangladesh Rural Advancement Committee, *Cyclone Relief Programme 1991: The BRAC Response* (Dhaka: Bangladesh Rural Advancement Committee, 1991).

15

Making the Humanitarian System Work Better

LARRY MINEAR

As codirector of a three-year study, Humanitarianism and War: Learning the Lessons from Recent Armed Conflicts, I am engaged with colleagues in reviewing, from the ground up, how well the international humanitarian system is currently functioning.[1] At this early point in our study, we have done preliminary research on conflicts in more than a dozen countries, including Angola, Cambodia, El Salvador, Ethiopia/Eritrea, Guatemala, Iraq, Lebanon, Liberia, Mozambique, Nicaragua, Somalia, Sri Lanka, Sudan, and former Yugoslavia. We are also conducting comparative field research in the Horn of Africa, the Persian Gulf, and Central America, on the basis of which we are preparing a number of publications.

We have yet to reach definitive conclusions or to formulate overall recommendations. However, early evidence suggests that the performance of the current humanitarian system falls far short of reasonable expectations. It is difficult to find anyone associated with efforts to provide humanitarian aid and protect human rights who is happy with the status quo. Wherever we go, we are confronted by a litany of complaints about how the system works—or, as the case may be, fails to work. The criticisms come from governments and people in the affected areas, the international public, and aid practitioners themselves. None of the three major sets of international actors—United Nations organizations, bilateral aid agencies, and nongovernmental organizations—is immune to criticism.

Our evaluation of UN coordination of humanitarian activities during the Gulf crisis provides a case in point.[2] The UN is widely criticized for having responded slowly and ineffectively to the massive upheavals following Iraq's invasion of Kuwait in August 1990 and during Iraq's civil war half a year later. NGOs, widely credited with having responded with more alacrity, were nonetheless a fractious lot whose energy and drive were undercut by naïvete and confusion. Confronted with scores of NGOs descending upon Jordan, government authorities found it difficult, they told us, "to distinguish the charlatan from the humanitarian." For their part, donor governments, despite contributing substantial levels of resources, often seemed more interested in receiving credit than in the impact of their assistance.

One of the major weaknesses of the aid system in the Gulf was its heavy expatriate bias. Foreign medical personnel were brought in by international aid groups despite a surplus of resident Jordanian doctors. Drivers of relief vehicles in northern Iraq were paid more than local judges. Food imported for Iraqi refugees in Iran was offensive to religious traditions or unsuited to local tastes. Expatriate staff deportment left a great deal to be desired. The aid effort became a negative as well as a positive intervention. Local sensitivities were ignored, local institutions bypassed, and local resources marginalized.

Our general impression, based on interviews with more than two hundred participants in various aspects of the Gulf drama, was of an international system that, despite the efforts of many dedicated people, was not well functioning. It resembled a loose constellation of moving parts whose random motion at critical points received only the most general centripetal focus from the crisis. We understood the reluctance of people in the region, based on their earlier experience, to activate the international humanitarian apparatus in 1990–1991 and, based on experience during the Gulf crisis itself, to do so the next time around.

As researchers, we do not take all such criticisms at face value. Neither, however, do we dismiss them out of hand as coming from people who expect too much from the international system. On the contrary, we view the negative aspects of the Gulf experience—confirmed in large measure by that in theaters elsewhere and duly balanced against some clear successes—as grist for the learning mill. We take heart from the fact that major aid agencies, many of which are participants in our work, are themselves committed to making the system work better.

What follows is, in essence, a report on our work in progress. In the first three sections we examine the basic areas in which conventional wisdom requires rethinking: the nature of coordination, the comparative advantages of the actors, and the professionalism required for effective action. From clearer concepts in each respect, we believe, will flow needed operational changes.

In a concluding section and along the way, we indicate some of the concrete contributions our project will make. Our early findings and tentative recommendations, addressing humanitarian assistance in more detail than health and human rights issues, will suggest ways in which the world's framework for survival should be strengthened.

Coordination

Coordination is a desideratum of all aid activities, whether emergency or longer-term in nature. Since major crises routinely involve at least half a dozen UN organizations, scores of governments, and hundreds of NGOs, coordination is required to avoid duplication, waste, and competition. It helps keep costs down and assure that relief gets to those for whom it is intended. At this level of generality, there is little controversy.

What is less apparent, however, at least until the particulars of specific interventions are examined, is that coordination can be a very mixed blessing. Everyone reveres coordination, but few wish to be coordinated—for legitimate as well as self-serving reasons. Coordination can involve significant opportunity costs, impede quick action, centralize functions that are better decentralized, and politicize aid. Certainly coordination is not an end in itself. What is needed is not more coordination but better coordination.

We define coordination as the systematic utilization of policy instruments to deliver humanitarian assistance in a cohesive and effective manner. Such instruments include strategic planning, gathering data and managing information, mobilizing resources and assuring accountability, orchestrating field activities, negotiating a framework of action with the political authorities, and providing leadership to aid efforts. A review of the actual utilization of these instruments demonstrates some of the more problematic aspects of coordination.

The area of strategic planning provides an illustration of the *oppor-*

tunity costs involved. One of the charges given by the UN General Assembly and the secretary-general to the new Department of Humanitarian Affairs (DHA) is that it carry out systemwide planning for UN responses to major emergencies, on the basis of which consolidated appeals will be launched. Without doubt, an overall assessment of a given crisis and a multiagency response plan is preferable to individual UN agencies doing their own assessments and floating their own appeals. In its first half year of existence, DHA did precisely this for emergencies in southern Africa, the Horn of Africa, Kenya, Afghanistan, and former Yugoslavia. Governments have already expressed appreciation.

Carrying out this function, however, has been possible only because individual UN agencies have provided senior staff for lengthy consultations under DHA auspices in Geneva, underwriting their time and the sizable costs of their participation. But there are also hidden costs. Staff time thus allocated becomes unavailable for directing individual UN agency task forces and supervising actual relief operations. Ironically, the same governments that insist on improved coordination also demand that the UN's operational activities proceed apace and are reluctant to provide the necessary resources for both objectives to be achieved simultaneously.

On the national and local levels, too, there are trade-offs. At the peaks of emergencies, when coordinating sessions are often held on a daily basis, agencies must decide whether to commit limited time and resources to attending meetings or to relieving urgent need. Many agencies understandably opt for the latter, wishing to help people directly. Under the duress of emergencies, "coordinating," particularly when its results are frequently intangible, seems far less urgent than "doing."

Many who insist on coordination, be they governments or the general public, also insist that "overhead expenses" be kept to a minimum. With this in mind, some aid organizations waive all administrative costs for emergency operations. They also resist spending funds on activities that may have only indirect effects on those in need of relief, such as evaluation and staff training. Be that as it may, the management costs necessary for more effective activities are underestimated by the parliaments or public that support aid efforts. Yet coordination is anything but cost-free.

Coordination can also be a deterrent to *responsiveness,* for which the orchestration of field activities serves as an illustration. As just implied, there is a tension between responding quickly and as part of a concerted plan. Many of those with a tradition of being first off the mark—UNICEF on the UN side, Médecins sans Frontières and the International Committee of the Red Cross (ICRC) among the private groups—are the most wary of coordination. "UNICEF's priority is saving lives," says one official with operational responsibilities, "not coordination."

Therefore, according to Charles LaMunière, now DHA point person in Geneva charged with coordinating the UN's operational activities, the coordination challenge concerns "how you preserve the capacity of some of the constituent parts of the system to do some things more quickly and better than others would—and still keep the system as a whole in sync with itself." He continues, "Coordination should not be a delaying process reducing all interventions to their 'slowest' common denominator but rather a generator and enhancing mechanism for coherent multifaceted action."[3] In short, the system should welcome quicker-acting members' taking the lead on its behalf rather than any delaying action until all agencies are on board.

There are also unavoidable trade-offs between coordination and *decentralization.* The perceived role of headquarters in keeping activities in sync with each other exists in obvious tension with the delegation of authority to the field, where fast-moving developments demand quick action. "Reference back to headquarters on every move," commented one Jordanian official on the UN's approach to management and accountability during the Gulf crisis, "seems to take unnecessary time. The team on the ground should have the responsibility and be able to make decisions."[4]

Awareness has been growing that the ultimate test of program effectiveness is the strengthening of participatory institutions at the community level. "Promoting such institutions means promoting the empowerment of the unorganized, the poor, the marginalized," says Secretary-General Boutros Boutros-Ghali in a wide-ranging report on the United Nations of the future. "The focus of the United Nations should be on the 'field,' the locations where economic, social, and political decisions take effect."[5]

At the same time, widely divergent understandings exist about what "the field" really means. Does it mean Colombo and Managua rather than New York and Geneva, or does it mean the Jaffna Peninsula and Bluefields rather than Colombo and Managua? Obviously, the further decentralization is carried, the more difficult certain aspects of coordination become. As will be suggested in the following section, a more effective international framework for humanitarian action will require discriminating judgment about which aspects of coordination can best be performed at which levels.

In principle, devolution of certain responsibilities is a step toward a more effective humanitarian system. It takes into account the reality, observed by former World Food Programme Executive Director James C. Ingram, that "the appearance of improved coordination at the center is not necessarily a factor in more effective and timely interventions in the field."[6] At the same time, such devolution requires a revision of the traditional understanding of coordination as a highly centralized activity. Only some of the aforementioned coordination instruments should be used by headquarters; others need to be more fully delegated.

Finally, the better coordinated humanitarian activities are, the greater their susceptibility to *politicization*. The crucial task of negotiating a framework with host political authorities provides an illustration. Generally speaking, a well-coordinated system that presents a common front in negotiations with the authorities has a better chance in a conflict or disaster theater of arranging adequate humanitarian space within which all organizations may function. However, the authorities can also use such a system to control the activities of those agencies that choose to participate, and to increase the isolation of those that do not.

In 1990 the government of Sudan looked to the UN to coordinate the activities of NGOs involved in relief activities. It wanted to rein in the freewheeling approach of some groups that were functioning in insurgent-held areas of the south without government permission and were suspected of having airlifted military personnel and weapons to the Sudan People's Liberation Army.

In consultation with NGOs, the UN drafted a memorandum of association spelling out the terms of their relationships. Most NGOs signed, some after tacit assurance that the UN would not enforce its provisions strictly. Others resisted, despite pressure from the UN and government funders, fearing that the Sudanese government would put pressure on NGO activities through the UN, which was itself laboring under heavy political constraints from the Khartoum authorities.[7] Particularly in the politicized circumstances of civil strife, a more unitary system in which aid activities by the UN, donor governments, and NGOs alike take their marching orders from a single general can be a recipe for disaster.

Similarly, the government of Iraq viewed its memorandum of understanding negotiated in April 1991 and subsequently extended as a means of setting limits within which international aid agencies would function. To its credit, the agreement regularized relationships with the government and encouraged coordination between the UN and those NGOs that signed letters of association. However, the government's refusal to extend the memorandum after its expiration at the end of June 1992 cast a cloud of uncertainty over UN operations and personnel and over associated NGO activities.

In sum, insistence on an ill-conceived model of coordination can hobble effective action. A better-functioning system requires, instead, a more realistic concept of, and a more nuanced approach to, the various aspects of coordination delineated above. The result would be a better balance between the discipline needed among a crowded field of actors and the flexibility required if each is to play its optimum roles.

Discipline will make demands on all actors. Individual UN agencies will need to restrain their freewheeling and flag-flying instincts. Bilateral donors cannot expect the United Nations to coordinate activities while they continue to earmark funds for pet sectoral or geographic priorities. NGOs will need to commit more time and energy to being team players, or at least to staying in closer touch with the team, even at the occasional expense of pressing ahead with their own activities.

Yet systemwide discipline, lest it become the enemy of creative action, needs to be leavened with flexibility. Governments and UN organizations should welcome initiative taking by the quicker-acting members of the system. NGOs, viewing themselves as more integral to the common effort, will still need to be assured reasonable running room. Supporters of aid programs will need a clearer understanding of the limits of coordination and greater support for its costs. Coordination must serve the cause of effectiveness, not vice versa.

Comparative Advantage

Making the system work better also requires a more effective division of labor among aid actors. A fresh look at comparative advantage is particularly important in the post–Cold War era, when conventional notions about agency roles are called into question and new possibilities are emerging for each of the major actors.

With a crowded field—on the international side, UN and regional organizations, bilateral aid donors, and NGOs; on the national side, host governments and indigenous NGOs—a serviceable framework for survival needs a better understanding of who does what best.

Although comparative advantages may be difficult to honor in the near-panic atmosphere of conflicts and disasters, they are still an indispensable starting point for achieving the requisite improvement in relief operations.

The questions framed in this section are illustrative of the fundamental rethinking that needs to be brought to bear on the current humanitarian framework. Other questions need to be framed, as well. Depending on the answers, some of which we hope to suggest in later stages of our own project, changes will be needed in the current missions and mandates of the organizations involved in health, human rights, and humanitarian assistance activities.

Who responds to life-threatening suffering most quickly? This is an area in which NGOs and the ICRC have excelled. In Jordan, for example, the first evacuees following Iraq's invasion of Kuwait on August 2, 1990, started arriving within days. After several weeks they were crossing the border with Iraq at the rate of fourteen thousand per day. International and local NGOs and the ICRC, already present in Jordan at the time, sprang into action. They set up camps near the border and soon opened additional sites, purchasing items inside the country and abroad and deploying them quickly where needed.

Representatives of UN organizations and donor governments in Jordan used their own emergency authority and quick-action resources, however limited, to respond, and UNICEF flew in a planeload of supplies from its Copenhagen warehouse. Yet it was almost a month before the major elements of an intergovernmental response were in place. Of the twenty-three thousand metric tons of food aid pledged for the emergency, less than one thousand had arrived by the end of August, and only nine thousand by mid-November.

The Jordan experience suggests that the world's first line of defense is really the governments and people of neighboring countries. "If the Jordanian government had not decided to use its own resources to provide food and shelter to the evacuees," concluded a UN study, "it would have taken several days, if not weeks, for the international community to provide the same sort of services."[8] The Jordanians themselves shared personal food supplies generously. An improved framework of survival would take governments and people in neighboring countries more seriously, helping to equip and support them in their front-line labors.

Who moves large amounts of relief material quickly? A somewhat different picture emerges from the second chapter in the Gulf crisis: assisting Kurdish populations along the Turkish border in April 1991.

Here the first to respond were once again NGOs—in this instance groups such as Médecins sans Frontierès and the International Rescue Committee—with intergovernmental organizations such as the World Food Programme and the International Organization for Migration also involved. However, the magnitude of the need and the remoteness of the location quickly overwhelmed the initially available resources. It took a massive mobilization of allied coalition personnel and logistic support to reach the Kurds and prevent major loss of life.

The use of military assets to provide emergency assistance in internal armed conflicts such as that in Iraq, and in natural disasters such as (later in 1991) the cyclone in Bangladesh and the volcanic eruption in the Philippines, has placed the issue of comparative advantage in this regard on the international policy agenda. Clearly, the United Nations, bilateral aid agencies, NGOs, and the ICRC lack the logistical ability themselves to respond to such massive crises. At the same time, however, the utilization of military resources raises a number of major policy and financial questions. The possibility of having national military contingents on call to serve under United Nations direction is being explored.[9]

Conventional wisdom has it that intergovernmental organizations have a comparative advantage in moving large tonnages of relief material. However, the accomplishments of private aid groups can prove surprising. Between January and mid-August 1992, for example, ICRC delivered eighty-eight thousand metric tons of food to Somalia, four times the amount transported by the United Nations. The tonnages managed by the private groups such as CARE in major disasters can also be sizable.

Who provides aid best in the crossfire of battle? In settings of internal armed conflict, the provision of humanitarian aid is a perilous proposition at best. The regional and local conflicts that characterized the Cold War era took a heavy toll on agency personnel. CARE sustained heavy losses in Mozambique, and World Vision was hard hit in Ethiopia. Aid personnel were lost on aircraft shot down by insurgents in Sudan, and church workers were targeted by the Salvadoran government during the 1989 Farabundo Marti National Liberation Front offensive. The demise of the Cold War, it is evident, has brought an end neither to the strife that has required humanitarian assistance nor to the jeopardy of the personnel providing it.

Generally speaking, those agencies that sustained the heaviest losses were probably the ones that did the best job of getting assistance through. In Lebanon, for example, the Middle East Council of

Churches and Save the Children managed to retain the confidence of the warring factions and to provide ongoing assistance throughout the strifetorn land. The ICRC has the most consistent record of functioning well under duress. In Somalia, the contrast between the ICRC, which maintained personnel and programs in-country almost without interruption throughout 1990–1992, and the UN, which was virtually without presence in the country for most of a year, is particularly telling. However, the ICRC's insistence that all parties agree to its presence can produce delays, as in Sudan, where during most of 1988 it was sidelined in the absence of a common agreement with the protagonists.

Who provides the best protection for humanitarian operations? Over the years the moral imperatives and transparency of humanitarian action have worked to shield aid activities from physical attack. For practical as well as philosophical reasons, many aid institutions have traditionally dissociated their efforts from force. "Humanitarian aid, like peacekeeping, requires the consent and good will of all parties," writes one analyst, "because it necessarily exposes to attack those providing the aid—on foot, in trucks and in undefended cargo planes."[10] Most aid providers, particularly private relief groups, have thus been reluctant to request or accept armed protection.

As aid activities and personnel have come under greater fire in recent years, some institutions have rethought their reservations. While agreeing to the use of armed escorts for food convoys nowadays can indeed lead to problems, refusing altogether to use such escorts may mean that people will starve. As the inherent inviolability of humanitarian action has eroded, no institution—military or civilian, international or national—has yet emerged as the favorite to pick up the physical protection function. Suffice it to say that in militarized settings, security for humanitarian activities and personnel raises a host of problems—conceptual and practical, institutional and personal.

At a time when innovation is essential, the creation and deployment of the UN guards contingent for Iraq in mid-1991 is noteworthy, although its utility in other situations may prove limited. The UN guards were a largely symbolic presence in Iraq, a compromise devised to fill a vacuum left by the departure of allied coalition troops in mid-1991 that stopped well short of a larger UN presence in the form of an observer or a peacekeeping mission.

For a year the guards played a useful and largely unchallenged role in watching over humanitarian activities, personnel, and stores. Civilians carrying only sidearms for their own protection, UN guards were backed up by coalition military presence in Turkey. In mid-1992, however, they themselves became a target of hostility amid heightened tensions between the government of Iraq and the United Nations on a range of postwar political and military issues. As of August 1992, one UN guard had been killed and a number wounded. Kurdish officials claim to have evidence of promises of rewards by the Baghdad authorities for successful attacks on UN protection personnel.

In Somalia and former Yugoslavia, too, the protection of humanitarian activities has been a matter of extensive debate. On July 27, 1992, the Security Council voted to rush food to Somalia, accompanied by five hundred UN troops, although UN negotiators then experienced difficulties in laying the groundwork for their arrival. Three weeks later, on August 13, the Security Council demanded "unimpeded and continuous access" for ICRC and other relief groups to prison camps and detention centers in Bosnia and Herzegovina. It also called upon "all states to take nationally or through regional agencies or arrangements all measures necessary to facilitate in coordination with the United Nations the delivery . . . of humanitarian assistance."

In practice multilateral—or, more precisely, multinational—protection initiatives appear to enjoy an emerging comparative advantage over bilateral ones. Yet it remains to be seen how successful each of the approaches taken in Iraq, Somalia, and former Yugoslavia proves, what level of force turns out to be required, and how the humanitarian protection function relates to the ongoing conflict that requires continued international presence.

Who negotiates best on behalf of humanitarian interests? As indicated above, the United Nations is generally assumed to be best at negotiating with host political authorities on behalf of the humanitarian system as a whole. This spares hosts the task of hammering out numerous individual agreements and aid agencies the need to make their own arrangements. In point of fact, however, the historical record suggests that negotiating arrangements with political authorities is a highly contextual task, with no single actor enjoying lead status.

In many natural disasters, to be sure, the UN has played a lead role, though in some situations, such as the Armenian earthquake, the absence of UN presence and relationships have prevented it from doing so. In internal armed conflicts, however, where negotiations must be carried out not only with the government but also with insurgent political or military forces, the UN is generally at a comparative disadvantage. Former UN official James C. Ingram confirms that the UN is not well equipped to function where impartiality is required to gain the consent of the warring parties. "The United Nations is a political body," he observes, "and even its humanitarian agencies are not apolitical."[11]

In Operation Lifeline Sudan, the special representative of the secretary-general, James P. Grant, did indeed win the agreement of both insurgents and government on the terms of relief operations. However, NGOs, who had preceded the UN on the scene and whose earlier work had been discouraged by the UN, took umbrage at the assumption that the UN would coordinate all aid efforts, including their own. A similar dynamic affected relationships between the NGOs and representatives of the United Nations High Commissioner for Refugees (UNHCR) in northern Iraq. Kurdish leaders also criticize the UN for being too deferential to Baghdad and too reluctant to deal directly with elected Kurdish officials.

The UN is also at a clear disadvantage in conflict settings in which it is non grata or absent altogether. In such circumstances negotiation of humanitarian space falls to other actors. Faced with a major famine at the end of the 1980s in northern Ethiopia, the Joint Relief Partnership, a collaborative effort of three indigenous national church organizations, negotiated arrangements with the Ethiopian government and the insurgents to allow it to operate cross-border and cross-line from government-controlled areas into Tigre and Eritrea. For historical and political reasons, the United Nations was not a trusted party in that situation.

Who has the special resources needed in conflict resolution? Here, too, actors with a contribution to make are more numerous than generally imagined. The possibility that, pursuing their own approaches, the various actors can reinforce each other's actions is also an intriguing one. The fact that the particulars vary from conflict to conflict makes it once again erroneous to assume that peacemaking should be the sole preserve of the United Nations and governments. Moreover, experience suggests that agreements reached among the authorities are only as viable as their resonance among affected populations.

In the case of Somalia, for example, the United Nations has led with a decidedly top-down approach, seeking to prevail directly upon the leaders of the two major warring factions, Mohammed Farah Aidid and Mohammed Ali Mahdi, to sign an agreement allowing safe passage for humanitarian supplies. Yet the agreement, negotiated in Mogadishu and New York and signed in early 1992 in Mogadishu, failed to hold, delaying further the UN's access to starving civilians.

Meanwhile the ICRC and other private groups were pressing ahead, if with limited success, to reach those in need in Mogadishu and beyond with emergency relief.

In contrast, others tried a bottom-up approach, convening meetings of Somalis in exile to understand and bridge the tensions beneath the conflict. One such group, the nongovernmental Somali Peace and Consultation Committee, meeting regularly since late 1990, has made significant progress in getting agreement upon broad principles and procedures for a peace initiative. Only belatedly has the United Nations itself reached out to the elders of the warring clans and subclans to hasten a viable accommodation.

In Sudan key international actors have given distressingly little attention to resolving the civil war. The UN, which mounted an expensive relief program in 1989, failed to use the cooperation extracted from the protagonists to press for a negotiated end to the conflict. As far as peace was concerned, said James P. Grant, who headed Operation Lifeline Sudan, "there was nothing in my mandate at all."[12] While broadening the focus from aid to reconciliation would have been a delicate task, domestic forces pressing for peace would surely have benefited had their own efforts toward a political settlement been reinforced from outside.

Who can best reach people at the grass roots? Traditional development theory holds that intergovernmental organizations and bilateral aid donors work best in dealing with host governments through appropriate ministries, while NGOs enjoy their own comparative advantage at the community level. That, too, is changing as major institutions such as the World Bank and the U.S. Agency for International Development pay more direct attention to local needs and as NGOs make their influence felt well beyond the grass roots.

A number of recent UN operations have been extremely personnel-intensive, reflecting both the severity of the need and the additional challenges of monitoring posed by armed conflicts. The numbers of UN personnel making up the aid contingents in Sudan, Iraq, Cambodia, former Yugoslavia, and, more recently, Somalia are substantial, with UN staff fanning out well beyond national capitals to far-flung provinces and villages.

Expanding their roles into the highways and byways, such institutions as UNICEF, UNHCR, and the World Food Programme are functioning much more as have NGOs. Meanwhile, NGOs are no longer confining their efforts to local communities. In broader compass, the growing awareness of the importance of local institution-building, reflected in the secretary-general's remarks above, and of national and international policies that reinforce the empowerment of the poor pose major questions of policy, institutional mandates, and cost.

What, for example, are the implications of outposting more UN personnel for existing UN staff, the UN staff of the future, and the cultures of UN organizations? With the outposting of each overseas UN staff person costing about twice that of international NGO personnel, is increased field presence the best use of limited UN resources? Should the international system place greater reliance on indigenous NGOs, which are less expensive still and generally have greater access to those in need? What are the implications for other actors as NGOs themselves expand the scope of their contributions beyond the grass roots to the realms of planning, project replication, training, and advocacy? Can private agencies play larger roles in a more integrated system without compromising their essential nongovernmental nature?

Who best makes the connections between emergency relief and longer-term development? At a conceptual level, the linkages are well understood by all parties. They were clearly stated and often repeated, especially by developing countries, in the UN General Assembly's discussions of humanitarian coordination in the fall of 1991, and again in the UN Economic and Social Council (ECOSOC) July 1992 review of the performance of DHA.

"The need for humanitarian assistance results from many different origins," recalled Ambassador Ronaldo Mota Sardenberg of Brazil on the latter occasion, including "natural disasters, military conflicts, political turmoil, etc. But in a deeper sense, this need is also a result of the shortcomings of international cooperation for economic and social development. With economic development comes not only a higher per capita income or higher standards of living, but also a greater resilience of the society to external shocks, greater preparedness to cope with natural catastrophes and greater political stability. That linkage must be kept in mind at all times."[13]

Conceptual linkages notwithstanding, there are deep-seated political and institutional reasons why the path between relief and development remains, in practice, anything but continuous. Bilateral donors, particularly when dealing with opprobrious host political authorities, tend to make hard-and-fast distinctions between "humanitarian" and other aid, placing similar strictures on UN bodies, as well. NGOs, generally better at seeing the whole picture, frequently become preoccupied with emergency aid. All agencies are, to one extent or another, prisoners of the public's preference for relieving immediate emergencies rather than investing, as Ambassador Sardenberg urges, in the prevention of future crises.

The functional areas in which comparative advantage needs to be examined extend well beyond the eight enumerated above. Who monitors human rights violations best? Who is most effective at curtailing human rights abuses? Which actors are best at conveying international solidarity with vulnerable populations? Which excel at activating regional interest and involvement? Which have special gifts for nurturing a constituency among Northern publics and parliaments for progressive policies? What agencies are the most cost-effective? A full elaboration must await more research and additional space.

Even without proceeding further here, the thrust of our findings to date is clear. Rather than expecting a single agency to perform this entire array of diverse functions, the humanitarian system needs to nurture and maximize the differing gifts of the rich variety of existing agencies. Additional research is also unlikely to reverse the hypothesis that the specific division of labor adopted must reflect the idiosyncrasies of each given conflict or disaster setting.

Recent aid to Cambodia is a case in point. The role of NGOs in the current relief effort, begun in 1979 following civil war and Khmer Rouge atrocities, was unprecedented in scope and scale. "NGOs responded to the disaster in Cambodia," observes one reviewer, "with assistance in sectors of their traditional expertise and concern, such as agriculture, health, and rural water supply, as well as in areas not normally their domain, such as urban water systems, industry, transport, and the rehabilitation of basic infrastructure." From the time of the imposition of the international embargo in 1982, "NGOs were the only source of rehabilitation and reconstruction assistance . . . until the embargo began to relax in 1990."[14]

With UN organizations and donor governments increasingly back in the picture, "NGOs welcome the opportunity to return to their traditional role of supporting community-based programs." They do so, however, having established unusually productive working relationships with government officials at every level and having earned a place at the table for national development discussions surprising for NGOs. In the absence of the other major actors, such groups broke new ground in the degree of concerted action across the NGO community and in the high level of professionalism exhibited.[15]

There are thus few hard-and-fast answers in the evolving realm of comparative advantage. Nevertheless, because the actors, however numerous, are constant in type and the challenges confronting them, however particular to a given situation, are generic in nature, it is possible and essential to hammer out a more clear division of labor. The world does not have the luxury of gearing up from scratch for each new emergency. That said, there is also need for more flexibility and improvisation. The cause of effective humanitarian action is not well served by forcing "square" agency pegs into "round" disaster holes.

Professionalism

The third area of priority in making the humanitarian system work better involves increasing the professionalism of practitioners. Here, too, humanitarian actors have a great deal to learn from experience and from each other. From such interaction, those in need of assistance and protection also stand to benefit. While many aid practitioners acknowledge the need for more effective action, there are differences of opinion about what essential changes are needed and, more fundamentally still, about what "professionalism" implies.

Humanitarian institutions find themselves chastened by the distorting impacts of the Cold War on their efforts, sobered by the complex challenges of post–Cold War conflicts and natural disasters, and laboring under increasingly rigorous public expectations. Not generally known for taking time out from the press of emergencies for reflection, they are now reviewing fundamental principles, rethinking philosophy and objectives, refining operational strategies, and seeking to equip staff for functioning better in such settings.

The process of reflection is moving forward on a number of fronts. At the international level, UNHCR and UNDRO (the United Nations Disaster Relief Organization) have completed internal studies of their activities during the Gulf crisis. UNDRO and UNDP (the United Nations Development Programme) are preparing materials on the needs of displaced persons in civil conflicts for use in disaster management training. The Federation of Red Cross and Red Crescent Societies is working on guidelines for its members as they relate to national military forces. The International Council of Voluntary Agencies plans to review NGO experience in selected country conflicts.

In the United States, the Agency for International Development (AID) is charting strategies for famine prevention and disaster mitigation in settings where civil strife complicates action. AID and the

Pentagon have evaluated Operation Provide Comfort and assessed its implications for the future.[16] The Congressional Research Service has released a study of the expanded use of the U.S. military in overseas relief.[17] InterAction, the professional association of 136 U.S. private relief and development groups, is developing standards to encourage "professional competence, ethical practices, and quality services." Individual NGOs, such as Catholic Relief Services, have developed and approved new policies. The Humanitarianism and War project is the beneficiary of and, we hope, a contributor to, this widespread ferment.

No code of conduct currently exists, however, for the community of humanitarian practitioners as a whole, or even for the subcommunities of United Nations, government, and NGO professionals. This is just as it should be, say some. The diversity of viewpoints on principle and practice, they point out, reduces chances of forging meaningful communitywide consensus. However committed to broad humanitarian principles, agencies understand the principles differently, with widely divergent views, for example, on sovereignty and accountability. Thus an attempt to achieve consensus, the argument goes, would be unproductive. Proceeding agency by agency and avoiding broader and sometimes bruising public discussions of policy and ethics is thus the preferred route.

Others disagree, viewing the development of a code of conduct as long overdue and now imperative. The development of standards for humanitarian action is urgently needed, they argue, because the task of functioning effectively in armed conflicts is so complex, the exposure of civilian populations so perilous, and the stakes for the international community so high. They view the humanitarian enterprise as we know it as living on borrowed time. Unless aid agencies take steps to improve their functioning, more rigorous accountability will be imposed from outside and fewer resources will be forthcoming.

Our own view is that while the diversity within the aid community is so great as to test the very concept of community itself, humanitarian organizations of all sorts and conditions can and should work to affirm agreement on certain broad principles. Beyond that, like-minded agencies should articulate humanitarian standards for themselves and train their staffs accordingly. To facilitate this process, we are developing and field-testing a handbook for practitioners, which is scheduled for publication in early 1993.[18]

For purposes of the present discussion, it is useful to identify several key areas of improvement that, in our judgment, would enhance the professionalism of the humanitarian enterprise. The first is *a broader sense of community* among professionals. We have been struck during our field research—in 1990 on Sudan and more recently on the Middle East and the Horn of Africa—by the absence during emergencies of a sense of common purpose, and sometimes even of routine communication, among aid professionals.

At the time of Operation Lifeline Sudan, for example, there were disturbing frictions both between NGOs and the UN, and among NGOs. The dearth of consultation by UN officials prior to launching Lifeline in early 1989 and their lack of collegiality throughout much of the program hampered concerted action. For their part, individual NGOs were preoccupied with their own activities and did not function as part of a community joined by common purposes and with a recognized stake in the success of the United Nations effort.

The situation was much the same in Iraq, where the overriding priority each NGO attached to its own survival undercut a sense of common effort in which NGOs and the United Nations were partners. One NGO official interviewed in May 1990 in Baghdad, frustrated by the need to terminate his agency's operations because of the government's refusal to grant visa extensions to expatriate staff, could hardly wait to exit the country and lambaste the Iraqi authorities in the Western media. He was undeterred by the negative effects that such publicity might have on the larger international operation and on the agencies, particularly their Iraqi staffs, remaining behind.

There are, of course, legitimate reasons of policy and program that lead individual organizations zealously and jealously to guard their separate identities. The credibility of ICRC might suffer, for example, if it shared routinely or widely the human rights or other information garnered from its visits to prisons, or if its symbol were appropriated by groups that do not espouse its principles. Nevertheless, the effectiveness of aid efforts—and sometimes even the continued presence of aid personnel themselves—would benefit from greater collegiality and common action. The greater threat to aid programs amid civil wars surely comes from political authorities, not from other aid operatives.

A second area of needed improvement is the achievement of *greater contextual sensitivity*. Our field research to date is replete with instances of gross insensitivity to local and national traditions and practices. Examples of these and of the dysfunctional bias of many aid activities, emergency and longer-term alike, in favor of the expatriate and the alien have already been noted.

In a more profound sense external interventions can have substantial effects on fundamental realities such as the status of the poor, the human rights of minorities and women, the possibilities of longer-term economic and social development, and the role of the military in civil society. Apparent at times of natural disasters, such impacts are even more significant when the fundamental identity and survival of nations are tested by ethnic tensions and civil wars.[19] "Natural" disasters and civil wars alike have origins in underlying economic, social, and political inequities. These inequities may be inadvertently reinforced by international humanitarian institutions, even when they seek to avoid such side effects.

"The time has come for us in the Horn of Africa," observes the Nairobi-based peace activist Kibiru Kinyanjui, "to ask whether the efforts of relief agencies are contributing, indirectly or even remotely, to an escalation of the wars or to a peaceful resolution of the conflicts."[20] There is troubling evidence to suggest that outside food and other aid to Ethiopia and the Sudan not only benefited soldiers but also allowed the protagonists to prosecute their wars more single-mindedly. The current situation in Somalia has its own set of excruciating choices. Tribute in the form of food to armed bands terrorizing civilians is now the price paid for reaching those who are starving.

Similarly, humanitarian institutions concerned about the fate of Bosnian Muslims face painful choices. "The humanitarian effort that has been the focus of the outside world's concern deals with the consequences—not the cause—of this catastrophe," observes one visitor to former Yugoslavia. "Obscured in the debate over whether the U.N. should authorize force to deliver relief to existing victims is the fact that there is no debate and no plan to prevent more victims from being created. Every international relief worker here knows this awful truth and grapples with the dilemma it presents. Are they, by helping the victims of ethnic cleansing, inadvertently implementing and sanctioning it?"[21]

Agencies that understand the contextual complexities in which humanitarian action is set will not always make the right choice; indeed, the "right" choice may be difficult to identify, even after the fact. However, humanitarian interests will be better served by practitioners who carefully contextualize their choices than by institutions that proceed in a vacuum. A willingness to reflect self-critically on the paths taken and not taken is also essential. These, at least, are hypotheses our research is testing.

A third area of needed improvement is *greater access to specialized skills*. It seems self-evident that in the humanitarian crises of today and tomorrow, there is both the need for and the possibility of greater emergency management expertise. This is especially the case where massive human displacement is involved, and more especially still where the presence of conflict makes humanitarian action more difficult, tenuous, and suspect.

In the Gulf crisis, for example, the effective transportation of large numbers of people required, and received, specialized expertise from the International Organization for Migration. During a period of only two months the organization oversaw the movement of some 700,000 evacuees from Iraq and Kuwait to homes in Asia and elsewhere in the Middle East. Its expertise was pivotal, even though the government of Jordan, host countries such as India, and the NGOs noted earlier played altogether indispensable roles in internal transport, logistics, and exit visa processing.

Telecommunications is another area of growing importance. Effective humanitarian operations need to be closely linked through reliable communications, keeping personnel in the field, in national capitals, and at agency headquarters regularly in touch. Yet such arrangements raise difficult political and security issues, particularly in civil wars. In northern Iraq, the installation in a Kurdish-controlled area of a UN communications relay station with Baghdad became an item of contention with Kurdish leadership. In Ethiopia communications sensitivities delayed delivery of World Food Programme cargo into the insurgent-controlled port of Massawa and of a convoy across no-man's land between government- and insurgent-controlled territory. In humanitarian crises, technical matters may have significant political reverberations.

In areas less technical, too, increased competence is essential. As indicated above, there is growing consensus that humanitarian institutions must do more to address the underlying problems that occasion the need for their assistance. This does not mean that every aid organization must seek to bring combatants to the negotiating table; that requires expertise of a special sort. There may even be valid reasons for lodging peacemaking and aid responsibilities in separate hands, as did the United Nations in Afghanistan. However, aid agencies should be aware of the importance of peacemaking and of the need for specialized expertise, enlisting it as appropriate.

The negotiation of access demands special skills. Negotiators require an astute sense of the carrots and the sticks, and of the appropriate use of the two. They need a finely honed sense of when behind-the-scenes pressure should be used and when the full glare of international publicity should be brought to bear. Negotiators also need to know what has worked or not worked in the past, and they need an ability to adapt such experience to new settings. Thus, negotiations of corridors of tranquillity in Somalia, Angola, and Bosnia can be informed by the experiences in Ethiopia and Sudan, and perhaps avoid some of the problems encountered.

In the final analysis, the large gaps in the current system may prove to be less in the realm of technical capacity and more in the area of wisdom and seasoned judgment. Developing a cadre of people who possess the resourcefulness to function successfully amid the complexities of today's "natural" disasters and the political land mines of ethnic conflicts represents a long-term, formidable challenge.

In these three respects, then, there is doubtless widespread agreement on the need for greater professionalism among aid providers. Yet significant differences exist in the relative importance attached to these as against operational demands.

Faced with the choice of developing greater contextual awareness or responding with alacrity, most agencies will opt for the latter. At the same time, many are coming to acknowledge that some circumstances are simply too constricting for assistance to be provided with integrity. Rather than automatically engaging in every conceivable crisis, aid agencies are learning that on occasion discretion may be the better part of valor. There is no inherent contradiction, some are now willing to acknowledge, in the refusal of a humanitarian institution to provide humanitarian aid.

Significant differences also exist in terms of what is understood by "professionalism." For many in humanitarian pursuits, to be said to be functioning with professionalism is a high compliment. Others see the term as pejorative, believing that the problems to which aid agencies are now responding are the result of too much professionalism rather than too little.

One element in the rash of ethnic conflicts in Africa and elsewhere, it is contended, is the failure of development strategies recommended by card-carrying aid professionals that have undermined indigenous institutions and values. How can responsibility for the post–Cold War rash of violence, they ask, be separated from superpower strategies of seeding the world's developing regions with lethal weaponry?

In this perspective, what is now needed is not greater technical capacity and emboldened prescriptiveness, but more willingness among those in positions of institutional responsibility to listen, to adapt, to implement decisions locally arrived at, and to be accountable to the people for whom humanitarian assistance is ostensibly designed. Given the divergent viewpoints on these matters, post–Cold War professionalism itself is an item in need of docketing on the international agenda.

The code of conduct our project is developing and testing—and other thoughtful codes are also gestating—would not bring about improvement in the quality of humanitarian action overnight. It will not likely win the endorsement of all institutions. Even those that endorsed it would be accepting a set of norms toward which they would strive rather than a legally binding and enforceable instrument. Its credibility and effectiveness would be a function largely of the seriousness with which it was taken.

Nor would a code guarantee that humanitarian activities would be better managed. Individual agencies would still have to make judgments: some of them wise and vindicated by events, others less so and overtaken by events. Over time, however, a code could help restrain the extremes of pure pragmatism unguided by humanitarian principle and unswerving fidelity to such principle untempered by the exigencies of conflicts and disasters. Refined in the light of new experience, such a code could be a vehicle for ongoing efforts to upgrade the "professionalism" of humanitarian action.

The present moment is indeed opportune for improving the functioning of the world's humanitarian system. The need for a more effective regime is underscored by a proliferation of civil conflicts and natural disasters. Within the community of humanitarian organizations, as well, the time is a propitious one for reflection and action. Other papers in this volume suggest various encouraging developments on a number of fronts.

Our review of the positive and negative lessons from recent experience, however, cautions against quick fixes. Despite the recent and growing popularity of the United Nations, the UN and its various organizations are not in and of themselves the solution to the current problems. Bilateral governments, and particularly their military assets, are not a deus ex machina that will assure that recalcitrant regimes no longer abuse their populations. Nor are NGOs, despite their energy and their expanding areas of competence, a panacea. A universal template to chart courses of action in any and all situations does not exist and is unlikely to be developed.

Over the long haul, the world's humanitarian system will benefit most from coordinated action guided by an understanding of its various component elements, from a more creative utilization of the comparative advantages of existing organizations, and from enhanced professionalism among those committed to seeing that persons in life-threatening situations receive effective protection and assistance.

IV

UNITED NATIONS RESPONSE

The arcane semantics of diplomacy are no longer acceptable substitutes for action in international relief operations; they have happily fallen victim to the increasingly obvious need to deal rapidly and effectively with catastrophes created by nature and man. In 1974 after the Sahel drought decimated much of West Africa, a report from the Carnegie Foundation, "Disaster in the Desert," concluded that the bureaucracy of the United Nations and other major powers were responsible for serious flaws in the delivery of relief programs. The authors spoke of "institutional inertia, rivalries between offices and agencies, an unwillingness to acknowledge failures to the public or even within official circles."

Almost twenty years have passed since these observations were made about an organization that still represents the best and, maybe, the only hope in mankind's endless quest for a more equitable and peaceful world. Today it can certainly be recognized as a major achievement that preventive diplomacy and humanitarian interventions are acceptable tools of the United Nations as it answers frequent and urgent calls to deal with natural and man-made disasters.

It is, however, still pertinent to ask whether the organization and its affiliated agencies have learned the hard lessons of the past. Have they developed a coordinated and cooperative approach that can deal adequately with disasters, especially in the developing countries that so often lack the civil infrastructure necessary to cushion a society battered by great stress?

These and other questions relating to the role of the UN in emergency situations are considered in this section by senior representatives of its major agencies. The contributions conclude with an overview by the newly appointed under-secretary-general for Humanitarian Affairs.

16

Responding to Emergencies: A View from Within

ABDULRAHIM A. FARAH

In spite of advances in science and technology that were unimaginable thirty or forty years ago, a large proportion of the world's population—for the most part its poorest people—live on the edge of survival. They are the chief victims of the vagaries of nature and of man-made disasters. The end of the Cold War seemed to hold promise for a more peaceful world, but instead, long-simmering ethnic and tribal conflicts in many areas have erupted, leading to brutal wars where the innocent and the most vulnerable are the principal victims. Not surprisingly, the question of international responses to disaster situations is receiving increased attention as the grim realities of human suffering caused by drought, disease, famine, displacement, conflict, and other ills are brought routinely by the news media into living rooms on all continents.

During my tenure as under-secretary-general at the United Nations from 1972 to 1990, my responsibilities brought me in close touch with disaster situations on the African continent. What follows are my recollections and impressions about issues and problems that were topical at the time. It has been said that memory is a capricious and arbitrary creature; one can never tell where it will lead and what it will bring forward, but I hope that my thoughts will be instructive to those now struggling in the field.

My vantage point was unique: it provided me with an appreciation of the needs and expectations of recipient countries, a better understanding of the response mechanisms of the UN system, and familiarity with the role of both the donor community and the international and national voluntary agencies. I became familiar with a variety of views—some from recipients and some from donors, some negative and some positive. In many cases these views were directed in good faith toward improving the overall effectiveness of relief operations; in other cases they were defensive of actions taken. All reflected the complexity and harsh realities of disaster situations.

Countries that sought aid were invariably underdeveloped with totally inadequate infrastructures. At the time of their independence they had inherited fragile economies made progressively worse either by internal strife, drought, an unfavorable international economic climate, excessive military spending and mismanagement, or a combination of any of these factors. Underdevelopment not only perpetuated low living standards for the populations concerned, but, in times of emergencies, hindered relief operations and served to retard the rehabilitation and reconstruction process.

Political and Legal Issues

Serious and sensitive political issues often had to be taken into account in mounting relief operations. Such issues frequently involved questions of international law relating to humanitarian intervention in conflict and disaster situations. They included seeking the consent of the governments concerned for cross-line or cross-border relief activities in conflict situations, obtaining the agreement of neighboring states for use of their land, sea, and air routes for the shipment of humanitarian supplies, and securing the cooperation of both government and opposition forces in the conduct of relief operations.

The situation on the Horn of Africa in the late 1980s underscored such considerations. Sudan, Ethiopia, and Somalia were each caught up in the throes of civil war, with slim prospects for peaceful solutions. Because of poverty, famine, and the devastating economic consequences of the prolonged strife, each government was obliged to appeal for humanitarian aid. The problem for the UN was to work out arrangements with each government to ensure that there would be no discrimination in the distribution of aid and that it reached those in need.

SUDAN

In the case of Sudan, a breakthrough occurred when the UN succeeded in winning the agreement of both the Sudan government and of the Sudan People's Liberation Army (SPLA) for the establishment of peace corridors through which food and medical supplies could be transported across combat lines to beleaguered communities. The principal conditions attached to such traffic was that advance notice should be given to the two parties of the route to be taken, and the cargo to be carried. Operation Lifeline Sudan (OLS), as the operation was known, had its ups and downs, but the encouraging fact then was that neither side wanted to terminate it. Thus, for the first time, an African government and the rebels who opposed it, cooperated with the UN to enable relief operations to be mounted.

ETHIOPIA AND SOMALIA

The Sudan experience contrasted markedly with operations in Ethiopia and Somalia, where there was clear opposition to any international presence in areas other than those firmly controlled by the government. The latter states were reluctant to acknowledge the existence of their civil wars, even though the war in Ethiopia had continued for almost thirty years and the war in Somalia had been steadily escalating for almost ten years.

It was only in the closing stages of Ethiopia's civil war that an understanding was reached with the UN which allowed the transport of supplies from agreed points within the territory to the borders of rebel-held territory. The Ethiopian authorities insisted that from there onward supplies were to be transported only by Ethiopian voluntary agencies, and not by the UN or any other foreign organization. This arrangement satisfied Ethiopian sensitivities on the question of "domestic jurisdiction." From the UN standpoint, it enabled urgently needed supplies to reach the affected population, although in terms of volume and speed more could have been accomplished had the UN been allowed full involvement. The Ethiopian regime would not compromise on the question of cross-border supply routes or direct access by sea or air into rebel-controlled areas. The regime made clear that cross-border relief operations, without its consent, would be viewed as a violation of the country's sovereignty. No doubt, dominant among these considerations was the fear that direct contact with the UN might strengthen the position of the rebels and eventually lead to some form of recognition for them.

This same fear was very much in the mind of the Somali regime. Taking an extreme stand, the Barre regime opposed all deliveries of humanitarian supplies to areas outside of its control. Repeated attempts were made to secure the government's consent for such supplies to be distributed by the International Committee of the Red Cross (ICRC), but to no avail. The regime refused to admit that an insurgency existed, or that the rebels had acquired control over any area within the country. In its view, the rebels were essentially dissidents, engaged in hit-and-run raids from across the border. The ICRC did establish informal contact with the rebels and was able to provide them with small quantities of medicines. Since it was the practice to restrict UN relief operations to areas authorized by the government concerned, practically no international aid reached the civilian population in the contested areas.

Mobilizing International Assistance

The process of mobilizing international relief lies at the heart of disaster relief operations. As a global organization with practically every country a member, the UN is well placed to serve as an intermediary between the donor community and national governments. During my tenure at the UN, mobilizing public support normally began as soon as the first alarm was sounded by the government concerned, or by the issuance of early warning reports by the UN agency concerned. There were exceptions to this form of reporting, as in the case of the 1974 famine in Ethiopia. In that case, the local authorities neglected to pay attention to a famine situation that had rapidly developed in the northern area of the country. It fell to the international media to discover and publicize the impending disaster, but not before thousands of people had perished.

In general, all disaster reports were taken up by the local UN representatives and relayed immediately to the appropriate organization within the UN system. In large-scale disasters, where there was a mix of natural and man-made disasters, appeals for assistance were directly addressed to the secretary-general by the government concerned. According to the nature of the disaster, the secretary-general, in turn, would decide which office or agency within the UN system should take the lead role in developing an appropriate response. The principal agencies concerned would be alerted, an interagency assessment team dispatched to the affected country, the team's findings given wide circulation, and ultimately a pledging conference of potential donors would be called. Unfortunately, this necessary but time-consuming process did not always yield the resources requested, despite the urgency involved and the importance of providing adequate aid to the victims before conditions deteriorated further.

It was always an uphill task to mobilize sufficient funds to cover even the minimum initial cost of launching operations; in the case of funding for rehabilitation and reconstruction purposes, the situation was even more difficult, and responses seldom matched the amounts needed.

Of course a great deal depended on the efficiency and effectiveness of the UN response mechanism. One of the most successful relief operations undertaken by the UN in recent times was organized in 1984 and 1985 to deal with the ravages of the devastating drought that swept the Sahelian countries. A combination of flair, efficiency, and organizational abilities enabled the two top men of the UN team— Bradford Morse and Maurice Strong—to galvanize the UN system into action, win the generous support of the donor community in the mobilization of resources, and deliver those resources to target areas deep into the heart of the Sahel. This entailed breaking bottlenecks at ports and airfields, strengthening road transport capacities, and securing the support of the various governments in a regionwide cooperative effort. Equally important was the efficient communications system that enabled information to flow continuously from the field to headquarters and from there to donors. All involved were kept constantly informed of developments, problems, and needs—a critical requirement to sustain the interest of donors in a specific situation.

THE DEVELOPMENT AGENCIES

The social and humanitarian agencies of the UN did not have enough resources of their own to effectively respond to disaster situations. The funds required had to be mobilized from scratch through voluntary contributions. Resource-giving agencies such as the World Bank, and to a much lesser degree the United Nations Development Programme (UNDP), had more available resources than other UN agencies, but they could only help marginally because their mandates prevented them from committing funds for projects or activities that were not strictly developmental in character.

Fortunately, in recent years, the UNDP has developed a strategy that has enabled funds to be devoted to disaster preparedness and disaster response. Some agencies have developed joint programs with the World Bank that cover the relief component and leave the development component to be funded by the Bank. These are welcome developments, given the magnitude of needs and the importance of early and sustained resource-support throughout the emergency period. It can certainly be expected that increased demands will be made on these two development agencies for a more direct and expanded role in disaster situations.

The importance of involving development agencies in relief operations became apparent to United Nations High Commissioner for Refugees (UNHCR) in 1978, following the influx of hundreds of thousands of refugees from Ethiopia into Somalia in the wake of war. While UNHCR allocated whatever funds it could muster to cope with the situation, it was clear that, given the fragility of Somalia's economy, the country would need, in addition to relief, immediate development aid to strengthen its infrastructure. An interagency team was dispatched to assess the situation, and its findings were circulated in the form of an appeal for additional aid to supplement the relief assistance being sought by UNHCR. This arrangement established the format for similar operations undertaken in the years that followed, with varying degrees of success.

"ADDITIONALITY"

In responding to appeals for emergency aid, donors sometimes found it convenient to allocate aid they had earmarked for development programs in the affected countries and use it instead to support relief activities within those countries. This practice is referred to as "additionality." While the transfer helped the relief process, it often meant that the development side would be deprived of important resources, for the funds were not always replaced. Thus the list of pledges would show the amount as a new contribution to the appeal, when in actual fact the balance sheet of the recipient government would show no change in real terms.

This issue is raised because the question of additionality in refugee related assistance programs gave rise to considerable debate at the 1984 International Conference on Assistance to Refugees in Africa

(ICARA II). Host countries made clear that they could not absorb refugees into their own communities unless steps were taken by the international community to increase their development aid commensurately. Given their precarious economic condition, these countries could hardly be expected to contract additional debts for nationals other than their own. The conference eventually recognized that additional assistance should be provided to host countries to enable them to discharge their responsibilities toward refugees, and that durable solutions could not be brought about unless the country of origin was helped to absorb the cost of resettling returnees.

In 1991, the General Assembly resolution 46/182 on humanitarian emergency assistance recognized the need of additionality in all relief situations. The resolution included, among its guiding principles, the provision that "contributions for humanitarian assistance should be provided in a way which is not to the detriment of resources made available for international cooperation for development."

Rehabilitation and reconstruction programs should commence as soon as relief operations are mounted. As one African leader explained it, relief, rehabilitation, and reconstruction are inseparable necessities in the developing world in times of emergencies, particularly among the least developed states. To paraphrase his words, they are as essential and complementary to each other as the skin, the flesh, and the bones are to the body. Experience has demonstrated, however, that as soon as the more dramatic aspects of relief begin to fade because of a perceived improvement in the condition of the disaster victims, the spotlight of public attention is turned off, and so is the flow of resources. The less dramatic but equally critical phases of rehabilitation and reconstruction are stymied before they can get under way.

The Costs of Delay and Inaction

A question that baffled many of us over the years was why donors took such a long time to respond to appeals for emergency assistance when the evidence of an impending or ongoing disaster was so overwhelming. What we experienced in the past is again happening today. The present emergency in Somalia is of course a glaring example. Civil strife has continued unabated since early 1991, causing massive casualties among the civilian population and widespread hunger and misery. Yet no one seemed to appreciate the gravity of the situation, and when the media finally began reporting the tragedy, the response of donors, as well as that of the UN, was abysmally slow, uncoordinated, and totally inadequate.

A number of reasons have been given to explain the slow reaction of donors. Inaction was sometimes attributed to a wait and see attitude—an unwillingness to believe what was happening or waiting to see what others would do. In other instances, reaction was decided by the politics of the day and by the special interests of donors. In most situations, the initial aid was inadequate to cover immediate needs, and when enough aid did arrive, it was too late to limit or contain the impact of the disaster: death would already have begun to exact its toll on the population. It took a television crew to arouse the world about the nature and dimensions of the disastrous drought that hit Ethiopia in 1974. Again, in 1984, early warning signals given by the UN on a further famine were ignored at great cost to the Ethiopian people. In the current case of Somalia, where a tragedy of unimaginable proportions has developed, we see once again the terrible consequences of delay and indifference.

VAGARIES OF VOLUNTARY FUNDING

Given the frequency with which states must seek international humanitarian assistance, it is obvious that existing procedures and constraints should be reviewed to ensure effective responses to their appeals. Despite the generosity of some donor states and organizations, it has clearly become necessary to remove relief operations from dependence on the vagaries of international charity, so that critical time and supply gaps between the launching of appeals and the delivery of aid can be avoided. Dr. Kevin Cahill of the Center for International Health and Cooperation has suggested emergency relief operations funded from assessed levies on UN member states as in the case of peacekeeping operations. Moreover, in the context of the secretary-general's proposal that countries earmark contingents for peacekeeping activities, another possibility is that countries contribute disaster relief teams for deployment at short notice in emergency situations. Both proposals deserve serious attention, and both would address many of the concerns outlined here.

Operational Problems

Although it may be stating the obvious to say that smooth relations between the governments of affected countries, the donor community, and the UN are essential for mounting effective responses to disaster situations, from my vantage point several factors were observed which worked against efficient and cooperative efforts. Many governments seeking help should have determined at the outset whether their policies and performance were likely to attract or repel donor support. Donors were often hesitant to become directly involved in relief operations if they felt that the government concerned was pursuing policies and practices that did not measure up to internationally recognized standards. Illegal diversion of aid, corrupt practices in aid distribution, inefficient relief mechanisms, and the exaggeration of needs were among the charges leveled against authorities in some countries.

Donors required assurances that the recipient governments would create the necessary distribution mechanisms and would introduce adequate safeguards to ensure that the aid received was used for the designated purpose. Donors also wanted assurances that they could monitor aid distribution and that consultative arrangements would be set up between the government and the donor community to review the progress of relief operations.

When problems occurred, there was often considerable shifting of blame. In some situations the donor community would be accused of being unappreciative of the problems facing the recipient country, or of offering help with too many strings attached to it. Recipient countries sometimes felt that their circumstances obliged them to put up with unjustifiable criticism and attitudes of political or cultural insensitivity, if not arrogance. Such issues had to be frankly examined and addressed by all concerned, as they often were.

Within the UN, jurisdictional issues were sometimes a divisive factor, hampering interagency cooperation. The major agencies each had their own mandates and governing bodies. This arrangement sometimes gave rise to independent rather than cooperative action, friction rather than harmony, particularly in cases where responsibilities overlapped and respective areas were not clearly defined.

Many of these matters have been remedied in recent years, but the problem of effective coordination within the UN has yet to be resolved to the credit of the system, and to the satisfaction of the donor community and of the countries which are being served. During my term in office, the Office of the Coordinator for Disaster Relief (UNDRO) was created in Geneva in the hope that it would resolve the situation, but since it was far from political headquarters and had few resources, it did not command much authority or influence among the major UN relief agencies.

THE RIGHT PERSON FOR THE RIGHT JOB

Another area of friction was the caliber of relief personnel. Relief operations are often thought of only as the broader components such as assessment of need, identification of priorities, sensitizing the international community, mobilizing resources, logistics, in-country capacities, and related questions. Little is said about the quality of the relief personnel who carry out the planning, assessment, handling, and distribution of resources. Will they measure up to the challenge? Does the selection process identify and match the personal and professional qualifications of such personnel to the particular task in the field? Is he or she sensitive to a country's political, social, and cultural environment? Is he or she a team leader, a team player, or a "loner"? These and related questions should be asked to minimize misunderstandings in the field.

Often the less experienced expatriate officials were posted to the less developed countries, even though the development problems of these countries were extremely challenging. Only a few senior staff were allotted to these postings, and the best of them were moved around fairly frequently. Administrative considerations were often given as the cause for this state of affairs. Some officials sought transfer to posts in less developed countries because of lack of promotion opportunities elsewhere; others received such postings as a form of penance for sins committed. In neither case did it appear that the competence or suitability of the individual concerned was the main consideration. The general feeling was that the special needs of disaster-prone or underdeveloped countries were not appreciated at the headquarters level.

When I expressed the view that post assignments should not be based only on budgetary considerations or the relative political importance of a country, but also by the development complexities and challenges of the posts themselves, I was told that this approach would not work, since experienced officials often found that they could only move up the ladder by transferring to so-called "prestige posts." Keeping experienced and capable personnel in the least developed countries, particularly disaster-prone countries, will remain a problem until a formula is found to adequately reward them for their services.

The work relationship between the local professional and the expatriate official posed another problem. At one time there was a suggestion that UN programs could best be implemented by increasing the number of young, aggressive, and well-educated officials in the field. That suggestion was not always appreciated within the countries concerned. It ignored the fact that in Africa, for example, African universities and overseas scholarship schemes had supplied large numbers of graduates to the local labor markets. The need was not for young graduates from abroad but for experience and expertise in areas that were not available locally. Some agencies appeared insensitive to these realities and continued to reserve professional appointments for expatriate staff when the same jobs could have been performed equally well by local nationals.

Age is another important factor in the assignment of personnel. Age and experience still wield considerable influence with African leaders. Agency representatives are often called upon for advice and counsel on development and other issues which a less experienced person would not be in a position to give. I recall discussing the relative merits of younger versus older experts with a group of African ministers. They acknowledged that on a personal level they tended to be on the same wavelength as the younger expert because of age, outlook, enthusiasm, and impatience to get the job done. But they all preferred the presence of the experienced hand so that when their enthusiasm took them to the brink of the dangerous unknown, instead of hearing the voice of the young exclaim "charge," they could rely on the steadying voice of the experienced expert to say "hold back—let's think this over!"

It would be remiss on my part not to mention the difficult and stressful conditions under which expatriate staff often must work. I recall visiting a particular country that, at one stage, was regarded by international staff as a graveyard for any further career hopes they may have had. Staff members who did not always see eye to eye with the local authorities, or who were not pliant enough, seldom lasted for long before they were declared persona non grata on some unsubstantiated charge. This had disastrous effects on the efficiency of field operations. When I discussed the situation with the government, one of the ministers retorted by accusing the expatriate staff of being hostile to the country, and the UN of being at fault for not sending better qualified people in the first place! The agencies persevered to the extent possible, but the country was the loser because of the experienced staff it rejected.

Whatever the nature of their personnel problems, agencies and organizations can ill afford to neglect the periodic review of their policies governing the recruitment and posting of field staff. Too much is at stake in crisis situations for an agency to have to deal with a wrong team member in the wrong place at the wrong time. Experience has demonstrated the need for agencies to have available a list of field staff who have distinguished themselves in disaster management, and who can both lead and be good team members. Some agencies have already instituted arrangements along these lines. It is to be hoped that they will share their lists with other agencies so that a special cadre of crisis managers can be developed.

THE NEED FOR LOCAL INVOLVEMENT

An equally important personnel problem is that international relief agencies seldom allow local professionals to be involved at the senior level in the planning, preparation, and execution of their programs. Such policies would obviate the mistakes caused by an inadequate knowledge of local conditions. The Third World has progressed considerably since the 1960s, when expatriate staff assigned to developing countries were, for the most part, the only experts available. Nowadays, the majority of developing states have their own highly trained professionals and skilled technicians. Unfortunately, in civil strife situations they, too, become casualties and can be found among the displaced and the exiled.

Wherever possible, UN agencies and international NGOs should give local professionals the opportunity to play a role in relief activities and in programs designed for the rehabilitation and reconstruction of their countries. A policy of this kind would lead to the return of many of the country's trained and experienced people. Once the emergency is over, and the expatriate agencies depart, the local professionals could ensure the smooth transfer from relief to reconstruction programs. Moreover, their presence would constitute a pool from which the national authorities could draw to staff the civil service once it is reestablished. Many of them would be willing to return to their countries on short-, medium-, or long-term contracts. The UNDP program known as Tokten (Transfer of Knowledge Through Expatriate Nationals) would be ideal for this purpose and could be adapted to meet the special needs of each country.

THE ROLE OF NGOs

In some countries international organizations have taken initiatives in training local personnel and in strengthening local structures, but much more needs to be done. As a reporter from the *London Observer* (August 23, 1992) who recently returned from an African country aptly commented,

> It is vital that we assist local infrastructures. And it is vital that the UN begins to channel resources through those structures. Emergency-type organizations are not going to be here forever and, when they go, who will take over? T.E. Lawrence once wrote: "Better to let them do imperfectly what you can do perfectly yourself, for it is their country, their war and your time is short."

The winds of political change have begun to blow across the borders of many countries. If they bring the democratic process in their wake, there will be much more decentralization of authority than has hitherto existed. Local communities will be expected to shoulder more responsibility for their own development at the grass-roots level, and they would be well served if they had on hand the services of local NGOs, working in concert with their international colleagues. These circumstances would certainly facilitate the transition to stable government.

In relief work, as well as in development at the community level, no discussion about needs and solutions would be complete without reference to the role of international NGOs. In my visits to disaster areas, I was always impressed by their zeal and commitment, and by the confidence that their activities generated among the communities in which they worked. Sometimes they were the only ones prepared to provide emergency assistance under difficult conditions, when others with greater resources had withdrawn. It was evident that for many of them, the task they were performing was more a vocation than a career. Of course, as with other organizations, international NGOs must periodically examine their goals and procedures to ensure that their objectives are maintained, their shortcomings corrected, and any members who are out of step—by attitude or behavior—are brought back into line.

PRINCIPLES GOVERNING INTERNATIONAL AID

I have dwelt at some length on many of the practical problems and needs encountered in the day-to-day oversight of relief operations.

Overshadowing these problems was the broader one of the absence of a clearly defined and widely accepted set of principles governing international humanitarian assistance.

In my time, the guidelines that governed UN activities in conflict or disaster situations varied according to the particular mandate of the agency concerned. They were not widely known, either within the UN, or by states for whose benefit the guidelines were designed. The need for compiling information on these guidelines became apparent when the secretary-general's consultative group on the Horn of Africa began its work in 1989. Since the group was composed of representatives of agencies involved in humanitarian activities, including the ICRC, they had to be conversant with each other's mandates and the principles guiding their relief operations. Some useful information emerged, and it would be helpful if the information they exchanged could be edited and incorporated in the form of a handbook. The same could be done for the operational principles and procedures of international governmental and nongovernmental organizations. Such information would be of value not only to relief agencies but also to recipient states, which need to be aware of the source and type of aid available, the procedures to be followed in order to secure the aid, and the conditions attached to it.

Reorganizing UN Aid Mechanisms

General Assembly Resolution 46/182 was a landmark achievement that codified a set of principles to guide future UN relief operations, and instituted organizational changes to make the collective response of the international community more effective. In comparison to the piecemeal approach taken in the past, Resolution 46/182 was a comprehensive and reasoned effort to establish a firm basis for efficient and coordinated responses to appeals for emergency assistance.

Many weaknesses in the response mechanism were identified, together with the requisite solutions for their correction. These included measures for strengthening the capacity of developing countries in disaster prevention and mitigation, increasing the availability of early warning systems, creating a $50 million emergency revolving fund, and reorganizing and improving the coordination of UN aid mechanisms. Special attention was given to the relationship between emergency, rehabilitation, and development. The resolution stressed that in order to ensure a smooth transition from relief to rehabilitation and development, emergency assistance should be provided in ways that will be supportive of recovery and long-term development.

SOVEREIGNTY AND HUMANITARIAN INTERVENTION

Resolution 46/182 also established a set of broad, legal principles to guide future relief operations. The consensus reached on these important points came about after intense behind-the-scenes discussions. The most controversial issue was a suggestion that provision for unilateral humanitarian intervention by the UN be permitted in certain situations without requiring the prior consent of the state concerned. Many participants contended that humanitarian aid was a human right and should be available to all in need. This issue had not been raised at previous sessions of the General Assembly. Those who had raised the issue in closed sessions did not press the point in the open debate, whereas delegates from the developing world discussed the legal implications and recorded their objection to any weakening of the principles of "sovereignty" and "domestic jurisdiction."

During the debate over these issues the chairman of the group of developing nations expressed concern that other states might not be sensitive to the pleas of the developing world for an abiding respect for the sovereignty of nations. Such concerns stemmed from the historical past when many states, as colonial subjects, had no rights. The respect for sovereignty enjoined in the UN charter was not an idle stipulation that could be rejected even in the name of the noblest gestures. An essential attribute of sovereignty is the principle of consent—one of the cornerstones of the democratic ideal itself. The UN ought not to be commandeered into forming an assistance brigade that would deliver its gifts by coercion.

Other speakers said that it would be a mistake to give the UN functions that were neither provided in its charter nor supported by international law, and warned against the UN being used as a platform for interfering in the internal affairs of states or undermining their sovereignty. The type of emergency situation that would justify international humanitarian intervention without the consent of the state concerned had to be clearly defined, otherwise the concept could give rise to arbitrary or unilateral interpretations, adversely affecting the fundamental principle of respect for the sovereignty of states.

These concerns eventually prevailed and the guiding principles adopted by the General Assembly made clear that the sovereignty, territorial integrity, and national unity of states had to be fully respected in accordance with the UN charter. It was agreed that humanitarian assistance should be provided with the consent of the affected country, and, in principle, on the basis of an appeal by the affected country.

The use of the word *country* rather than *government* is significant because it leaves a certain ambiguity on the question of who could appeal for help—the government or the distressed population. States that emphasized sovereignty and states that believed that humanitarian concerns should be paramount in certain circumstances will no doubt read into that provision what they would like to see. Of course, in the final analysis, the matter does not rest with the General Assembly. The Security Council is free to take whatever action it considers appropriate if it determines that a situation is a threat to the peace, and that unilateral humanitarian intervention provides the only means by which help can be delivered to a population in need.

Looking back, it occurs to me that a great deal of the suffering and immense loss of life inflicted on innocent populations by civil strife could have been avoided if member states of the UN had not felt as trapped as they did by provisions of the charter they had themselves either formulated or endorsed. There have been situations when questions of sovereignty and domestic jurisdiction should not have been allowed to paralyze humanitarian intervention—situations when there was compelling evidence that an overwhelming human tragedy was taking place, and when intervention was the only way that humanitarian assistance could reach the affected population. In my view, there comes a time when the law of humanity must prevail over all other considerations.

17

Lifelines to the Innocent: Children Caught in War

RICHARD REID

Any one of us who has ever put a dead child into the ground in a wooden box—or a wrapping of rags or banana leaves—has had to stifle a cry of rage. These children died because we let them die. No one was there to protect them. Where in God's name is our wonderful humane civilization?
                    —Diary note of a UN field worker in Sudan, 1989

Among all the creatures on the phylogenetic tree, our species in its early years is spectacular in its vulnerability. The most robust young child is as perishable as a blade of grass. There have been eras, some as recent as the seventeenth century, as often as not in the most advanced societies, when more than half of all live-born infants died before the age of five.

Things are not as different today as one may think. The world has all the means to stave off the childhood killer diseases, but in many African and Asian countries young children still die at a ratio of one to five or one to six of those born. Many infants are small at birth—many scarcely larger than one's hand, weighing three pounds—and in the critical months that follow they get too few of the foods and nutrients that might give them a fair grip on life. A two-year-old can look normal to his mother in the morning and be dead that night. It takes little to push them over the edge—an epidemic of measles in the village, a chest infection, a bout of diarrhea that turns half-convulsive, with stooling at shorter and shorter intervals. The pulse weakens, the kidneys fail, the blood cells collapse; the lights of the body go out. It can happen in six hours. Nearly thirteen million children die this way every year, 36,000 a day.

These numbers stun the mind. At a time of radically expanding immunization and diarrhea control by the health services of even the poorest countries, what keeps child deaths at these levels? Why haven't the vaccines, the ampicillins, the oral rehydration salts shielded them? The answer is that malnutrition and disease have been powerfully reinforced in the second half of this century, especially over the past two decades, by a multiplier agent of terrible effectiveness. That agent is armed conflict, and it is the principal reason many of these children have had no vaccines and oral rehydration—or sufficient food. The kind of war commonly waged in the world since the mid-sixties destroys civilian infrastructure and supply lines much faster than it knocks out tanks or bunkers. Towns are leveled anonymously by artillery and missiles from the air; the man at the firing lever never sees or guesses at the child whose home and parents he has blown up. In late August 1992, three weeks prior to this writing, the opposition forces positioned around Kabul launched a saturation bombardment that rained two thousand rockets and shells on the city in ninety minutes; residential neighborhoods were hit as often as "military" areas. In World War I only one-tenth of the casualties were civilian; now 90 percent of those who die due to war are noncombatants, particularly children. In the Sudanese civil war up to mid-1989, it was estimated that fourteen children died for every dead government soldier or rebel. These children died not from bullets or bombing, but from wholesale dispersal. The fighting drove them away from their families, homes, farms, wells, fishing places, support systems; it wrecked the health services. Until the two sides were pried apart for three months to create "corridors of tranquility" and restore supply lines, the fighting kept outside aid from reaching them.

A glance at the world's mortality tables is instructive. The first, second, and third highest child mortality rates in the world are those of countries whose names are synonymous with war—Mozambique, Afghanistan, and Angola. Roughly a third of the young children of these countries do not live to see their fifth birthdays. Close behind them are Ethiopia, Somalia, Liberia, and Cambodia. All of them have been so torn apart internally by fighting that even the supply and distribution of salt and matches, the ultimate basics that find their way to remote areas in the most primitive conditions, have been disrupted. A measure of the size of child losses in these countries is that they are occurring at a constant rate probably five times greater than Bosnia's.

The Somalias and Bosnias of today were prefigured by some wars in the past that fell squarely on civilian populations, but never on the scale or frequency that is the norm now. The Hittites, the Children of Israel, Philip of Macedon, King Herod, the religious wars of Europe, the New World campaigns of Pizzaro and Cortez, the Chaco wars, Manchuria, Guernica, all these brought episodes of indiscriminate slaughter, some encouraged by policy, some driven by a spirit of reprisal, but through all of this and despite it there ran a sense, approaching a taboo, that children, along with women and the elderly, were to be succored and were beyond the limits of attack. The nature of war before this century accommodated such discrimination. The soldier, even the mercenary, could take the high road of chivalry or magnanimity in times when, apart from sieges and raids, state-sponsored conflict took place mainly on battlegrounds well away from towns and settlements. Killing then was more an individual action, an intimate and arduous act. It had more links with conscience than the insouciant spraying of a village with an AK-47. Volition and choice were involved.

Added to this was the aura of innocence that was attached to children up through the start of this century. They were also revered as the seed of the race—insurance against extinction. In those precarious times, the decimation of populations by half or more due to famine or pestilence was a possibility dreaded by all. Population replenishment was crucial. And so, across hundreds of generations, there emerged a social contract that bound combatants to protect and spare children and the defenseless.

That contract began to lose its adhesion with the advent of mechanized war. It has pulled apart more and more rapidly since. Relief columns are routinely shot up, their drivers killed. Relief workers are forced to hire gunmen to protect refugee food supplies from gangs of other gunmen. At this moment, except in editorial columns and the policies of humanitarian organizations, or intermittently by governments seeking a pretext for an ulterior motive, there would appear to be no contract at all on the ground where the fighting rages, only cease-fires and safe passages that evaporate at a gunman's whim. Are these brief compacts with assassins the best endeavor of a world all too likcly to be faced in the near future with ethnic, religious, and civil wars that may make Bosnia seem mild? Where will the world be if Kenya or Macedonia crack apart and we cannot get humanitarian supplies and a measure of enforced civil order into Bosnia and Somalia? Can it be that we are already seeing the last of the legacy of "self-determination" that came with the Cold War's end?

The problem of getting lifelines to the innocent has other roots besides intercommunal hatred and local brutishness. It is more than a matter of Serbs, Croatians, and Muslims trying to kill each other, more than situation-specific mortar fire on funerals or lethal ambushes of UN supply columns. It spreads more widely into the motivations of nations and leaders. For many, worse is better. Chaos begets opportunity. This was certainly true in Lebanon, where warlords and leaders from all sides decried the suffering of the people while plucking at abundant political options amid the disorder and amassing huge wealth from arms sales and the drug trade. A similar alert entrepreneurialism has sprung up among the militias in Bosnia, reminding one observer of "hyenas at the carcass."

The problem may also be a contemporary reflection of the world's inertness in the face of the killing fields of Cambodia, or the later acceptance of the Khmer Rouge as that country's legal representative at the United Nations. Radical dissociation of this kind, which has often happened in the face of Bengal famines, Treblinkas, and boat people, may best be explained by the dynamics of mob psychology, which insulate individuals (here nations) from blame for actions or inaction, and distribute (or deny) guilt to the point of dissipation of conscience. "My country is only a bystander in this beastly business," is the gist of the message. "The carnage would only spread if we were to be involved. The odds against success are too high." This argument may have made sense in the framework of the Cold War, when a rescue foray into a Soviet client country (or the reverse on the part of the USSR) could have triggered a nuclear confrontation. But now the basis for that line of reasoning has evaporated. The Security Council is in a consensus mode, or near enough one to authorize major actions undreamed of in the UN's history. In the political world at large all alignments have loosened, and there are no menacing big protectors. Everything is scrambled and tentative. If in this clear field the Muslims in Bosnia, the population of Haiti, and all of the defenseless in Kabul are fair game, and none of their tormentors have either apologists, powerful protectors, or great power of their own, what is to keep the world from clamping down on the tormentors? Surely it can't all boil down to "no oil, no concern"—the logic of the limited strategic interests of nations, which brought lightning mobilization against Saddam Hussein but finds the Western allies avoiding real confrontation with Slobodan Milosevic.

It cannot boil down only to this, because the same allies that pounded Saddam Hussein over oil also built an elaborate umbrella of protection over Iraq's Kurds—a broad and costly humanitarian enterprise that has brought little comparable in the way of strategic benefit. This major humanitarian "aberration" came about for reasons of public pressure and political response that can raise hopes for aid to the Somalias and Bosnias. Ethiopia in 1982—the BBC footage of living child skeletons—comes to mind. There are permanent fonts of mercy and outrage in the world that are deeper than the fear of doubled gasoline prices. At the other end of the ethical spectrum, often among the most ruthless political leaders there is a readiness to be perceived as the fathers of their people. Among the ruthless as well as the benign is a reservoir of fear of humiliation, disparagement, isolation. These reservoirs can be tapped wisely, and they can help open lifelines.

Used alongside good logistics and supply mechanisms, these resorts to the heart (or the instincts) of those controlling the game in conflict zones have cleared the way since 1985 for a number of successful, if short-term, humanitarian supply actions that have caused fighting to stop for the sake of the innocent. These actions in turn have given rise to the growth of a kind of common-law acceptance of the right of humanitarian intervention on behalf of children, mothers, and the defenseless. A sense of this was captured in the latter part of 1991 by the French foreign minister. Looking back on the Gulf War, he said:

> For the first time through a Security Council resolution, the United Nations affirmed that the sufferings of a population justified immediate intervention. Today the foundations of a new right, of a new humanitarian order, have been laid. Why not adopt a code of conduct affirming the right of humanitarian assistance every time the integrity and survival of a people is threatened?[1]

The humanitarian interventions cited above were carried out between 1985 and 1991 in El Salvador, Lebanon, Sudan, and Iraq. Each was different, but all had in common an urgent supply imperative, international or local public awareness-raising campaigns, and a successful appeal to the combatants to stop fighting so as to permit the intervention. Two of the four focused on immunization, one on an array of supplies led by food, and one on emergency medical supplies. They are summarized in the following sections.

El Salvador

This intervention, (beginning in 1985 and continuing annually through 1989) as a joint campaign created by the Catholic Church of El Salvador, the Government of President Napoleon Duarte, the rebel command, the national media, the Rotarians, the Boy Scouts, the Red Cross, UNICEF, and the Pan American Health Organization, became an early model of humanitarian intervention. Its objective was to fan out across the country for three days with government, guerrilla, church, and private vehicles carrying refrigerated vaccines for all of the country's unimmunized under-one-year olds, who would be enumerated by village or neighborhood and brought to two thousand vaccination stations—clinics, schools, churches—and inoculated by on-site teams readied in advance by training programs on both sides of the fighting lines. The blitz-style campaign was also aimed at reviving the demoralized rural health services, most elements of which had been driven out of operation.

The drama of the campaign was that nothing was certain until the first day of the cease-fire. For three days an atmosphere of feverish and festive mobilization prevailed from San Salvador to remote forest settlements, unmarred by any outbreaks of fighting. The nearest approach to an incident occurred when guerrillas abducted two doctors and took them to an unmanned health center where children were waiting with their parents to be vaccinated. Once the shots had been administered, the two physicians were returned to their homes. Ultimately, the children of El Salvador were vaccinated to a 62 percent coverage level.

All the principals in this effort emerged winners, and a previously unreached cohort of children were given a shield of protection. Media coverage and public feedback showed that the campaign reminded Salvadorans of priorities more fundamental than political power. The campaign has been viewed as one of the earliest precursors of the national peace, finally obtained at the end of 1991. "This reconciliation for progress and the common good announced loudly El Salvador's commitment to a positive future, and has been an inspiration to the rest of the world," said UN Secretary-General Javier Pérez de Cuéllar in a letter to President Duarte.

Lebanon

This immunization intervention was dependent, like El Salvador's, on the tight timing of vaccine, syringe, and cold chain equipment air shipments from UNIPAC, UNICEF's emergency supply center in Copenhagen. Nineteen eighty-seven was the twelfth year of Lebanon's civil war. The national health ministry in Beirut, drained of funds and with no central government to support it, had essentially closed its doors. There had been no systematic countrywide vaccination for at least five years. Sporadic measles outbreaks had been reported, and UNICEF feared a full-scale epidemic in the winter. The malnutrition that had become general across the country would push measles mortality to levels higher than they had been since the 1940s. But the Lebanon campaign that grew out of these fears—three vaccination rounds of four days each in September, October, and November 1987, with the aim of reaching out to all unvaccinated children under the age of five and immunizing at least 80 percent of them—was to hinge on a fickle conjunction of elements. Seven often-violent factions—among them the Sunni, Maronite, Shiite, Druze, and Eastern Orthodox groupings, the real rulers of the country—would have to be brought to agreement on the idea of monthly "days of tranquility," and all would have to accept and honor the cease-fire dates. Negotiations with these groups took on the character of seven-dimensional chess. As artillery exchanges rocked Beirut, UNICEF met with the factions at their fortified villas or at rendezvous points. Leaders such as Nabin Berri (Shiites), Amin Gemayel (Maronites), Walid Jumblatt (Druze), and Sheikh Fadlallah (Hizbollah) played critical roles. The message of making Lebanon something more than an object of the world's disgust, and of protecting its children despite adult political madness, went out from churches, mosques, and the media, especially Lebanese television, which produced dramatic spots of riveting frankness. In the end, the country transcended itself. The September, October, and November cease-fires not only held but saw the warring factions bend themselves to the effort of getting vaccines, syringes, children, and mothers to the immunization stations. Cold boxes and vaccine carriers were hauled across factional boundaries that had only been crossed in the past by tanks and tracer bullets. Taxi drivers crisscrossed Beirut and the suburbs to report by radio on vaccination stations that had run out of syringes. Eighty-two percent of the child target group were immunized, and there was no measles epidemic—or outbreak—that winter.

Sudan

Here the supply intervention was mainly a matter of food, and what was at risk dwarfed the human scope—if not the political complexity—of El Salvador and Lebanon. At least half a million people, the majority children and women, seemed likely to die that summer from disease and hunger in southern Sudan unless a mammoth effort could be mounted to get food to them before the onset of the May to August rainy season, which would make access all but impossible. This dawned on the world as the southern provinces lay prostrate from drought, critically low grain stocks, and the accumulated damage of a grinding, eight-year civil war that had turned an area of savannah, marshland, and desert the size of France and Germany into a diaspora zone. Most of the population, both fit and infirm, had set out in straggling refugee migrations toward government garrison towns and understocked UN and NGO feeding centers, or, in desperation, toward Ethiopia and Uganda, each hundreds of miles away.

The task of getting 110,000 tons of food, mainly grain, but also drugs, vaccines, agricultural tools, seeds, and fishing nets and lines to the people of this area in the spring and summer of 1989 came to be called Operation Lifeline Sudan (OLS). Initiated by the UN on a rising tide of press and NGO warnings of a famine worse than Ethiopia's six years earlier, Operation Lifeline was headed by UNICEF Executive Director James Grant as special representative of the secretary-general. He coordinated the work of an emergency coalition of UN agencies (principally the World Food Programme [WFP], UNICEF, and United Nations Development Programme [UNDP]), bilateral aid agencies (such as USAID), and a host of NGOs (including Save the Children/U.K., World Vision, Irish Concern, OXFAM, Médecins sans Frontières, and Lutheran World Relief). Apart from the orchestration of these agencies, the global fund-raising for the operation, and the short time remaining, there were three main challenges bound up in the overall task. First, WFP experts had to locate and obtain the grain needed. Second, WFP and other OLS team members needed to open access routes from Khartoum or other points to the emergency area by rail, river, road, and air for delivery. Third, the OLS negotiating team, led by Grant, had to bring the government of Prime Minister Sadiq el Mahdi and the Sudan People's Liberation Army (SPLA) of John Garang to a cessation of hostilities long enough to permit delivery and distribution. Each of the challenges seemed intractable, but the most daunting were the second and third—physical access and political agreement.

Opening access routes meant working from almost a zero base, not simply reactivating reasonably maintained routes ready for supply transit. The main rail line to the south, seen by all as the main channel for moving the grain, had been essentially abandoned years earlier in the civil war, due to its vulnerability to attack by the SPLA. Rails and cross-ties were overgrown with heavy grass, long stretches were strewn with sand and rubble, and some segments had been mined. Also abandoned was the north-south barge route along the Nile, from Kosti to Juba, the next most important conduit. All barge stock of significant tonnage in the country was beached, damaged, in the hands of SPLA units, or in dry dock in Khartoum. The roads to the south, unpaved dirt tracks that would turn to sticky gumbo during the rainy season, were regarded as shooting galleries, with driver deaths common and truck rates extortionate. Nor was the air safe; relief planes had been shot at, even fired upon by SAM-7 missiles. It was impossible to know who was doing the firing—were the gunners SPLA forces surrounding the government garrison towns and airstrips, government troops defending them, or government-inspired militias doing free-lance work? A vast area that needed to be laced with supply lines to avert mass death looked impassable due to human and physical obstacles. As OLS began to tackle these problems, alarming tallies of sinking nutritional levels, estimated deaths by sector among children and old people, and increasing village depopulation came in from NGOs already engaged in the south, as well as from the well-established International Committee of the Red Cross (ICRC), which was to work parallel to OLS throughout the emergency.

Political agreement for Operation Lifeline followed a pattern of three steps forward and two back. Neither the government in Khartoum nor the SPLA in its Ethiopian rear base was pleased to contemplate the confusion of its war plans by a large-scale humanitarian intervention. Yet both sides, in different ways, could see international image and support value to be gained from cooperating or being perceived to cooperate with OLS. To an important degree both, particularly the government, were beleaguered and isolated internationally, as is generally the case with governments or movements presiding over wars that go out of control and principally ruin the civilian population.

Unlike today, in 1989, the tide of Sudan's civil war was carrying the SPLA forward. The rebels effectively held, or could move with impunity through, a third of the country. Making Dinka their official language in place of the Arabic imposed by Khartoum, they loosely administered large areas, set up schools and clinics, and put their own relief organization to work in the field. John Garang disavowed all talk of secession, but the vague *de facto* outlines of a separate political, ethnic, and linguistic entity, disdainful of the Muslim central government, began to take shape. Khartoum, politically divided internally by a powerful fundamentalist opposition, was adamantly against any loosening of sovereignty for the sake of OLS. There was a deep fear of "recognition" of the SPLA in any form. Hence Prime Minister Sadiq el Mahdi's government could never acknowledge the rebels as more than "buzzing mosquitoes," let alone deal with them in the arrangement of the fire-free zones—corridors of tranquility—required to reach the south with food. Word spread that OLS was a Western-backed front for the SPLA. Fundamentalists fanned these reports and embroidered on them. The credibility of Operation Lifeline's neutrality—its aim of equally aiding the stricken in government garrison towns and areas as well as those in rebel-dominated areas—was suddenly fragile. The whole intervention was at risk. So, not incidentally, was the El Mahdi government.

Sorely needed at this point was an event or situation that would give maximum "face" to the government, appease or co-opt its opponents, and gain a broad base of Sudanese acceptance of the scope of the crisis and the appropriateness of a major UN role in addressing it. This came in February 1989, when, at Grant's urging, the UN and the government organized an International Sudan Emergency Conference in Khartoum. The meeting was opened and chaired by Prime Minister el Mahdi. The main opposition leader and National Islamic Front head, Hassan el Turabi, participated prominently, as did Grant and World Food Programme executive director James Ingram. The conference rescued OLS and gave it a "prospector's permit" valid for government-controlled areas in the south. This foothold would soon expand. In addition, the conference gave the government a relatively free hand to work openly with the OLS leadership.

In the meantime, as February and March passed and the weight of donor government and world media pressure increased, Khartoum agreed to permit Grant and OLS staff to sound out the rebels. The aim was to explore "modalities" of reduced military activity along the main supply routes. Soon afterward, two low-profile visits to the SPLA leadership in Addis Ababa were made by this writer. Simultaneously, the broad lines of a cross-border supply capability for air and road shipments from Kenya to southern Sudan were established by the World Food Programme and UNICEF in Nairobi. To reinforce the Kenya routes as needed, backup plans were made for supply movements from Uganda—from Entebbe by air and Kampala by land. Step by step through March and April, as the rainy season approached and more force and expectation were attached to OLS, not only by the outside aid-givers but by the increasingly engaged government and SPLA, the operation took on a life of its own that eased open all routes, at first to a trickle of supply and then to a stream. Thousands now had hands-on involvement in OLS—the Khartoum bureaucracy, the increasingly large UN field staff, UN guards and volunteers for the barge and train routes, SPLA soldiers and nonmilitary administrators, large and small NGOs, and the ICRC in vital parallel actions. By late May the remaining main challenge was one of pushing the food and other supplies along the corridors rapidly enough and overseeing their distribution. The two sides in the war had backed away from the routes except to join in clearance and secondary transport to NGO-manned distribution sites. Attacks from scattered militias and raider tribes such as the Toposa were never fully controlled, but basically the fighting had stopped. The corridors of tranquility were to hold for the better part of three months.

The hard-won success of Operation Lifeline Sudan has been described in greater detail in other accounts. In the end, the effort did stave off disaster: the 110,000 tons of grain reached those who needed it, unevenly but sufficiently. There was no famine. Child deaths for the year beginning in May 1989 were not measurably higher than in nonemergency years. In the crescent-shaped area of the south reached by cross-border operations from Kenya, immunization levels tripled during OLS. By and large, the people dispersed by the crisis gradually found their way back to their villages, and the precarious civil society of southern Sudan began to reconstitute itself.

Probably more important than this supply/logistical accomplishment—the sustained feeding and health protection of hundreds of thousands—was the precedent it established. A full-scale humanitarian intervention, supported by world opinion but opposed at length by a seated government, had succeeded through negotiation in stopping a war for a substantial period. Moreover, OLS gave an understood legitimacy to the practice of establishing cross-border humanitarian routes. The introduction of this cross-border element, acquiesced to by a government made malleable by international pressure, cut at the premise of unconditional sovereignty that had long given free rein to murderous leaders such as Idi Amin. The significance of what OLS established in 1989 was to be enshrined a year later in the Declaration of the World Summit for Children, which bears the signatures of more than 150 heads of state or government. The declaration urged that "periods of tranquility and special relief corridors be observed for the benefit of children, where war and violence . . . are taking place." Operation Lifeline Sudan had carried the principle of humanitarian intervention a long step forward from El Salvador and Lebanon. The precedent it set would soon pave the way for similar supply corridors in Ethiopia and Angola.

Iraq

Humanitarian aid to Iraq since the country's defeat in 1991 has been tangled in political ambivalence. Balked at every turn by the embargo controls of the allies and the machinations of the Iraqis themselves, aid for the country's needy majority has been too little and too scattered. However, that is not the subject of this account; the topic here will be a single intervention made on behalf of Iraqi children and mothers during the war. Unique because it took place in a major conflict among nations and not a civil war, this action, a one-week emergency supply mission carried out by road, brought with it the added nuance of originating across the border of an enemy nation—Iran. Rarer still, it delivered UN aid to an "outlaw" government fighting to repel a UN-sponsored attack. The critical last leg of the mission took place, more-over, under the protective umbrella of a prearranged six-hour pause in allied bombing. Judged along lines of response to pure need, orches-trated cooperation between the two sides, and adherence to political neutrality, the UNICEF-WHO mission from Tehran to Baghdad the week of February 16 can be viewed as a high-water mark in humanitar-ian intervention.

The sailing was not all smooth in the weeks before the February mission. UNICEF, citing dwindling Iraqi stores of children's vaccines and birth supplies, had been hard-pressed over three weeks in December 1990 to win UN Sanctions Committee approval even for an emer-gency supply flight from UNIPAC/Copenhagen to Baghdad. UNICEF and WHO had calculated that Iraq's average of 1,100 new-borns a day, coupled with the effects of the embargo, would soon bring the birth supply stocks and vaccines in the Baghdad central medical stores to nearly zero—a critical condition for a Ministry of Health that had never accumulated deep stocks, relying always on easy resupply by air from Europe. After back-and-forth discussion between UNICEF and Sanctions committee members on whether the bowls, scissors, and rubber sheets in standard UNIPAC midwife kits could be put to war uses by the Iraqis, a green light from the allies was finally secured. UNICEF flew a cargo of midwives' kits and vaccines, the first UN emergency supply flight of the war, from Copenhagen to Saddam Hussein Airport on December 18.

Those birth supplies would be no more than a brief solution. By February, the effects of the sanctions in squeezing health resupply, along with the wiping out of energy sources by allied bombing, had reduced Iraq to the infant mortality potential of an Ethiopia. The UNICEF country office in Baghdad monitored the situation daily and, as telephone contact grew uncertain, sent regular status reports to the Amman regional office by road. Sometimes these reports were brought by staff who then returned to Baghdad with basic food items and bottled water for colleagues' families. The reports depicted apartment building occupants huddled in basements around the clock, as well as a collapse of water-sanitation systems, the food supply, and the health services. What emerged was a natural-disaster-like profile of need, calling more for emergency field medical items to fend off epidemics than the sophisticated medicines and hospital equipment requested by the Ministry of Health. Iraq's hospitals, like the rest of the country's modern sector, were wholly dependent on a state-of-the-art electrical grid that had been rendered brain-dead during the first twelve hours of allied bombing. There was no chance that large-city hospitals could be functional in the foreseeable future.

What Iraq needed most was a large-volume infusion of preventive medical aid. This was needed for ethical and political reasons as much as for epidemiological ones. In several Arab countries, commentators had raised an awkward question: did Iraqi children have less of a right to protection because they were on the wrong side in the war? The UN also needed to remind the world that its humanitarian operations had not gone into suspension.

Serious consideration of a larger delivery of UN supplies, focusing on children, began at UNICEF New York in early January 1991. The possibility of direct origin-to-destination air transport was at first set aside tentatively because of bulk factors and tonnage limitations, and then definitively because of the expected incapacitation of Iraqi airports by allied bombing. Time factors and the UN blockade of Aqaba put any seaport transshipment out of question. What was needed was a road route with the shortest traverse of Iraqi territory. This ruled out the desert highway from the Jordanian border to Baghdad, a normally excellent but long route so strategically situated that it would soon be a target of air attacks. One acceptable road option remained—the highway from the Iranian border town of Karan to Baghdad, a maximum four-to-five-hour trip by heavy truck.

Use of this route—and, for that matter, the implementation of any supply mission to Iraq—would require permissions from several sides. Iran, Iraq, the UN secretary-general, the allied coalition, and the Sanctions committee would all need to agree. UNICEF began to put out feelers in New York and elsewhere. Iran signaled its agreement in principle, suggesting that it might be ready to help assemble a truck convoy in Tehran. Secretary-General Pérez de Cuéllar encouraged UNICEF's Grant to explore further. In Copenhagen, UNIPAC was put on alert to prepare for multiple air shipments to Tehran. The war had begun on January 17, and within a week the first accounts of pinpoint bombing began to appear in the media along with reports of a free-fall deterioration of social conditions in Iraq. The Iran shipment plan was presented to members of the Sanctions committee and received general support. In Amman, the Iraqi ambassador reported to UNICEF that his government would accept the mission. The key bases had been touched.

In the meantime, Grant had been in contact with WHO leadership in Geneva, where he met on January 28 with WHO director-general Hiroshi Nakajima and each organization's regional director for the Middle East to lay out plans for a joint mission in February. A week later, the seven team members chosen to carry out the mission—four from UNICEF and three from WHO, a group including four physicians, a nutritionist, a water-sanitation engineer, and the UNICEF regional director—met for two days at the WHO regional office in Alexandria to map out aims and roles. They would meet six days later in Tehran, the UNICEF team members traveling circuitously from Amman by way of Cyprus and Vienna because of commercial flight cancellations, and the WHO group arriving directly from Geneva.

In Tehran, the UNICEF and WHO offices had enlisted Iranian drivers and completed loading fifty-two tons of air-delivered and locally-produced supplies into long-haul trucks as the mission members arrived for a briefing layover of a day. The mission left Tehran on snowy roads the morning of February 15 with twelve trucks and three landcruisers. The main cargo of the trucks was 300 emergency medical kits and enough vaccines and syringes to bring the Iraqi medical stores

up to a six-week supply level. Each of the emergency medical kits—
meant for use by doctors and trained clinical staff—was designed to
meet the crisis needs of 10,000 people for three months. The kits
contained essential surgical supplies, basic drugs and medicines, an-
tiseptics, and dressings. For security reasons on the Iraqi side of the
border, the trucks themselves had been dressed for safety—each was
emblazoned with three meter-high UN markings on its top and sides.
This added confidence to an agreement struck earlier with the allied
bombing command, which assured the UN that the convoy would be
granted a bomb-free corridor for six hours once it entered Iraq.

For ten hours the three landcruisers carrying the team members and
their provisions led the convoy across south-central Iran and up
through the Zagros Mountains to Bakhtaran, where they spent the
night in a hotel that had housed Soviet peace negotiators a few days
earlier. Early on the morning of the sixteenth, the convoy drove the
remaining distance to the Karan-Khosrovi border area, a ten-
kilometer-wide belt of razed countryside. As Iranian border guards
checked the convoy through, one question was in all minds: would the
Iraqis be waiting with trucks and drivers on their side? No one had
been able to confirm this in anxious phone conversations with New
York the night before.

Once across the border, however, it was clear that the team was
expected. An Iraqi Health Ministry delegation, headed by a deputy
minister, was waiting across the chain barrier with everything
needed—drivers, trucks, and a minibus for the UN team. The unloading and reloading were done in ninety minutes. The convoy refueled
and began its dash for Baghdad under heavily overcast skies, with two
of its allotted six hours already elapsed. Along the route the only signs
of war were the flattened remains of electrical transmission towers and
power stations, large and small. During two brief stops en route, the
one sound clearly audible from the empty highway was the rumble of
allied jets crisscrossing overhead. While team members saw few additional signs of destruction during the approach to Baghdad, the collapse of the water system was manifest; people on all sides, in fields and
on village streets, were carrying tins and buckets of water scooped from
irrigation canals and gutters. Leaving behind four of its trucks for
unloading at suburban Health Ministry distribution sites outside the
customary allied bombing pattern, the team continued on to the El
Rashid Hotel for a 5 P.M. arrival, six hours after leaving Khosrovi.

The UNICEF/WHO team remained in Baghdad and the south-
central Iraq area for five days, as bombing resumed and reached a peak

February 17–18. Working in pairs from 7 A.M. to nightfall so as to make maximum use of daylight (there was no electricity), team members traveled to neighborhood clinics and dispensaries to pore over patient intake records and interview staff, parents, and children. Many unannounced home visits in poor areas, such as Saddam City, were also made. One repeated observation was the hushed, fearful behavior of many older children. These ten-to-twelve-year-olds tended to stay within touching distance of their parents at all times. Younger children seemed less affected; they were often seen playing ball or flying kites as the ground shook from bombing and anti-aircraft fire not far away. Team members also spent much time assessing damage to health and water facilities and looking into the distribution of the newly arrived supplies. On-site inventories showed that the vaccines brought by the convoy had increased the stocks of the central medical stores by almost 80 percent. The availability of the new vaccines helped the team convince the still-dazed Health Ministry that it was timely and urgent to put an epidemic control program into operation in Baghdad. No piped water had run and no toilets had flushed in the city since the start of the bombing. For almost a month the slow-moving Tigris River had served the population variously as a public bath, waste sluice, and water source. Steps had to be taken to avert widespread outbreaks of typhoid and cholera.

Well before the seven members of the Iraq mission team traveled back to Tehran to complete their assessment report and return to their duty stations, it was clear that the mission had had a catalytic effect in opening up Iraq to a rainbow variety of humanitarian assistance. Only the ICRC had put staff on the ground earlier. UNICEF reopened its office in Baghdad to full operation the day after the mission's arrival; other UN agencies began to follow suit shortly and were ready for full operation when the war stopped at the end of February. Under an agreement between the government and UNICEF, there was a rapid influx of foreign NGOs—the first ever to be permitted to deploy staff in Iraq. The mission also had its effects in New York, where its assessment report helped broaden the Sanctions committee's definition of permissible humanitarian assistance to Iraq.

If the UNICEF/WHO mission broke new ground in moving supplies into a country at war, it and the relief developments that followed it also gave rise to hard ethical questions, some new, some as old as Hitler, that might have been expected to evoke a consensus response, but have still produced none.

Item: Is there any justification for economic embargoes? Even if an embargo were eventually to stop humanitarian offenses in a country, or to cause ill-gained territory to be relinquished—which has not happened in any important test—would the day-to-day punishment levied by the embargo on the country's common people be defensible? How much are the ruling groups in Baghdad, Belgrade, and Port au Prince suffering?

Item: Is the principle of humanitarian intervention a sliding scale, to be used when circumstances are politically safe and morally convenient (Sudan) or inflamed by fears of endangered wealth (Iraq/Kuwait), but not in cases of mere distant mayhem (Serbia)?

Item: Peacekeeping versus peacemaking. Gunmen in Somalia joke that the UN peacekeeping forces to be deployed there will be "targets in blue helmets." Emergency convoys in Bosnia come under repeated attack; an Italian relief plane is shot down by a missile. How long will it take the world to respond to Secretary-General Boutros Boutros-Ghali's request for 1,000-man troop contingents from UN member countries—with, it is hoped, a measure of firepower and mobility sufficient to contain roaming militias, and to *make* the peace in situations of murderous chaos? If powerful countries are willing to send large forces of their best-trained young people off to distant wars for often obscure reasons of ideology or territorial ownership—and to take the risk of unpopular body counts at home in doing so—why should they not now begin sending limited forces to protect the defenseless wherever conditions require it for reasons of human solidarity? Within a frame of international determination of this kind, would any government or group risk a campaign of "ethnic cleansing," or level tank guns at relief workers unloading a UN supply ship to cover the theft of ten trucks of food?

There is a strong case, of course, for prudence—in seeing that any intervention is limited and contained, in striving to gain at least acquiescence from combatant governments or groups, in safeguarding around the world the broad principles of national sovereignty. Calls for humanitarian intervention can provide an easy guise for arbitrary incursions. "Sovereignty is not an idle stipulation which can be rejected outright in the name of even the most noble gesture," a spokesman for the Group of 77 has said. "The UN cannot and must not be commandeered into forming an assistance brigade that will deliver its gifts by coercion."[2] True in principle and in most applications; but what if sovereignty bars the door to helping a mortally abused or stricken population?

We cannot go on debating these questions indefinitely. Changed conditions and expectations are constantly raising the stakes. Escalating military violence in more and more of the world is exposing the defenseless—mainly children—to unprecedented harm. Moral norms, and levels of outrage, have also risen. Forces supporting the Convention on the Rights of the Child, now ratified by 122 countries, are demanding a strict application of the convention's armed conflict protection articles. The need to respond to suffering in a new way was expressed by Italy's foreign minister at the 1991 General Assembly:

> The right to intervene for humanitarian ends and the protection of human rights . . . is the most truly innovative concept of the remaining decade of this century. Intervention that is primarily aimed at securing protection of human rights . . . is a prerogative of the international community, which must have the power to suspend sovereignty when it is exercised in a criminal manner.[3]

Aroused conviction of this kind was voiced around the world at the highest political levels a year ago. Is its force dissipating? Is the case for reaching the defenseless in war any less strong now? For those concerned with humanitarian issues and the protection of children, the clock is ticking toward an hour of moral default that may not be far away. Three hundred to four hundred deaths from hunger and disease are taking place in Somalia each day; more than half of these are the deaths of children. The fact of the global village means that the luxury of indifference to the suffering of others is gone forever. Like it or not, we are our brothers' keepers—and the guardians of their children.

18

The Plight of Refugees: Issues and Problems Affecting Their Humanitarian Needs

SADAKO OGATA

The United Nations High Commissioner for Refugees (UNHCR) dubbed 1992 as the year beginning the decade of voluntary repatriation. With the end of the Cold War, and the improved international political climate, UNHCR hoped that political settlements would pave the way for the return home, in peace and safety, of hundreds of thousands of refugees.

During the year, UNHCR undoubtedly made significant progress in the area of voluntary return. For example, some 900,000 refugees returned to Afghanistan, more than 100,000 to Cambodia, some 50,000 to Angola, and more than 10,000 to South Africa. Unfortunately, this progress was more than offset by the perpetuation and escalation of massive new crises in Bangladesh, Kenya, and former Yugoslavia—to name but the most conspicuous of the world's recent rash of tragedies. Each day in the latter half of 1992, 10,000 refugees have been forced to flee their homes, often in conditions of unspeakable misery and destitution. As a result, UNHCR has been confronted by humanitarian emergencies on a scale that stretches human and financial resources to their very limits.

Of course, the fact that of late, up to ten thousand refugees have been returning home each day is immensely satisfying. So, too, is the prospect of further large-scale repatriation in the near future to Angola, Mozambique, and other parts of Africa. But this satisfaction is tempered by the problems that in many instances continue to plague countries of origin and that, if not contained, could undermine the impetus to return. Harassment and detention of returnees in South Africa, unresolved tensions in Cambodia and Afghanistan, and returnee emergencies in the Horn of Africa all demonstrate that the foundations of voluntary repatriation are often more fragile than we would wish. Never has the need been so great for concerted and effective action by the international community to reinforce achievements in the resolution of regional conflicts, to support and consolidate related humanitarian solutions for their victims, and to contain and reverse the new crises of the post–Cold War era.

Current Protection Concerns

The complexity of the situation confronted by UNHCR raises not only a number of demanding operational issues but also complex protection concerns that go to the crux of UNHCR's mandate.

With the horrendous conflict in former Yugoslavia, problems of massive population displacement have affected the very heart of Europe for the first time since World War II. With the turbulent events elsewhere, too, that leave almost no part of the contemporary world untouched, the debate on refugee issues has taken a sharp new turn, and at times, first asylum has been in jeopardy. These events pose, in ever more acute form, the question of how the international community as a whole can best equip itself to respond in a coherent, humane, and coordinated way to new outflows of refugees and to problems of massive displacement.

Thus, the first concern I should like to raise here is how the international community can define a strategy that takes account of current realities and moves us beyond an approach that often seems at best fragmented and at worst incoherent. How can we ensure that the victims of contemporary events are accorded asylum and protection until such time as they can return home in safety and dignity? How can we make voluntary repatriation a durable solution? And how can UNHCR develop the preventive dimension of its operations so as, whenever possible, to provide alternatives to external flight?

This brings me to a second, related preoccupation. The fragmentation of states and the proliferation of internal conflicts is increasingly blurring the distinction between refugees and the internally displaced. When world events are moving so rapidly that they repeatedly threaten to overtake us, we would do well to give high priority to addressing this increasingly important question, which has profound implications for UNHCR in particular and for interagency cooperation in general.

Interagency Coordination

It goes without saying that many of today's humanitarian emergencies pose extraordinary challenges to the international community. Refugee situations, returnee emergencies, conflict, internal displacement, famine, drought, and underdevelopment—to cite but the most obvious elements—create situations that require concrete and comprehensive approaches from the international community and the United Nations system.

There is a wide gap in the international system for bringing aid and protection to internally displaced persons. UNHCR has been filling the gap in some situations, UNICEF in others, but always more on an ad hoc basis than through a structured institutional approach.

If UNHCR is to have a real impact on anything other than the superficial symptoms of current refugee-producing crises, a concerted effort is required within the United Nations family as a whole in its efforts to address the political, humanitarian, and economic dimensions of current emergencies.

Increasingly close operational partnerships have already been forged between UNHCR and a number of other agencies. The situation in former Yugoslavia is illustrative. As the lead agency designated by the secretary-general, UNHCR has built up close collaboration with UNICEF, the World Health Organization, and the International Committee of the Red Cross in providing relief and protection to more than two million refugees and displaced persons who are victims of the most terrible humanitarian crisis in Europe since the end of World War II. Equally significantly, in the Horn of Africa, together with the World Food Programme and other agencies, UNHCR is trying to respond, through cross-mandate and cross-border assistance programs, to the critical needs of all categories of persons—refugees, returnees, internally displaced, and needy local populations. At a more general level of interagency cooperation, I hope that UNICEF can eventually become the automatic supplier of water to refugees, just as the World

Food Programme now has responsibility for the supply of basic food.

Despite the significant progress that UNHCR has been able to achieve with other agencies, the scale and complexity of a number of recent challenges have called for more comprehensive coordination measures. There has been a clear need within the United Nations system for an interlocutor for the operational agencies on political issues and, where a multifaceted interagency response is required, for a focal point to address both overlaps in responsibilities and the gaps in mandates and performance that have been evident in various operations. For this reason, UNHCR has warmly welcomed the initiatives taken by the secretary-general to reinforce systemwide coordination, notably the establishment of the Department of Humanitarian Affairs.

UNHCR also welcomes the progress made in setting up institutional mechanisms for cooperation, including the Inter-agency Standing Committee in Geneva. Focal points have been designated within UNHCR for relating to the coordinator at levels of both policy and operations.

If the new efforts to enhance coordination are to succeed, however, they must not be diluted; on the contrary, they need to be carefully focused. In this respect, a clear distinction must be maintained between *normal* operations, which remain the responsibility of individual agencies, and *complex humanitarian emergencies* requiring a special degree of coordination not already provided for. Where the efforts of the coordinator can be of inestimable value is not at the operational level, but in facilitating the delivery of assistance in complex emergencies and overcoming political obstacles that may stand in its way.

At the operational level, coordination can, in difficult situations, help agencies to dovetail their efforts more effectively. It cannot, however, substitute either for the unique mandate of a particular organization or for its operational capacity. An important ongoing challenge for organizations is therefore the enhancement of their individual response capacities.

In this respect the crises UNHCR has confronted in the early 1990s have proven the value of its emergency preparedness and response capacity. While yet to be perfected, that capacity is now operational and has been deployed to considerable effect in Bangladesh, Kenya, former Yugoslavia, and elsewhere. UNHCR now has a solid basis on which to respond with the speed and effectiveness that both the victims of refugee emergencies and the international community have every right to expect.

But at a time when the UN is being asked to do more and more with fewer and fewer resources, the role of nongovernmental organizations—with their speed, flexibility, and adaptability—is becoming increasingly indispensable. If UNHCR has been able to respond with reasonable efficiency to recent emergencies, it is first and foremost thanks to our partnership with NGOs, carefully built up over the years and recently refined and reinforced.

While institutional reinforcement both within UNHCR and in the United Nations system as a whole has undoubtedly increased UNHCR's ability to respond rapidly and effectively, another main preoccupation has not yet been so effectively addressed—that is, the need to look beyond emergency to rehabilitation and development. Progress in emergency response needs to be complemented by a more concerted approach to the reintegration of repatriates and the overall development of the communities to which they return. Most of the countries to which increasing numbers of refugees are now repatriating have been devastated by years of conflict. Without comprehensive rehabilitation programs, the capacity of these societies to heal their wounds and achieve stability remains in question. Cambodia might serve as an example in this regard: a mechanism for the United Nations systemwide cooperation exists there, in the form of the UN Transitional Authority for Cambodia, and UNHCR repatriation activities will be complemented by rehabilitation efforts led by the United Nations Development Programme and involving longer-term reconstruction programs supported by governments, international organizations, and NGOs.

Funding

The challenges confronting UNHCR have made inevitable and urgent claims on financial resources. Indeed, the dramatic acceleration in world events since the end of the Cold War has allowed us no respite. New or spiraling crises such as those in former Yugoslavia, Kenya, Bangladesh, Nepal, and Yemen have required immediate and sometimes massive responses from UNHCR. Simultaneously, repatriation programs require significant resources.

UNHCR is, of course, deeply grateful for the strong donor support that it enjoys in these difficult times, when competing demands on donors multiply and overall resources available to governments continue to be tight. As of September 1992, UNHCR's general programs—budgeted at $385 million for 1992—to which we must accord priority, were funded for eleven months, a good position to have achieved at that time of year. There is, nevertheless, reason for deep concern. New emergencies, massive repatriation operations, and other unforeseen (and therefore unbudgeted-for) events have pushed the agency's special programs to more than $600 million—with the result that UNHCR, which in 1991 raised and spent more than $800 million, expected in 1992 to need almost $1 billion.

Furthermore, in a situation where needs may outpace resources and the agency may have to set priorities, it could easily be solutions, and notably voluntary repatriations, that suffer. The financial needs of accelerating repatriation programs are massive, amounting to some $300 million in 1992. While some programs, such as in Cambodia, elicit strong support, others, such as in Angola or even Afghanistan, could easily be constrained by insufficient funds. For example, the encashment program for Afghan refugees repatriating from Pakistan (repatriation peaked in July at a rate of some seventy thousand persons a week) requires a weekly injection of close to $2 million, not including essential rehabilitation assistance back in the country of origin. Overall, funding projections indicate that UNHCR may face a financial short-fall in 1992 of some $200 million against overall needs of some $1 billion.

This worrisome funding situation highlights an essential dilemma. While totally dependent on voluntary funds for the financing of its programs, UNHCR has, in contrast to many other United Nations agencies, very little scope to be selective in assuming its responsibilities. How can UNHCR refuse assistance when a new refugee crisis erupts and when the international community is rightly urging us to act? Where are the limits to what is expected of us in refugee and similar emergencies? How should UNHCR set priorities when the very operations in which governments have urged our involvement draw resources away from durable solutions elsewhere? And what should be the criteria for phasing out UNHCR operations and handing responsibility over to those who will implement either political solutions or development initiatives?

These are some of the many questions haunting UNHCR, to which we are required to respond immediately, often before having time to reflect.

19

From Disaster to Development

ELLEN JOHNSON SIRLEAF

I t is estimated that from 1970 to 1990, natural disasters claimed 3 million lives, adversely affected the lives of at least 800 million more people, and resulted in immediate damages in excess of $23 billion. These direct losses are exceeded by secondary and indirect losses, such as loss of revenue from tourism, negative effects on balance of payments, increased food import needs, investment losses, and opportunity costs caused by the diversion of development resources to relief activities.

As one example, the 1985 earthquake in Mexico City caused $3.8 billion worth of damage to the city's infrastructure. The effects at the macroeconomic level were devastating: it has been estimated that in the subsequent five years the negative effects on the balance of payments reached $8.6 billion. The current drought emergency in Africa has put 130 million people at risk. Even more tragic has been the sharp rise in refugees and in the internally displaced. Refugees are estimated to exceed twenty million in number globally. This figure is exceeded by the number of internally displaced who do not even have the minimal legal protection afforded to refugees under various international conventions.

The negative effects of natural and man-made disasters on development may seem obvious, but understanding of disaster and development linkages is still far from widespread. Still less understood and implemented are processes to ensure that development activities help to lessen rather than increase vulnerability to disasters.

Disaster Concepts: The Last Fifty Years

International institutional response to disasters has a relatively short history, with the League of Red Cross and Red Crescent Societies largely paving the way. Until quite recently, however, the disaster field was essentially concerned with the delivery of postdisaster relief; specialists began to focus upon disaster preparedness measures even later. As recently as 1988, United Nations Resolution 42/169, which established the International Decade for Natural Disaster Reduction, focused only on natural disasters. Complex and compound emergencies with grave development consequences (where civil conflict and famine coexist, each exacerbating the effects of the other) are not addressed in the resolution.

Yet studies show that disasters occur when hazards interact with vulnerable populations. There is no doubt that vulnerability is frequently a reflection of poverty and that consequently vulnerability reduction is largely a product of social and economic development. There is a multiple relationship between disaster and development.

First, poorly planned development programs can increase vulnerability. Indiscriminate deforestation to increase export earnings is an example in this regard. Second, disasters can, and often do, set back development. This is particularly true in the case of prolonged civil strife and war that result in the displacement of indigenous populations, precipitous brain drain, and the destruction of local infrastructures. Third, even though development may have an ugly side of pollution and environmental degradation, sustainable development can and should reduce vulnerability. Lastly, in a classical case of good coming out of evil, disaster sometimes can provide development opportunities hitherto overlooked by exposing the multifaceted relationship between disasters and development, leading to remedial action in policies and programs.

Risk Management and Vulnerability Reduction

Important first steps in dealing with disasters as a development phenomenon are vulnerability reduction and disaster preparedness. The risk faced by a population is a combination of the level of hazard and of vulnerability to that particular hazard. A disaster occurs when a hazard interacts with a vulnerable population. Disaster reduction can sometimes be achieved through reducing the scale of the hazard. It invariably involves the reduction of vulnerability to that hazard. Awareness of risk by governments and local communities largely determines whether anything is done to reduce that risk.

Risk management involves two processes: *risk assessment,* which is the scientific quantification of risk from data and an understanding of the processes involved, and *risk evaluation,* which pertains to the social, political, and developmental judgment concerning the importance of risks to which communities and development assets are exposed. Studies have shown that four factors are important in the perception of risk:

Exposure: Actual qualitative risk level;
Familiarity: Personal experience of the hazardous event;
Preventability: The degree to which the hazard is perceived as controllable or its effects preventable;
Dread: The horror of the hazard: its scale and consequences.

Key areas for the education of development decision-makers clearly are *exposure* (through quantifying the risk level) and *preventability* (in order to have adequate resources devoted to reducing vulnerability). Once risk analysis has been carried out, measures to reduce vulnerability (and sometimes hazards) can be formulated.

Although the role of government in vulnerability reduction is crucial since it disposes of tools (such as legislative powers, local government structures, and investment plans), government alone cannot implement vulnerability reduction measures. The support of the private sector (including construction and insurance), NGOs, and community-level organizations is indispensable. Community coping mechanisms can be greatly strengthened by a community-based preparedness plan.

The Economics of Vulnerability and Hazard Reduction

Perhaps the greatest constraint on implementing vulnerability reduction measures is budgetary. For example, the Japanese government spends over $2 billion per year on vulnerability reduction and disaster preparedness. This is more than the total government revenue of half the world's nations. In addition, the private sector in Japan invests heavily in vulnerability reduction. In most disaster-prone developing countries, investment capital is at a premium. However, the extra spending on a new facility to provide resistance to known hazards is usually prudent.

The level of investment that is justified to protect society and its economic activities is a matter of political and development decision-making. The costs and benefits of alternative strategies need to be carefully evaluated. The use of a systematic framework of risk assessment as part of the development planning process is a task that the development community can no longer afford to ignore.

No realistic vulnerability reduction scheme will claim to totally remove vulnerability. Capacities in disaster preparedness and disaster management are also required to minimize the adverse effects of a hazard. Effective disaster preparedness and disaster management ensure the timely, appropriate, and effective delivery of relief and assistance following a disaster.

Rehabilitation, Reconstruction, and Resumed Development

Issues of rehabilitation, reconstruction, and resumed development determine whether a disaster results in the derailment of development efforts or becomes a one-time aberration in the development process. Development experts are gradually beginning to appreciate that dealing with the consequences of a major disaster invariably becomes the major development issue for the country concerned. How effective this exclusive focus will be depends heavily how well prepared are national and external development institutions to play their role in relief, recovery, and rehabilitation efforts, thus speeding the return to sustainable development.

In the case of a sudden onset of natural disaster, intense efforts are made during the relief phase, but rehabilitation and reconstruction efforts are often totally inadequate. In other words, the development dimensions of relief are often ignored under the urgent pressure to "do something fast." The record of the donor community does not bear close examination in this regard.

There are four important concepts that need to be considered in any discussion of rehabilitation and reconstruction. First, rehabilitation and reconstruction traditionally has referred to the process of returning disaster-affected populations and development assets to the *status quo ante*. This approach, however, will merely replicate the vulnerability that caused the disaster in the first place. Second, rehabilitation can also mean the process whereby economic and social development activities are undertaken as an essential precursor and/or accompaniment to the resettlement of displaced populations. A third concept of considerable importance is that disasters can provide development opportunities. These opportunities should be identified during the stage of rehabilitation and reconstruction. Finally, the weeks and months after the occurrence of a disaster are an opportune time for a review and update of existing preparedness and disaster management plans.

Any discussion of rehabilitation and reconstruction, therefore, must be multifaceted. Disasters expose existing vulnerabilities in a most dramatic and unarguable manner. Political and operational factors, however, may militate against the kind of careful vulnerability reduction design that is required. The political pressures on government to start reconstruction as soon as possible may be overwhelming and inimical to inbuilt hazard protection. Operationally, it may be essential, for example, to move people out of temporary accommodation given winter's approach. An ill-conceived relief operation may have damaged local economies to the extent that the possibilities of upgrading local food production are severely compromised.

One of the few encouraging signs in the worldwide disaster situations is that completed—or ongoing—conflict-resolution negotiations are opening up prospects for the return of displaced populations. The challenge for governments and development agencies is to conceptualize, plan, and implement the "grid" of socioeconomic development measures necessary for the return of displaced populations. Clearly, development activities put into place must be community-based and quick-acting.

Because disasters highlight particular vulnerabilities, they can become major vehicles for development programs, particularly where serious loss of life has occurred or where the economic damage is disproportionate to the impact of the disaster involved. The outcome of many disaster relief operations is usually to highlight the general level of underdevelopment. For a few weeks or months after a disaster, the political environment may favor a much higher rate of economic and social change than before in areas such as land reform, new job training, housing improvements, and restructuring of the economic base. There also may be longer-term benefits from the restructuring of the economy as a result of a disaster. For example, economies that were previously dependent on a single crop may expand their economic base, often with international assistance.

Recent UN Responses

Two recent UN resolutions have firmly placed disasters in the context of economic and social development. In the first of these (42/169), the General Assembly proclaimed the 1990s as the International Decade for Natural Disaster Reduction (IDNDR). The significance of this resolution lies primarily in the fact that the assembly recognized that disaster reduction is best accomplished by development-based disaster mitigation efforts.

Undoubtedly the most important resolution of the General Assembly on the subject of disasters is resolution 46/182, adopted by consensus on December 19 1991. Resolution 46/182 clearly sets aside the longstanding UN distinctions between natural and man-made disasters. In so doing, the assembly recognized that there are clear political dimensions to many disasters and emergencies and opened the way to much closer links between UN humanitarian assistance operations, on the one hand, and its political and peacekeeping functions, on the other hand.

The whole philosophy of Resolution 46/182 is encapsulated in the concept of the "relief-to-development continuum." The nature of a relief to development continuum includes three important ideas:

- That we are, indeed, dealing with a continuum, rather than a set of rigidly defined stages of preparedness, relief, and rehabilitation;
- That the former concept of a disaster management continuum has been expanded to include resumed sustainable development;
- That the aim of activities in the continuum must be to move from relief to rehabilitation/reconstruction to resumed development at the earliest opportunity.

The resolution emphasizes the need for emergency assistance to be provided in a manner that "will be supportive of long-term development" and that emergency measures should be seen as a "step towards long-term development." The resolution also states unambiguously that "economic growth and sustainable development are essential for the prevention of, and preparedness against, natural disasters and other emergencies." Consequently, it is not surprising that the assembly also resolved that "development assistance organizations of the United Nations system should be involved at an early stage and should collaborate closely with those responsible for emergency relief and recovery. . . ." Finally, the resolution emphasizes that the UN has a "central and unique role to play" in providing leadership and coordinating the efforts of the international community to support the affected countries.

The Role of the United Nations Development Programme

The United Nations Development Programme (UNDP) is the central technical assistance funding mechanism of the UN system. Over the last year, both the UNDP governing council and the UNDP secretariat have devoted much time to examining wherein lies UNDP's comparative advantage in implementing the concept of the disaster-to-development continuum.

There are three principal advantages that UNDP brings to the disaster field:

1. Its global network of field offices. UNDP now has over 120 field offices in all developing regions;
2. Its multisectoral role. UNDP provides technical assistance for development in all economic sectors; and
3. Its constituency. UNDP's primary interface in developing countries is with central policy-making institutions, such as national ministries of finance and of planning.

The concept of the continuum means that UNDP should assist in ensuring that recovery activities are immediately begun as an integrated part of relief operations, and that these same relief operations do not adversely affect long-term development. As part of its capacity-building mandate, UNDP should facilitate the development and implementation of prevention and preparedness strategies to avoid the recurrence of such emergencies. Equally, UNDP has an important role to play in ensuring that reconstruction and recovery activities do not merely replicate the same vulnerability that caused the disaster in the first place. In short, while other organizations of the UN system approach the continuum from its relief end, UNDP approaches the same continuum from the development end.

UNITED NATIONS RESIDENT COORDINATORS

Apart from UNDP's institutional involvement in the continuum is the separate issue of UNDP resident representatives in their dual capacity as the in-country coordinators for UN relief activities and to ensure the linkage between disaster relief and development programs. In performing their emergency-related functions, resident coordinators report to the under-secretary-general for Humanitarian Affairs. The resident coordinators—with their dual coordination responsibilities for relief and for development—are in a unique position to promote the concept of the continuum at the country level. It is vital that the in-country UN disaster management teams be standing bodies dealing with the whole continuum rather than bodies that are only belatedly assembled after a disaster has struck.

The dual role of the UNDP resident representative has helped to bring the collective efforts and resources of different agencies such as the UNDP, United Nations High Commissioner for Refugees (UNHCR), World Food Programme (WFP), and UN Disaster Relief Organization (UNDRO) to bear upon disaster situations in Africa. For example, during the last five years, UNDP has provided about $30 million of disaster-related development assistance to complement even higher amounts in relief work by UNHCR, UNDRO, and WFP, among others, in dealing with natural and man-made disasters from Liberia to the Horn of Africa, from Sudan to Mozambique.

FUNDING OF DISASTER-RELATED DEVELOPMENT PROJECTS

In accordance with the concept of development-based disaster reduction approaches, the value of UNDP-administered humanitarian assistance projects continues to rise. At present the figure stands at approximately $120 million, of which 39 percent is for prevention and preparedness, 21 percent for relief, and 40 percent for reconstruction and rehabilitation. Many of these funds are administered on a bilateral cost-sharing basis. There are many other UNDP projects that indirectly serve to reduce the vulnerability of populations to disasters (for example, reforestation, low-cost housing, and food security).

STRENGTHENING UNDP'S CAPACITY

Efforts to strengthen UNDP's capacity have focused on several areas. General Assembly resolution 46/182 called for the "broadening and strengthening" of the joint UNDP/Department for Humanitarian Affairs Disaster Management Training Programme (DMTP). As a result of emerging crises in Africa and elsewhere, the scope of the DMTP has been expanded so that, by mid-1994, the program will have implemented training courses covering over seventy developing countries. In this manner, over three thousand persons drawn from governments, the NGO community, bilateral donors, and the UN system will have received training. While the great majority of courses remain to be conducted, the evidence to date indicates that DMTP has played an important role in promoting disaster preparedness among the groups mentioned above. The program would not be implement-able were it not for the generous financial, personnel, and conceptual assistance that UNDP has received from the Food and Agriculture Organization (FAO), UNHCR, United Nations Children's Fund (UNICEF), WFP, and World Health Organization (WHO).

General Assembly resolution 46/182 also calls for UN organizations to develop special financial, administrative, and personnel procedures for use in emergency situations.

Conclusion

When the concept of a relief-to-development continuum is considered, it becomes clear that it is more than an empty piece of development jargon. Development is so clearly affected by disasters and has such a key role to play in reducing vulnerability that the full and systematic commitment of the development establishment is required. In the areas of disaster preparedness and disaster management, development institutions have such an essential supportive role that effective systems will be severely compromised by their absence. In the areas of vulnerability reduction and rehabilitation and reconstruction leading to resumed development, there is no alternative to the development community accepting its leadership role.

20

The World Response to Humanitarian Emergencies

JAN ELIASSON

The world of the 1990s is a world of turbulent change. Not many would have predicted a few years ago that this last decade of the twentieth century would be a time of such far-reaching and dramatic transformation. In the new world that has emerged since the end of the Cold War—in a chilly new dawn that left the protagonists stumbling uncertainly in the pale light rather than marching with the confidence of victors—humanitarian issues have come to the center of the global stage. An explosion of ethnic and civil conflicts has followed the end of the Cold War.

With the removal of the threat of nuclear conflagration, the arena of conflict has spread unchecked through the poorest, most vulnerable, and most deprived of the world's regions. Poverty, hunger, despair, and violence have long fed upon each other in a relentless cycle, inhibited only by shifting strategic and ideological considerations and temporary alliances. Ironically, the disappearance of East-West tensions may have bred a new indifference to the plight of the most disadvantaged of the world's populations. And today ancient prejudices and resentments born of oppression engender renewed bitterness and bloodshed, fueled by the desperation of abject poverty and lack of hope for the future.

Many societies are torn between demands for autonomy, or self-determination, and the dangers of fragmentation, or what the United Nations secretary-general has termed "micronationalism." The already fragile structures in a large number of developing countries are being severely tested by the vicious cycle of poverty, population pressure, and environmental degradation. The Food and Agriculture Organization has warned that poverty is accelerating environmental degradation to such an extent that natural resources soon may not be able to meet the food requirements of the world's fast-growing population. More than one billion people today suffer from poverty; over 500 million, or roughly 10 percent of the world population, are undernourished, and some 50 million face famine. With the rate of global population increase at 97 million people each year, the structural pressures creating displacement and refugee flows for the years to come are evident.

The outcome of these upheavals cannot be entirely foreseen. What is clear is that the profound and complex causes of the present situation are rooted as much in social and economic circumstances as in political developments. But their effects are felt at the human level, and they threaten the very lives and well-being of men, women, and children who cannot wait for diplomatic solutions. The process can be long and difficult, bringing in its wake a tragic toll in lives and further cycles of deprivation. Natural disasters and man-made havoc together menace the very foundations of society in countries such as Somalia and Mozambique. Political and ethnic chaos in former Yugoslavia lies at the gates of Europe: indeed, with the constant stream of refugees, the poor may well come knocking on the doors of their rich neighbors. Ethnic and social unrest creates new displacements and outflows of refugees—with all the accompanying humanitarian problems for those displaced and for their beleaguered hosts alike—in the Horn of Africa, Bangladesh/Myanmar, and elsewhere. At the same time, the country so much in the focus of the endeavors to promote the "new world order"—Iraq—continues to thwart the international community's efforts to secure humanitarian assistance for the most vulnerable of its population. Indeed, in late 1992, almost two years after the exodus of some two million Kurds across their mountainous borders, the onset of winter finds them once again bereft of the means to ensure their safety and survival.

In the Horn of Africa the already acutely dangerous situation has been steadily worsening. Drought, environmental degradation, civil conflicts, and underdevelopment have combined to wreak havoc. Millions of men, women, and children are threatened by disease and by lack of food and water. In Somalia famine, clan conflicts, and the collapse of law and order have resulted in the loss of countless lives through starvation and senseless slaughter. In other parts of the region conflict has continued to prevent relief efforts from reaching people in desperate need. The result of this continued turmoil is mass displacement and increased vulnerability of populations.

The drought ravaging the countries of southern Africa has no parallel in living memory. With less than 50 percent of average crop yields anticipated during 1992–1993, eighteen million people face the specter of starvation. The scope and magnitude of the drought threatens the social fabric and economic structures of several states. In Mozambique and Angola, where civil strife has also taken its toll, the drought has added another dimension to already severe problems.

The international community has an obligation to provide humanitarian assistance to all the affected populations, regardless of political or other considerations. Experience has shown that this is not an easy undertaking. We have seen how international relief efforts have been impeded by serious threat to the security of relief personnel both in former Yugoslavia and in Somalia. This has tended to erode the morale of relief personnel, as well as donor support. Given the wide range of actors and the complexity of the problems, strengthened coordination and clear leadership are essential. This would require intensified and innovative response from the United Nations systems, as well as the support and commitment of all partners in this challenging endeavor.

General Assembly Resolution 46/182

In 1991 member states held a pioneering debate on the capacity of the United Nations to coordinate humanitarian assistance. These deliberations, and a subsequent report of the secretary-general on the subject, provided the basic elements for resolution 46/182, adopted by the General Assembly on December 19, 1991. This, in turn, led to the establishment by the secretary-general, in March 1992, of the Department of Humanitarian Affairs.

Resolution 46/182 constitutes the "road map" for the new department. In discharging its responsibilities, the department will always need to bear in mind the balance struck among the guiding principles of the resolution. That is, at all times, United Nations humanitarian assistance will be provided in accordance with the principles of humanity, neutrality, and impartiality. The sovereignty, territorial integrity, and national unity of states will be fully respected. Assistance will be provided with the consent of the affected country and, in principle, on the basis of a request from that country. The guiding principles, however, also stress the responsibility of states to take care of the victims of emergencies occurring on their territory, and the need for access to those requiring humanitarian assistance.

The resolution also emphasizes the importance of addressing the root causes of disasters, as well as ensuring the smooth transition from relief to rehabilitation and development. The provision of humanitarian relief in isolation is, in a way, like putting a Band-Aid over an infected wound. This is in the interest neither of the recipients nor of the donor community. The United Nations has the unique mandate to mobilize the necessary international support for humanitarian assistance and to address the root causes of crises.

Mechanisms for Response

The resolution provides the United Nations with four tools for coordination: the emergency relief coordinator and his function, the Central Emergency Revolving Fund, the Inter-agency Standing Committee, and the consolidated appeals process. These instruments should substantially enhance the capacity of the United Nations to respond to emergencies effectively and in a timely fashion.

EMERGENCY RELIEF COORDINATOR

The first of the tools is the function of emergency relief coordinator and the establishment of the Department of Humanitarian Affairs, with offices in New York and Geneva. The New York office focuses on policy planning, functional issues, the substantive servicing of the UN's deliberative organs, and the policy and diplomatic dimensions of emergencies. It works closely with the concerned political, economic, and financial departments to ensure humanitarian access and to address the root causes of emergencies, as well as to facilitate a smooth transition from relief to rehabilitation and development. It also manages the Central Emergency Revolving Fund.

The Geneva office is the focal point for emergency operational support and relief coordination, as well as for disaster mitigation. It leads the interagency process for needs assessment on the subsequent preparation of consolidated appeals. Once relief operations are in place, the Geneva office monitors follow-up, identifies unmet needs, and prepares updated situation reports in close cooperation with all the partners in a particular program. These include the donors; the United Nations agencies and organizations concerned; and other humanitarian, governmental, and nongovernmental organizations. In addition, the Geneva office provides technical support to the Inter-agency Standing Committee. The Geneva office also has primary responsibility for action and issues relating to natural disasters.

CENTRAL EMERGENCY REVOLVING FUND

The second innovation of the resolution is the establishment of the Central Emergency Revolving Fund (CERF). Studies following natural disasters have shown that a disproportionately high percentage of damages are sustained within the initial phase of the emergency. The CERF is designed to ensure that resources are available to operational organizations for prompt response to emergencies, whether manmade or natural. Resolution 46/182 set a target level of U.S.$50 million for the CERF. The generous contributions of twenty-five states have enabled that target to be reached, and the CERF is now fully operational.

Guidelines and financial procedures have been established to indicate how agencies can initiate use of the CERF and how it is to be replenished from resources subsequently collected. The first disbursement of $2 million was made upon the request of UNICEF to assist vulnerable groups in Kenya, as part of the new department's overall effort in the Horn of Africa. A further $5 million has been disbursed, also at UNICEF's request, for use in Somalia for initiating immediate programs.

INTER-AGENCY STANDING COMMITTEE

The third tool for coordination is the Inter-agency Standing Committee, which meets at the executive level a few times a year to address policy issues concerning the United Nations response to emergencies. The International Committee of the Red Cross (ICRC), the International Federation of Red Cross and Red Crescent Societies (IFRC), and the International Organisation for Migration (IOM) are to participate fully in the work of the committee, while other NGO representatives will be invited on an ad hoc basis. The standing committee will also meet when a situation calls for urgent consultation.

During the interval between meetings of the standing committee, an interagency working group holds regular consultations at the middle-management level. An interagency unit has been established in Geneva, as part of the Department of Humanitarian Affairs, to provide the necessary secretariat support. NGOs are also associated with the work of these groups. In addition, on an ad hoc basis, informal interagency meetings have been convened in New York to enhance cooperation and coordination on humanitarian issues before the Security Council.

At the field level the United Nations resident coordinators are the main channel and instrument for coordination, and have an important role to play in the early warning of emergencies. Once an emergency has occurred, the resident coordinators will head the disaster management teams in affected countries. The country teams are also crucial to the preparation of consolidated appeals.

CONSOLIDATED APPEAL

The consolidated appeal process is used to address emergencies that require collective action. The new department works closely with the operational agencies and NGO representatives, both in the field and at headquarters, to ensure that an effective and efficient, well-coordinated plan for assistance is prepared. Bearing in mind the importance of strategic planning, the department has sought the active participation of the World Bank and the International Monetary Fund in specific cases, such as the southern African drought, to strengthen the development dimension by addressing the transition from relief to rehabilitation and development.

The United Nations has initiated interagency assessment and consultation procedures, culminating in the issuance of the Consolidated UN-Southern African Development Coordination Conference Appeal for the Drought Emergency in Southern Africa (June 1992), the Special Consolidated Inter-agency Appeal for Kenya (June 1992), the Consolidated Appeal for Emergency Humanitarian Assistance in Afghanistan (June 1992), the Updated Consolidated Inter-agency Appeal for the Special Emergency Programme for the Horn of Africa (July 1992), and the Consolidated Inter-agency Programme of Action and Appeal for former Yugoslavia (September 1992).

The international donor community's response to this process of

consolidated appeals has been positive. For example, at the joint UN/
SADCC Pledging Conference on the southern African drought, con-
vened on June 1, 1992, in Geneva under the chairmanship of President
Masire of Botswana, $578 million was received in pledges, against
$856 million requested in the consolidated appeal.

Security Council Consideration

A notable new development in terms of the humanitarian role of the
United Nations has been the active involvement of the Security Council in the consideration of humanitarian issues and the provision of
assistance in Cambodia, Iraq, Somalia, and former Yugoslavia. In the
last two cases, in particular, the council has accorded the secure delivery of humanitarian assistance a very high priority. Its resolutions in
these two cases indicated that, in the absence of cooperation, "the
Security Council does not exclude other measures to deliver humanitarian assistance." In the absence of a UN peacekeeping presence, the
council has, in some instances, specifically provided armed protection
for the implementation of humanitarian programs and the delivery of
relief assistance.

United Nations Experience and Reflections

The months following the adoption of General Assembly resolution
46/182 and the emplacement of the institutions and mechanisms for its
implementation allowed some perspectives on the dimensions of the
UN's humanitarian role.

First, while humanitarian assistance must be provided regardless of
whether there is an immediate solution at hand, the United Nations has
been increasingly called upon to address simultaneously both the humanitarian and the political dimensions of conflict situations. Somalia,
Yugoslavia, and Mozambique are cases in point. Humanitarian assistance, delivered impartially, can have a positive impact on peacemaking efforts. Bringing relief to those afflicted can supply new avenues for
negotiation. On the other hand, corridors of peace and zones of tranquillity can reinforce peacemaking initiatives. These are parts of a
chain that constitutes the essence of what one may call humanitarian
diplomacy.

Second, the United Nations is required in an increasing number of emergencies to negotiate not only access of personnel and relief supplies but also arrangements to ensure their safety. The situations in Somalia, Sudan, former Yugoslavia, and Iraq are tragic reminders of this dilemma. The presence of a relief operation has not always been sufficient to deter hostile action and, sadly, sometimes has even invited such action. At the same time, humanitarian organizations in several instances have preferred not to have armed protection. There is need for caution, but also for imagination and flexibility, in addressing each security situation. In finding solutions to the ever more serious safety problems, the secretary-general will need the full cooperation of all parties concerned. Attacks against UN personnel and humanitarian aid workers are cowardly and self-defeating, and constitute serious violations of international and humanitarian law.

Third, the serious problem of land mines, millions of which remain scattered in current and former combat zones, must be urgently addressed. The indiscriminate maiming that mines inflict on innocent people is an affront to the international conscience. In addition, the presence of land mines has seriously hampered relief assistance, repatriation, and rehabilitation, and will continue to do so; de-mining must therefore be vigorously pursued. As pointed out by the secretary-general in his report "An Agenda for Peace," de-mining is a crucially important element of building peace.

Fourth, in recent years the United Nations system has been developing a valuable network of early-warning systems for environmental threats, natural disasters, mass movements of populations, the threat of famine, and the spread of disease. This capacity must be systematically mobilized for preventive action. This task would require the close cooperation of not only UN organizations but interested governments and NGOs. The Department of Humanitarian Affairs has the responsibility to serve as the focal point for the collection, analysis, and dissemination of early-warning information relating to disasters and emergencies. This can be achieved only through closer collaboration between all the actors involved in both humanitarian and development activities under the leadership of the United Nations. The effective development of this capacity can enhance the prevention of, or at least mitigation of, the effects of crises.

Fifth, cooperation among operational organizations is essential for effective UN response to disasters and emergencies. There can only be benefits from cooperation, and disadvantage from the lack thereof—the biggest loser of all being the innocent victims needing assistance. Moreover, this cooperation must be all-inclusive, applying equally to the relationships among UN organizations and with the ICRC, IFRC, IOM, and NGOs. Cooperation must also be extended to and strengthened with the relevant regional organizations. In addition to putting into place various mechanisms for coordination, the international community must continue to promote a climate, indeed a culture and a natural environment, of cooperation.

Last, while the UN stands ready to meet growing challenges in response to emergencies of increasing number and complexity, it must be provided with the necessary resources to do what it is asked to do. This applies not only to the immediate humanitarian requirements but also to rehabilitation and development. Resources should be mobilized to prevent emergencies from recurring, forcing societies to cope with the same devastating consequences. As the secretary-general emphasized in his report to the Security Council:

> Trust also requires a sense of confidence that the world organization will react swiftly, surely and impartially and that it will not be debilitated by political opportunism or by administrative or financial inadequacy. This presupposes a strong, efficient and independent international civil service whose integrity is beyond question and an assured financial basis that lifts the Organization, once and for all, out of its present mendicancy.

The humanitarian agenda today is both much longer and more critical than ever. Yet we are very far from consensus on how to address this agenda. The debate on the appropriate means of tackling humanitarian issues has raged among opinion leaders in the North and South. The issue is obviously as timely as it is controversial: charges and countercharges are constantly exchanged over the propriety of the international community's various actions in following up the cease-fire at the end of the Gulf War, and accusations and comparisons highlight differing international responses to the humanitarian catastrophes in Somalia and former Yugoslavia.

Take, for example, the following three very contrasting opinions expressed in the space of a single week in August 1992:

• In the *Times of London,* Marc Weller of Cambridge University writes that the international community's recent activities in both northern and southern Iraq can be taken as evidence that "overwhelming humanitarian necessity" is sufficient legal justification for "limited armed action on behalf of a population in danger from its own Government." Where the circumstances are grave enough, "genuine humanitarian intervention" is required. He concludes that "there is now emerging an international practice which permits the international community to pierce through the armour of state sovereignty when atrocities of this magnitude are being committed. This has been recently demonstrated in the cases of the Kurds, the Liberians, the Somalis and to an extent, the former Yugoslavia."[1]

- A completely contrasting view is expressed by Peter Sinai, a former Indian diplomat, in the *Pioneer* of New Delhi. The Western countries' actions in imposing a "no-fly zone" in southern Iraq constitute, in his view, a distortion of the principles and purposes of the UN Charter. He criticizes the U.K. foreign secretary for claiming that "enforcing humanitarian aid to the populace of Southern Iraq by all possible means, including the use of force, is now in accordance with international law." Instead, he maintains, "there is in fact no legal sanction for the enforcement of humanitarian aid . . . Iraqi consent will be needed for the delivery of humanitarian relief." He considers that the Security Council is being asked to "lend a cloak of legality to blatant interference in Iraq's internal affairs" and suggests instead that the nonaligned movement propose procedures, at the coming General Assembly, "to regulate the proper delivery of humanitarian aid."[2]

- A wholly different perspective is given in *Le Monde* by Claude Malhuret, former French secretary of state for human rights and former chairman of Médecins sans Frontières. Malhuret laments that governments' new interest in humanitarian action has become a frequent alibi for political passivity. With the example of Bosnia-Herzegovina uppermost in mind, he suggests that the West has responded to Serbian tanks by sending ambulances, and to missiles by sending medicine chests. Governments have avoided political action by "humanitarian gestures, completely useless under certain circumstances but enough to persuade public opinion that something has been done and good will demonstrated." While lauding humanitarian assistance as such, Malhuret asserts that the examples of Kurdistan, Sudan, Somalia, and Bosnia show that "there is a time for assistance and a time for political decisions"—the humanitarian assistance does no service if it is used merely to put off a political solution.[3]

These widely differing views demonstrate the depth of feelings surrounding the new attention given to the humanitarian agenda. For my part, I am all to well aware of the need for the United Nations simultaneously to be at the forefront of international humanitarian action and to proceed on the basis of the hard-won consensus that characterized resolution 46/182. I believe the only appropriate path is to convince governments and peoples alike that humanitarian action is in their best interest. We must clearly and compellingly demonstrate that our concern for people transcends political expediency, that the international community's conscience will respond with dispatch and generosity to the suffering and affliction of fellow men and women, and that humanitarian assistance must and will be incorporated in the overall continuum from emergency relief to rehabilitation and development. Indeed, in concentrating on humanitarian requirements, the United Nations acknowledges that social and economic needs have too long been left in second place and must now be addressed as a priority within the overall framework of cooperation. To ensure that the most impoverished and vulnerable are not again the most afflicted victims of disaster, that the often fragile path of development is not dealt a mortal blow by unforeseen crises, and that the very essence of regional stability and security is not left in turmoil by man-made or natural catastrophes, humanitarian assistance is an imperative that should be universally agreed.

To be truly effective, our endeavor must be founded upon cooperation, not coercion, upon a shared responsibility and mutual respect. The safety of humanitarian personnel must once more be assured and taken as an indispensable element of their mission. The capacity necessary to guarantee this objective and to protect humanitarian resources must be seen as geared solely to these ends and must be sufficient to achieve them. Humanitarian assistance must place human dignity and well-being as its main criterion for success. It must express solidarity in action. And it must exemplify the impartiality and integrity of the United Nations enterprise, historically the most critical asset at our disposal.

The international community has an obligation to provide humanitarian support to the many people caught in crisis situations. We must demonstrate solidarity in action, above all by bringing relief to vulnerable groups like women and children, often the first affected and the ones who suffer most in such conflicts.

Finally, we must recognize that there will always be the need to redefine our response and refine our instruments for effective and timely humanitarian assistance, wherever it may be required.

CONCLUSION

As I reread these papers and recall the exciting but exhausting debates at our symposium, I am confident that there is more reason for hope than for pessimism. The profound differences of philosophy and method, the accidents of history and geography, the divisions of time and civilization are all present in the chapters, and they are real. Even more impressive, however, are the human bonds, the mutual interests, and the shared dedication to the relief of suffering and the prevention of cruelty and death in needless conflicts. For perhaps the first time, at least in the United States, leaders in diplomacy and humanitarian assistance have met together. They recognize that they are not trains running on separate tracks but cars joined together in a common cause. They understand that the work of health, human rights, and disaster relief must be moved from the periphery into the center ring of foreign policy and never again considered merely as matters of transient emotional interest.

Just as mass communications have transported distant tragedies into the center of the world's consciousness and conscience, so too can we no longer blot out the knowledge of terrible human rights violations. We cannot escape epidemics that sweep across continents and attack the rich as well as poor. We are inextricably linked on this earth to the fates of all the innocent victims of oppression. Whether we like it or not, we cannot avoid this transcendental fact: we are, and must be, involved in the suffering of others.

And that is my ground for hope. I am convinced that by cooperating in efforts to heal the wounds of war and eliminate the causes of widespread violence we can find new ways to peace, approaches that are more promising than the alliances and military force that have dominated international relations through so many troubled years.

Kevin M. Cahill

NOTES

Introduction

1. Kevin Cahill, ed., *The Untapped Resource: Medicine and Diplomacy* (Baltimore: Orbis Press, 1973).
2. ————, *A Bridge to Peace* (New York: Haymarket Doyma, 1988).

Chapter 1: Human Rights, Humanitarian Assistance, and the Sovereignty of States

1. The phrase "post-Cold War" is itself a Eurocentric reading of history. Conceiving of the world from a Northeast Asian or Pacific outlook, the persistence of Cold War concerns remains significant: Korea is divided, China remains committed ideologically and structurally to an authoritarian form of state socialism, an unresolved revolutionary war in the Philippines, an unresolved territorial dispute between the former Soviet Union and Japan about the status of the Kuriles islands. Despite such considerations for purposes of this chapter the post-Cold War terminology seems appropriate. There is no longer any strategic conflict of global scope. Policy response at the United Nations, and elsewhere, is no longer blocked by the sort of rigid bipolarity that was characteristic of the era of superpower rivalry.

2. See "Intelligence Sources See Air Ban as Ineffective and 'Political'," *The Guardian* (August 20, 1992).

3. "Report of the Secretary-General of the United Nations" (New York, 1991), p. 5.

4. "The Limits of Sovereignty," *UN Focus: Human Rights,* undated newsletter, page 1.

5. See articulation of this position in Thomas M. Franck's book on the World Court, *Judging the World Court* (New York: Priority Press, 1986), especially pp. 53–76.

6. The sort of shift toward liberalism noted and favored by Joseph Nye in "What New World Order?" *Foreign Affairs* 71 (1992):83–96.

7. "U.S. Isolates Major over Iraq," *The Guardian* (August 20, 1992).

8. See John Vincent, *Nonintervention and International Order* (Princeton, N.J.: Princeton University Press, 1974), especially pp. 64–141.

9. See W. Michael Reisman and Andrew Willard, eds., *International Incidents: The Law That Counts in World Politics* (New Haven, Conn.: Yale University Press, 1988).

10. For convenient texts of these treaties see Burns H. Weston, Anthony D'Amato, and Richard Falk, eds., *Basic Documents in International Law and World Order,* 2d rev. ed. (St. Paul, Minn.: West Publishing Co., 1990), pp. 147–80 and 230–52.

11. "Report of the Secretary-General," p. 11.

12. Richard Falk, *Explorations at the Edge of Time* (Philadelphia: Temple University Press, 1992).

Chapter 2: The Contribution of International Humanitarian Law to the Restoration of Peace

1. United Nations, *International Humanitarian Law and Human Rights,* Fact Sheet no. 13 (Geneva: Centre for Human Rights, 1991), p. 17.

2. Erich Fromm, *You Shall Be as Gods* (New York: Holt, Rinehart and Winston, 1966). The Golden Rule is universally accepted in all great spiritual traditions. Confucius writes in the *Analects* (15,23): "If there is one maxim which ought to be acted upon throughout one's life, surely it is the maxim of loving kindness. Do not do unto others what you would not have them do unto you." Christ says, "In everything do to others as you would have them do to you" (Matthew 7:12). In Islam the *Sunnah* proclaims, "No one is a believer until he desires for his brother what he desires for himself." These quotes and others in John Catoir, *World Religions: Belief Behind Today's Headlines* (New York: The Christophers, 1989).

3. Max Huber, *The Good Samaritan: Reflections on the Gospel and Work of the Red Cross* (London: Gollancz, 1945).

4. Francis Lieber, *Instructions for the Government of the Armies of the United States in the Field* (1863).

5. See the 1954 Hague Convention for the Protection of Cultural Property in the Event of Armed Conflict, and article 53 of protocol I and article 16 of protocol II of 1977.
6. See article 43 of additional protocol I and article 14 of protocol II of 1977.
7. Article 56 of protocol I and article 15 of protocol II.
8. See article 55 of protocol I and the United Nations Convention on the Prohibition of Military or Any Other Hostile Use of Environmental Modification Techniques (December 10, 1976).
9. Henri Meyrowitz, "Réflexions sur le fondement du droit de la guerre," in Christophe Swinarski, ed., *Studies and Essays on International Humanitarian Law and Red Cross Principles* (Geneva and The Hague: ICRC, 1984), pp. 419–31.
10. Denise Bindschedler-Robert, "A Reconsideration of the Law of Armed Conflicts." (Report to the Conference on the Law of Armed Conflict, Carnegie Endowment, Geneva, September 15–20, 1969), p. 61.
11. Dietrich Schindler, *The Different Types of Armed Conflicts According to the Geneva Conventions and Protocols* (The Hague: Recueil des Cours, 1979), vol. 2, pp. 117–64.
12. Henri Meyrowitz, "Le droit de la guerre dans le conflict vietnamien," *Annuaire français de droit international,* XIII, 1967, pp. 153–201.
13. *International Review of the Red Cross* (December 1973), p. 641.
14. Mohamed Bedjaoui, *La Révolution algérienne et le droit* (Brussels: International Association of Democratic Lawyers, 1961).
15. Louis Joinet, "Study on Amnesty Laws and Their Role in the Safeguard and Promotion of Human Rights." Report to the Commission on Human Rights (E/CN.4/Sub. 2/ 1984/15, page 8, para. 30.)
16. International Committee of the Red Cross, "Commentary on the Additional Protocols of 8 June 1977 to the Geneva Conventions of 12 August 1949" (Geneva: ICRC, 1986), p. 402.
17. Alfred M. de Zayas, "Amnesty Clause," in *Encyclopedia of Public International Law,* vol. 3 (Heidelberg: Max Planck Institute for Public International Law, 1982), p. 15.
18. "Trial of Pakistani Prisoners of War, Order of 15 December 1973," *International Court of Justice Reports* (The Hague: I.C.J., 1973), p. 347.
19. Octavio Paz, *Tiempo Nublado, One Earth, Four or Five Worlds: Reflections on Contemporary History* (San Diego, Calif.: Harcourt Brace Jovanovich, 1985).
20. "La compassion, pilier de la paix mondiale" (Lecture by the Dalai Lama at the University of Geneva, August 31, 1983).
21. *Freedom in Exile. The Autobiography of the Dalai Lama* (Calcutta, Rupa, 1992), p. 298. See also p. 297: "My concern extends to all members of the human family and indeed, to all suffering sentient beings. I believe that this suffering is caused by ignorance, and that people inflict pain on others in pursuit of their own happiness or satisfaction. Yet true happiness comes from a sense of inner peace and contentment, which in turn must

be achieved through cultivation of altruism, of love, of compassion, and through the elimination of anger, selfishness and greed."
22. Quoted in Martin Luther King, Jr., *Strength to Love* (Cleveland: North Light Books, 1963), p. 53.

Chapter 3: Obligations and Responsibilities of Donor Nations

1. Report of the Independent Commission on International Humanitarian Issues, *Winning the Human Race?* (London: Zed Books Ltd., 1988).
2. F. Fenner, D. A. Henderson, I. Arati, Z. Yezek, and I. D. Lednyi, *Smallpox and Its Eradication* (Geneva: The World Health Organization, 1988).
3. London School of Hygiene and Tropical Medicine, "Malaria: Waiting for the Vaccine," edited by G. A. T. Targett (Chichester: John Wiley & Sons, 1991), pp. 67–78.
4. Report of the Independent Commission on International Development Issues, *North-South: A Programme for Survival* (London: Pan Books Ltd., 1980).
5. Carnegie Endowment National Commission on America and the New World, *Changing Our Ways* (Washington, D.C.: Carnegie Endowment for International Peace, 1992), p. 30.
6. Report of the Independent Commission on Disarmament and Security Issues, *Common Security: A Programme for Disarmament* (London: Pan Books Ltd., 1982).

Chapter 4: The Concerns of Recipient Nations

1. Walter Rodney, *How Europe Underdeveloped Africa* (Cambridge, Mass.: Harvard University Press, 1982).
2. Graham Hancock, *Lords of Poverty* (New York: Atlantic Monthly Press, 1989), p. viii.
3. Ibid., p. 4.
4. Ibid., p. 5.
5. Ibid., p. 8.
6. *World Vision Newspaper* (November 1982), quoted in Hancock, *Lords of Poverty*, p. 9.
7. *Voluntary Funds Administered by UNHCR: Audited Financial Statements for the Year Ended December 1984* (New York: United Nations General Assembly), quoted in Hancock, *Lords of Poverty*, p. 10.
8. Hancock, *Lords of Poverty*, p. 10.
9. Ibid., pp. 11–12.
10. Ibid., p. 12.

Chapter 5: The Economics of Neglect

1. P. Dasgupta, *An Inquiry into Well-being and Destitution* (Oxford: Clarendon Press, forthcoming, 1993).

2. P. Dasgupta, "Well-being and the Extent of Its Realization in Poor Countries," *Economic Journal* 100 (1990).

3. J. Waldron, "What Do We Know About the Causes of Sex Differences in Mortality? A Review of the Literature," *Population Bulletin of the United Nations* 18 (1985); and S. R. Johansson, "Welfare, Mortality and Gender: Continuity and Change in the Explanation of Male/Female Mortality Differences over Three Centuries," *Continuity and Change* 6 (1991).

4. R. Martorell et al., "Long-term Consequences of Growth Retardation during Early Childhood" (Ithaca, N.Y.: Cornell University, 1991).

5. R. Martorell et al., "Maternal Stature, Fertility and Infant Mortality," *Human Biology* 53 (1981).

6. F. Falkner and J. M. Tanner, eds., *Human Growth 2: Postnatal Growth* (New York: Plenum Press, 1978).

7. L. J. Mata, "The Fight Against Diarrhoeal Diseases: The Case of Costa Rica," in J. Vallin and A. D. Lopez, eds., *Health Policy, Social Policy, and Mortality Prospects* (Paris: Institut National d'Etudes Demographiques, 1985).

8. World Bank, *World Development Report* (New York: Oxford University Press, 1992).

9. L. J. Mata, *The Children of Santa Maria Cauque: A Prospective Field Study of Health and Growth* (Cambridge, Mass.: MIT Press, 1978).

10. K. Hill and A. R. Pebley, "Child Mortality in the Developing World," *Population and Development Review* 15 (1989).

11. V. Fauveau et al., "The Contribution of Severe Malnutrition to Child Mortality in Rural Bangladesh: Implications for Targeting Nutritional Interventions," *Food and Nutrition Bulletin* 12 (1990).

12. M. K. Chowdhury et al., "Does Malnutrition Predispose to Diarrhoea during Childhood? Evidence from a Longitudinal Study in Matlab, Bangladesh," *European Journal of Clinical Nutrition* 44 (1990).

13. J. C. Waterlow, ed., *Protein Energy Malnutrition* (London: Edward Arnold, 1992).

14. A. Briend, "Is Diarrhoea a Major Cause of Malnutrition among the Under-fives in Developing Countries? A Review of Available Evidence," *European Journal of Clinical Nutrition* 44 (1990).

15. Dasgupta, *Inquiry into Well-being.*

16. A. Chavez and C. Martinez, "Behavioural Measurements of Activity in Children and Their Relation to Food Intake in a Poor Community," in E. Pollitt and P. Amante, eds., *Energy Intake and Activity* (New York: Alan R. Liss, 1984).

17. J. M. Meeks Gardner et al., "Dietary Intake and Observed Activity of Stunted and Non-stunted Children in Kingston, Jamaica. Part II: Observed Activity," *European Journal of Clinical Nutrition* 44 (1990).

18. A. Chavez and C. Martinez, "Consequences of Insufficient Nutrition in Child Character and Behaviour," in D. A. Levitsky, ed., *Malnutrition, Environment and Behaviour* (Ithaca, N.Y.: Cornell University Press,

1979); and Chavez and Martinez, "Behavioural Measurements of Activity."

19. For references see Dasgupta, *Inquiry into Well-being*, ch. 14.

20. M. Colombo and I. Lopez, "Evolution of Psychomotor Development in Severely Undernourished Infants Submitted to an Integral Rehabilitation," *Pediatrics Research* 14 (1980).

21. J. Dobbing, "Early Nutrition and Later Achievement," *Proceedings of the Nutrition Society* 49 (1990).

22. F. Falkner and J. M. Tanner, eds., *Human Growth: A Comprehensive Treatise*, vol. 3, 2d ed. (New York: Plenum Press, 1986).

23. The study of the effect of malnutrition on mental development is shot through with difficulties of interpretation. See the chapter by S. M. Grantham-McGregor in Waterlow, *Protein Energy Malnutrition*.

24. G. B. Spurr and J. C. Reina, "Influence of Dietary Intervention on Artificially Increased Activity in Marginally Undernourished Colombian Boys," *European Journal of Clinical Nutrition* 42 (1988).

25. E. Pollit, *Malnutrition and Infection in the Classroom* (Paris: UNESCO, 1990).

26. Waterlow, *Protein Energy Malnutrition*.

27. World Health Organization, *Energy and Protein Requirements*, Technical Series, no. 724 (Geneva, 1985), p. 85.

28. Ibid., pp. 87–89.

29. A. M. Prentice, "Variations in Maternal Intake, Birthweight and Breast Milk Output in the Gambia," in H. Aebi and R. G. Whitehead, eds., *Maternal Nutrition during Pregnancy and Lactation* (Bern, Switzerland: Hans Huber, 1980); A. M. Prentice et al., "Prenatal Dietary Supplementation of African Women and Birth Weight," *Lancet*, vol. 1 (1983); and A. M. Prentice et al., "Dietary Supplementation of Lactating Gambian Women. II: Effect on Maternal Health, Nutritional Status and Biochemistry," *Human Nutrition: Clinical Nutrition*, vol. 37C (1983).

30. L. S. Adair and E. Pollitt, "Seasonal Variation in Maternal Body Dimensions and Infant Birthweights," *American Journal of Physical Anthropology*, vol. 62 (1983); and L. S. Adair, "Marginal Intake and Maternal Adaptation: The Case of Rural Taiwan," in Pollitt and Amante, *Energy Intake*.

31. D. P. Chandhuri, *Education, Innovation and Agricultural Development* (London: Croom Helm, 1979). See also I. Singh, *The Great Ascent: The Rural Poor in South Asia* (Baltimore: Johns Hopkins University Press, 1990).

32. For references see Dasgupta, *Inquiry into Well-being*.

33. S. H. Cochrane, "Effects of Education and Urbanization on Fertility," in R. Bulatao and R. Lee, eds., *Determinants of Fertility in Developing Countries*, vol. 2 (New York: Academic Press, 1983).

34. Dasgupta, *Inquiry into Well-being*.

35. A. K. M. A. Chowdhury, "Child Mortality in Bangladesh: Food versus Health Care," *Food and Nutrition Bulletin* 10 (1988).
36. J. Bhagwati, "Education, Class Structure and Income Inequality," *World Development* 1 (1973).
37. Dasgupta, "Well-being and the Extent of Its Realization."
38. L. Summers, "The Most Influential Investment," *Scientific American* 267 (1992).
39. Dasgupta, "Well-being and the Extent of Its Realization"; and P. Dasgupta and M. Weale, "On Measuring the Quality of Life," *World Development* 20 (1992).
40. Dasgupta, *Inquiry into Well-being.*

Chapter 6: When the System Doesn't Work: Somalia 1992

1. G. B. Masefield, *Food and Nutrition Procedures in Times of Disaster* (Rome: Food and Agriculture Organization, 1967); R. C. Kent, *Anatomy of Disaster Relief: The International Network in Action* (London: Pinter Publishers, 1987); J. Ingram, "Food and Disaster Relief: Issues of Management and Policy," *Disasters,* vol. 12 (1988), pp. 12–18; J. Borton and J. Shoham, "Experiences of Non-governmental Organisations in the Targeting of Emergency Food Aid," *Disasters,* vol. 13 (1989), pp. 77–93; C. Eldridge, "Thought for Food: Suggestions for a Systematised Approach to Emergency Food Distribution Operations," *Disasters,* vol. 13 (1989), pp. 135–52.
2. International Committee of the Red Cross, *The Geneva Conventions of August 12, 1949* (Geneva: ICRC Publications); International Committee of the Red Cross, *Protocols Additional to the Geneva Conventions of August 12, 1949* (Geneva: ICRC Publications, 1977); International Committee of the Red Cross, "Rules of International Humanitarian Law Governing the Conduct of Hostilities in Non-international Conflicts and Declaration on the Rules of International Humanitarian Law Governing the Conduct of Hostilities in Non-international Conflicts," *International Review of the Red Cross,* no. 278 (September-October 1990), pp. 383–409.
3. G. H. Aldrich, "Compliance with International Humanitarian Law," *International Review of the Red Cross,* no. 282 (May–June 1991), pp. 294–312.
4. I. M. Boothman, "A Historical Survey of the Incidence of Drought in Northern Somalia," in I. M. Lewis, ed., *Abaar: The Somali Drought* (London: 1975).
5. Amnesty International, *Somalia: Report on an Amnesty International Visit and Current Human Rights Concerns* (New York: Amnesty International, 1990).
6. S. J. Ungar, "Africa: The Military Money Drain," *Bulletin of the Atomic Scientists* (September 1985), pp. 31–34.

7. Personal and privileged communication with representative of UN agencies in Nairobi, February 17, 1992.
8. A. de Waal and J. Leaning, "Somalia: No Mercy in Mogadishu," in *The Human Cost of the Conflict and the Struggle for Relief* (New York: Physicians for Human Rights and Africa Watch, 1992).
9. J. Kunder, "Somalia—Civil Strife," Situation Report no. 7, Office of U.S. Foreign Disaster Assistance, Agency for International Development, Washington, D.C., January 30, 1992, p. 3.
10. International Committee of the Red Cross, "Emergency Plan of Action: Somalia. March 5, 1992," as cited in de Waal and Leaning, "No Mercy in Mogadishu."
11. J. Bongaarts and M. Cain, "Demographic Responses to Famine," Working Paper 77, Center for Policy Studies, The Population Council, New York (November 1981).
12. International Committee of the Red Cross, "Somalia: Global Approach the Only Means of Averting Famine," *Bulletin* (March 1992).
13. J. Perlez, "U.S. Says Airlifts Fail Somali Needy," *New York Times,* July 31, 1992, p. A9.
14. J. Perlez, "Officials Say Somali Famine Is Even Worse Than Feared," *New York Times,* September 6, 1992, p. A1.
15. Personal and privileged communication with representative of the ICRC in Somalia, February 16, 1992; Y. Sandoz, " 'Droit' or 'devoir d'ingerence' and the Right to Assistance: The Issues Involved," *International Review of the Red Cross,* no. 288 (May–June 1992), pp. 215–27.
16. J. Perlez, "No Easy Fix for Somalia," *New York Times,* September 7, 1992, p. A1.
17. S. Engelberg, "U.N. Official Pleads for Help for Beseiged Bosnians," *New York Times,* August 18, 1992, p. A3.
18. Estimate attributed to Gen. Lewis MacKenzie, in charge of UN forces at Sarajevo, in R. W. Apple, Jr., "Baker Aide Says War Crimes Inquiry Into Bosnian Camps," *New York Times,* August 6, 1992, p. A1.
19. Estimate attributed to Lt. Gen. Barry R. McCaffrey, in M. R. Gordon, "60,000 Needed for Bosnia, a U.S. General Estimates," *New York Times,* August 12, 1992, p. A8.
20. J. Perlez, "Food Relief Grows but So Do Somalia's Dead," *New York Times,* July 19, 1992, p. A1; J. Perlez, "UN Observer Unit to Go to Somalia," *New York Times,* July 20, 1992, p. A3.
21. S. Faison, "U.N. Head Proposes Expanded Effort for Somali Relief," *New York Times,* July 25, 1992, p. A1; P. Tyler, "UN Chief's Dispute with Council Boils Over," *New York Times,* August 3, 1992, p. A1.
22. J. Perlez, "No Easy Fix for Somalia."
23. M. Putzel, "U.S. Preparing Units to Help UN in Bosnia," *The Boston Globe,* July 1, 1992, p. 1.
24. P. Lewis, "UN Set to Debate Peacemaking Role," *New York Times,* September 6, 1992, p. 7.

Chapter 7: Casualties of Conflicts and Mine Warfare

1. Christopher F. Foss and Terry J. Gander, eds., *Jane's Military Vehicles and Logistics*, 13th ed. (Alexandria, Va.: Jane's Information Group, 1992), p. 197.

Chapter 8: The Clinical Face of Famine

1. Kevin M. Cahill, *Famine* (New York: Orbis Press, 1982).
2. ———, *Health on the Horn of Africa* (London: Spottiswoode Ballantine, 1969).
3. ———, *Somalia: A Perspective* (Albany: State University of New York Press, 1980).
4. J. Erdrishinghe, "Infections in the Malnourished: With Special Reference to Malaria," *Ann. of Tropical Pediatrics* 6 (1986), p. 233.

Chapter 9: The Public Health Consequences of Inaction

1. U.S. Committee for Refugees, *World Refugee Survey, 1992* (Washington, D.C., 1992).
2. M. J. Toole and R. J. Waldman, "Prevention of Excess Mortality in Refugee and Displaced Populations in Developing Countries," *Journal of the American Medical Association,* vol. 263 (1990), pp. 3296–3302.
3. Ibid.; U.S. Centers for Disease Control (CDC), "Public Health Consequences of Acute Displacement of Iraqi Citizens—March–May 1991," *Morbidity and Mortality Weekly Report,* vol. 40 (1991), pp. 443–46; Médecins sans Frontières (Holland), "Bhutanese Refugees: Rapid Assessment of Health and Nutrition Situation (11–16 May, 1992)" (Katmandu, Nepal, 1992, unpublished); and United Nations High Commissioner for Refugees (UNHCR), "Ruhinga Refugee Camps" (Cox's Bazaar, Bangladesh, 1992, unpublished).
4. Toole and Waldman, "Prevention of Excess Mortality"; CDC, "Nutritional and Health Status of Displaced Persons—Sudan, 1988–1989," *Morbidity and Mortality Weekly Report,* vol. 38 (1989), pp. 848–850, 855; and Serge Manoncourt et al., "Public Health Consequences of the Civil War in Somalia, April, 1992," *Lancet,* vol. 34. (1992), pp. 176–177.
5. Toole and Waldman, "Prevention of Excess Mortality."
6. CDC, "Public Health Consequences of Acute Displacement of Iraqi Citizens."
7. UNHCR, "Ruhinga Refugee Camps."
8. Toole and Waldman, "Prevention of Excess Mortality."
9. M. J. Toole, R. W. Steketee, R. J. Waldman, and P. Nieburg, "Measles Prevention and Control in Emergency Setting," *Bulletin of the World Health Organization,* vol. 67 (1989), pp. 381–88.
10. Toole and Waldman, "Prevention of Excess Mortality."
11. CDC, unpublished data.

12. Toole and Waldman, "Prevention of Excess Mortality"; Médecins sans Frontières, "Bhutanese Refugees"; and UNHCR, "Ruhinga Refugee Camps."
13. Manoncourt et al., "Public Health Consequences of the Civil War in Somalia."
14. UNHCR, *Handbook for Emergencies* (Geneva, 1982), p. 122.
15. CDC, "Public Health Consequences of Acute Displacement of Iraqi Citizens."
16. Ibid.

Chapter 10: The American Medical Establishment

1. R. E. Morgan and G. Mutalik, "Bringing International Health Back Home," Policy Paper for the 19th Annual Conference of the National Council for International Health (Washington, D.C.: National Council for International Health, 1992).
2. *Directory of U.S. International Health Organizations, 1992* (Washington D.C.: National Council for International Health).
3. Graduate Medical Education National Advisory Council, *GMENAC Summary Report,* Vol. 1. Dept. of Health and Human Services publication (HRA) 81–651 (Hyattsville, Md.: Health Resource Administration, 1980).
4. A. Mejia, H. Pizurki, E. Royston, eds., *Foreign Medical Graduates: The Case of the United States* (Lexington, Mass.: Lexington Books, 1980); H. A. Ronaghy, K. Cahill, and T. D. Baker, "Physician Migration in the United States: One Country's Transfusion Is Another Country's Hemorrhage," *JAMA* 227 (1974):538–42; World Bank. Health Sector Policy Paper, 2d ed. (Washington, D.C.: World Bank, 1980).
5. J. Crofton, "Tobacco: World Action on the Pandemic" (editorial), *British Journal of Addiction* 84 (1989):1397–1400.
6. M. Silverman, P. R. Lee, and M. Lydecker, "The Drugging of the Third World," *International Journal of Health Services* 12 (1982):585–95.
7. T. D. Baker, C. Weisman, and E. Piwoz, "U.S. Physicians in International Health," *JAMA* 251 (1984):502–4.
8. Ibid.; T. D. Baker, C. Weisman, and E. Piwoz, "United States Health Professionals in International Health Work," *American Journal of Public Health* 74 (1984):438–41.
9. P. H. Grundy and P. B. Budetti, "The Distribution and Supply of Cuban Medical Personnel in Third World Countries," *American Journal of Public Health* 70 (1980):717–19.
10. Baker et al., "United States Health Professionals," p. 439.
11. R. E. Pust, "U.S. Abundance of Physicians and International Health," *JAMA* 252 (1984):385–88.
12. S. P. Asper, "Report on the Survey of International Activities of U.S.

Health Professions Schools," *Academic Medicine* 64 (1989, supplement):S33–36; S. P. Asper and W. W. Steele, eds., *1988 Directory of International Programs and Projects of U.S. Schools of Medicine, Dentistry, Pharmacy and Public Health* (Philadelphia, Pa.: Educational Commission for Foreign Medical Graduates, 1988).

13. *Medical Student Graduation Questionnaire* (Washington, D.C.: Association of American Medical Colleges, 1989).

14. *Medical Student Graduation Questionnaire* (Washington, D.C.: Association of American Medical Colleges, 1984).

15. Kevin Cahill, personal communication.

16. H. Burstin, "Responding to Medical Needs Abroad," *The New Physician* 44 (October 1985).

17. D. A. Kindig and G. L. Lythcott, "A Proposal: Share Our Doctors Abroad," *The New Physician* 10 (September 1984).

18. V. W. Sidel, "International Health: A World View for Medical Students," *Einstein Quarterly Journal of Biology and Medicine* 3 (1985):50–51.

19. J. Javits, R. Schweiker, and M. Humphrey, SB-3103—International Health Act of 1978, 95th Congress, 2nd sess.

20. J. E. Banta, Statement before the Labor and Human Resources Subcommittee on Health and Scientific Research, United States Senate. Washington, D.C. July 2, 1980.

21. AMSA International Health Task Force, *International Health Electives for Medical Students,* 5th ed. (St. Louis, Mo.: St. Louis University School of Medicine, 1989); *Faculty Contacts and Curricular Information on International Health at U.S. Medical Schools* (Reston, Va.: American Medical Student Association, 1987). Also note C. Krogh and R. Pust, *International Health: A Manual for Advisers and Students* (Kansas City, Mo.: Society of Teachers of Family Medicine, 1990); L. Barthauer, *International Health Funding Guide* (Reston Va.: American Medical Student Association, 1990).

22. *The International Partnership Program in Community-Based Medical Education* (Reston, Va.: American Medical Student Association, 1992).

23. M. Barry and F. J. Bia, "Departments of Medicine and International Health," *American Journal of Medicine* 80 (1984):1019–21.

24. *International Dimensions: News on Activities and Opportunities in International Medicine* (Chapel Hill, N.C.: University of North Carolina School of Medicine, Office of International Affairs, June–July 1992).

25. B. Unland, R. Waterman, W. Wiese, et al., "Learning from a Rural Physician Program in China," *Academic Medicine* 67 (1992):307–309.

26. R. S. Northrup, "Preparing Students for Overseas Electives," *Academic Medicine* 66 (1991):92.

27. J. E. Heck and D. Wedemeyer, "A Survey of American Medical Schools to Assess Their Preparation of Students for Overseas Practice," *Academic Medicine* 66 (1991):78–81.

28. R. E. Pust and S. P. Moher, "A Core Curriculum for International Health: Evaluating Ten Years' Experience at the University of Arizona," *Academic Medicine* 67 (1992):90–94.

29. *Proceedings of the International Health Medical Education Consortium (IHMEC), Washington, D.C., June 22–23, 1991* (Rochester, NY: IHMEC, University of Rochester Medical Center, 1991).

30. R. S. Northrup, "Preparing Students for Overseas Electives," p. 92.

31. S. L. Kark, *The Practice of Community-Oriented Primary Health Care* (New York: Appleton-Century Crofts, 1981).

32. H. J. Geiger, "Community Health Centers as an Instrument of Social Change," in W. V. Sidel and R. Sidel, eds., *Reforming Medicine* (New York: Pantheon, 1984).

33. "U.S. Agencies Utilizing U.S. Physicians Abroad," *JAMA* 263 (1990):3237–45.

34. R. G. Pierloni, W. H. Waddell, and E. Suter, "The Interinstitutional Development of an International Health Course," *Journal of Medical Education* 54 (1979):75–80.

35. Educational Commission for Foreign Medical Graduates. "Strategies for Developing Innovative Programs in International Medical Education." Proceedings of the 1988 International Invitational Conference. *Academic Medicine* 64 (1989) supplement.

36. E. M. Einterz, "Getting Doctors to the Third World" (editorial), *Postgraduate Medicine* 79 (1986):15–22.

Chapter 11: The Changing Roles of Voluntary Organizations

1. William Shawcross, *The Quality of Mercy* (London: Andre Deutsch, Ltd., 1984), p. 427.

2. Statement of Andrew Natsios on Somalia, press conference, Washington, D.C., August 24, 1992.

3. Jane Perlez, "UN Let the Somali Famine Get Out of Hand, Aide Says," *New York Times*, August 16, 1992.

4. Phil Davison, "Somalis Pay Price of UN 'Shambles'," the London *Independent*, August 30, 1992.

Chapter 12: Relief and Reality

1. Notable exceptions included the Bihar famine in 1966–1967 and the Pakistan/Bangladesh crisis of the early 1970s. These crises, more typical of the relief situation of today, foreshadowed the trends outlined below.

2. The State Department claimed the United States was technically in compliance with the 1951 United Nations Convention Relating to the Status of Refugees because it was sending the Haitians back to Haiti before they entered U.S. territory. The claim that U.S. Coast Guard cutters were intercepting boats because they were "unseaworthy" was quickly chal-

lenged by human rights organizations, but the Supreme Court upheld the legality of the interdiction.

3. *News from Americas Watch National Coalition for Haitian Refugees,* vol. 4, no. 4, June 30, 1992.

4. At the end of 1991 Germany harbored over 250,000 refugees. During the first six months of 1992 Germany received an additional 125,000 refugees from Yugoslavia alone. In addition, a steady stream of 10,000–15,000 refugees from other countries sought asylum each month.

5. For number of refugees within the country, see U.S. Committee for Refugees, *World Refugee Survey 1992* (Washington, D.C.: American Council for Nationalities Service, 1992), pp. 52–53.

6. Ibid., p. 47.

7. Ibid.

8. See Neil Boothby, "Living in the War Zone," in U.S. Committee for Refugees, *World Refugee Survey 1989 in Review* (Washington, D.C.: American Council for Nationalities Service, 1992), pp. 40–42; and Robert Gersony, *Summary of Mozambican Accounts of Principally Conflict-Related Experience in Mozambique* (Washington, D.C.: U.S. Department of State, 1988).

9. Larry Minear, "Civil Strife and Humanitarian Aid: A Bruising Decade," in U.S. Committee for Refugees, *World Refugee Survey 1989 in Review,* pp. 13–19.

10. Stuart Auerbach, "Developing Countries Get Short Shrift in Group of Seven Deliberations," *Washington Post,* July 8, 1992, p. A34.

11. See Michael J. Bayzler, "Reexamining the Doctrine of Humanitarian Intervention in Light of the Atrocities in Kampuchea and Ethiopia," *Stanford Journal of International Law,* vol. 23, no. 2 (Summer 1987), pp. 547–619; and David Schaeffer, "Toward a Modern Doctrine of Humanitarian Intervention," *University of Toledo Law Review,* vol. 23, no. 2 (1992), pp. 253–93.

12. Address to the United Nations Association of the United States, April 30, 1985, *UN Chronicle,* vol. 22, no. 1 (1985), p. 23.

Chapter 14: Coping with Disasters

1. A. M. R. Chowdhury and J. P. Vaughan, "The Problem of Diarrhoeal Disease in Developing Countries," *Bangladesh Journal of Child Health,* vol. 11 (September 1987), pp. 72–78.

2. R. L. Guerrent and R. D. Cash, "Infectious Disease. Treatment of Cholera and Other Diarrhoeal Illness," in L. C. Cher, ed., *Disaster in Bangladesh* (Oxford: Oxford University Press, 1973).

3. F. H. Abed, "Household Teaching of Oral Rehydration Therapy in Rural Bangladesh," *Assignment Children,* vol. 61/62 (1983), pp. 249–65.

4. A. M. R. Chowdhury and Z. N. Kabir, "Folk Terminology for Diarrhoea

in Rural Bangladesh," *Reviews of Infectious Diseases,* vol. 13, supplement 4 (1991), pp. S252–54.

5. A. M. R. Chowdhury and J. P. Vaughan, "Perception of Diarrhoea and the Use of a Homemade ORS in Rural Bangladesh," *Journal of Diarrhoeal Disease Research,* vol. 6 (1988), pp. 6–14.

6. A. M. R. Chowdhury, J. P. Vaughan, and F. H. Abed, "Use and Safety of Homemade ORS: An Epidemiological Evaluation from Bangladesh," *International Journal of Epidemiology,* vol. 17 (1988), pp. 655–65.

7. A. M. R. Chowdhury, "Teaching ORT to Millions," in *Proceedings of the Third International Conference on ORT (ICORT III)* (Washington D.C.: United States Agency for International Development, 1988).

8. A. M. R. Chowdhury, F. Karim, and J. Ahmed, "Teaching ORT to Women: Individually or in Groups?" *Journal of Tropical Medicine and Hygiene,* vol. 91 (1988), pp. 283–87.

9. A. M. R. Chowdhury, "Teaching ORT to Millions."

10. A. M. R. Chowdhury et al., *Measuring Basic Education of Children in Bangladesh* (Dhaka: Bangladesh Rural Advercement Committee and UNICEF, 1992).

11. W. M. Gray, "Global View of the Origin of Tropical Disturbances and Cyclones," *Monthly Weather Review,* vol. 96 (1968).

12. R. Haider, A. Rahman, and S. Hug, *"Cyclone '91: An Environmental and Perceptional Study"* (Dhaka: Bangladesh Centre for Advanced Studies, 1991).

13. A. M. R. Chowdhury et al., "Cyclone Aftermath: Research and Directions for the Future," in H. Hossain, C. Dodge, and F. H. Abed, eds., *From Crisis to Development: Coping with Disasters in Bangladesh* (Dhaka: Dhaka University Press, 1992), pp. 101–133.

14. M. Haque, "Relief in Full Swing," in H. Hossain et al., eds., *From Crisis to Development,* pp. 27–54.

15. Ibid.

16. Government of Bangladesh, "District and Upazila Wise Damage Report" (Chittagong: Zonal Relief Coordinator, June 6, 1991).

17. "Cyclone Damage Estimated at US $2.4 Billion," *Financial Indicators, Bangladesh* (Dhaka: ANZ Grindlays Bank and Bangladesh Centre for Advanced Studies, 1991).

18. Government of Bangladesh, *Multipurpose Cyclone Shelter Programme* (Dhaka: Government of Bangladesh and Bangladesh University of Engineering and Technology, 1992).

19. A. K. Siddique and A. Yusof, "Cyclone Deaths in Bangladesh, May 1985: Who Was at Risk," *Tropical and Geographical Medicine,* vol. 39 (1987), pp. 3–8.

20. A. M. R. Chowdhury et al., "Cyclone Aftermath."

21. Ibid.

22. M. Haque, "Relief in Full Swing."

23. Bangladesh Rural Advancement Committee, *Cyclone Relief Programme 1991: The BRAC Response* (Dhaka: Bangladesh Rural Advancement Committee, 1991).

24. A. M. R. Chowdhury, A. U. Bhuiya, A. Y. Chowdhury, and Rita Sen, *Bangladesh Cyclone of 1991: Why So Many People Died* (Dhaka: Bangladesh Rural Advancement Committee, 1991).

25. S. Rahman, "The First Five Days," in H. Hossain et al., eds., *From Crisis to Development*, pp. 13–26.

26. UNICEF, "Health Effects of the 1991 Bangladesh Cyclone: Report of the UNICEF Review Group" (Dhaka: UNICEF, 1991).

27. Ibid.

28. M. Hossain, "Development Policy, Growth Process and Coping with Natural Disasters," in H. Hossain et al., eds., *From Crisis to Development*.

29. Ibid.

Chapter 15: Making the Humanitarian System Work Better

1. The project is a research and action initiative undertaken by the Thomas J. Watson Jr. Institute for International Studies of Brown University and the Refugee Policy Group of Washington, D.C. Funds come from five United Nations organizations (the Department of Humanitarian Affairs/UNDRO, UNHCR, UNICEF, the World Food Programme, and the Special Programme for the Horn of Africa), three governments (the Netherlands, France, and the United States), eight nongovernmental groups (Catholic Relief Services, the Danish Refugee Council, the Lutheran World Federation, Lutheran World Relief, the Mennonite Central Committee, the Norwegian Refugee Council, Oxfam-U.K., and the Save the Children Fund–U.K.), and two foundations (the Pew Charitable Trusts and the Arias Foundation). I would like to thank the codirector, Thomas G. Weiss, for his assistance in this chapter, which utilizes data and concepts we have developed jointly.

2. Larry Minear, U. B. P. Chelliah, Jeff Crisp, John Mackinlay, and Thomas Weiss, "United Nations Coordination of the International Humanitarian Response to the Gulf Crisis 1990–92," Thomas J. Watson Jr. Institute for International Studies Occasional Paper, no. 13 (Providence, R.I., 1992). On the wider implications of the issues, see Larry Minear and Thomas G. Weiss, "Groping and Coping in the Gulf Crisis: Discerning the Shape of a New Humanitarian Order," *World Policy Journal*, vol. 9 (Fall 1992).

3. Quoted in Minear and Weiss, "Groping and Coping," p. 28.

4. Minear et al., *United Nations Coordination*, p. 10.

5. Boutros Boutros-Ghali, "An Agenda for Peace: Preventive Diplomacy, Peacemaking and Peace-keeping." Report of the secretary-general pursuant to the statement adopted by the Summit Meeting of the Security Council, January 31, 1992 (New York: United Nations, 1992), p. 23.

6. James C. Ingram, "The United Nations and the Future Architecture for International Humanitarian Assistance," in Thomas G. Weiss and Larry Minear, eds., *Humanitarianism Across Borders* (Boulder, Colo.: Lynne Reinner, 1993).

7. For a more detailed elaboration, see Larry Minear, *Humanitarianism Under Siege: A Critical Review of Operation Lifeline Sudan* (Trenton, N.J.: Red Sea Press, 1991), chs. 3 and 4.

8. UN Disaster Relief Organization, "The Iraq/Kuwait Crisis: International Assistance to Displaced People Through Jordan, August–November 1990" (Geneva: UNDRO, 1991), p. 17.

9. For a discussion of the use of outside military forces to assist in emergencies, see Leon Gordenker and Thomas G. Weiss, eds., *Soldiers, Peacekeepers and Disasters* (London: Macmillan, 1992); and Thomas G. Weiss and Kurt M. Campbell, "Military Humanitarianism," *Survival*, vol. 33, no. 5 (1991), pp. 451–65.

10. Barton Gellman, "U.S. Military Fears Balkan Intervention," *Washington Post*, August 12, 1992, p. A24. See also John Mackinlay and Jarat Chopra, "Second Generation Multinational Operations," *The Washington Quarterly*, vol. 15, no. 3 (1992), pp. 113–34.

11. Ingram, "The United Nations and the Future Architecture for International Humanitarian Assistance."

12. Quoted in Minear, *Humanitarianism Under Siege*, p. 131.

13. Statement by the permanent representative of Brazil, Ambassador Ronaldo Mota Sardenberg, on agenda item 9 (special economic, humanitarian and disaster relief assistance), United Nations Economic and Social Council, 1992 Substantive Session, July 22, 1992, p. 1.

14. Joel R. Charney, "NGOs and the Rehabilitation and Reconstruction of Cambodia" (Phnom Penh: Cooperation Committee for Cambodia, 1992), pp. i–ii.

15. Ibid.

16. "Kurdish Relief & Repatriation: DOD-AID/OFDA Partnership: The AID/OFDA Kurdish Response After-Action Report" (Washington, D.C.: U.S. Agency for International Development, Dec. 1991).

17. Patrice K. Curtis, "Providing Humanitarian Assistance: Using the U.S. Military Overseas," Congressional Research Service Report for Congress, July 31, 1992.

18. The handbook is currently in its second draft, incorporating suggestions made at an expert consultation held at Brown University in early 1992. Further revisions will be made following additional review at sessions later in the year in San José, Costa Rica; Nairobi, Kenya; and Addis Ababa, Ethiopia. The currently circulating version is Larry Minear and Thomas G. Weiss, "Humanitarian Principles and Policy Guidelines: A Handbook for Practitioners," discussion draft II (Providence, R.I.: Humanitarianism and War Project, May 1, 1992).

19. For an elaboration of the comparative impacts of aid interventions on drought-related and war-borne famine, see Francis M. Deng and Larry Minear, *The Challenges of Famine Relief: Emergency Operations in the Sudan* (Washington, D.C.: The Brookings Institution, 1992).
20. Quoted in Minear, *Humanitarianism Under Siege,* p. 126.
21. Richard Holbrooke, "Bosnia: The 'Cleansing' Goes On," *Washington Post,* August 16, 1992, p. C7.

Chapter 17: Lifelines to the Innocent

1. James Grant, "Advocating Humanitarian Ceasefires," Conference on Humanitarian Ceasefires: Peace-building for Children, Ottawa, November 26, 1991.
2. Ibid.
3. Ibid.

Chapter 20: The World Response to Humanitarian Emergencies

1. Marc Weller, "Intervention Plans Lack Specific UN Sanction," *Times of London,* August 20, 1992.
2. Peter Lynn Sinai, "A Distortion of UN Purposes and Principles," *New Delhi Pioneer,* August 25, 1992.
3. Claude Malhuret, "L'action humanitaire alibi de l'inaction politique?" *Le Monde,* August 20, 1992.

ABOUT
THE AUTHORS

FAZLE H. ABED is the Founder and Executive Director of the Bangladesh Rural Advancement Committee (BRAC). He is a member of the International Commission on Health Research for Development and is a visiting scholar at Harvard University. He is the recipient of the Feinstein World Hunger Award, the Roman Magsaysay Award, the UNESCO Noma Prize, and the UNICEF Maurice Pate Award.

KOFI N. AWOONOR, Permanent Representative of the Republic of Ghana to the United Nations, is Chairman of the U.N. Committee on Apartheid. He previously served as Ambassador to Brazil, Cuba, Argentina, Venezuela, Uruguay, Guyana, Jamaica, and Trinidad and Tobago. A poet and the author of several books, he has been a visiting professor in the United States and is the recipient of literary awards in Ghana and the United Kingdom.

RONY BRAUMAN, M.D., is the President of Médecins sans Frontières, Paris. He is a member of the French National Commission of Human Rights, and has served as a medical doctor in refugee camps and during civil wars in Thailand, Indonesia, Honduras, Chad, Angola, and El Salvador.

KEVIN M. CAHILL, M.D., is the President of the Center for International Health and Cooperation. He also serves as Director of the Tropical Disease Center in New York, Professor and Chairman of the Department of International Health at the Royal College of Surgeons in Ireland, and senior medical consultant to the United Nations Health Service and to numerous foreign governments.

PARTHA DASGUPTA is Professor of Economics at the University of Cambridge and Fellow of St. John's College. Previously, he was Professor of Economics, Professor of Philosophy, and Director of the Program in Ethics in Society at Stanford University. He has written extensively on the economics of destitution, economic demography, and political philosophy.

JAN ELIASSON is the Under-Secretary-General for Humanitarian Affairs of the United Nations. He previously served as Sweden's Permanent Representative to the United Nations, Vice President of the Economic and Social Council (ECOSOC), Chairman of the General Assembly working group on emergency relief, and Ambassador and Under-Secretary for Political Affairs in the Foreign Ministry of Sweden.

RICHARD FALK is Albert G. Milbank Professor of International Law and Practice at Princeton University. He is the author of *Human Rights and State Sovereignty* and, most recently, *Explorations at the Edge of Time: Prospects for World Order.*

ABDULRAHIM A. FARAH, Consultant Director of the Center for International Health and Cooperation, served for twenty years as Under-Secretary-General and Senior Political Advisor on African Affairs to the Secretary-General of the United Nations. He has also served as Somalia's Ambassador to Ethiopia and Permanent Representative to the United Nations.

REV. AENGUS FINUCANE, C.S.S.p., is the Chief Executive of CONCERN. He has worked for over thirty years in disaster zones in Biafra, Uganda, Bangladesh, the Thai-Cambodian border, and in Somalia.

H. JACK GEIGER, M.D., is President of Physicians for Human Rights and Professor of Community Medicine at the City University of New York Medical School. He is a founding member and former President of Physicians for Social Responsibility. He has published numerous articles and book chapters on medical and biological effects of nuclear weapons.

PHILIP JOHNSTON, President and Chief Executive Officer of CARE, is also a member of the Overseas Development Council and the African Development Foundation Advisory Council. He now also serves as the special United Nations coordinator for Somali relief operations.

JENNIFER LEANING, M.D., Medical Director of the Health Centers Division, Harvard Community Health Plan, is on the faculty of the Harvard Medical School and is an attending physician at Brigham & Women's Hospital. She is the Editor-in-Chief of the *PSR Quarterly,* published by the Physicians for Social Responsibility.

LARRY MINEAR is co-director of the Humanitarianism and War Project, a joint undertaking of the Thomas J. Watson Institute for International Studies at Brown University and the Refugee Policy Group of Washington, D.C.

SADAKO OGATA is the United Nations High Commissioner for Refugees. Prior to her appointment as Commissioner, Mrs. Ogata was Dean of the Faculty of Foreign Studies at Sophia University in Tokyo, the Representative of Japan on the United Nations Commission on Human Rights, and Chairman of the Executive Board of UNICEF.

LORD DAVID OWEN, M.D., Former Foreign Secretary of the United Kingdom, has also served in his government as a Member of Parliament, Minister of the Navy, and Minister of Health. He helped to found the Social Democratic Party (SDP) and was its leader for almost a decade. He has been a member of the Independent Commission on Disarmament and Security Issues and the Independent Commission on International Humanitarian Issues.

RICHARD REID, Director of Public Affairs for the United Nations Children's Fund (UNICEF), has been Regional Officer for the Middle East and North Africa and has had extensive experience providing medical care to children caught in war zones in the Sudan, Lebanon, and Iraq.

RÉMI RUSSBACH, M.D., is Chief Medical Officer and Founder of the Medical Division of the International Committee of the Red Cross. An expert on war injuries, he serves as the Vice President of the International Society for Disaster Medicine.

ELLEN JOHNSON SIRLEAF is the Director of the Bureau of Africa for the United Nations Development Programme. Prior to her appointment, she served as Deputy Minister of Finance in Liberia, President of the Liberian Bank for Development and Investment, and worked in the World Bank, Washington, D.C.

MICHAEL J. TOOLE, M.D., is Medical Epidemiologist in the International Health Program Office of the Centers for Disease Control (CDC) in Atlanta. He coordinates CDC's technical assistance to refugee and displaced populations, including recent projects in Ethiopia, Kenya, Malawi, Kurdistan, Nepal, Bangladesh, Sudan, Pakistan, and the republics of the former Soviet Union.

CYRUS VANCE, former Secretary of State for the United States of America, is currently a Personal Envoy of the Secretary-General of the United Nations. A naval officer in World War II, he later served as Secretary of the Army and as Deputy Secretary of Defense.

MICHEL VEUTHEY has worked for the International Committee of the Red Cross for over twenty-five years, serving as the ICRC Representative in conflict areas from Vietnam to Angola, and as Chief of its Division of International Organizations. He is the author of *Guerrilla Warfare and International Law*.